THE NEO-PLATONISTS

THE NEO-PLATONISTS

A STUDY IN THE HISTORY OF HELLENISM

BY

THOMAS WHITTAKER

SECOND EDITION
WITH A SUPPLEMENT ON THE
COMMENTARIES OF PROCLUS

 BOOKS FOR LIBRARIES PRESS
FREEPORT, NEW YORK

First Published 1918
Second Edition
Reprinted 1970

B
5 17
W5
1970

STANDARD BOOK NUMBER:
8369-5305-3

LIBRARY OF CONGRESS CATALOG CARD NUMBER:
76-114901

PRINTED IN THE UNITED STATES OF AMERICA

PREFACE

TO THE SECOND EDITION

DURING the time that has elapsed since the publication of the
first edition of this work, I have at intervals kept myself in
contact with the subject; but it was not until lately that I saw
clearly how the book might receive the completion which from
the first had appeared desirable. The task that obviously remained was to give a more circumstantial account of the
Athenian period of Neo-Platonism. I once thought of doing
this in a second volume; but it became evident in the end
that, for the aim I had in view, what was necessary and
sufficient was a more adequate exposition of Proclus. I had
never proposed to deal with all minutiae on a uniform scale.
My purpose was, while not neglecting to give some account
of the lesser as well as the greater thinkers, to set forth substantially the doctrine of the school so as to bring out its
real originality and its historical importance. Now, for this
purpose, even Porphyry and Iamblichus, while they must
always retain an honourable place in the history of philosophy, are of minor significance. The case is otherwise with
Proclus, whose name has by general consent taken rank next
to that of Plotinus as representing the last powerful expression
of Hellenic thought before it ceased to have any effective
originality.

Since the book was written, the publication of improved
texts has put it in my power to do more justice to the thought
of Proclus than would have been possible at first. I hope that,
with the aid of these, I have been able to set before the reader
an account of his principal commentaries bringing out their
distinctive features and the new developments by which its
finished form was given to the great system of philosophy
initiated by Plotinus two centuries earlier.

In the text and notes of the book as it appeared in 1901, I have made only slight alterations. The Appendix on the outlying subject of Gnosticism, however, I found must be re-written in view of recent research. The nature of the modification needed, I have indicated in the Appendix itself in its new form.

T. W.

February, 1918.

CONTENTS

PAGE

INTRODUCTION ix

CHAPTER I

GRAECO-ROMAN CIVILISATION IN ITS POLITICAL DE-
VELOPMENT. 1

CHAPTER II

THE STAGES OF GREEK PHILOSOPHY 7

CHAPTER III

RELIGIOUS DEVELOPMENTS IN LATER ANTIQUITY . 17

CHAPTER IV

PLOTINUS AND HIS NEAREST PREDECESSORS . . 26

CHAPTER V

THE PHILOSOPHICAL SYSTEM OF PLOTINUS . . . 40

    1. PSYCHOLOGY 43

    2. METAPHYSICS 53

    3. COSMOLOGY AND THEODICY 70

    4. AESTHETICS 87

    5. ETHICS 91

CHAPTER VI

THE MYSTICISM OF PLOTINUS 98

CHAPTER VII

THE DIFFUSION OF NEO-PLATONISM 107

    1. PORPHYRY 107

    2. IAMBLICHUS 121

    3. THE SCHOOL OF IAMBLICHUS 131

CHAPTER VIII

PAGE

THE POLEMIC AGAINST CHRISTIANITY 136

CHAPTER IX

THE ATHENIAN SCHOOL 155

    1. THE ACADEMY BECOMES NEO-PLATONIC . . 155

    2. PROCLUS 157

    3. THE END OF THE PLATONIC SUCCESSION . . 180

CHAPTER X

THE INFLUENCE OF NEO-PLATONISM 185

CHAPTER XI

CONCLUSION 205

APPENDIX

I. THE COMMUNISM OF PLATO 216

II. THE GNOSTICS 218

III. IAMBLICHUS AND PROCLUS ON MATHEMATICAL
    SCIENCE 225

SUPPLEMENT

THE COMMENTARIES OF PROCLUS 229

    ON THE *FIRST ALCIBIADES* 242

    ,, ,, *PARMENIDES* 248

    ,, ,, *TIMAEUS* 264

    ,, ,, *REPUBLIC* 295

INDEX OF NAMES 315

INTRODUCTION

THAT the history of ancient culture effectively ends with the second century of the Christian era is an impression not infrequently derived from histories of literature and even of philosophy. The period that still remains of antiquity is obviously on its practical side a period of dissolution, in which every effort is required to maintain the fabric of the Roman State against its external enemies. And, spiritually, a new religious current is evidently beginning to gain the mastery; so that, with the knowledge we have of what followed, we can already see in the third century the break-up of the older form of inner as well as of outer life. In the second century too appeared the last writers who are usually thought of as classical. The end of the Stoical philosophy as a living system coincides with the death of Marcus Aurelius. And with Stoicism, it is often thought, philosophy ceased to have an independent life. It definitely entered the service of polytheism. In its struggle with Christianity it appropriated Oriental superstitions. It lost its scientific character in devotion to the practice of magic. It became a mystical theology instead of a pursuit of reasoned truth. The structure of ancient culture, like the fabric of the Empire, was in process of decay at once in form and content. In its permeation by foreign elements, it already manifests a transition to the new type that was to supersede it.

An argument for this view might be found in a certain "modernness" which has often been noted in the later classical literature. Since the ancient type was dissolved in the end to make way for the modern, we might attribute the early appearance of modern characteristics to the new growth accompanying incipient dissolution. The general falling-off in literary quality during the late period we should ascribe to decay; the wider and more consciously critical outlook on life, which we call modern, to the movement of the world into its changed path. Thus there would be a perfectly continuous process from the old civilisation to the new. On the other hand, we may hold that the "modernness" of the late classical period does not indicate the beginning of the intermediate phase of culture, but is a direct approximation to the modern type, due to the existence of a long intellectual tradition of a similar kind. If the latter view be taken, then we must regard the dissolution of the ancient world as proceeding, not by a penetration of new elements into the older form of culture so as to change the type, but indirectly through the conquest of the practical world by a new power; so that, while ancient culture was organically continuous as long as it lasted, it finally came to an end as an organism. The new way into which the world had passed was directed by a new religion, and this appropriated in its own manner the old form of culture, bringing it under the law of its peculiar type. Thus one form was substituted for another, but the first did not spontaneously pass into the second. There was no absolute break in history; for the ancient system of education remained, though in a reduced form, and passed by continuous transition into another; but the directing power was changed. The kind of "modern" character which the ancient culture assumed in the end was thus an anticipation of a much later period, not a genuine phase of transition. In confirmation of the latter view, it might be pointed out that the culture of the intermediate period, when it assumed at length its appropriate form, had decidedly less of the specifically modern character than even that of early antiquity with all its remoteness.

Be this as it may in pure literature, it is certain that the latest phase of ancient philosophy had all the marks of an intrinsic development. All its characteristic positions can be traced to their origin in earlier Greek systems. Affinities can undoubtedly be found in it with Oriental thought, more particularly with that of India; but with this no direct contact can be shown. In its distinctive modes of thought, it was wholly Hellenic. So far as it was "syncretistic," it was as philosophy of religion, not as pure philosophy. On this side, it was an attempt to bring the various national cults of the Roman Empire into union under the hegemony of a philosophical conception. As philosophy, it was indeed "eclectic," but the eclecticism was under the direction of an original effort of speculative thought, and was exercised entirely within the Hellenic tradition. And, in distinction from pure literature, philosophy made its decisive advance after practical dissolution had set in. It was not until the middle of the third century that the metaphysical genius of Plotinus brought to a common point the Platonising movement of revival which was already going on before the Christian era. The system founded by Plotinus, and known distinctively as "Neo-Platonism," was that which alone gave unity to all that remained of Greek culture during the period of its survival as such. Neo-Platonism became, for three centuries, the one philosophy of the Graeco-Roman world. It preserved the ancient type of thought from admixture with alien elements; and, though defeated in the struggle to give direction to the next great period of human history, it had a powerful influence on the antagonist system, which, growing up in an intellectual atmosphere pervaded by its modes of thought, incorporated much of its distinctive teaching.

The persistence of philosophy as the last living force of the ancient world might have been predicted. Philosophic thought in antiquity was the vital centre of liberal education as it has never been for the modern world. There were of course those who disparaged it in contrast with empirical practice or with rhetorical ability, but, for all that, it had the direction of practical thought so far as there was general direction at all. The dissolution by which the ancient type was broken down did not begin at the centre but at the extremities. The free development of the civic life both of Greece and of Rome had been checked by the pressure of a mass of alien elements imperfectly assimilated. These first imposed a political principle belonging to a different phase of culture. To the new movement thus necessitated, the culture of the ancient world, whatever superficial changes it might undergo, did not inwardly respond. Literature still looked to the past for its models. Philosophy least of all cared to adapt itself. It became instead the centre of resistance to the predominant movement,—to overweening despotism under the earlier Caesars, to the oncoming theocracy when the republican tradition was completely in the past. The latest philosophers of antiquity were pre-eminently

> The kings of thought
> Who waged contention with their time's decay.

And their resistance was not the result of pessimism, of a disposition to see nothing but evil in the actual movement of things. The Neo-Platonists in particular were the most convinced of optimists, at the very time when, as they well knew, the whole movement of the world was against them. They held it for their task to maintain as far as might be the type of life which they had themselves chosen as the best; knowing that there was an indefinite future, and that the alternating rhythms in which, with Heraclitus and the Stoics, they saw the cosmic harmony[1] and the expression of providential reason, would not cease with one period. If they did not actually predict the revival of their thought after a thousand years, they would not have been in the least surprised to see it.

More than once has that thought been revived, and with various aims; nor is its interest even yet exhausted. The first revival the philosophers themselves would have cared for was that of the fifteenth century, when, along with their master Plato, they became the inspirers of revolt against the system of mediaeval theology that had established itself long after their defeat. Another movement quite in their spirit, but this time not an insurgent movement, was that of the Cambridge Platonists in the seventeenth century, which went back to

---

[1] παλίντονος ἁρμονίη κόσμου ὅκωσπερ λύρης καὶ τόξου.—Heraclitus.

Neo-Platonism for the principles of its resistance to the exclusive dominance of the new "mechanical philosophy." As
the humanist academies of Italy had appealed against Scholastic dogmatism to the latest representatives in antiquity of
free philosophic inquiry, so the opponents in England of
"Hobbism" went for support to those who in their own day
had intellectually refuted the materialism of the Stoics and
Epicureans. Since then, many schools and thinkers have
shown affinity with Neo-Platonic thought; and, apart from
direct historic attachment or spontaneous return to similar
metaphysical ideas, there has been a deeper continuous influence of which something will have to be said.

From about the middle of the nineteenth century, the Neo-
Platonists, though somewhat neglected in comparison with
the other schools of antiquity, have been made the subject of
important historical work. To French philosophers who began
as disciples of Cousin, a philosophy that could be described as
at once "eclectic" and "spiritualist" naturally became an
object of interest. The result of that interest was seen in the
brilliant works of Vacherot and Jules Simon. For definite and
positive information on the doctrines of the school, the portion
of Zeller's *Philosophie der Griechen* that deals with the period
is of the highest value. In English, Mr Benn's chapter on
"The Spiritualism of Plotinus," in his *Greek Philosophers*,
brings out well the advance in subjective thought made by
the latest on the earlier philosophies of Greece. Of special
importance in relation to this point are the chapters on
Plotinus and his successors in Siebeck's *Geschichte der Psychologie*. An extensive work on the psychology of the school
has appeared since in the last two volumes of M. Chaignet's
Psychologie des Grecs. Recent English contributions to the
general exposition of the Neo-Platonist philosophy are Dr C.
Bigg's volume in the "Chief Ancient Philosophies" Series
(Christian Knowledge Society), and Dr F. W. Bussell's
stimulating book on *The School of Plato*, which, however, deals
more with preliminaries than with the school itself.

In the later historical treatment of Neo-Platonism a marked tendency is visible to make less of the supposed "Oriental" character of the school and more of its real dependence on the preceding philosophies of Greece. This may be seen in Zeller as compared with Vacherot, and in Mr Benn as compared with Zeller. Of the most recent writers, M. Chaignet and Dr Bigg, approaching the subject from different sides, conclude in almost the same terms that the system of Plotinus was through and through Hellenic. And, as M. Chaignet points out, Plotinus, in all essentials, fixed the doctrine of the school. Whatever attractions the thought of the East as vaguely surmised may have had for its adherents, their actual contact with it was slight. When the school took up a relation to the practical world, it was as the champion of "Hellenism" ('Ελληνισμός) against the "barbarian audacity" of its foes. On the whole, however, it did not seek to interfere directly with practice, but recognised the impossibility of modifying the course which the world at large was taking, and devoted itself to the task of carrying forward thought and preserving culture. Hence a history of Neo-Platonism must be in the main a history of doctrines internally developed, not of polemic with extraneous systems of belief. At the same time the causes must be indicated of its failure, and of the failure of philosophy, to hold for the next age the intellectual direction of the world,—a failure not unqualified. To bring those causes into view, it will be necessary to give a brief sketch of the political, as well as of the philosophical and religious, movement to the time of Plotinus. For the ultimate causes of the triumph of another system were social more than they were intellectual, and go far back into the past. Of the preceding philosophical development, no detailed history can be attempted. As in the case of the political and religious history, all that can be done is to put the course of events in a light by which its general bearing may be made clear. In relation to the inner movement, the aim will be to show precisely at what point the way was open for an advance on previous philosophies,—an advance which,

it may be said by anticipation, Neo-Platonism did really succeed in making secure even for the time when the fortunes of
independent philosophy were at their lowest. Then, when the
history of the school itself has been set forth in some detail, a
sketch, again reduced to as brief compass as possible, must be
given of the return of the modern world to the exact point
where the thought of the ancient world had ceased, and of
the continued influence of the Neo-Platonic conceptions on
modern thought. Lastly, an attempt will be made to state
the law of the development; and, in relation to this, something will be said of the possibilities that still remain open for
the type of thought which has never been systematised with
more perfection than in the school of Plotinus.

"On pourrait dire, sans trop d'exagération, que l'histoire morale des premiers siècles de notre ère est dans l'histoire du platonisme."

MATTER, *Histoire Critique du Gnosticisme*, livre VIII. ch. 28.

CHAPTER I

GRAECO-ROMAN CIVILISATION IN ITS POLITICAL DEVELOPMENT

Broadly, the political history of classical antiquity almost from the opening of the historic period may be described as a slow passage from the condition of self-governing commonwealths with a subordinate priesthood to the condition of a theocratic despotism. This was a reduction of the West to the polity of the civilised East. In the old Oriental monarchies known to the classical world, the type was that of a consecrated despot ruling with the support and under the direction of a priesthood socially supreme. Immemorial forms of it were to be seen in Egypt and in the Assyrio-Babylonian civilisation on which the conquering Persian monarchy was superimposed. In Persia had appeared the earliest type of a revealed as distinguished from an organised natural religion. And here were the beginnings of the systematic intolerance at first so puzzling to the Greeks[1]. Intolerance, however, did not till later and from a new starting-point assume a permanently aggressive form. With the Persians, conquest over alien nationalities led to some degree of tolerance for their inherited religions.

The origin of the monarchies of Egypt and of Western Asia is a matter of conjecture. To the classical world they appeared as a finished type. The ancient European type of polity was

[1] Herodotus, though he knew and sympathised with the refusal of the Persian religion to ascribe visible form to the divinity, saw in the persecution of the Egyptian cult by Cambyses and in the burning of Greek temples by order of Xerxes, nothing but acts of wanton impiety. They had come to be better understood in the time of Cicero, who definitely ascribes the latter to the motive of pious intolerance. See *De Rep.* iii. 9, 14. After a reference to the animal deities of Egypt as illustrating the variety of religious customs among civilised men, the exposition proceeds: "Deinde Graeciae sicut apud nos, delubra magnifica humanis consecrata simulacris, quae Persae nefaria putaverunt, eamque unam ob causam Xerxes inflammari Atheniensium fana iussisse dicitur, quod deos, quorum domus esset omnis hic mundus, inclusos parietibus contineri nefas esse duceret."

new and independent. It did not spring out of the Oriental
type by way of variation. In investigating its accessible beginnings we probably get nearer to political origins than we
can in the East. We have there before our eyes the plastic
stage which cannot in the East be reconstructed. The Greek
tragic poets quite clearly distinguished their own early constitutional monarchies with incompletely developed germs of
aristocracy and democracy from Oriental despotism. While
these monarchies lasted, they were probably not very sharply
marked off, in the general consciousness, from other monarchical institutions. The advance to formal republicanism
revealed at once a new type of polity and the preparation for
it at an earlier stage. That this was to be the conquering type
might very well be imagined. Aeschylus puts into the mouth
of the Persian elders a lamentation over the approaching
downfall of kingship in Asia itself[1]. Yet this prophecy, as we
know, is further from being realised now than it may have
appeared then. And, though organised despotism on the great
scale was thrown back into Asia by the Persian wars, the later
history of Europe for a long period is the history of its return.

The republican type of culture was fixed for all time[2], first
in life and then in literature, by the brief pre-eminence of
Athens. The Greek type of free State, however, from its re-
striction to a city, and the absence of a representative system,
with other causes, could not maintain itself against the inroads
of the monarchical principle, which at that time had the power
of conferring unity on a larger aggregate. The Macedonian
monarchy, originally of the constitutional type, became,
through its conquests at once over Greece and Asia, essentially
an Oriental monarchy—afterwards a group of monarchies—
distinguished only by its appropriation of the literary culture

---

[1]   οὐδ' ἐς γᾶν προπίτνοντες
ἄρξονται· βασιλεία
γὰρ διόλωλεν ἰσχύς.
οὐδ' ἔτι γλῶσσα βροτοῖσιν
ἐν φυλακαῖς· λέλυται γὰρ
λαὸς ἐλεύθερα βάζειν,
ὡς ἐλύθη ζυγὸν ἀλκᾶς.   *Pers.* 588–594.

[2]   ἐς τὸν ἄπαντα ἀνθρώπων βίον.   Herod. vi. 109.

of Greece. Later, the republican institutions of Rome, which
succeeded those of Greece as the type of political freedom,
broke down, in spite of their greater flexibility and power of
incorporating subjects[1], through a combination of the causes
that affected Greece and Macedon separately. Perhaps the
imperial monarchy was a necessity if the civilised world was
to be kept together for some centuries longer, and not to break
up into warring sections. Still, it was a lapse to a lower form
of polity. And the republican resistance can be historically
justified. The death of Caesar showed his inheritors that the
hour for formal monarchy was not yet come. The complete
shaping of the Empire on the Oriental model was, in fact,
postponed to the age of Diocletian and Constantine. Mean-
while, the emperor not being formally monarch, and the republic remaining in name, the whole system of education continued to be republican in basis. The most revered classics
were those that had come down from the time of freedom.
Declamations against tyrants were a common exercise in the
schools. And the senatorial opposition, which still cherished
the ethical ideal of the republic, came into power with the
emperors of the second century. What it has become the
fashion to call the "republican prejudices" of Tacitus and
Suetonius were adopted by Marcus Aurelius, who, after citing
with admiration the names of Cato and Brutus, along with
those of later heroes of the Stoical protestation against
Caesarean despotism, holds up before himself "the idea of
a polity in which there is the same law for all, a polity ad-
ministered with regard to equal rights and equal freedom of
speech, and the idea of a kingly government which respects
most of all the freedom of the governed[2]." Here the demand

[1] That the Romans themselves were conscious of this, may be seen for
example in a speech of the Emperor Claudius as recorded by Tacitus (*Ann.*
xi. 24): "Quid aliud exitio Lacedaemoniis et Atheniensibus fuit, quamquam
armis pollerent, nisi quod victos pro alienigenis arcebant? at conditor nostri
Romulus tantum sapientia valuit, ut plerosque populos eodem die hostes,
dein cives habuerit."

[2] i. 14 (Long's Translation). With the above passage may be compared
Julian's appeal to Plato and Aristotle in support of his conviction that the
spirit of laws should be impersonal (*Epistola ad Themistium*, 261–2). The
second imperial philosopher, in his satirical composition entitled *Caesares*,

for administrative unity might seem to be reconciled with the older ideal; but the Stoic emperor represented the departing and not the coming age.

There was a discrepancy between the imperial monarchy on the one hand, potentially absolute, though limited by the deference of the ruler for ancient forms, and on the other hand the ideal that had come down from the past. The ethics of antiquity had never incorporated absolutism. Now the new religion that was already aiming at the spiritual dominance of the Empire had no tradition that could separate it from the monarchical system. Christian ethics from the first accepted absolutism as its political datum. The Christian apologists under the Antonines represent themselves as a kind of legiti-mists,—praying, in the time of Marcus Aurelius, that the right of succession of Commodus may be recognised and the blessing of hereditary kingship secured[1]. Christianity therefore, once accepted, consecrated for the time an ideal in accordance with the actual movement of the world. In substituting the notion of a monarch divinely appointed for the apotheosis of the emperors, it gave a form less unendurable in civilised Europe to a servility which, in its pagan form, appearing as an Asiatic superstition, had been something of a scandal to the rulers who were in a manner compelled to countenance it. The result, unmodified by new factors, is seen in the Byzantine Empire. The Roman Empire of the East remained strong enough to throw off the barbarian attack for centuries. It preserved much of ancient Greek letters. In distinction from the native monarchies of Asia, it possessed a system of law that had received its bent during a period of freedom[2]. But, with these differences, it was a theocratic monarchy of the Oriental type. It was the last result, not of a purely internal

most frequently reaffirms the judgments of Suetonius and Tacitus, but not without discrimination. Tiberius he sums up as a mixed character, and does not represent him as flung into Tartarus with Caligula and Nero.

[1] See Renan, *Marc-Aurèle*, where illustrations are given of this attitude on the part of the apologists.

[2] "The period of Roman freedom was the period during which the stamp of a distinctive character was impressed on the Roman jurisprudence." Sir Henry Maine, *Ancient Law*, 10th ed., ch. ii. p. 40.

development, but of reaction on the Graeco-Roman world from the political institutions and the religions of Asia.

The course of things in the West was different. Having been for a time reduced almost to chaos by the irruptions of the Germanic tribes, the disintegrated and then nominally revived Western Empire furnished the Church with the opportunity of erecting an independent theocracy above the secular rule of princes. This type came nearest to realisation in the twelfth and thirteenth centuries. It broke down partly through internal decay and partly through the upgrowth of a stronger secular life. With immense difficulty and with the appearance almost of accident[1], a new kind of free State arose. The old Teutonic monarchies, like the old Greek monarchies, were not of the Asiatic type. They contained elements of political aristocracy and democracy which could develop under favouring circumstances. In most cases the development did not take place. With the cessation of feudal anarchy, the royal power became too strong to be effectively checked. There was formed under it a social hierarchy of which the most privileged equally with the least privileged orders were excluded as such from all recognised political authority. Thus on the Continent, during the early modern period, the prevailing type became Catholic Absolutism, or, as it has been called, "European monarchy,"—a system which was imitated in the Continental Protestant States. By the eighteenth century this had become, like the Byzantine Empire or the old Asiatic monarchies, a fixed type, a terminal despotism from which there could be no peaceful issue. It was destroyed—so far as it has since been destroyed—by the revolutionary influence of ideas from the past and from without. In England the germs of freedom, instead of being suppressed, were developed, and in the seventeenth century, after a period of conflict, the modern system of constitutional monarchy was established. To the political form of the modern free State, early English institutions by their preservation contributed most. Classical reminiscences, in England as elsewhere, enkindled the love of

[1] Comte at least regarded Absolutism as the normal development, Constitutionalism as a local anomaly, in European history before 1789.

freedom; but deliberate imitation was unnecessary where the
germs from which the ancient republics themselves had sprung
were still ready to take a new form. From England the influence of revived political freedom diffused itself, especially
in France, where it combined with the emulation of classical
models and with generalisations from Roman law, to form
the abstract system of "natural rights." From this system,
on the intellectual side, have sprung the American and the
French Republics.

In the general European development, the smaller constitutional States may be neglected. The reappearance of a
kind of city-republic in mediaeval Italy is noteworthy, but
had little practical influence. The Italian cities were never
completely sovereign States like the Greek cities. Politically,
it is as if these had accepted autonomy under the supremacy
of the Great King. Spiritually, it is as if they had submitted
to a form of the Zoroastrian religion from which dissent was
penal. Nor did the great Italian poets and thinkers ever quite
set up the ideal of the autonomous city as the Greeks had
done. In its ideal, their city was rather a kind of municipality:
with Dante, under the "universal monarchy" of the restored
Empire; with Petrarch and more distinctly with Machiavelli,
under Italy as a national State, unified by any practicable
means. Even in its diminished form, the old type of republic
was exceedingly favourable to the reviving culture of Europe;
but the prestige of the national States around was too strong
for it to survive except as an interesting accident.

The present type of free State is one to which no terminal
form can be assigned. In England and in America, in France
and in Italy, not to speak of the mixed forms existing elsewhere, it is still at the stage of growth. The yet living rival
with which it stands confronted is the Russian continuation
or reproduction of Christian theocracy in its Byzantine form[1].

---

[1] This epilogue, sketching the political transition to modern Europe,
seemed necessary for the sake of formal completeness, although the bearing
of political history on the history of philosophy is much less direct in modern
than in ancient times. Since 1901 (the date of the first edition), war and
revolution have changed the aspect of things indicated in the last sentence of
the chapter.

CHAPTER II

THE STAGES OF GREEK PHILOSOPHY

AT the time of the Persian wars the civilisation of the East was in complexity, specialism, organised industry—whatever relative importance we may attach to those features of progress—in all probability ahead of the civilisation of Greece. The conscious assumption of self-government by the Greek cities had, however, been closely followed by the beginnings of what we may call speculative science, which was a distinctive product of the Greek intellect. For this, the starting-point was furnished by the empirical observations of Egyptians and Chaldaeans, made with a view to real or fancied utility—measurement of land or prediction of future events. The earliest Greek philosophers, natives of the Ionian cities of Asia Minor, and thus on the borders of the fixed and the growing civilisations, took up a few generalised results of the long and laborious but unspeculative accumulation of facts and methods by the leisured priesthoods[1] of Egypt and Babylonia, and forthwith entered upon the new paths of cosmical theorising without regard to authoritative tradition, and of deductive thinking about numbers and figures without regard to immediate utility. As early as Pythagoras, still in the sixth century B.C., speculative science had begun to show signs of its later division into philosophy properly so-called, and positive science; the first special sciences to become detached, after mathematics, being those to which mathematical treatment seemed applicable. All this took place before the continuous movement of reflective thinking on human knowledge,

---

[1] This way of putting the matter seems to reconcile the accounts of the invention of geometry in Egypt given by Herodotus and Aristotle, which Prof. Burnet (*Early Greek Philosophy*, 1st ed., Introduction, p. 19) finds discrepant. Herodotus assigns the motive, *viz.* "the necessity of measuring the lands afresh after the inundations"; Aristotle the condition that made it possible, *viz.* "the leisure enjoyed by the priestly caste."

which marks a new departure in philosophy, not its first origin,
began at Athens.

The emotion in which philosophy and science had their
common source was exactly the same in ancient Greece and
in renascent Europe. Plato and Aristotle, like Descartes and
Hobbes, define it as "wonder." The earliest thinkers did not
define it at all. Their outlook has still something very impersonal. With them, there is little inquiry about happiness
or the means of attaining it. When the speculative life has
been lived by several generations of thinkers, and a self-conscious theory of it is at length set forth, as at the opening of
Aristotle's *Metaphysics*, the happiness involved in it is regarded as something that necessarily goes with mere thinking
and understanding.

This is the subjective form of early Greek philosophy. In
objective content, it is marked by complete detachment from
religion. No traditional authority is acknowledged. Myths
are taken merely as offering points of contact, quite as frequently for attack as for interpretation in the sense of the
individual thinker. The handling of them in either case is
perfectly free. Results of the thought and observation of one
thinker are summed up by him, not to be straightway accepted by the next, but to be examined anew. The aim is
insight, not edification.

The general result is a conception of the cosmos in principle
not unlike that of modern science; in detail necessarily crude,
though still scientific in spirit, and often anticipating the
latest phases of thought in remarkable ways. Even the representations of the earth as a disc floating on water, and of the
stars as orifices in circular tubes containing fire, are less remote in spirit from modern objective science than the astronomy of later antiquity and of the instructed Middle Ages.
This was far more accurate in its conception of shapes and
magnitudes and apparent motions, but it was teleological in
a way that purely scientific astronomy cannot be. The earliest
Ionian thinkers, like modern men of science, imposed no teleological conceptions on their astronomical theories.

At the same time, early Greek philosophy was not merely

objective, as modern science has become. It was properly philosophical in virtue of its "hylozoism." Life and mind, or their elements, were attributed to the world or its parts. Later, a more objective "naturalism" appears, as in the system of Democritus. Here the philosophical character is still retained by the addition of an explicit theory of knowledge to the scientific explanation of the cosmos. "Primary" and "secondary" qualities of matter are distinguished, and these last are treated as in a sense unreal. Thus the definite formulation of materialism is accompanied by the beginnings of subjective idealism. But with the earliest thinkers of all, there is neither an explicit theory of knowledge nor an exclusion of life and mind from the elements of things.

The atomism of Democritus and his predecessors was the result of long thinking and perhaps of much controversy. The "Ionians," down to Heraclitus, regarded the cosmos as continuously existing, but as ruled by change in all its parts if not also as a whole. The Eleatics, who came later, affirmed that unchanging Being alone exists: this is permanent and always identical; "not-being" absolutely does not exist, and change is illusory. The Being of Parmenides, it is now held[1], was primarily the extended cosmos regarded as a closed sphere coincident with all that is. Yet, though the conception was in its basis physical and not metaphysical, the metaphysical abstraction made by Plato was doubtless implicit in it. And Parmenides himself evidently did not conceive reality as purely objective and mindless. If he had intended to convey that meaning, he would have been in violent contradiction with his predecessor Xenophanes, and this would hardly have escaped notice. The defect of Eleaticism was that apparent change received no satisfactory explanation, though an attempt was made to explain it in what Parmenides called a "deceptive" discourse as dealing with illusory opinion and no longer with demonstrative truth. Atomism mediated between this view and that of the Ionians by asserting a plurality of real beings, each having the characters of the Eleatic

[1] See Tannery, *Pour l'Histoire de la Science Hellène*, and Burnet, *Early Greek Philosophy*.

"being." "Not-being" for the atomists was empty space; change in the appearances of things was explained by mixture and separation of unchanging elements. The mechanical conception of the purely quantitative atom, which modern science afterwards took up, was completed by Democritus. Anaxagoras, though fundamentally a mechanicist, did not deprive his atoms of quality. And Empedocles, along with ideas of mixture and separation—explained by the attractive and repulsive agents, at once forces and media, to which he gave the mythological names of Love and Strife—retained something of the old hylozoism. Over against the material elements of things, Anaxagoras set Mind as the agent by which they are sifted from their primitive chaos. This was the starting-point for a new development, less purely disinterested than the first because more coloured by ethical and religious motives, but requiring even greater philosophic originality for its accomplishment.

The new departure of philosophy, though adopting the Anaxagorean Mind as its starting-point, had its real source in the ethical and political reflection which began effectively with the Sophists and Socrates. To give this reflective attitude consistency, to set up the principles suggested by it against all exclusive explanations of reality from the material ground of things, and yet to do this without in the end letting go the notion of objective science, was the work of Plato. Aristotle continued Plato's work, while carrying forward science independently and giving it relatively a more important position. One great characteristic result of the earlier thinking—the assertion that materially nothing is created and nothing destroyed—was assumed as an axiom both by Plato and by Aristotle whenever they had to deal with physics. They did not take up from the earlier thinkers those specific ideas that afterwards turned out the most fruitful scientifically—though Plato had a kind of atomic theory—but they affirmed physical law in its most general principle. This they subordinated to their metaphysics by the conception of a universal teleology. The teleological conception of nature there is good historical ground for attributing also to Socrates.

The special importance which Plato's *Timaeus* acquired for his successors is due to its being the most definite attempt made by the philosopher himself to bring his distinctive thought into relation with objective science. Thus, in view of knowledge as it was in antiquity, the later Platonists were quite right in the stress they laid on this dialogue.

For the period following upon the death of Aristotle, during which Stoicism and Epicureanism were the predominant schools, the most important part of Plato's and Aristotle's thought was the ethical part. Both schools were, on the theoretical side, a return to naturalism as opposed to the Platonic and Aristotelian idealism. Both alike held that all reality is body; though the Stoics regarded it as continuous and the Epicureans as discrete. The soul, for the Stoics as for the Epicureans, was a particular kind of matter. The most fruitful conception in relation to the science of the future was preserved by Epicurus when he took up the Democritean idea of the atom, defined as possessing figured extension, resistance and weight; all "secondary" qualities being regarded as resulting from the changes of order and the interactions of the atoms. And, on the whole, the Epicureans appealed more to genuine curiosity about physics for itself[1], though ostensibly cultivating it only as a means towards ridding human life of the fear of meddlesome gods. If the determinism of the Stoics was more rigorous, it did not prevent their undertaking the defence of some popular superstitions which the Epicureans have the credit of opposing. On the other hand, Stoicism did more for ethics. While both schools, in strict definition, were "eudaemonist," the Stoics brought out far more clearly the social reference of morality. Their line of thought here, as the Academics and Peripatetics were fond of pointing out, could be traced back to Plato and Aristotle. So also could the teleology which they combined with their naturalism. But all the systems of the time were more or less eclectic.

The social form under which the Stoics conceived of morality was the reference, no longer to a particular State,

[1] Mr Benn, in his *Greek Philosophers*, points out the resemblance of Lucretius in type of mind to the early physical thinkers of Greece.

but to a kind of universal State. Since the social reference
in Greek morality had been originally to the "city," the name
was retained, but it was extended to the whole world, and the
ideal morality was said to be that of a citizen of the world.
This "cosmopolitanism" is prepared in Plato and Aristotle.
Socrates (as may be seen in the *Memorabilia* of Xenophon)
had already conceived the idea of a natural law or justice
which is the same for all States. And in Aristotle that conception of "natural law" which, transmitted by Stoicism, had
so much influence on the Roman jurisprudence, is definitely
formulated[1]. The humanitarian side of Stoicism—which is
not quite the same thing as its conception of universal justice
—is plainly visible in Cicero[2].

Although Zeno, the founder of Stoicism, was by race half a
Phoenician, it cannot be said that the East contributed anything definable to the content of his ethics. Its sources were
evidently Greek. Down to the end of the ancient world,
philosophy was continued by men of various races, but always
by those who had taken the impress of Greek or of Graeco-
Roman civilisation,

The same general account is true of the Neo-Platonists.
They too were men who had inherited or adopted the Hellenic
tradition. On the ethical side they continue Stoicism; although in assigning a higher place to the theoretic virtues

[1] See the quotation and references given by Zeller, ii. 2, p. 646, n. 1.
(*Aristotle*, Eng. Trans., ii. 175, n. 3.)

[2] See, in *De Finibus*, the exposition of Cato, deducing from the Stoic
principles the existence of a "communis humani generis societas" (iii. 19, 62).
"Bonitas" is expressly distinguished from "justitia" (c. 20, 66); cf. *De Off.*
iii. 6, 28. In the fifth book of the *De Finibus*, Piso goes back for the origin of
the whole doctrine to the Platonists and Peripatetics. The following sentence
(c. 23, 65) sums up the theory: "In omni autem honesto, de quo loquimur,
nihil est tam illustre nec quod latius pateat quam coniunctio inter homines
hominum et quasi quaedam societas et communicatio utilitatum et ipsa
caritas generis humani, quae nata a primo satu, quod a procreatoribus nati
diliguntur et tota domus coniugio et stirpe coniungitur, serpit sensim foras,
cognationibus primum, tum affinitatibus, deinde amicitiis, post vicinitatibus,
tum civibus et iis, qui publice socii atque amici sunt, deinde totius complexu
gentis humanae; quae animi affectio suum cuique tribuens atque hanc, quam
dico, societatem coniunctionis humanae munifice et aeque tuens iustitia dicitur,
cui sunt adiunctae pietas, bonitas, liberalitas, benignitas, comitas, quaeque
sunt generis eiusdem."

they return to an earlier view. Their genuine originality is in psychology and metaphysics. Having gone to the centre of Plato's idealistic thought, they demonstrated, by a new application of its principles, the untenableness of the Stoic materialism; and, after the long intervening period, they succeeded in defining more rigorously than Plato had done, in psychology the idea of consciousness, in metaphysics the idea of immaterial and subjective existence. Scientifically, they incorporated elements of every doctrine with the exception of Epicureanism; going back with studious interest to the pre-Socratics, many fragments of whom the latest Neo-Platonist commentators rescued just as they were on the point of being lost. On the subjective side, they carried thought to the highest point reached in antiquity. And neither in Plotinus, the great original thinker of the school, nor in his successors, was this the result of mystical fancies or of Oriental influences. These, when they appeared, were superinduced. No idealistic philosophers have ever applied closer reasoning or subtler analysis to the relations between the inner and the outer world. If the school to some extent "Orientalised," in this it followed Plato; and it diverged far less from Hellenic ideals than Plato himself.

A certain affinity of Plato with the East has often been noticed. This led him to the most remarkable previsions of the later movement of the world. The system of caste in the *Republic* is usually said to be an anticipation of the mediaeval order of society. Now in the introduction to the *Timaeus* and in the *Critias*, the social order of Egypt is identified in its determining principles with that of the ideal State, and both with the constitution of pre-historic Athens, also regarded as ideal. Hence it becomes evident that, for his specialisation and grading of social functions, Plato got the hint from the Egyptian caste of occupations[1]. Thus his ideal society is in contact, on one side with the pre-Hellenic East, on the other side with the Orientalised Europe of the Middle Ages. By its communism it touches modern schemes of reform[2].

---

[1] Cf. Arist. *Pol.* iv. (vii.) 9, 1329 b 23: ὁ δὲ χωρισμὸς ὁ κατὰ γένος τοῦ πολιτικοῦ πλήθους ἐξ Αἰγύπτου.   [2] See Appendix I.

Mr Benn has remarked that the stages of degeneration from the ideal aristocracy to a tyranny, set forth in the *Republic*, are the same as the actual stages of degeneration of the Roman State. To this it may be added that in the *Laws* Plato lays down the exact conditions that concurred for the establishment of Christianity. The problem is to get a new system of legislation received in the projected colony. For this he finds that, though citizens from the same State are better in so far as they are likely to be more orderly, yet they will be too attached to their own laws. There is therefore an advantage in beginning with a mixture of colonists from several States. The character of such colonists will make the task in any case difficult, but the most favourable condition is that the ideas of a great legislator should be taken up by a young and vigorous tyrant. Generalise a little, putting for a single legislator the succession of those who formulated ecclesiastical doctrine and discipline, and for a single tyrant the consummated autocracy of the later Roman Empire, and the conditions are historically given. For there was, in the cosmopolitan Empire, exactly that mixture of different inherited customs which Plato desiderates. Add, what is continually insisted on in the *Laws*, that towards getting particular precepts enforced it would conduce much if they could be regarded as proceeding from a god, and it will be seen that here also the precise condition of success was laid down.

The philosopher even anticipated some of the actual legislation of the Church. In the tenth book of the *Laws*, he proposes a system of religious persecution. Three classes of the impious are to be cast out,—those who deny the existence of all gods, those who say that the gods take no heed of human affairs, and those who say that they can be bought off with prayers and gifts; or, as we may put it compendiously,— Atheists, Epicureans and Catholics. As, however, the last class would have been got rid of with least compunction, the anticipation here was by no means exact. And probably none of these glimpses, extraordinary as they were, into the strange transformation that was to come in a thousand years, had any influence in bringing it to pass.

The Neo-Platonists would have carried out an ethical reform of polytheism in the spirit of the *Republic* and the *Laws*; but they did not propose to set up persecution as a sanction. On the contrary, they were the champions of the old intellectual liberty of Hellenism against the new theocracy. One of the most Orientalising sayings to be found in the later Platonists, namely, that the "barbarians" have an advantage over the Greeks in the stability of their institutions and doctrines as contrasted with the Greek innovating spirit[1], occurs both in the *Timaeus* and in the *Laws*[2]. And Plato's attack, in the *Republic*, on the myths of Greek religion, was continued by the Christians, not by his Neo-Platonic successors; who sought to defend by allegorical interpretations whatever they could not accept literally; or at least, in repudiating the fables, did not advocate the expulsion of the poets.

It is to be remembered further that in the philosophical tradition of antiquity even more than in its general culture, the republican ideal was always upheld. Aristotle as well as Plato, it is true, was less favourable than the statesmen, orators and historians of the great Athenian period to personal spontaneity uncontrolled by the authority of the State. But of course what the philosophers desired was the supremacy of reason, not of arbitrary will. Licence in the city seemed to them condemnable on this ground among others, that under the show of liberty it paved the way for a tyrant. And the later schools, in which philosophy had fixed a sort of official

---

[1] Quoted by Ritter and Preller (*Historia Philosophiae Graecae*, 7th ed. 547 b) from the *De Mysteriis* formerly attributed to Iamblichus (vii. 5, ed. Parthey, p. 259): μεταβαλλόμενα ἀεὶ διὰ τὴν καινοτομίαν καὶ παρανομίαν τῶν Ἑλλήνων οὐδὲν παύεται...βάρβαροι δὲ μόνιμοι τοῖς ἤθεσιν ὄντες καὶ τοῖς λόγοις βεβαίως τοῖς αὐτοῖς ἐμμένουσι.

[2] Allowance being made for the point of view, the two aspects of Plato are appreciated with perfect exactitude by Joseph de Maistre in his vituperation of the Greek spirit. (*Du Pape*, livre iv. ch. 7.) Plato's "positive and eternal dogmas," says the brilliant reactionary, "portent si clairement le cachet oriental que, pour le méconnaître, il faut n'avoir jamais entrevu l'Asie....Il y avait en lui un sophiste et un théologien, ou, si l'on veut, un Grec et un Chaldéen. On n'entend pas ce philosophe si on ne le lit pas avec cette idée toujours présente à l'esprit."

attitude, were always understood to be hostile to despotism[1]. The Stoics in particular had this reputation, which they justified under the early Empire. That the Neo-Platonists, although by their time philosophy had almost ceased to have a political branch, were still of the ancient tradition, is proved by the republican spirit of Julian, who had received from them his self-chosen training[2]. In the chiefs of the school also, slight indications to the same effect may be discerned. This attitude of the philosophers had its importance in preserving the memory of the higher ideal notwithstanding the inevitable descent due to circumstance. And even in the early Middle Ages, deriving their knowledge of antiquity as they did mainly from a few late compilations, such discussions as there are on the origin of society and of government seem traceable to reminiscences from the philosophic schools; the idea of a social contract in particular coming probably from the Epicureans.

---

[1] Cf. Sueton. *Nero*, 52: "Liberalis disciplinas omnis fere puer attigit. Sed a philosophia eum mater avertit, monens imperaturo contrariam esse."

[2] Julian's refusal to be addressed by the title δεσπότης customary in the East, did not conciliate the "average sensual man" of Antioch. See *Misopogon*, 343 C—344 A: δεσπότης εἶναι οὐ φὴς οὐδὲ ἀνέχῃ τοῦτο ἀκούων, ἀλλὰ καὶ ἀγανακτεῖς,...δουλεύειν δ' ἡμᾶς ἀναγκάζεις ἄρχουσι καὶ νόμοις. καίτοι πόσῳ κρεῖττον ἦν ὀνομάζεσθαι μέν σε δεσπότην, ἔργῳ δὲ ἐᾶν ἡμᾶς εἶναι ἐλευθέρους;... ἀφεὶς δὲ τὴν σκηνὴν καὶ τοὺς μίμους καὶ τοὺς ὀρχηστὰς ἀπολώλεκας ἡμῶν τὴν πόλιν.

CHAPTER III

RELIGIOUS DEVELOPMENTS IN LATER ANTIQUITY

THOUGH philosophy at its beginning among the Ionians had broken with traditional authority as completely as it has ever done since, religion and free speculation did not cease to inter-act. In some points, however, their developments were inde-pendent. Religious developments independent of philosophy were the establishment and the increased attention paid to the "mysteries," and the importation of new worships from Egypt and Asia Minor. It was also due rather to a new development of religion than to philosophy, that more definite and vivid beliefs came to be popularly held about the immor-tality of the soul and about future rewards and punishments; though philosophers of religious mind sought to impress these doctrines along with the general conception of a providential government of the universe. In the Homeric poems, the soul goes away to the underworld as soon as the corpse is burnt, and can never afterwards reappear in the world of living men. Yet much later, in the dramatists, the ghost is invoked as still having active powers in this world. Here there is perhaps a survival of a stage of belief more primitive than the Homeric, rather than a development[1]; but in the notion of definite places of reward and punishment there was clearly some growth of belief. Perhaps the mythical treatment of immor-tality by which Plato follows up his arguments for it on speculative grounds, is more a reaction of older religion on philosophy than an application of philosophy to religion. To the exact truth of the representations given, the philosopher never commits himself, but merely contends that something of the kind is probably true, as against the imaginations in Homer of a world of lifeless shades contrasted in their un-reality with the vigour and bloom of life on earth. This side

[1] Rohde (*Psyche*, i.) finds evidences of such survival in Hesiod.

of Plato's teaching had for a long time not much influence. It became influential in proportion as religion revived. With Aristotle and the naturalistic schools, personal immortality almost went out of sight. The Epicureans denied the immortality of the human soul altogether, and with the Stoics survival of consciousness after death, if admitted at all, was only till the end of a cycle or "great year." The religious belief, and especially the belief in Tartarus, became, however, in the end vigorous enough to furnish one point of contact for a new religion that could make it still more definite and terrible. And one side of the new religion was prepared for by the notion, more or less seriously encouraged, that those who partook of the mysteries had somehow a privileged position among the dead[1]. This of course was discountenanced by the most religious philosophers; though they came to hold that it showed a certain want of piety towards ancestral beliefs to make light of initiation into the native mysteries.

Ancient religion and philosophy had not always been on such amicable terms as are implied in this last approximation. Especially at the beginning, when philosophy was a new thing, what may be called a sporadic intolerance was manifested towards it. Indeed, had this not been so, it would be necessary to allow that human nature has since then changed fundamentally. Without such germs of intolerance, its later developments would have been inconceivable. What can be truly said is that the institutions of antiquity were altogether unfavourable to the organisation of it. The death of Socrates had political more perhaps than religious motives. It has even been maintained that serious intolerance first appeared in the Socratic school itself[2]. Plato, it is clear, would have been quite willing that an ethical reform of religion should be carried out by force. After the first collision, however, religion on the one side remained unorganised, and philosophy on the other side practically free.

[1] Cf. Hatch, *The Influence of Greek Ideas and Usages upon the Christian Church*, Lecture X.

[2] This is the thesis of a very suggestive little book by M. G. Sorel, entitled *Le Procès de Socrate* (1889).

How far was popular polytheism taken seriously? That it was not taken seriously by the philosophers is quite evident. Perhaps the Epicureans reacted on it less than any other school; for they conceived of their ethical ideal as realised by the many gods named in mythology, and they had no other divinities. Their quarrel was not with polytheism as such, but with the belief in gods who interrupted their divine tranquillity to interfere in the affairs of mortals. The belief of the philosophic schools generally was some form of theism, or, as in the case of the Stoics, pantheism, by which the gods of mythology, if recognised at all, were subordinated to a supreme intelligence or allegorised into natural forces. The later philosophers made use of more elaborate accommodations. Aristotle had rejected polytheism in so many words. Plato had dismissed it with irony. Their successors needed those explicit theories of a rationalising kind which Plato thought rather idle. For the educated world, both in earlier and later antiquity, Cudworth's position is probably in the main true, that a sort of monotheism was held over and above all ideas of gods and daemons.

Thus the controversy between Christian assailants and pagan defenders of the national religions was not really a controversy between monotheism and polytheism. The champions of the old gods contended only for the general reasonableness of the belief that different parts of the earth have been distributed to different powers, divine though subordinate[1]. And in principle the Christians could have no objection to this. They themselves often held with regard to angels what the pagans attributed to gods; or even allowed the real agency of the pagan gods, but called them "daemons," holding them to be evil beings. The later paganism also allowed the existence of evil daemons, and had a place for angels among supernatural powers. Perhaps there is here a trace of influence from the Eastern gnosis; though Proclus insisted that the name is not peculiar to "the barbarian theosophy," but was applied of old to genuinely Hellenic divinities[2].

---

[1] Cf. Keim, *Celsus' Wahres Wort*, p. 67.

[2] See *Comm. in Remp.*, ed. Kroll, ii. 255: οὐ ξενικὸν τὸ ὄνομα καὶ βαρβάρου

It is often represented as a paradox that the Christian idea
of a suffering God should have triumphed over what is supposed to have been the universal prejudice of paganism that
to suffer is incompatible with divinity. There is no real
paradox. Ideas of suffering gods were everywhere, and the
worship of them became the most popular. The case is really
this. The philosophers held that absolutely divine beings—
who are not the gods of fable—are "impassible." In oratorical
apologies for the Crucifixion and the Resurrection, this philosophic view of the divinity had to be met. On the other hand,
the Christians made most of their converts among those who
were not philosophers. By their mode of appeal, they got the
advantage at once of a rigorous monotheism such as philosophy was tending to diffuse, and of the idea that expiations
could be performed by incarnate and suffering deities, such
as were believed in over all the pagan world. Exactly with
this kind of popular paganism philosophy had had its quarrel.
Of Xenophanes, the earliest explicitly monotheistic philosopher, it is related that, being asked by the people of Elea
whether they should sacrifice to Leucothea and lament for
her, he replied: "If you think her a god, do not lament; if
human, do not sacrifice[1]." The same view was taken by later
philosophers. It was against this, and not against the
popular imaginations, that such sayings as the well-known
one of Tertullian were directed[2].

Coinciding with the rise of Christianity there was, as has
lately come to be recognised, a revival, not a decline, of
ancient religion. The semblance of decline is due to the
effect produced on modern readers by the literature of the
later Roman Republic and earlier Empire, which proceeded
for the most part from the sceptical minority. This impression

θεοσοφίας μόνης, ἀλλὰ καὶ Πλάτων ἐν Κρατύλῳ τὸν Ἑρμῆν καὶ τὴν Ἶριν θεῶν
ἀγγέλους εἶναί φησιν.

[1] Arist. Rhet. ii. 23, 1400 b 5. (R. P. 81 a.) Ξενοφάνης Ἐλεάταις ἐρωτῶσιν εἰ
θύωσι τῇ Λευκοθέᾳ καὶ θρηνῶσιν ἢ μή, συνεβούλευεν, εἰ μὲν θεὸν ὑπολαμβάνουσι,
μὴ θρηνεῖν, εἰ δ᾽ ἄνθρωπον, μὴ θύειν.

[2] Tert. De Carne Christi, c. 5: "Natus est Dei Filius; non pudet, quia
pudendum est: et mortuus est Dei Filius; prorsus credibile est, quia ineptum
est: et sepultus, resurrexit; certum est, quia impossibile."

has been corrected by the evidence of archaeology. So far as
there was a real decline in the worship of the old gods, it
meant only a desertion of indigenous cults for more exciting
ones from the East. First there appeared the cult of the
Oriental Bacchus, then of Cybele and of Isis. And all these
present curious analogies with Christianity. It is an interesting circumstance that from the *Bacchae* of Euripides,—which
is essentially a picture of the uncontrollable frenzy aroused
by devotion to a lately born son of Zeus, persecuted and afterwards triumphant, coming from the East,—many lines were
transferred to the *Christus Patiens*[1]. The neglect of the altars
of the gods spoken of by Lucian may be explained by this
transfer of devotion. In the dialogue Θεῶν Ἐκκλησία, the
Hellenic gods are called together with a view to the expulsion
of intruding barbarian divinities, such as those that wear
Persian or Assyrian garments, and above all "the brutish
gods of Nile," who, as Zeus himself is obliged to admit, are
a scandal to Olympus. Momus insinuates that the purge will
not turn out easy, since few of the gods, even among the
Hellenic ones themselves, if they come to be closely examined,
will be able to prove the purity of their race. Such an attempt
at conservative reform as is here satirised by Lucian no doubt
represented what was still the attitude of classical culture in
the second century; as may be seen by the invective of
Juvenal against the Egyptian religion. Later, the syncretism
that took in deities of every nationality came to be adopted
by the defenders of classicism. It is this kind of religious
syncretism, rather than pure classicism, that revives at the
Renaissance. The apology not only for the Greek gods but
for those of Egypt, as in truth all diverse representations of
the same divinity, is undertaken in one of Bruno's dialogues.
What makes this the more remarkable is that Bruno probably
got the hint for his *Spaccio della Bestia Trionfante* precisely
from the dialogue of Lucian just referred to.

The nearest approach in the Hellenic world to the idea of a

---

[1] See the notes in Paley's edition of Euripides. The *Christus Patiens* was
formerly attributed to Gregory Nazianzen, but is now held to be of much
later date.

personal religious revelation was made by the philosophic sect of the Pythagoreans. The early history of the sect is mainly the account of an attempt at ethico-political regulation of cities in the south of Italy by oligarchies imbued with the philosophical and religious ideas of Pythagoras. These oligarchies made themselves intensely unpopular, and the Pythagorean associations were violently suppressed. Afterwards remains of the societies combined to form a school specially devoted to geometry and astronomy, and in astronomy remarkable for suggestions of heliocentric ideas. Till we come to the Neo-Pythagoreans of about the first century B.C., the history of the school is obscure. Its religious side is observable in this, that those who claim to be of the Pythagorean succession appeal more than other philosophers to the recorded sayings of the founder, and try to formulate a minute discipline of daily life in accordance with his precepts. The writings, mostly pseudonymous, attributed by them to early Pythagoreans[1] are in composition extremely eclectic, borrowing freely from the Stoics as well as from Plato and Aristotle. Coincidences were explained by the assumption that other philosophers had borrowed from Pythagoras. The approach of the Neo-Pythagorean school to the idea of a revelation is illustrated by the circumstance that Apollonius of Tyana, to whom in the first century A.D. miracles and a religious mission were attributed, was a Pythagorean. The lives of Pythagoras himself, by Porphyry and Iamblichus, are full of the marvels related in older documents from which both alike drew. According to Zeller, the peculiar doctrines and the ascetic discipline of the Essenes are to be ascribed to Neo-Pythagorean rather than to Indian or Persian influences. Their asceticism—an essentially non-Judaic character—has in any case to be explained from a foreign source; and its origin from this particular Hellenic source is on the whole the most probable, because of the number of detailed coincidences both in method of life and in doctrine.

Closely connected with the idea of the cosmical harmony, so strongly accentuated in the Pythagorean school, is the

[1] Zeller, iii. 2, pp. 100–3, gives a long list of them.

adoration of the stars thought of as animated beings, which
became in quite a special manner the philosophic religion.
This may have been first suggested by the star-worship
associated with the empirical observations of the Chaldaeans,
from which the Greek rational astronomy arose. There is not
much trace of this form of religion in Greek polytheism at its
first mythological stage. The genuine gods of Greece were
essentially anthropomorphic. In a passage of Aristophanes[1]
it is even said that the sun and moon are distinctively the gods
of the barbarians. The earliest philosophers did not treat the
heavenly bodies as in any special way divine, but regarded
them as composed of the same kinds of matter as the other
and lower bodies of the universe. When popular religion
thought it an impiety on the part of Anaxagoras to explain
the nature and action of the sun without introducing divine
agency, the divine agency required was no doubt of an anthropomorphic kind,—that of a charioteer for example. By Plato
and Aristotle the divinity of the stars themselves was affirmed;
and it afterwards became an article of faith with what we
may call pagan philosophical orthodoxy. It was for the
philosophers a mode of expressing the teleological relation
between the supreme Deity and the animated universe. The
heavenly bodies, according to the theory, were placed in
spheres to give origin by their motions to the ideas of time
and number, and to bring about the succession of day and
night and the changes of the seasons for the good of men and
other animals. That they might do this, they were endowed
with ruling intelligences superior to man's and more lasting.
For the animating principle of the stars, unimpeded by any
process of growth or decay, can energise continuously at its
height, whereas human souls, being temporarily united to
portions of unstable matter, lapse through such union from

---

[1] Quoted in Blakesley's Herodotus, vol. ii. p. 210, n.

TP. ἡ γὰρ σελήνη χὠ πανοῦργος ἥλιος,
ὑμῖν ἐπιβουλεύοντε πολὺν ἤδη χρόνον,
τοῖς βαρβάροισι προδίδοτον τὴν Ἑλλάδα.
EP. ἵνα τί δὲ τοῦτο δρᾶτον; TP. ὁτιὴ νὴ Δία
ἡμεῖς μὲν ὑμῖν θύομεν, τούτοισι δὲ
οἱ βάρβαροι θύουσι.   Pax, 406–11.

the condition of untroubled intellectual activity. This theory, founded by Plato in the *Timaeus*, was an assertion of teleological optimism against the notion that the stars are products of chance-aggregation. As such, it was defended by Plotinus against the pessimism of the Christian Gnostics, who—going beyond the Epicureans, as he says—regarded the present world as the work of an imperfect or of an evil creator. And in the latest period of the Neo-Platonic school at Athens, a high place was given, among the devotional usages adopted from the older national religions, to those that had reference to the heavenly bodies.

A current form taken by this modification of star-worship was astrology. Its wide dissemination in Italy is known from the edicts expelling the so-called "mathematici" or "Chaldaei," as well as from the patronage they nevertheless obtained at the courts of emperors. Along with magic or "theurgy," it came to be practised by some though not by all the members of the Neo-Platonic school. Plotinus himself, as a true successor of Plato, minimised where he could not entirely deny the possibility of astrological predictions and of magical influences, and discouraged the resort to them even if supposed real. In his school, from first to last, there were always two sections: on the one hand those who, in their attachment to the old religion and aversion from the new, inquired curiously into all that was still preserved in local traditions about human intercourse with gods or daemons; and on the other hand those who devoted themselves entirely to the cultivation of philosophy in a scientific spirit, or, if of more religious mind, aimed at mystical union with the highest God as the end of virtue and knowledge. This union, according to the general position of the school, was in no case attainable by magical practices, which at best brought the soul into relation with subordinate divine powers. According to those even who attached most importance to "theurgy," it was to be regarded as a means of preparation for the soul itself in its progress, not as having any influence on the divinity. One here and there, it was allowed, might attain to the religious consummation of philosophy without external aids, but for the majority they were necessary. As "magical" powers, when real, were held to be due to a strictly "natural" sympathy of each part of the universe with all the rest, and as this was not denied, on scientific grounds, by the opponents of magic, the theoretical difference between the two parties was less than might be supposed. It did not prevent philosophers of opposite views on this point from being on friendly terms with each other. The real chasm was between the philosophers who, however they might aspire after what they had heard of Eastern wisdom, had at heart the continuance of the Hellenic tradition, and those believers in a new revelation who, even if giving to their doctrines a highly speculative form, like the Gnostics[1], yet took up a revolutionary attitude towards the whole of ancient culture.

[1] See Appendix II.

CHAPTER IV

PLOTINUS AND HIS NEAREST PREDECESSORS

A NAME once customarily but incorrectly applied to the Neo-Platonist school was "the School of Alexandria." The historians who used the name were aware that it was not strictly correct, and now it seems to be again passing out of use. That the Neo-Platonic teachers were not in any close association with the scientific specialists and literary critics of the Alex-andrian Museum was elaborately demonstrated by Matter in a work which is really a History of the School—or rather Schools—of Alexandria, and not, like those of Vacherot and Jules Simon bearing the same general title, of Neo-Platonism. In his third volume (1848) Matter devotes a special section to the Neo-Platonic philosophy, "falsely called Alexandrian," and there he treats it as representing a mode of thought secretly antipathetic to the scientific spirit of the Museum. This, however, is an exaggeration. Of the obscure antipathy which he thinks existed, he does not bring any tangible evidence; and, in fact, when Neo-Platonism had become the philosophy of the Graeco-Roman world, it was received at Alexandria as elsewhere. What is to be avoided is merely the ascription of a peculiar local association that did not exist.

To the Jewish Platonism of Philo and to the Christian Platonism of Clement and Origen the name of "Alexandrian" may be correctly applied; for it was at Alexandria that both types of thought were elaborated. To the Hellenic Platonism of Plotinus and his school it has no proper application. Plotinus indeed received his philosophical training at Alexandria under Ammonius Saccas; but it was not till long after, at Rome, that he began to put forth a system of his own. After his death, knowledge of his system, through Porphyry and Iamblichus, diffused itself over all parts of the Roman Empire where there was any care for philosophy. Handed on by the successors of Iamblichus, the doctrine of Plotinus at last gained the assent of the occupants of Plato's chair in the Academy. The one brilliant period of Neo-Platonism at Alexandria was when it was expounded there by Hypatia. Its last great names are not those of Alexandrian teachers, but those of the "Platonic successors" at Athens, among whom by far the most distinguished was Proclus.

The school remained always in reality the school of Plotinus. From the direction impressed by him it derived its unity. A history of Neo-Platonism must therefore set out from the activity of Plotinus as teacher and thinker. Of this activity an account sufficient in the main points is given by his disciple Porphyry, who edited his writings and wrote his life[1].

Through the reticence of Plotinus himself, the date and place of his birth are not exactly recoverable. This reticence Porphyry connects with an ascetic repugnance to the body. It was only by stealth that a portrait of the master could be taken; his objection, when asked to sit to a painter, being the genuinely Platonic one that a picture was but an "image of an image." Why perpetuate this when the body itself is a mere image of reality? Hence also the philosopher did not wish to preserve the details of his outward history. Yet in his aesthetic criticism he is far from taking a merely depreciating view of the fine arts. His purpose seems to have been to prevent a cult of him from arising among his disciples. He would not tell his birthday, lest there should be a special celebration of it, as there had come to be of the birthdays of other philosophers[2]; although he himself used to keep the traditional birthday-feasts of Socrates and Plato[3].

According to Eunapius[4], he was born at Lyco (or Lycopolis) in Egypt. From Porphyry's Life the year of his birth is inferred to be 204 or 205. In his twenty-eighth year, being

[1] Porphyry's Life is prefixed to the edition of Plotinus by R. Volkmann (Teubner, 1883, 4), from which the citations in the present volume are made.

[2] Cicero treats the direction of Epicurus that his birthday should be celebrated after his death as a weakness in a philosopher. *De Fin.* ii. 31, 102: "Haec non erant eius, qui innumerabilis mundos infinitasque regiones, quarum nulla esset ora, nulla extremitas, mente peragravisset." In the last two words there is an evident allusion to Lucr. i. 74.

[3] Porph. *Vita Plotini*, 2.

[4] *Vitae Philosophorum ac Sophistarum* (Plotinus).

dissatisfied with the other Alexandrian teachers of philosophy whom he frequented, he was taken by a friend to Ammonius. When he had heard him, he said to his companion: "This is the man of whom I was in search" (τοῦτον ἐζήτουν). With Ammonius he remained eleven years. At the end of that time, he became eager to learn something definite of the philosophy that was cultivated among the Persians and Indians. Accordingly, in his thirty-ninth year he joined the expedition which Gordian was preparing against Persia (242). The Emperor was killed in Mesopotamia, and, the expedition having failed, Plotinus with difficulty escaped to Antioch. At the age of forty, he went to Rome (244); where, for ten whole years, though giving philosophical instruction, he wrote nothing. He began to write in the first year of the reign of Gallienus (254). In 263, when Plotinus was about fifty-nine, Porphyry, then thirty years of age, first came into relation with him. Plotinus had by that time written twenty-one "books," on such topics as had presented themselves in lectures and discussions. These Porphyry found issued to a few. Under the stimulus of new discussions, and urged by himself and an earlier pupil, Amelius Gentilianus, who had come to him in his third year at Rome, Plotinus now, in the six years that Porphyry was with him, wrote twenty-four more books. The procedure was as before; the books taking their starting-point from the questions that occurred[1]. While Porphyry was in Sicily, whither he had retired about 268, Plotinus sent him in all nine more books. In 270, during this absence, Plotinus died in Campania. After his death, Amelius consulted the Delphic oracle on his lot, and received a response placing him among the happy daemons, which Porphyry transcribes in full[2].

Among the hearers of Plotinus, as Porphyry relates, were not a few senators. Of these was Rogatianus, who carried philosophic detachment so far as to give up all his possessions, dismiss all his slaves, and resign his senatorial rank. Having before suffered severely from the gout, he now, under the

---

[1] *V. Plot.* 5: ἐκ προσκαίρων προβλημάτων τὰς ὑποθέσεις λαβόντα.
[2] *V. Plot.* 22.

abstemious rule of life he adopted, completely recovered[1]. To
Plotinus were entrusted many wards of both sexes, to the
interests of whose property he carefully attended. During the
twenty-six years of his residence at Rome, he acted as umpire
in a great number of disputes, which he was able to settle
without ever exciting enmity. Porphyry gives some examples
of his insight into character, and takes this occasion to explain
the reason of his own retirement into Sicily. Plotinus had
detected him meditating suicide; and, perceiving that the
cause was only a "disease of melancholy," persuaded him to
go away for a time[2]. One or two marvellous stories are told
in order to illustrate the power Plotinus had of resisting
malignant influences, and the divine protection he was under[3].
He was especially honoured by the Emperor Gallienus[4] and
his wife Salonina, and was almost permitted to carry out a
project of restoring a ruined city in Campania,—said to have
been once a "city of philosophers[5],"—which he was to govern
according to the Platonic Laws, giving it the name of "Plato-
nopolis[6]." The fortunes of the scheme are curiously recalled
by those of Berkeley's projected university in the Bermudas.

At the time of this project, Plotinus must have been already
engaged in the composition of his philosophical books. As
Porphyry relates, no external demands on his attention, with
whatever good will and practical success he might respond to
them, could break the continuity of his meditations, which he
had always the power to resume exactly at the point where
he had left off. Of the characteristics of his lecturing, his
disciple gives a sympathetic picture[7]. He did not care for
personal controversy; as was shown by his commissioning his
pupils to reply to attacks on his positions. Porphyry mentions

---

[1] V. Plot. 7.   [2] Ibid. 11.   [3] Ibid. 10.

[4] Gallienus tolerated Christianity. He was a man of considerable accomplishments, though the historians do not speak highly of him as a ruler.

[5] This apparently means, as has been conjectured (R. P. 508 f.), that it had
formerly been ruled by a Pythagorean society.

[6] V. Plot. 12.

[7] V. Plot. 13: ἦν δ' ἐν τῷ λέγειν ἡ ἔνδειξις τοῦ νοῦ ἄχρι τοῦ προσώπου αὐτοῦ τὸ
φῶς ἐπιλάμποντος· ἐράσμιος μὲν ὀφθῆναι, καλλίων δὲ τότε μάλιστα ὁρώμενος· καὶ
λεπτός τις ἱδρὼς ἐπέθει καὶ ἡ πρᾳότης διέλαμπε καὶ τὸ προσηνὲς πρὸς τὰς ἐρωτήσεις
ἐδείκνυτο καὶ τὸ εὔτονον.

a case in which he himself was set to answer an unedifying discourse of the rhetor Diophanes[1]. The books of Plotinus, as we have seen, were not composed on any general plan. Porphyry relates that, through a weakness of the eyes, he never read over again what he had once written. His grammatical knowledge of Greek remained imperfect, and the revision as well as editing of his writings was committed to Porphyry, from whom proceeds the arrangement of the six "Enneads,"—the name the fifty-four books received from their ordering in groups of nine. While he worked in this irregular way, the character of his thought was extremely systematic. He evidently possessed his doctrine as a whole from the time when he began to write. Yet in detail, even to the very last books, in which Porphyry thought he observed a decline of power, he has always something effectively new to add.

In addition to the grouping according to subjects, which he adopted for his arrangement of the Enneads as we have them, Porphyry has put on record an alternative ordering which may be taken as at least approximately chronological. The chronological order is certain as regards the succession of the main groups. Of these there are three, or, more exactly, four; the third group being divided into two sub-groups. At the beginning of the second main group also the order of four books is certain. For the rest, Porphyry does not definitely state that the books are all in chronological order; but, as his general arrangement in this enumeration is chronological, we may take it that he carried it through in detail as far as he could; and, as a matter of fact, links of association can often be detected in passing consecutively from one book to another. For reading, I have found this order on the whole more convenient than the actual grouping of the Enneads.

When the books are read in this chronological order, the psychological starting-point of the system becomes particularly obvious, the main positions about the soul coming early in the series. In the exposition that is to follow[2], these will be set forth first. After Psychology will come Metaphysics,

---

[1] *V. Plot.* 15.   [2] See ch. **v.**

then in succession Cosmology (with Theodicy), Aesthetics and Ethics[1]. A separate chapter will be devoted to the Mysticism of Plotinus[2]. For this order of exposition support might be found in what Plotinus himself says, where he points out that from the doctrine of the soul, as from a centre, we can equally ascend and descend[3].

Before beginning the exposition, an attempt must be made to ascertain the points of contact furnished to Plotinus by those nearest him in time. His general relation to his predecessors is on the whole clear, but not the details. Of the teachings of his Alexandrian master, nothing trustworthy is recorded. Ammonius left nothing written, and the short accounts preserved of his doctrine come from writers too late to have had any real means of knowing. What those writers do is to ascribe to him the reasoned positions of Plotinus, or even the special aims of still later thinkers contemporary with themselves. Porphyry, in a passage quoted by Eusebius, mentions that Ammonius had been brought up as a Christian, but, as soon as he came in contact with philosophy, returned to the religion publicly professed. He is spoken of as a native of Alexandria; and the name "Saccas" is explained by his having been originally a porter (Σακκᾶς being equivalent to σακκοφόρος). Hierocles calls him "the divinely taught" (θεοδίδακτος). Besides Plotinus he had as pupils Longinus the famous critic[4], Origen the Christian, and another Origen. With this Origen and a fellow-student named Herennius, Plotinus is said to have entered into a compact that none of them should divulge the doctrine of Ammonius. The compact was first broken by Herennius, then by Origen; lastly Plotinus thought himself at liberty to expound the master's doctrine orally. Not for ten more years did he begin to write[5]. Evidently this, even if accepted, does little towards explaining

---

[1] Roughly, this corresponds to the order:—Enn. IV. V. VI. II. III. I.
[2] See ch. vi.   [3] Enn. IV. 3, 1.
[4] The Περὶ Ὕψους, formerly attributed to Longinus, is now generally ascribed to some unknown writer of the first century. See the edition by Prof. W. Rhys Roberts (1899), who, however, points out that in its spirit it is such a work as might very well have proceeded from the historical Longinus.
[5] Porph. V. Plot. 3.

the source of the written doctrine of Plotinus,—in which there is no reference to Ammonius,—and Zeller throws doubt on the whole story[1], regarding it as suspiciously like what is related about a similar compact among the early Pythagoreans. It is to be observed that Porphyry does not say that he had it directly from Plotinus.

What is clear is this, that from Ammonius Plotinus must have received some impulse which was of great importance for his intellectual development. In the class-room of Plotinus, we learn from Porphyry[2], the later Platonic and Aristotelian commentators were read; but everywhere an original turn was given to the discussions, into which Plotinus carried the spirit of Ammonius. This probably indicates with sufficient clearness the real state of the case. Ammonius was one of those teachers who have the power of stirring up independent thought along a certain line; but he was not himself the formative mind of the movement. The general line of thought was already marked out. Neither Ammonius nor Plotinus had to create an audience. A large section of the philosophical world had for long been dissatisfied with the Stoic, no less than with the Epicurean, dogmatism. The opposition was partly sceptical, partly Neo-Pythagorean and Platonic. The sceptical opposition was represented first by the New Academy, as we see in Cicero; afterwards by the revived Pyrrhonism of Aenesidemus and Sextus. In Cicero we see also, set against both Epicureanism and Stoicism as a more positive kind of opposition, a sort of eclectic combination of Platonic and Peripatetic positions. A later stage of this movement is represented by Plutarch; when Platonism, though not yet assuming systematic form, is already more metaphysical or "theological," and less predominantly ethical, than the eclecticism of Cicero's time. On its positive side the movement gained strength in proportion as the sceptical attack weakened the prevailing dogmatic schools. These at the same time ceased to give internal satisfaction, as we perceive in the melancholy tone of Marcus Aurelius. By the end of the second century, the new positive current was by far the strongest; but no thinker

---

[1] iii. 2, p. 452.   [2] *V. Plot.* 14.

of decisive originality had appeared, at least on the line of
Greek thought. In Plotinus was now to appear the greatest
individual thinker between Aristotle and Descartes. Under
the attraction of his systematising intellect, all that remained
of aspiration after an independent philosophy was rallied to
a common centre. Essentially, the explanation of the change
is to be found in his individual power. Yet he had his precursors as well as his teachers. There were two thinkers at
least who, however little they may have influenced him,
anticipated some of his positions.

The first was Philo of Alexandria, who was born about
30 B.C., and died later than A.D. 40. The second was Numenius
of Apamea, who is said to have flourished between 160 and
180 A.D. Philo was pretty certainly unknown to Plotinus.
Numenius was read in his class-room; but his disciple Amelius
wrote a treatise, dedicated to Porphyry, in which, replying to
an accusation of plagiarism, he pointed out the differences between their master's teaching and that of Numenius. Amelius,
it may be remarked, had acquired a great reputation by his
thorough knowledge of the writings of Numenius. Porphyry
cites also the testimony of Longinus. The judgment of the
eminent critic was for the unquestionable originality of Plotinus among the philosophers of his own and the preceding
age[1]. In what that originality consisted, Plotinus, who spoke
of him as "a philologist but by no means a philosopher,"
might not have allowed his competence to decide. He himself confessed that he did not understand some treatises of
Plotinus that were sent to him. What he ascribes to him in
the passage quoted by Porphyry is simply a more accurate
mode of interpreting the Pythagorean and Platonic principles
than had been attempted by others who took the same general
direction. This, however, only renders his judgment the more

---

[1] Longinus ap. Porph. *V. Plot.* 20: οἱ δὲ...τρόπῳ θεωρίας ἰδίῳ χρησάμενοι
Πλωτῖνός εἰσι καὶ Γεντιλιανὸς Ἀμέλιος,...οὐδὲ γὰρ οὐδ᾽ ἐγγύς τι τὰ Νουμηνίου καὶ
Κρονίου καὶ Μοδεράτου καὶ Θρασύλλου τοῖς Πλωτίνου περὶ τῶν αὐτῶν συγγράμμασιν
εἰς ἀκρίβειαν · ὁ δὲ Ἀμέλιος κατ᾽ ἴχνη μὲν τούτου βαδίζειν προαιρούμενος καὶ τὰ
πολλὰ μὲν τῶν αὐτῶν δογμάτων ἐχόμενος, τῇ δὲ ἐξεργασίᾳ πολὺς ὤν...ὢν καὶ μόνων
ἡμεῖς ἄξιον εἶναι νομίζομεν ἐπισκοπεῖσθαι τὰ συγγράμματα.

decisive as to the impression Plotinus made in spite of the difficulties of his style.

To make clear what doctrines of Plotinus were anticipated, the principles of his metaphysics must be stated in brief preliminary outline. Of the causes above the visible world, he placed highest of all the One beyond thought and being. To the One, in the Neo-Platonic philosophy, the name of God is applicable in a peculiar manner. Everything after it that is called divine is regarded as derivative. Next in order, as the effect of the Cause and Principle, comes the divine Mind, identical with the "intelligible world" which is its object. Last in the order of supramundane causes comes the Soul of the whole, produced by Mind. Thence the descent is to the world of particular souls and changing things. The series composed of the primal One, the divine Mind, and the Soul of the whole, is sometimes called the "Neo-Platonic Trinity[1]." Now Numenius put forth the idea of a Trinity which in one point resembles that of Plotinus.

According to Proclus, Numenius distinguished "three Gods." The first he called the Father, the second the Maker[2], while the third was the World, or that which is made[3]. The point of resemblance here to Plotinus is the distinction of "the first God" from the Platonic Demiurgus, signified by "the Maker." With Numenius, however, the first God is Being and Mind; not, as with Plotinus, a principle beyond these. Zeller remarks that, since a similar distinction of the highest God from the Creator of the world appears before Numenius in the Christian Gnostics, among whom the Valentinians adopted

---

[1] It is of course inexact to speak of a first, second and third "Person" in the Trinity of Plotinus. Even the generalised term "hypostasis" is more strictly applicable in Christian than in Neo-Platonic theology, as Vacherot points out. See *Histoire Critique de l'École d'Alexandrie*, t. ii. p. 425 n.

[2] Cf. *Timaeus*, 28 c.

[3] *Comm. in Tim.* p. 93 A; ed. Diehl, i. 303–4. (R. P. 506 a; Zeller, iii. 2, p. 220, n. 6.) πατέρα μὲν καλεῖ τὸν πρῶτον, ποιητὴν δὲ τὸν δεύτερον, ποίημα δὲ τὸν τρίτον· ὁ γὰρ κόσμος κατ' αὐτὸν ὁ τρίτος ἐστὶ θεός. A protest follows against this "hypostasising," as we should call it, of the Father and the Maker. To divide apart the one Cause, following the names, says Proclus, is as if, because Plato calls the Whole both "heaven" and "world," we were to speak of the Heaven and the World as two different things.

the name "Demiurgus" from Plato, it was probably from them that Numenius got the hint for his theory; and that in addition Philo's theory of the Logos doubtless influenced him[1]. To this accordingly we must turn as possibly the original starting-point for the Neo-Platonic doctrine.

With Philo, the Logos is the principle that mediates between the supreme God and the world formed out of matter. Essentially the conception, in so far as it means a rational order of production running through nature, is of Greek origin, being taken directly from the Stoics, who got at least the suggestion of it from Heraclitus[2]. Philo regards the Logos as containing the Ideas in accordance with which the visible world was formed. By this Platonising turn, it becomes in the end a different conception from the divine "Reason" of the Stoics, embodied as that is in the material element of fire. On the other hand, by placing the Platonic Ideas in the divine Mind, Philo interprets Plato in a sense which many scholars, both in antiquity and in modern times, have refused to allow. Here Plotinus coincides with Philo. Among those who dissented from this view was Longinus. Porphyry, who, before he came to Rome, had been the pupil of Longinus at Athens, was not without difficulty brought over, by controversy with Amelius, to the view of Plotinus, "that intelligibles do not exist outside intellect[3]." Thus by Plotinus as by Philo the cause and principle of things is distinguished from the reason or intellect which is its proximate effect; and, in the interpretation of Plato, the divine mind is regarded as containing the ideas, whereas in the *Timaeus* they are figured as existing outside the mind of the Demiurgus. On the other hand, Plotinus differs both from Philo and from the Gnostics in consistently treating as mythical the representation of a maker setting out from a certain moment of time to shape things according to a pattern out of pre-existent matter. And, in spite of his agreement with Philo up to a certain point,

[1] iii. 2, p. 219, n. 3.

[2] See, for the detailed genealogy of the conception, Principal Drummond's *Philo Judaeus*, vol. i.

[3] *V. Plot.* 18. The position which he had adopted from Longinus was ὅτι ἔξω τοῦ νοῦ ὑφέστηκε τὰ νοητά.

there is nothing to show that their views were historically
connected. Against the attempt to connect Plotinus, or even
Numenius, with Philo, a strong argument is urged by Dr Bigg.
Neither Plotinus nor Numenius, as he points out, ever uses
λόγος as a technical term for the "second hypostasis[1]." Yet,
if they had derived their theory from Philo, this is evidently
what they would have done; for the Philonian λόγος, on the
philosophical side, was not alien from Greek thought, but was
a genuine product of it. In truth, to adapt the conception to
their own systems by means of a change of name, would have
been more difficult than to arrive at their actual terminology
directly by combining Stoical and Aristotelian positions with
their Platonism. This kind of combination is what we find in
the eclectic thinkers, of whom Numenius was one. Plotinus
made use of the same elements; the presence of which in his
system Porphyry has expressly noted[2]. And, so far as the
relation of the Neo-Platonic Trinity to Plato is concerned, the
exact derivation of the three "hypostases" is pointed out in
a fragment of Porphyry's lost History of Philosophy[3]. The
highest God, we there learn, is the Idea of the Good in the
Republic; the second and third hypostases are the Demiurgus
and the Soul of the World in the *Timaeus*. To explain the
triadic form of such speculations, no theory of individual

---

[1] See *Neoplatonism*, pp. 123, 242, etc. Dr Bigg's actual assertions are too
sweeping. It is not quite correct to say, as he does in the second of the passages referred to, that Plotinus expressly refuses to apply to his principle of
Intelligence the title Logos, which in his system means, as with the Stoics,
"little more than physical force." There are indeed passages where he refuses
to apply the title in some special reference; but elsewhere—as in Enn. v. 1, 6
—he says that Soul is the λόγος of Mind, and Mind the λόγος of the One.
While the term with him has many applications, and among them the
Stoical application to the "seminal reasons" (or formulae) of natural things,
it may most frequently be rendered by "rational law."

This indeed might well be adopted as the usual rendering of the term from
Heraclitus onward whenever it seems to approximate to an ontological sense.
Psychologically of course it often means simply "reason," though this is
never its exact sense in Heraclitus, with whom the transition of the idea is
from "word" or "discourse" to "law" or "measure."

[2] *V. Plot.* 14: ἐμμέμικται δ' ἐν τοῖς συγγράμμασι καὶ τὰ Στωικὰ λανθάνοντα
δόγματα καὶ τὰ Περιπατητικά· καταπεπύκνωται δὲ καὶ ἡ μετὰ τὰ φυσικὰ τοῦ
Ἀριστοτέλους πραγματεία.

[3] Fragm. 16 in Nauck's *Opuscula Selecta*.

borrowing on any side is necessary. All the thinkers of the period, whether Hellenic, Jewish or Christian, had grown up in an atmosphere of Neo-Pythagorean speculation about numbers, for which the triad was of peculiar significance[1]. Thus on the whole it seems that Numenius and Plotinus drew independently from sources common to them with Philo, but cannot well have been influenced by him.

Plotinus, as we have seen, had some knowledge of Numenius; but, where a special point of contact has been sought, the difference is as obvious as the resemblance. The great difference, however, is not in any detail of the triadic theory. It is that Plotinus was able to bring all the elements of his system under the direction of an organising thought. That thought was a definitely conceived immaterialist monism which, so far as we know, neither Philo nor Numenius had done anything substantially to anticipate. He succeeded in clearly developing out of Plato the conception of incorporeal essence, which his precursors had rather tended by their eclecticism to confuse. That the conception was in Plato, the Neo-Platonists not only admitted but strongly maintained. Yet Plato's metaphorical expressions had misled even Aristotle, who seriously thought that he found presupposed in them a spatial extension of the soul[2]. And if Aristotle had got rid of semi-materialistic "animism" even in expression, this had not prevented his successors from running into a new materialism of their own. Much as the Platonising schools had all along protested against the tendency to make the soul a kind of body or an outcome of body, they had not hitherto overcome it by clear definitions and distinctions. This is one thing that Plotinus and his successors achieved in their effort after an idealist metaphysic.

It was on this side especially that the thought of the school influenced the Fathers and Doctors of the Church. On the

---

[1] Jules Simon, in his *Histoire de l'École d'Alexandrie*, dwells on this point as an argument against the view, either that Neo-Platonism borrowed its Trinity from Christianity or Christianity from Neo-Platonism.

[2] Proclus wrote a book to show that Plato's view of the soul is not open to the objections raised by Aristotle. See *Comm. in Tim.* 226 D; ed. Diehl, ii. 279.

specific dogmas of Christian theology, Neo-Platonism probably exercised little influence. From Platonising Judaism or
Christianity, it received none at all. At most an isolated expression occurs showing that the antipathy to alien religions
was not so unqualified as to prevent appreciation, for example,
of the Platonism in the Fourth Gospel. Numenius, it is interesting to note, was one of the few earlier writers who attach
themselves to the Hellenic tradition and yet show traces of
sympathetic contact with Hebraic religion. He is said to have
called Plato "a Moses writing Attic[1]." On the other side Philo,
though by faith a Jew, was as a philosopher essentially Greek
both in thought and in terminology. What divided him from
the Hellenic thinkers was simply his acceptance of formal
limitations on thought prescribed by a positive religion.

In concluding the present chapter, a word may be said on
the literary style of Plotinus, and on the temper of himself and
his school in relation to life. His writing is admittedly difficult; yet it is not wanting in beautiful passages that leave an
impression even of facility. He is in general, as Porphyry says,
concentrated, "abounding more in thoughts than in words."
The clearness of his systematic thought has been recognised by
expositors in spite of obscurities in detail; and the obscurities
often disappear with close study. On the thought when it
comes in contact with life is impressed the character of ethical
purity and inwardness which always continued to mark the
school. At the same time, there is a return to the Hellenic
love of beauty and knowledge for themselves. Stoical elements
are incorporated, but the exaggerated "tension" of Stoicism
has disappeared. While the Neo-Platonists are more consistently ascetic than the Stoics, there is nothing harsh or
repulsive in their asceticism. The ascetic life was for them
not a mode of self-torture, but the means to a happiness
which on the whole they succeeded in attaining. Perhaps the
explanation is that they had restored the idea of theoretic

---

[1] Suid. and Clem. *Strom.* (R. P. 7 b, 504.) τί γάρ ἐστι Πλάτων ἢ Μωυσῆς
ἀττικίζων; (M. Théodore Reinach, in *Textes d'auteurs grecs et romains relatifs
au Judaïsme*, p. 175, n. 2, disputes the genuineness of this often-quoted
fragment).

virtue, against the too narrowly practical tone of the preceding schools. Hence abstinence from the ordinary objects of pursuit left no blank. It was not felt as a deprivation, but as a source of power to think and feel. And in thinking they knew that indirectly they were acting. For theory, with them, is the remoter source of all practice, which bears to it the relation of the outward effect to the inward cause.

CHAPTER V

THE PHILOSOPHICAL SYSTEM OF PLOTINUS

As idealists and their opponents alike recognise, one great stumbling-block of an idealist philosophy is language. This was seen by Plato, by Plotinus, and by Berkeley, just as from the other side it is seen by the materialist and the dualist. Language was formed primarily to indicate the things of sense, and these have not the characters which idealism, whether ancient or modern, ascribes to reality. Ancient idealism refuses to call external things real in the full sense, because they are in flux. The reality is the fixed mental concept or its unchanging intelligible object. Modern idealism regards things as merely "phenomenal," because they appear to a consciousness, and beyond this appearance have no definable reality. Whether reality itself is fixed or changing, may by the modern idealist be left undetermined; but at any rate the groups of perceptions that make up the "objects" of daily experience and even of science are not, in his view, objects existing in themselves apart from mind, and known truly as such. Only by some relation to mind can reality be constituted. The way in which language opposes itself to ancient idealism is by its implication that existence really changes. To modern idealism it opposes itself by its tendency to treat external things as absolute objects with a real existence apart from that of all thinking subjects.

The two forms of developed idealism here regarded as typically ancient and modern are the earliest and the latest— that of Plato on the one side, that of post-Cartesian, and still more of post-Kantian, thinkers on the other. The idealism of Plotinus contains elements that bring it into relation with both. English readers know how Berkeley insists that, if we are to grasp his doctrine, we must attend to the meanings he desires to convey, and must not dwell on the mere form of expression. Let us see how Plato and Plotinus deal with the same difficulty.

Plato's treatment of it may be most readily studied in the *Cratylus*. Language, Socrates undertakes to show, has a certain natural conformity to things named. To those who named them, external things mostly presented themselves as in flux. Accordingly, words are full of devices by the makers of language for expressing gliding and flowing movements. With a little ingenuity and an occasional evasion, those who hold that the true nature of everything is to flow and not to be in any manner fixed, might exhibit the early legislators over human speech as in exact agreement with their philosophical opinions. Yet after all there are some words, though fewer, that appear at first sight to express stability. So that the primitive legislators were not, on the face of things, perfectly consistent. On the whole, however, words suggesting flux predominate. Similarly the early myth-makers, in their derivation of all things from Ocean and Tethys, seem to have noticed especially the fact of change in the world. The Heracliteans, therefore, have the advantage in the appeal to language and mythology. Still, their Eleatic opponents may be right philosophically. The makers of language and myth may have framed words and imagined the origin of things in accordance with what is apparent but not real. Real existence in itself may be stable. If this is so, then, to express philosophic thought accurately, it will be necessary to reform language. In the meantime, the proper method in all our inquiries and reasonings must be, to attend to things rather than words.

According to the Platonic doctrine, the "place of ideas" is the soul[1]. In virtue of its peculiar relations to those stable and permanent existences known by intellect, the individual soul is itself permanent. It gives unity, motion and life to the fluent aggregate of material particles forming its temporary body. It disappears from one body and reappears in another, existing apart in the intervals between its mortal lives. Thus by Plato the opposition of soul and body is brought, as a

---

[1] Arist. *De An.* iii. 4, 429 a 27. (R. P. 251 c.)

subordinate relation, under the more general opposition of the stable ideas—the existence of which is not purely and simply in the soul, but is also in some way transcendent—and the flux of material existence. For Plotinus, this subordinate opposition has become the starting-point. He does not dismiss the earlier antithesis; but the main problem with him is not to find permanence somewhere as against absolute flux. He allows in the things of sense also a kind of permanence. His aim is first of all to prove that the soul has a real existence of its own, distinguished from body and corporeal modes of being. For in the meantime body as such—and no longer, as with the Heracliteans, a process of the whole—had been set up by the dominant schools as the absolute reality. By the Epicureans and Stoics, everything that can be spoken of at all was regarded as body, or a quality or relation of body, or else as having no being other than "nominal." The main point of attack for scepticism had been the position common to the naturalistic schools, that external things can be known by direct apprehension as they really are. Neither the Academical nor the Pyrrhonist scepticism, however, had taken the place of the ruling dogmatic system, which was that of the Stoics. Thus the doctrine that Plotinus had to meet was still essentially materialism, made by the sceptical attack less sure of itself, but not dethroned.

The method he adopts is to insist precisely on the paradoxical character of the soul's existence as contrasted with that of corporeal things. How specious is the view of his opponents he allows. Body can be seen and touched. It resists pressure and is spread out in space. Soul is invisible and intangible, and by its very definition unextended. Thus language has to be struggled with in the attempt to describe it; and in the end can only be made to express the nature of soul by constraining it to purposes for which most men never think of employing it. What is conclusive, however, as against the materialistic view, is that the soul cannot be described at all except by phrases which would be nonsensical if applied to body or its qualities, or to determinations of particular bodies. Once the conception of soul has been fixed as that

of an incorporeal reality, body is seen to admit of a kind of
explanation in terms of soul—from which it derives its "form"
—whereas the essential nature of soul admitted of no explanation in terms of body.

Above soul and beneath body, as we shall see, Plotinus has
other principles, derived from earlier metaphysics, by which
he is able to construct a complete philosophy, and not merely
what would be called in modern phrase a "rational psychology." His psychology, however, is the centre. Within
the soul, he finds all the metaphysical principles in some way
represented. In it are included the principles of unity, of pure
intellect, of moving and vitalising power, and, in some sense,
of matter itself. Further, by what may be called his "empirical psychology," he prepared the starting-point for the
distinctively modern "theory of knowledge." This he did, as
Prof. Siebeck has shown[1], by the new precision he gave to the
conception of consciousness. On this side he reaches forward
to Descartes, as on the other side he looks back to Plato and
Aristotle.

1. *Psychology.*

It is absurd, or rather impossible, says Plotinus at the opening of one of his earliest expositions[2], that life should be the
product of an aggregation of bodies, or that things without
understanding should generate mind. If, as some say, the
soul is a permeating air with a certain habitude ($\pi\nu\epsilon\hat{\upsilon}\mu\alpha$ $\pi\omega\varsigma$
$\H{\epsilon}\chi o\nu$)—and it cannot be air simply, for there are innumer-
able airs without life—then the habitude ($\pi\omega\varsigma$ $\H{\epsilon}\chi o\nu$ or $\sigma\chi\acute{\epsilon}\sigma\iota\varsigma$)
is either a mere name, and there is really nothing but the
"breath," or it is a kind of being ($\tau\hat{\omega}\nu$ $\H{o}\nu\tau\omega\nu$ $\tau\iota$). In the latter
case, it is a rational principle and of another nature than body
($\lambda\acute{o}\gamma o\varsigma$ $\mathring{\alpha}\nu$ $\epsilon\H{\iota}\eta$ $\tau\iota\varsigma$ $\kappa\alpha\mathring{\iota}$ $o\mathring{\upsilon}$ $\sigma\hat{\omega}\mu\alpha$ $\kappa\alpha\mathring{\iota}$ $\phi\acute{\upsilon}\sigma\iota\varsigma$ $\mathring{\epsilon}\tau\acute{\epsilon}\rho\alpha$). If the soul
were matter, it could produce only the effects of the particular
kind of matter that it is—giving things its own quality, hot
or cold, and so forth—not all the opposite effects actually
produced in the organism. The soul is not susceptible of
quantitative increase or diminution, or of division. Thus it

---

[1] *Geschichte der Psychologie,* i. 2.   [2] Enn. IV. 7.

has not the characters of a thing possessing quantity (ἄποσον ἄρα ἡ ψυχή). The unity in perception would be impossible if that which perceives consisted of parts spatially separated. It is impossible that the mental perception, for example, of a pain in the finger, should be transmitted from the "animal spirit" (ψυχικὸν πνεῦμα) of the finger to the ruling part (τὸ ἡγεμονοῦν) in the organism. For, in that case, there must either be accumulated an infinity of perceptions, or each intermediate part in succession must feel the pain only in itself, and not in the parts previously affected; and so also the ruling part when it becomes affected in its turn. That there can be no such physical transmission as is supposed of a mental perception, results from the very nature of material mass, which consists of parts each standing by itself: one part can have no knowledge of what is suffered by another part. Consequently we must assume a percipient which is everywhere identical with itself. Such a percipient must be another kind of being than body. That which thinks can still less be body than that which perceives. For even if it is not allowed that thought is the laying hold on intelligibles without the use of any bodily organ, yet there are certainly involved in it apprehensions of things without magnitude (ἀμεγέθων ἀντιλήψεις). Such are abstract conceptions, as for example those of the beautiful and the just. How then can that which is a magnitude think that which is not? Must we suppose it to think the indivisible with that in itself which is divisible? If it can think it at all, it must rather be with some indivisible part of itself. That which thinks, then, cannot be body. For the supposed thinking body has no function as an extended whole (and to be such is its nature as body), since it cannot as a whole come in contact with an object that is incorporeal.

The soul in relation to the body, according to Plotinus's own mode of statement, is "all in all and all in every part[1]." Thus it is in a sense divisible because it is in all the parts of a divisible body. Properly it is indivisible because it is all in the whole and *all* in each part of it. Its unity is unlike that

[1] Enn. IV. 2, 1.

of a body, which is one by spatial continuity, having different
parts each of which is in a different place; and unlike that of
a quality of body such as colour, which can be wholly in many
discontinuous bodies. In the case of a quality, that which is
the same in all portions of body that possess it in common is
an affection ($\pi\acute{\alpha}\theta\eta\mu\alpha$), and not an essence ($o\mathring{v}\sigma\acute{\iota}\alpha$). Its identity
is formal, and not numerical, as is the case with the soul[1].

In this general argumentation, it will be observed, Plotinus
starts from the supposition that the body has a reality other
than phenomenal. Allowing this, he is able to demonstrate
against his opponents that a reality of a different kind from
that of body must also be assumed. In his metaphysics he
goes further, and reduces corporeal things in effect to phenomena; but in his psychology he continues to take a view
nearer that of "common-sense." Thus he is confronted with
the difficulties that have since become familiar about the
"connexion of body and mind," and the possibility of their
interaction. He lays bare in a single saying the root of all
such difficulties. How if, in talking of a "mixture" of a
corporeal with an incorporeal nature, we should be trying to
realise an impossibility, as if one should say that linear magnitude is mixed with whiteness[2]? The solution for psychology
is found in the theory that the soul itself remains "unmixed"
in spite of its union with body; but that it causes the production of a "common" or "dual" or "composite" nature,
which is the subject in perception. By the aid of this inter-
mediary, the unity of the soul is reconciled—though not without perplexities in detail—with localisation of the organic
functions that subserve its activity.

The different parts of the animated body participate in the

---

[1] Cf. Enn. vi. 4, 1. The peculiar relation of the soul, in itself indivisible, to
the body, in itself divisible, and so communicating a kind of divisibility to the
soul, Plotinus finds indicated by the "divine enigma" of the "mixture" in the
Timaeus. Enn. iv. 2, 2: τοῦτο ἄρα ἐστὶ τὸ θείως ἠνιγμένον ' τῆς ἀμερίστου καὶ
ἀεὶ κατὰ τὰ αὐτὰ ἐχούσης [οὐσίας] καὶ τῆς περὶ τὰ σώματα γιγνομένης μεριστῆς
τρίτον ἐξ ἀμφοῖν συνεκεράσατο οὐσίας εἶδος.'

[2] Enn. i. 1, 4: ζητητέον δὲ καὶ τὸν τρόπον τῆς μίξεως, μήποτε οὐ δυνατὸν ᾖ,
ὥσπερ ἂν εἴ τις λέγοι μεμῖχθαι λευκῷ γραμμήν, φύσιν ἄλλην ἄλλῃ. This book,
though coming first in Porphyry's arrangement according to subjects, is given
as the last but one in the chronological order.

soul's powers in different ways[1]. According as each organ of
sense is fitted for one special function, a particular power of
perception may be said to be there; the power of sight in the
eyes, of hearing in the ears, of smell in the nostrils, of taste in
the tongue, of touch everywhere. Since the primary organs of
touch are the nerves, which have also the power of animal
motion, and since the nerves take their origin from the brain,
in the brain may be placed the starting-point of the actual
exercise of all powers of perception and movement. Above
perception is reason. This power has not properly a physical
organ at all, and so is not really in the head; but it was
assigned to the head by the older writers because it communicates directly with the psychical functions of which the
brain is the central organ. For these last, as Plotinus remarks,
have a certain community with reason. In perception there is
a kind of judgment; and on reason together with the imagination derived from perception, impulse follows.

In making the brain central among the organs that are
in special relation with mind, Plotinus of course adopts the
Platonic as against the Aristotelian position, which made the
heart central. At the same time, he incorporates what had
since been discovered about the special functions of the ner-
vous system, which were unknown to Aristotle as to Plato.
The vegetative power of the soul he places in relation with
the liver, because here is the origin of the veins and the blood
in the veins, by means of which that power causes the nourishment of the body. Hence, as with Plato, appetite is assigned
to this region. Spirited emotion, in accordance with the
Platonic psychology, has its seat in the breast, where is the
spring of lighter and purer blood.

Both perceptions and memories are "energies" or activities,
not mere passive impressions received and stored up in the
soul[2]. Take first the case of the most distinct perception. In
sight, when we wish to perceive anything clearly, we direct
our vision in a straight line to the object. This outwardly
directed activity would not be necessary if the object simply
left its impression on the soul. Were this the whole process,

[1] Enn. IV. 3, 23.   [2] Enn. IV. 6.

we should see not the outward objects of vision, but images
and shadows of them; so that what we see would be other
than the things themselves (ὥστε ἄλλα μὲν εἶναι αὐτὰ τὰ
πράγματα, ἄλλα δὲ τὰ ἡμῖν ὁρώμενα). In hearing as in sight,
perceptions are energies, not impressions nor yet passive
states (μὴ τύποι, μηδὲ πείσεις). The impression is an articulated stroke in the air, on which it is as if letters were written
by that which makes the sound. The power of the soul as it
were reads those impressions. In the case of taste and smell,
the passive affections (πάθη) are one thing; the perceptions
and judgments of them are another. Memory of things is produced by exercise of the soul, either generally or in relation
to a special class of them. Children remember better because
they have fewer things to attend to. Mere multitude of
impressions retained, if memory were simply an affair of
retaining impressions, would not cause them to be less remembered. Nor should we need to consider in order to remind ourselves; nor forget things and afterwards recall them
to mind. The persistence of passive impressions in the soul,
if real, would be a mark rather of weakness than of strength,
for that which is most fixedly impressed is so by giving way
(τὸ γὰρ ἐντυπώτατον τῷ εἴκειν ἐστὶ τοιοῦτον). But where
there is really weakness, as in the old, both memory and perception are worse.

The activity of perception, though itself mental, has direct
physical conditions. That of memory has not. Memory itself
belongs wholly to the soul, though it may take its start from
what goes on in the composite being. What the soul directly
preserves the memory of, is its own movements, not those of
body. Pressure and reaction of bodies can furnish no explanation of a storing-up of mental "impressions" (τύποι), which
are not magnitudes. That the body, through being in flux, is
really a hindrance to memory, is illustrated by the fact that
often additions to the store cause forgetfulness, whereas
memory emerges when there is abstraction and purification[1].
Something from the past that was retained but is latent may

---

[1] Enn. IV. 3, 26: προστιθεμένων τινῶν λήθη, ἐν δ' ἀφαιρέσει καὶ καθάρσει
ἀνακύπτει πολλάκις ἡ μνήμη.

be recalled when other memories or the impressions of the
moment are removed. Yet, though it is not the composite
being but the soul itself that possesses memory, memories
come to it not only from its spontaneous activity, but from
its activity incited by that which takes place in consequence
of its association with the body[1]. There are memories of what
has been done and suffered by the dual nature, though the
memories themselves, as distinguished from that which in-
cites them, are purely mental. Thus indirectly the physical
organism has a bearing on memory as well as on perception.
It follows, however, from the general view, that memory as
well as reason belongs to the "separable" portion of the soul.
Whether those who have attained to the perfection of virtue
will, in the life of complete separation from the body, retain
indefinitely their memories of the past, is another question.
The discussion of it belongs rather to the ethics than to the
pure psychology of Plotinus.

To specific questions about sense-perception, Plotinus devotes two short books, both of which are concerned primarily
with vision. Discussing the transmission of light[2], he finds
that, like all perception, seeing must take place through some
kind of body. The affection of the medium, however, need not
be identical with that of the sense-organ. A reed, for example,
through which is transmitted the shock of a torpedo, is not
affected like the hand that receives the shock. The air, he
concludes, is no instrument in vision. If it were, we should be
able to see without looking at the distant object; just as we
are warmed by the heated air we are in contact with. In the
case of heat too, Plotinus adds, we are warmed at the same
time with the air, rather than by means of it. Solid bodies
receive more of the heat than does the air intervening between
them and the heated object. In pursuance of this argument,
he remarks that even the transmission of sound is not wholly
dependent on a stroke in an aerial medium. Tones vary according to the differences of the bodies from which the sound
starts, and not simply according to the shock. Furthermore,
sounds are transmitted within our bodies without the inter-

[1] Enn. IV. 3, 27.   [2] Enn. IV. 5.

mediation of air; as when bones are bent or sawn¹. The shock
itself, whether in air or not, when it arrives at perception is
the sound. Light Plotinus defines as an incorporeal energy
of the luminous body directed outwards. Being an "energy,"
and not a mere quality (ποιότης), it is capable of overleaping
an interval without becoming inherent in that which occupies
the interval; as, in fact, it leaves no impress on the air through
which it passes. It can exist in the interspace without a percipient, though a percipient, if present, would be affected by it.

For positive explanation here, Plotinus falls back on the
idea, borrowed from the Stoics, of a "sympathy" binding together remote but like parts of the universe. The other book
mentioned², which discusses the question why things seen at a
distance appear small, is interesting from its points of contact
with Berkeley. To solve the problem, Plotinus sets out in
quest of something more directly psychological than the
"visual angle³." Is not one reason for differences of estimate,
he asks, because our view of magnitude is in an "accidental"
relation to colour, which is what we primarily behold⁴? To
perceive how large any magnitude really is, we must be near
it, so as to be able to go over its parts in succession. At a
distance, the parts of the object do not permit accurate dis-
cernment of their relative colouring, since the colours arrive
faint (ἀμυδρά). Faintness in colours corresponds to smallness
in magnitude; both have in common "the less" (τὸ ἧττον).
Thus the magnitude, following the colour, is diminished pro-
portionally (ἀνὰ λόγον). The nature of the affection, however,
becomes plainer in things of varied colours. Confusion of
colours, whether in near or distant objects, causes apparent
diminution of size, because the parts do not offer differences by
which they can be accurately distinguished and so measured⁵.
Magnitudes also of the same kind and of like colours are

---

¹ Enn. IV. 5, 5: οὐκ ἐν ἀέρι, ἀλλὰ συγκρούσαντος καὶ πλήξαντος ἄλλο ἄλλου·
οἷον καὶ ὀστῶν κάμψεις πρὸς ἄλληλα παρατριβομένων ἀέρος μὴ ὄντος μεταξὺ καὶ
πρίσεις.

² Enn. II. 8.   ³ Cf. Theory of Vision, § 79.

⁴ Enn. II. 8, 1: ὅτι κατὰ συμβεβηκὸς ὁρᾶται τὸ μέγεθος τοῦ χρώματος πρώτως
θεωρουμένου.

⁵ Cf. Theory of Vision, § 56.

deceptive because the sight slips away; having, for precisely
the same reason as in the case of confused colours, no hold on
the parts. Again, distant objects look near at hand because
there is loss of visible detail in the intervening scenery. Close
as all this comes to Berkeley, at least in psychological method,
the incidental remark comes still closer, that that to which we
primarily refer visible magnitude appears to be touch. This
occurs in a question about the "magnitude" of sound, to
which reference is made by way of illustrating the analogy
of great and small in different sense-perceptions[1].

Feeling, in the sense of pleasure and pain, according to
Plotinus, belongs primarily to the animated body, in the
parts of which it is localised[2]. The perception of it, but not
the feeling itself, belongs to the soul. Sometimes, however, in
speaking of the feeling of pleasure or pain, we include along
with it the accompanying perception. Corporal desires too
have their origin from the common nature of the animated
body. That this is their source is shown by the differences, in
respect of desires, between different times of life, and between
persons in health and disease. In his account of desire and
aversion, Plotinus notes the coincidence between mental and
bodily movements[3]. The difference between the affection of
the animated body on the one side and the soul's clear perception of it on the other, applies both to appetitive and to
irascible emotion[4]. Of these the second is not derived from
the first, but both spring from a common root. That its origin
cannot be entirely independent is shown by the fact that those
who are less eager after bodily pleasures are less prone to anger
and irrational passions. To explain the impulse ($\delta\rho\mu\dot{\eta}$) to repel
actively the cause of injury, we must suppose perception added
to the mere resentment ($\dot{\alpha}\gamma\alpha\nu\dot{\alpha}\kappa\tau\eta\sigma\iota\varsigma$), which, as a passion, is
primarily a boiling-up of the blood. The "trace of soul" on

---

[1] Enn. II. 8, 1: τίνι γὰρ πρώτως τὸ ἐν τῇ φωνῇ μέγεθος, ὥσπερ δοκεῖ τῇ ἀφῇ τὸ
ὁρώμενον;

[2] Enn. IV. 4, 18–21.

[3] Enn. IV. 4, 20: ἐκ τῆς ὀδύνης ἐγίνετο ἡ γνῶσις, καὶ ἀπάγειν ἐκ τοῦ ποιοῦντος
τὸ πάθος ἡ ψυχὴ βουλομένη ἐποίει τὴν φυγήν, καὶ τοῦ πρώτου παθόντος διδάσκοντος
τοῦτο φεύγοντός πως καὶ αὐτοῦ ἐν τῇ συστολῇ.

[4] Enn. IV. 4, 28.

which this kind of emotion depends (τὸ ἐκπεσὸν εἰς θυμὸν ἴχνος) has its seat in the heart.

Error too arises from the common nature, by which right reason becomes weak, as the wisest counsellor in an assembly may be overborne by the general clamour[1]. The rational power, with Plotinus as with Aristotle, is in its own nature "unmixed"; but it has to manifest itself under conditions of time and in relation to the composite being. Further discussion of these points will in the main come better under the head of metaphysics than of psychology. A distinctively psychological theory, however, is the explicit transformation of the Platonic "reminiscence" into a doctrine of "innate ideas" potentially present. The term "memory," Plotinus observes, is improperly applied to the intellectual energising of the soul in accordance with its innate principles[2]. The reason why the older writers ascribed memory and reminiscence to the soul when it thus energises, was apparently because it is then energising in accordance with powers it always had (as it has now latent memories) but does not always bring into action, and especially cannot bring into action on its first arrival in the world. In this place for one Plotinus does not in the least fail to recognise that there has been scientific progress since the time of those whom he calls "the ancients."

The higher and the lower powers of the soul meet in the imaginative faculty (φαντασία, τὸ φανταστικόν), which is the psychical organ of memory and self-consciousness. By this view the dispersion is avoided that would result from assigning memory of desires to the desiring part of the soul, memories of perception to the perceiving part, and memories of thought to the thinking part. Thought is apprehended by the imagination as in a mirror; the notion (νόημα) at first indivisible and implicit being conveyed to it by an explicit discourse (λόγος). For thought and the apprehension of thought are not the same (ἄλλο γὰρ ἡ νόησις, καὶ ἄλλο ἡ τῆς νοήσεως ἀντί-ληψις); the former can exist without the latter. That which thus apprehends thought apprehends perceptions also[3].

[1] Enn. IV. 4, 17. [2] Enn. IV. 3, 25.
[3] Enn. IV. 3, 28–30.

Here we come to the psychological conception of "consciousness," which Prof. Siebeck has traced through its formative stages to its practically adequate expression by Plotinus[1]. By Plato and Aristotle, as he points out, such expressions are used as the "seeing of sight," and, at a higher degree of generality, the "perceiving of perception" and the "thinking of thought"; but they have no perfectly general term for the consciousness with which we follow any mental process whatever, as distinguished from the process itself. Approximations to such terms were made in the post-Aristotelian period by the Stoics and others, but it was Plotinus who first gained complete mastery of the idea. Sometimes he speaks of "common perception" ($\sigma\nu\nu\alpha\dot{\iota}\sigma\theta\eta\sigma\iota\varsigma$) in a generalised sense. His most usual expression is that of an "accompaniment" ($\pi\alpha\rho\alpha\kappa\circ\lambda\circ\dot{\nu}\theta\eta\sigma\iota\varsigma$) of its own mental activities by the soul. "Self-consciousness," in its distinctive meaning, is expressed by "accompanying oneself" ($\pi\alpha\rho\alpha\kappa\circ\lambda\circ\nu\theta\epsilon\hat{\iota}\nu$ $\dot{\epsilon}\alpha\nu\tau\hat{\omega}$). With these terms are joined expressions for mental "synthesis" ($\sigma\dot{\nu}\nu\theta\epsilon\sigma\iota\varsigma$ and $\sigma\dot{\nu}\nu\epsilon\sigma\iota\varsigma$) as a unitary activity of the soul in reference to its contents.

Important as the conception of consciousness became for modern thought, it is not for Plotinus the highest. Prof. Siebeck himself draws attention to one remarkable passage[2] in which he points out that many of our best activities, both theoretical and practical, are unaccompanied at the time by consciousness of them; as for example reading, especially when we are reading intently; similarly, the performance of brave actions; so that there is a danger lest consciousness should make the activities it accompanies feebler ($\ddot{\omega}\sigma\tau\epsilon$ $\tau\dot{\alpha}\varsigma$ $\pi\alpha\rho\alpha\kappa\circ\lambda\circ\nu\theta\dot{\eta}\sigma\epsilon\iota\varsigma$ $\kappa\iota\nu\delta\nu\nu\epsilon\dot{\nu}\epsilon\iota\nu$ $\dot{\alpha}\mu\nu\delta\rho\circ\tau\dot{\epsilon}\rho\alpha\varsigma$ $\alpha\dot{\nu}\tau\dot{\alpha}\varsigma$ $\tau\dot{\alpha}\varsigma$ $\dot{\epsilon}\nu\epsilon\rho\gamma\epsilon\dot{\iota}\alpha\varsigma$ $\alpha\hat{\iota}\varsigma$ $\pi\alpha\rho\alpha\kappa\circ\lambda\circ\nu\theta\circ\hat{\nu}\sigma\iota$ $\pi\circ\iota\epsilon\hat{\iota}\nu$). The rank assigned to introspective consciousness of mental activities is similar to that which is assigned to memory[3]. It is above sense, but lower than pure intellect, which energises with more perfection in its absence. The organ of introspection and of memory, as we have seen, is the same.

The highest mode of subjective life, next to the complete

---

[1] *Geschichte der Psychologie*, i. 2, pp. 331 ff.
[2] Enn. I. 4, 10.   [3] Enn. IV. 4, 2.

unification in which even thought disappears, is intellectual
self-knowledge. Here the knower is identical with the known.
On this too Plotinus is not without keen psychological observations, apart from the metaphysical developments next to be
considered. The strong impression of a sense-perception, he
remarks, cannot consist with the attainment of this intellectual unity. Whatever exaggerates feeling lowers the activity
of thought. The perception of evils, for example, carries with
it a more vehement shock, but less clear knowledge. We are
more ourselves in health than in disease, but disease makes
itself more felt, as being other than ourselves. The attitude
of self-knowledge, Plotinus adds, is quite unlike that in which
we know an object by external perception. Even the knower
cannot place himself outside like a perceived object and gaze
upon himself with the eyes of the body[1].

Within the mind as its very centre is the supreme unity
beyond even self-knowledge. This is one with the metaphysical cause of all things, and must first be discussed as
such, since the proof of its reality is primarily metaphysical.
Its psychological relations will best be dealt with in the
chapter on the mysticism of Plotinus.

2. *Metaphysics.*

Apart from a unifying principle, nothing could exist. All
would be formless and indeterminate, and so would have
properly no being. A principle of unity has already been
recognised in the soul. It is not absent in natural things, but
here it is at a lower stage; body having less unity than soul
because its parts are locally separate. In soul, however, we
cannot rest as the highest term. Particular souls, by reason of
what they have in common, can only be understood as derived
from a general soul, which is their cause but is not identical
with all or any of them. Again, the general soul falls short of
complete unity by being the principle of life and motion to
the world, which is other than itself. What it points to as a
higher unifying principle is absolutely stable intellect, think-

---

[1] Enn. v. 8, 11: οὐδὲ γὰρ οὐδ' αὐτὸς δύναται ἔξω θεὶς ἑαυτὸν ὡς αἰσθητὸν ὄντα
ὀφθαλμοῖς τοῖς τοῦ σώματος βλέπειν.

ing itself and not the world, but containing as identical with
its own nature the eternal ideas of all the forms, general and
particular, that become explicit in the things of time and
space. Even intellect has still a certain duality, because,
though intelligence and the intelligible are the same, that
which thinks distinguishes itself from the object of thought.
Beyond thought and the being which, while identical with
it, is distinguishable in apprehension, is the absolute unity
that is simply identical with itself. This is other than all
being and is the cause of it. It is the good to which all things
aspire; for to particular things the greatest unification attainable is the greatest good; and neither the goodness and unity
they possess, nor their aspiration after a higher degree of it,
can be explained without positing the absolute One and the
absolute Good as their source and end.

By the path of which this is a slight indication, Plotinus
ascends to the summit of his metaphysics. The proof that the
first principle has really been attained, must be sought partly
in the demonstration of the process by which the whole system
of things is derived from it, partly in individual experience.
This last, being incommunicable—though not to be had without due preparation—belongs to the mystical side of the
doctrine. Of the philosophical doctrine itself, the method is
not mystical. The theory of "emanation" on which it depends is in reality no more than a very systematic expression
of the principle common to Plato and Aristotle, that the lower
is to be explained by the higher[1].

The accepted term, "emanation," is derived from one of the
metaphors by which Plotinus illustrates the production of each
order of being from the next above. He compares the cause
of all to an overflowing spring which by its excess gives rise to
that which comes after it[2]. This similarly produces the next,
and so forth, till at length in matter pure indetermination is
reached. The metaphorical character of this representation,

---

[1] See for example Enn. v. 9, 4: οὐ γὰρ δή, ὡς οἴονται, ψυχὴ νοῦν τελειωθεῖσα
γεννᾷ· πόθεν γὰρ τὸ δυνάμει ἐνεργείᾳ ἔσται, μὴ τοῦ εἰς ἐνέργειαν ἄγοντος αἰτίου
ὄντος;...διὸ δεῖ τὰ πρῶτα ἐνεργείᾳ τίθεσθαι καὶ ἀπροσδεᾶ καὶ τέλεια.

[2] Enn. v. 2, 1.

however, is carefully insisted on. There is no diremption of the higher principle. God and mind do not disperse themselves in individual souls and in natural things, though these are nowhere cut off from their causes. There is a continual process from first to last, of which the law is the same throughout. Each producing cause remains wholly in its proper seat (ἐν τῇ οἰκείᾳ ἕδρᾳ), while that which is produced takes an inferior station[1]. The One produces universal Mind, or Intellect that is one with the Intelligible. Intellect produces the Soul of the Whole. This produces all other existences, but without itself lapsing. Nothing within the series of the three intelligible principles can be said to lapse in production; the term being applicable only to the descent of the individual soul. The order throughout, both for the intelligible causes and for the visible universe, is a logical order of causation, not an order in time. All the producing causes and their effects in every grade always existed and always will exist. The production by the higher causes has the undeviating character of natural necessity, and is not by voluntary choice and discursive reason, which are secondary resultants within the world of particulars.

This philosophical meaning Plotinus makes clear again and again. His metaphors are intended simply as more or less inadequate illustrations. One that comes nearer to his thought than that of the overflowing spring, is the metaphor of illumination by a central source of light; for according to his own theory light is an incorporeal energy projected without loss. Since, however, it is still an energy set going from a body, he admits that even this comparison has some inexactitude. In this mode of expression, Mind is the eternal "irradiation" of the One[2]. As Mind looks back to the One, Soul looks back to Mind; and this looking back is identical with the process of generation.

Plotinus himself traces the idea of this causal series to Plato, for whom, he says, the Demiurgus is Intellect, which is produced by the Good beyond mind and being, and in its turn

[1] Enn. v. 2, 2.
[2] Enn. v. 1, 6: περίλαμψιν ἐξ αὐτοῦ μέν, ἐξ αὐτοῦ δὲ μένοντος, οἷον ἡλίου τὸ περὶ αὐτὸν λαμπρὸν φῶς περιθέον, ἐξ αὐτοῦ ἀεὶ γεννώμενον μένοντος.

produces Soul[1]. This historical derivation, as we have seen, was accepted by Porphyry. Plotinus goes on to interpret earlier philosophers from the same point of view. He recognises, however, that the distinctions between the One in its different senses drawn by the Platonic Parmenides were not made with that exactitude by Parmenides himself. Aristotle, he says, coming later, makes the primal reality separable indeed and intelligible, but deprives it of the first rank by the assertion that it thinks itself. To think itself belongs to Mind, but not to the One[2].

As in the nature of things there are three principles, so also with us[3]. For there is reality in this world of ours, and not a mere semblance. The virtue and knowledge here are not simply images of archetypes yonder in the intelligible world. If indeed we take the world here not as meaning simply the visible aspect of things, but as including also the soul and what it contains, everything is "here" that is "there[4]."

The order of first, second and third in the intelligible principles is not spatial[5]. In the intelligible order, body may be said to be in soul, soul in mind, and mind in the One[6]. By such expressions is to be understood a relation of dependence, not the being in a place in the sense of locality. If any one objects that place can mean nothing but boundary or interval of space, let him dismiss the word and apply his understanding to the thing signified[7]. The incorporeal and unextended in which extended body participates is not to be thought of as a point; for mass, which includes an infinity of points, participates in it. Nor yet must we think of it as stretched out over the whole of the mass; but of the whole extended mass as participating in that which is itself without spatial interval[8].

---

[1] Enn. v. 1, 8: ὥστε Πλάτωνα εἰδέναι ἐκ μὲν τἀγαθοῦ τὸν νοῦν, ἐκ δὲ τοῦ νοῦ τὴν ψυχήν.

[2] Enn. v. 1, 9.

[3] Enn. v. 1, 10: ὥσπερ δὲ ἐν τῇ φύσει τριττὰ ταῦτά ἐστι τὰ εἰρημένα, οὕτω χρὴ νομίζειν καὶ παρ' ἡμῖν ταῦτα εἶναι.

[4] Enn. v. 9, 13: πάντα ἐνταῦθα, ὅσα κἀκεῖ.

[5] Enn. vi. 5, 4.   [6] Enn. v. 5, 9.

[7] Enn. vi. 4, 2: τὴν τοῦ ὀνόματος ἀφεὶς κατηγορίαν τῇ διανοίᾳ τὸ λεγόμενον λαμβανέτω.

[8] Enn. vi. 4, 13.

This is the general relation of the visible to the intelligible
world. As non-spatial dependence and implication, we have
found that it runs through the intelligible causes themselves.

In what relates to the difference between the extended and
the unextended, the character of intelligible being is already
perfectly determinate not only in soul, but in soul as the
principle of organic life. For that principle transcends the
opposition between small and great. If it is to be called small
as having no extension of its own, it may equally be called
great as being adequate to the animation of the whole body
with which it is connected, while this is growing in bulk[1]. The
soul is all in the germ; yet in a manner it contains the full-
grown plant or animal. In itself it undergoes no change of
dimensions. Though the principle of growth, it does not grow;
nor, when it causes motion, is it moved in the motion which it
causes[2].

The primal One from which all things are is everywhere and
nowhere. As being the cause of all things, it is everywhere.
As being other than all things, it is nowhere. If it were only
"everywhere," and not also "nowhere," it would be all things[3].
No predicate of being can be properly applied to it. To call it
the cause is to predicate something, not of it but of ourselves,
who have something from it while it remains in itself[4]. This
is not the "one" that the soul attains by abstracting from
magnitude and multitude till it arrives at the point and the
arithmetical unit. It is greatest of all, not by magnitude but
by potency; in such a manner that it is also by potency that
which is without magnitude. It is to be regarded as infinite,
not because of the impossibility of measuring or counting it,
but because of the impossibility of comprehending its power[5].
It is perfectly self-sufficing; there is no good that it should
seek to acquire by volition. It is good not in relation to itself,
but to that which participates in it. And indeed that which

---

[1] Enn. VI. 4, 5: μαρτυρεῖ δὲ τῷ μεγάλῳ τῆς ψυχῆς καὶ τὸ μείζονος τοῦ ὄγκου
γινομένου φθάνειν ἐπὶ πᾶν αὐτοῦ τὴν αὐτὴν ψυχήν, ἢ ἐπ' ἐλάττονος ὄγκου ἦν.

[2] Enn. III. 6, 4.   [3] Enn. III. 9, 3.

  Enn. VI. 9, 3.

[5] Enn. VI. 9, 6: ληπτέον δὲ καὶ ἄπειρον αὐτὸ οὐ τῷ ἀδιεξιτήτῳ ἢ τοῦ μεγέθους
ἢ τοῦ ἀριθμοῦ, ἀλλὰ τῷ ἀπεριλήπτῳ τῆς δυνάμεως.

imparts good is not properly to be called "good," but "the
Good" above all other goods. "That alone neither knows, nor
has what it does not know; but being One present to itself it
needs not thought of itself." Yet in a sense it is all beings
because all are from it[1]; and it generates the thought that is
one with being. As it is the Good above all goods, so, though
without shape or form, it possesses beauty above beauty. The
love of it is infinite; and the power or vision by which mind
thinks it is intellectual love[2].

Any inconsistency there might appear to be in making assertions about the One is avoided by the position that nothing
—not even that it "is" any more than that it is "good"—is
to be affirmed of it as a predicate. The names applied to it
are meant only to indicate its unique reality[3]. The question
is then raised, whether this reality is best indicated by names
that signify freedom, or chance, or necessity. Before we can
know whether an expression signifying freedom (τὸ ἐφ᾽ ἡμῖν)
may be applied in any sense to the gods and to God (ἐπὶ θεοὺς
καὶ ἔτι μᾶλλον ἐπὶ θεόν), we must know in what sense it is
applicable to ourselves[4]. If we refer that which is in our power
to will (βούλησις), and place this in right reason (ἐν λόγῳ
ὀρθῷ), we may—by stretching the terms a little—reach the
conclusion that an unimpeded theoretic activity such as we
ascribe in its perfection to the gods who live according to
mind, is properly called free. The objection that to be free in
this sense is to be "enslaved to one's own nature" is dismissed
with the remark that that only is enslaved which, being with-
held by something else, has it not in its power to go towards
the good[5]. The view that seems implied in the objection,
namely, that freedom consists in action contrary to the nature
of the agent, is an absurdity[6]. But to the supreme principle,
from which all things have being and power of their own, how
can the term be applied in any sense? The audacious thought
might be started that it "happens to be" as it is, and is not

---

[1] Enn. vi. 7, 32: οὐδὲν οὖν τοῦτο τῶν ὄντων καὶ πάντα· οὐδὲν μέν, ὅτι ὕστερα
τὰ ὄντα, πάντα δέ, ὅτι ἐξ αὐτοῦ.

[2] Enn. vi. 7, 35. Plotinus's actual expression is νοῦς ἐρῶν.

[3] Enn. vi. 7, 38. [4] Enn. vi. 8, 1.

[5] Enn. vi. 8, 4. [6] Enn. vi. 8, 7.

master of what it is, but is what it is, not from itself; and so,
that it has no freedom, since its doing or not doing what it
has been necessitated to do or not to do, is not in its own
power. To this the reply is, that we cannot say that the
primal cause is by chance, or that it is not master of its
origin; because it has not come to be[1]. The whole difficulty
seems to arise from our positing space (χώραν καὶ τόπον) as a
kind of chaos, and then introducing the principle into our
imaginary space; whereupon we inquire whence and how it
came there[2]. We get rid of the difficulty by assigning to the
One no place, but simply the being as it is,—and this because
we are bound so to express ourselves by necessity of speech.
Thus, if we are to speak of it at all, we must say that it is
lord of itself and free. Yet it must be allowed that there is
here a certain impropriety, for to be lord of itself belongs
properly to the essence (οὐσία) identical with thought, and
the One is before this essence[3]. With a similar impropriety,
its will and its essence may be said to be the same. Each
particular being, striving after its good, wills that more than
to be what it is, and then most thinks that it is, when it participates in the good. It wills even itself, so far only as it has
the good. Carry this over to the Good which is the principle
of all particular goods, and its will to be what it is, is seen to
be inseparable from its being what it is. In this mode of
speech, accordingly,—having to choose between ascribing to
it on the one hand will and creative activity in relation to
itself, on the other hand a contingent relation which is the
name of unreason,—we must say, not that it is "what it
happened to be," but that it is "what it willed to be[4]." We
might say also that it is of necessity what it is, and could
not be otherwise; but the more exact statement is, not that
it is thus because it could not be otherwise, but because the
best is thus. It is not taken hold of by necessity, but is itself

---

[1] Enn. VI. 8, 7: τὸ δὲ πρῶτον οὔτε κατὰ τύχην ἂν λέγοιμεν, οὔτε οὐ κύριον τῆς
αὐτοῦ γενέσεως, ὅτι μηδὲ γέγονε.

[2] Enn. VI. 8, 11.   [3] Enn. VI. 8, 12.

[4] Enn. VI. 8, 13: ὥστε οὐχ ὅπερ ἔτυχέν ἐστιν, ἀλλ' ὅπερ ἠβουλήθη αὐτός. Cf.
c. 20: αὐτός ἐστι καὶ ὁ παράγων ἑαυτόν.

the necessity and law of other things[1]. It is love, and the
object of love, and love of itself[2]. That which as it were desires and that which is desired are one[3]. When we, observing
some such nature in ourselves, rise to this and become this
alone, what should we say but that we are more than free
and more than in our own power? By analogy with mind, it
may be called operation (ἐνέργημα) and energy. Its energy
and as it were waking (οἶον ἐγρήγορσις) are eternal[4]. Reason
and mind are derived from the principle as a circle from its
centre[5]. To allow that it could not make itself other than it
did, in the sense that it can produce only good and not evil,
is not to limit its freedom and absolute power. The power
of choice between opposites belongs to a want of power to
persevere in what is best[6]. The One and Good alone is in
truth free; and must be thought and spoken of, though in
reality beyond speech and thought, as creating itself by its
own energy before all being[7].

To the question, why the One should create anything beyond itself, Plotinus answers that since all things, even those
without life, impart of themselves what they can, the most
perfect and the first good cannot remain in itself as envious,
and the potency of all things as without power[8]. As that is
the potency of all things, Mind, which it first generates, is all
things actually. For knowledge of things in their immaterial
essence is the things themselves[9]. Mind knows its objects not,
like perception, as external, but as one with itself[10]. Still this
unity, as has been said, involves the duality of thinking and

1 Enn. VI. 8, 10.
2 Enn. VI. 8, 15: καὶ ἐράσμιον καὶ ἔρως ὁ αὐτὸς καὶ αὐτοῦ ἔρως.
3 Ibid.: τὸ οἶον ἐφιέμενον τῷ ἐφετῷ ἔν.
4 Enn. VI. 8, 16.   5 Enn. VI. 8, 18.
6 Enn. VI. 8, 21: καὶ γὰρ τὸ τὰ ἀντικείμενα δύνασθαι ἀδυναμίας ἐστὶ τοῦ ἐπὶ
τοῦ ἀρίστου μένειν.
7 Since it is energy in the Aristotelian sense, or complete realisation, it is
ἀνενέργητον. That is, there is no higher realisation to which it can proceed.
Cf. Enn. V. 6, 6: ὅλως μὲν γὰρ οὐδεμία ἐνέργεια ἔχει αὖ πάλιν ἐνέργειαν. In this
sense, it is said (Enn. I. 7, 1) to be beyond energy (ἐπέκεινα ἐνεργείας).
8 Enn. V. 4, 1.
9 Enn. V. 4, 2. Cf. Enn. V. 9, 5: ἡ τῶν ἄνευ ὕλης ἐπιστήμη ταὐτὸν τῷ
πράγματι.
10 Enn. V. 5, 1.

being thought, and hence is not the highest, but the second in order, of the supramundane causes. Within its indivisible unity it contains the archetype of the whole visible world and of all that was or is or is to be existent in it. The relation of its Ideas to the whole of Mind resembles that of the propositions of a science to the sum of knowledge which consists of them. By this comparison, which frequently recurs, Plotinus seeks to convey the notion of a diversity in unity not expressed as local separation of parts[1]. The archetype of the world being thus existent, the world in space is necessarily produced because its production is possible. We shall see this "possibility" more exactly formulated in the theory of matter. The general statement is this: that, since there is the "intelligential and all-potent nature" of mind, and nothing stands between that and the production of a world, there must be a formed world corresponding to the formative power. In that which is formed, the ideas are divided; in one part of space the idea of the sun takes shape, in another the idea of man. The archetype embraces all in its unity without spatial division[2].

Thus, while supramundane intellect contains all real being, it has also the productive power by which the essential forms of things are made manifest in apparent separation from itself and from one another. Differences, so far as they belong to the real being, or "form," of things here, are produced by preexistent forms in the ideal world. So far as they are merely local and temporal, they express only a necessary mode of manifestation of being, under the condition of appearing at a greater degree of remoteness from the primal cause. What then is the case with individuality? Does it consist merely in differences of position in space and time, the only true reality being the ideal form of the "kind"; or are there ideal forms of individuals? Plotinus concludes decisively for the latter alternative[3]. There are as many formal differences as there

---

[1] See for example Enn. v. 9, 8.

[2] Enn. v. 9, 9: φύσεως νοερᾶς καὶ παντοδυνάμου οὔσης καὶ οὐδενὸς διείργοντος, μηδενὸς ὄντος μεταξὺ τούτου καὶ τοῦ δέξασθαι δυναμένου, ἀνάγκη τὸ μὲν κοσμηθῆναι, τὸ δὲ κοσμῆσαι. καὶ τὸ μὲν κοσμηθὲν ἔχει τὸ εἶδος μεμερισμένον, ἀλλαχοῦ ἄνθρωπον καὶ ἀλλαχοῦ ἥλιον· τὸ δὲ ἐν ἑνὶ πάντα.

[3] See especially Enn. v. 7: Περὶ τοῦ εἰ καὶ τῶν καθ' ἕκαστα ἔστιν εἴδη.

are individuals, and all pre-exist in the intelligible world.
What must be their mode of pre-existence we know from the
nature of Intellect as already set forth. All things there are
together yet distinct. Universal mind contains all particular
minds; and each particular mind expresses the whole in its
own manner. As Plotinus says in one of those bursts of enthusiasm where his scientific doctrine passes into poetry:
"They see themselves in others. For all things are transparent, and there is nothing dark or resisting, but every one
is manifest to every one internally and all things are manifest; for light is manifest to light. For every one has all
things in himself and again sees in another all things, so that
all things are everywhere and all is all and each is all, and
the splendour is infinite. For each of them is great, since the
small also is great. And the sun there is all the stars, and
again each and all are the sun. In each, one thing is pre-
eminent above the rest, but it also shows forth all[1]." The
wisdom that is there is not put together from separate acts
of knowledge, but is a single whole. It does not consist of
many brought to one; rather it is resolved into multitude
from unity. By way of illustration Plotinus adds that the
Egyptian sages, whether they seized the truth by accurate
knowledge or by some native insight, appear to have expressed the intuitive character of intellectual wisdom in
making a picture the sign of each thing[2].

In the intelligible world identical with intellect, as thus conceived, the time and space in which the visible world appears,
though not "there" as such, pre-exist in their causes. So too,
in the rational order, does perception, before organs of perception are formed. This must be so, Plotinus urges, because
perception and its organs are not a product of deliberation,
but are present for example in the pre-existent idea of man,
by an eternal necessity and law of perfection, their causes
being involved in the perfection of mind[3]. Not only man,
but all animals, plants and elements pre-exist ideally in the

---

[1] Enn. v. 8, 4.   [2] Enn. v. 8, 6. This is quite an isolated reference to Egypt.
[3] Enn. VI. 7, 3: ἔγκειται τὸ αἰσθητικὸν εἶναι καὶ οὕτως αἰσθητικὸν ἐν τῷ εἴδει
ὑπὸ ἀιδίου ἀνάγκης καὶ τελειότητος, νοῦ ἐν αὐτῷ ἔχοντος, εἴπερ τέλειος, τὰς αἰτίας.

intelligible world. For infinite variety is demanded in order that the whole, as one living being, may be perfect in all its parts and to the utmost degree. There, the things we call irrational pre-exist in their rational laws[1]. Nor is the thing here anywhere really mindless. We call it so when it is without mind in act; but each part is all in potency, depending as it does on its ideal cause. In the order of ideal causes there is as it were a stream of living beings from a single spring; as if all sensible qualities were combined in one quality without losing their distinctions[2]. The particular is not merely the one particular thing that it is called. Rational division of it always brings something new to light; so that, in this sense, each part of the whole is infinite[3]. This infinity, whether of whole or part, is one of successive involution. The process of division is not that of bisection, but is like the unfolding of wrappings[4]. The whole intelligible world may be presented to imagination as a living sphere figured over with every kind of living countenance[5].

Universal mind involves the essence of every form of reason, in one Reason as it were, great, perfect, embracing all (εἷς οἷον λόγος, μέγας, τέλειος, πάντας περιέχων). As the most exact reasoning would calculate the things of nature for the best, mind has all things in the rational laws that are before reasoning[6]. Each thing being what it is separately, and again all things being in one together, the complex as it were and composition of all as they are in one is Mind[7]. In the being that

---

[1] Enn. VI. 7, 9: ἐκεῖ δὲ καὶ τὸ ἄλογον λεγόμενον λόγος ἦν, καὶ τὸ ἄνουν νοῦς ἦν, ἐπεὶ καὶ ὁ νοῶν ἵππον νοῦς ἐστι, καὶ ἡ νόησις ἵππου νοῦς ἦν.

[2] Enn. VI. 7, 12: οἷον εἴ τις ἦν ποιότης μία πάσας ἐν αὑτῇ ἔχουσα καὶ σώζουσα τὰς ποιότητας, γλυκύτης μετ᾽ εὐωδίας, καὶ ὁμοῦ οἰνώδης ποιότης καὶ χυλῶν ἁπάντων δυνάμεις καὶ χρωμάτων ὄψεις καὶ ὅσα ἀφαὶ γινώσκουσιν. ἔστωσαν δὲ καὶ ὅσα ἀκοαὶ ἀκούουσι, πάντα μέλη καὶ ῥυθμὸς πᾶς.

[3] Enn. VI. 7, 13: νοῦς...οὐ...ταὐτὸν καὶ ἕν τι ἐν μέρει, ἀλλὰ πάντα· ἐπεὶ καὶ τὸ ἐν μέρει αὖ οὐχ ἕν, ἀλλὰ καὶ τοῦτο ἄπειρον διαιρούμενον. Cf. Enn. VI. 5, 5 on the infinite nature (ἄπειρος φύσις) of being.

[4] Enn. VI. 7, 14: μὴ κατ᾽ εὐθύ, ἀλλ᾽ εἰς τὸ ἐντὸς ἀεί.

[5] Enn. VI. 7, 15 fin.

[6] Enn. VI. 2, 21: ὡς γὰρ ἂν ὁ ἀκριβέστατος λογισμὸς λογίσαιτο ὡς ἄριστα, οὕτως ἔχει πάντα ἐν τοῖς λόγοις πρὸ λογισμοῦ οὖσι.

[7] Enn. VI. 2, 21: χωρὶς μὲν ἑκάστων ἃ ἐστιν ὄντων, ὁμοῦ δ᾽ αὖ ἐν ἑνὶ ὄντων, ἡ πάντων ἐν ἑνὶ ὄντων οἷον συμπλοκὴ καὶ σύνθεσις νοῦς ἐστι.

is mind, all things are together, not only undivided by position in space, but without reference to process in time. This characteristic of intellectual being may be called "eternity[1]." Time belongs to Soul, as eternity to Mind[2]. Soul is necessarily produced by Mind, as Mind by the primal One[3]. Thus it is in contact at once with eternal being, and with the temporal things which it generates by the power it receives from its cause. Having its existence from supramundane intellect, it has reason in act so far as that intellect is contemplated by it[4]. The Soul of the whole is perpetually in this relation to Mind; particular souls undergo alternation; though even of them there is ever something in the intelligible world[5]. Soul has for its work, not only to think—for thus it would in no way differ from pure intellect—but to order and rule the things after it. These come to be, because production could not stop at intelligibles, the last of which is the rational soul, but must go on to the limit of all possible existence[6].

In the relation of the many souls to the one which includes all, Soul imitates Mind. It too is necessarily pluralised; and in the inherent distinctions of the particular souls their coming to birth under different sensible manifestations is already necessitated. The one soul is the same in all, as in each part of a system of knowledge the whole is potentially present[7]. To soul, the higher intellect furnishes the reasons of all its operations[8]. Knowledge in the rational soul, so far as it is of

---

[1] Enn. III. 7, 4: αὕτη ἡ διάθεσις αὐτοῦ καὶ φύσις εἴη ἂν αἰών.

[2] Enn. III. 7, 11. Cf. Enn. IV. 4, 15: αἰὼν μὲν περὶ νοῦν, χρόνος δὲ περὶ ψυχήν.

[3] Enn. V. 1, 7: ψυχὴν γὰρ γεννᾷ νοῦς, νοῦς ὢν τέλειος. καὶ γὰρ τέλειον ὄντα γεννᾶν ἔδει, καὶ μὴ δύναμιν οὖσαν τοσαύτην ἄγονον εἶναι.

[4] Enn. V. 1, 3: ἥ τε οὖν ὑπόστασις αὐτῇ ἀπὸ νοῦ ὅ τε ἐνεργείᾳ λόγος νοῦ αὐτῇ ὁρωμένου.

[5] Enn. IV. 8, 8: οὐ πᾶσα οὐδ᾽ ἡ ἡμετέρα ψυχὴ ἔδυ, ἀλλ᾽ ἔστι τι αὐτῆς ἐν τῷ νοητῷ ἀεί....πᾶσα γὰρ ψυχὴ ἔχει τι καὶ τοῦ κάτω πρὸς τὸ σῶμα καὶ τοῦ ἄνω πρὸς νοῦν.

[6] Enn. IV. 8, 3: προσλαβοῦσα γὰρ τῷ νοερὰ εἶναι καὶ ἄλλο, καθ᾽ ὃ τὴν οἰκείαν ἔσχεν ὑπόστασιν, νοῦς οὐκ ἔμεινεν, ἔχει τε ἔργον καὶ αὐτή, εἴπερ καὶ πᾶν, ὃ ἂν ᾖ τῶν ὄντων. βλέπουσα δὲ πρὸς μὲν τὸ πρὸ ἑαυτῆς νοεῖ, εἰς δὲ ἑαυτὴν σώζει ἑαυτήν, εἰς δὲ τὸ μετ᾽ αὐτὴν κοσμεῖ τε καὶ διοικεῖ καὶ ἄρχει αὐτοῦ· ὅτι μηδὲ οἷόν τε ἦν στῆναι τὰ πάντα ἐν τῷ νοητῷ, δυναμένου ἐφεξῆς καὶ ἄλλου γενέσθαι ἐλάττονος μέν, ἀναγκαίου δὲ εἶναι, εἴπερ καὶ τὸ πρὸ αὐτοῦ.   [7] Enn. IV. 9, 5.

[8] Enn. IV. 9, 3. When the general soul impresses form on the elements of the world, νοῦς is the χορηγὸς τῶν λόγων.

intelligibles, is each thing that it thinks, and has from within
both the object of thought and the thinking (τό τε νοητὸν τήν
τε νόησιν), since mind is within[1]. Plotinus fully recognises
the difficulty of the question: How, if Being and Mind and
Soul are everywhere numerically one, and not merely of the
same formal essence (ὁμοειδές), can there yet be many beings
and minds and souls[2]? The answer, in the case of soul, as of
mind and being, is that the one is many by intrinsic difference, not by local situation (ἑτερότητι, οὐ τόπῳ). The plurality
of souls, as has been said, is in the rational order prior to
their embodiment. In the Soul of the Whole, the many souls
are present to one another without being alienated from themselves. They are not divided by spatial limits—just as the
many portions of knowledge in each soul are not—and the
one can contain in itself all. After this manner the nature of
soul is infinite[3]. The general soul can judge of the individual-
ised affections in each without becoming conscious to itself
in each that it has passed judgment in the rest also[4]. Each
of us is a whole for himself, yet all of us, in the reality that is
all, are together one. Looking outward, we forget our unity.
Turning back upon ourselves, either of our own accord or
seized upon as the goddess seized the hair of Achilles, we
behold ourselves and the whole as one with the God within[5].

The soul is the principle of life and motion to all things;
motion being an image of life in things called lifeless. The
heaven is one by the power of soul, and this world is divine
through it[6]. The soul of the whole orders the world in accordance with the general reasons of things, as animal bodies are
fashioned into "microcosms" under the particular law of the
organism[7]. It creates not by deliberative intelligence, like

[1] Enn. v. 9, 7.   [2] Enn. vi. 4, 4.

[3] Enn. vi. 4, 4 fin.: οὕτως ἐστὶν ἄπειρος ἡ τοιαύτη φύσις.

[4] Enn. vi. 4, 6: διὰ τί οὖν οὐ συναισθάνεται ἡ ἑτέρα τῆς ἑτέρας κρίμα; ἢ ὅτι κρίσις
ἐστίν, ἀλλ' οὐ πάθος. εἶτα οὐδ' αὐτὴ ἡ κρίνασα κέκρικα λέγει, ἀλλ' ἔκρινε μόνον.

[5] Enn. vi. 5, 7: ἔξω μὲν οὖν ὁρῶντες ἢ ὅθεν ἐξήμμεθα ἀγνοοῦμεν ἓν ὄντες, οἷον
πρόσωπα πολλὰ εἰς τὸ ἔξω κορυφὴν ἔχοντα εἰς τὸ εἴσω μίαν. εἰ δέ τις ἐπιστραφῆναι
δύναιτο ἢ παρ' αὐτοῦ ἢ τῆς Ἀθηνᾶς αὐτῆς εὐτυχήσας τῆς ἕλξεως, θεόν τε καὶ αὐτὸν
καὶ τὸ πᾶν ὄψεται.   [6] Enn. v. 1, 2.

[7] Enn. iv. 3, 10: οἷα καὶ οἱ ἐν σπέρμασι λόγοι πλάττουσι καὶ μορφοῦσι τὰ ζῷα
οἷον μικρούς τινας κόσμους.

human art, which is posterior and extrinsic. In the one soul are the rational laws of all explicit intelligence—"of gods and of all things." "Wherefore also the world has all[1]."

Individual souls are the intrinsic laws of particular minds within the universal intellect, made more explicit[2]. Not only the soul of the whole, but the soul of each, has all things in itself[3]. Wherein they differ, is in energising with different powers. Before descent and after reascent of the particular soul, each one's thoughts are manifest to another as in direct vision, without discourse[4]. Why then does the soul descend and lose knowledge of its unity with the whole? For the choice is better to remain above[5]. The answer is that the error lies in self-will[6]. The soul desires to be its own, and so ventures forth to birth, and takes upon itself the ordering of a body which it appropriates, or rather, which appropriates it, so far as that is possible. Thus the soul, although it does not really belong to this body, yet energises in relation to it, and in a manner becomes a partial soul in separation from the whole[7].

But what is finally the explanation of this choice of the worse, and how is it compatible with the perfection of the mundane order? How is the position of the *Phaedo*, that the body is a prison, and the true aim of the soul release from it, reconcilable with the optimism of the *Timaeus*? The answer is that all—descent and reascent alike—has the necessity of a natural law. The optimism has reference to the whole order. Of this order, such as it must be in a world that is still good though below the intelligible and perfectly stable supramundane order, temporary descent, dissatisfaction with the consequences of the descent, and the effort to return, are all conditions. Any expression that seems to imply arbitrariness at any point, is part of the mythological representation. Thus

---

[1] Enn. IV. 3, 10 *fin.*

[2] Enn. IV. 3, 5: λόγοι νῶν οὖσαι καὶ ἐξειλιγμέναι μᾶλλον ἢ ἐκεῖνοι...τὸ ταὐτὸν καὶ ἕτερον σώζουσαι μένει τε ἑκάστη ἕν, καὶ ὁμοῦ ἓν πᾶσαι.

[3] Enn. IV. 3, 6.

[4] Enn. IV. 3, 18: οἷον ὀφθαλμὸς ἕκαστος καὶ οὐδὲν δὲ κρυπτὸν οὐδὲ πεπλασμένον, ἀλλὰ πρὶν εἰπεῖν ἄλλῳ ἰδὼν ἐκεῖνος ἔγνω.

[5] Enn. IV. 3, 14.　　[6] Enn. V. 1, 1.　　[7] Enn. VI. 4, 16.

when in the *Timaeus* it is said that God "sows" the souls, this is mythical, just as when he is represented as haranguing them[1]. Necessity and self-caused descent are not discordant. The soul does not go by its will to that which is worse; yet its course is its own[2]. And it must expiate both the original error, and any evil that it may do actually. Of the first, the mere change of state is the punishment; to the second, further chastisement is assigned. The knowledge acquired below is a good, and the soul is not to be blamed overmuch if in its regulation of sensible nature it goes a little beyond what is safe for itself[3]. On the other hand, a slight inclination at the beginning to the worse, if not immediately corrected, may produce a permanent disposition[4]. Be the error light or grave, it comes under an undeviating law of justice. To the particular bodies fitted for them, the souls go neither by voluntary choice nor sent, but as by some natural process for which they are ready. The universal law under which the individual falls is not outside but within each[5]. The notion that there may be in small things an element of contingency which is no part of the order, is suggested but not accepted[6]. The whole course of the soul through its series of bodily lives, and its release from the body when this is attained, are alike necessarily determined[7]. The death of the soul, so far as the soul can die, is to sink to a stage below moral evil—which still contains a mixture of the opposite good—and to be wholly plunged in matter[8]. Even thence it may still somehow emerge; though souls that have descended to the world of birth need not all

---

[1] Enn. IV. 8, 4.   [2] Enn. IV. 8, 5.

[3] Enn. IV. 8, 7: γνῶσις γὰρ ἐναργεστέρα τἀγαθοῦ ἡ τοῦ κακοῦ πεῖρα οἷς ἡ δύναμις ἀσθενεστέρα, ἢ ὥστε ἐπιστήμῃ τὸ κακὸν πρὸ πείρας γνῶναι.

[4] Enn. III. 2, 4. Cf. III. 3, 4: καὶ σμικρὰ ῥοπὴ ἀρκεῖ εἰς ἔκβασιν τοῦ ὀρθοῦ.

[5] Enn. IV. 3, 13.

[6] Enn. IV. 3, 16: οὐ γὰρ τὰ μὲν δεῖ νομίζειν συντετάχθαι, τὰ δὲ κεχαλάσθαι εἰς τὸ αὐτεξούσιον. εἰ γὰρ κατ' αἰτίας γίνεσθαι δεῖ καὶ φυσικὰς ἀκολουθίας καὶ κατὰ λόγον ἕνα καὶ τάξιν μίαν, καὶ τὰ σμικρότερα δεῖ συντετάχθαι καὶ συνυφάνθαι νομίζειν.

[7] Enn. IV. 3, 24: φέρεται δὲ καὶ αὐτὸς ὁ πάσχων ἀγνοῶν ἐφ' ἃ παθεῖν προσήκει, ἀστάτῳ μὲν τῇ φορᾷ πανταχοῦ αἰωρούμενος ταῖς πλάναις, τελευτῶν δὲ ὥσπερ πολλὰ καμὼν οἷς ἀντέτεινεν εἰς τὸν προσήκοντα αὐτῷ τόπον ἐνέπεσεν, ἑκουσίῳ τῇ φορᾷ τὸ ἀκούσιον εἰς τὸ παθεῖν ἔχων. Cf. Enn. IV. 4, 45.

[8] Enn. I. 8, 13: καὶ τοῦτό ἐστι τὸ ἐν ᾅδου ἐλθόντα ἐπικαταδαρθεῖν. Cf. Enn. I. 6, 6.

make the full circle, but may return before reaching the
lowest point[1].

Here we come to the metaphysical doctrine by which
Plotinus explains the contrasts the visible world presents.
Neither moral good nor evil is with him ultimate. Of virtues,
even the highest, the cause is the Good, which in reality is
above good (ὑπεράγαθον). Of moral evil, so far as it is purely
evil, the cause is that principle of absolute formlessness and
indeterminateness called Matter. At the same time, matter
is the receptive principle by which alone the present world
could be at all. Evils accordingly are an inevitable constituent of a world that is subject in its parts to birth and
change. And indeed without evil there can be no good in our
sense of the term. Nor is there evil unmixed in the things of
nature, any more than there is unformed matter. Whence
then is this principle opposed to form and unity?

That Matter is an independently existing principle over
against the One, Plotinus distinctly denies. The supposition
is put as inadmissible that there are ἀρχαὶ πλείους καὶ κατὰ
συντυχίαν τὰ πρῶτα[2]. Matter is the infinite (τὸ ἄπειρον) in
the sense of the indeterminate (τὸ ἀόριστον), and is generated
from the infinity of power or of eternal existence that is an
appanage of the One, which has not in itself indeterminateness, but creates it[3]. To the term "infinite" in the sense of an
actual extent or number that is immeasurable (ἀδιεξίτητον),
or of a quantitative infinite (κατὰ τὸ ποσὸν ἄπειρον), there is
nothing to correspond. Matter, in itself indeterminate, is that
of which the nature is to be a recipient of forms. Like intelligible being, it is incorporeal and unextended. Place, indeed,
is posterior both to matter and bodies[4]. By its absolute want
of all form, that is, of all proper being, matter is at the opposite
extreme to things intelligible, and is in its own nature ugly
and evil[5]. It receives, indeed, all determinations, but it can-

---

[1] Enn. IV. 4, 5 fin.   [2] Enn. II. 4, 2.

[3] Enn. II. 4, 15: εἴη ἂν γεννηθὲν ἐκ τῆς τοῦ ἑνὸς ἀπειρίας ἢ δυνάμεως ἢ τοῦ ἀεί,
οὐκ οὔσης ἐν ἐκείνῳ ἀπειρίας ἀλλὰ ποιοῦντος.

[4] Enn. II. 4, 12: ὁ δὲ τόπος ὕστερος τῆς ὕλης καὶ τῶν σωμάτων.

[5] Enn. II. 4, 16.

not receive them indivisibly (ἀμερῶς). One form in matter
excludes another; so that they appear as separated by spatial
intervals[1]. The reason of this is precisely that matter has no
determination of its own. The soul in taking up the forms of
things perceptible, views them with their mass put away
(ἀποθέμενα τὸν ὄγκον ὁρᾷ), because by its own form it is indivisible, and therefore cannot receive the extended as such.
Since matter, on the contrary, has no form of its own by which
to unite distinctions, the intrinsic differences of being must be
represented in it by local separation. Yet, since the intelligible
world is in a sense a "world," and is many as well as one, it too
must have a kind of matter[2]. This "intelligible matter" is the
recipient of formal diversities in the world of being; as sensible
matter is the recipient of the varied appearances in space.
The matter of the intelligible world, differing in this respect
from matter properly so-called, does not receive all forms in-
differently; the same matter there having always the same
form[3]. The matter "here" is thus more truly "the indeterminate" than the matter "there"; which, in so far as it has
more real being, is so much less truly "matter[4]." Matter itself
may best be called "not-being[5]." As the indeterminate, it is
only to be apprehended by a corresponding indeterminateness
of the soul[6]—a difficult state to maintain, for, as matter itself
does not remain unformed in things, so the soul hastens to
add some positive determination to the abstract formlessness
reached by analysis. To be the subject and recipient ever
ready for all forms, it must be indestructible and impassible,
as it is incorporeal and unextended. It is like a mirror which
represents all things so that they seem to be where they are
not, and keeps no impression of any[7]. The appearances of
sense, themselves "invulnerable nothings[8]," go through it as
through water without dividing it. It has not even a falsehood

[1] Enn. III. 6, 18.　　　　[2] Enn. II. 4, 4.

[3] Enn. II. 4, 3: ἡ δὲ τῶν γινομένων ὕλη ἀεὶ ἄλλο καὶ ἄλλο εἶδος ἴσχει, τῶν δὲ
ἀιδίων ἡ αὐτὴ ταὐτὸν ἀεί.

[4] Enn. II. 4, 15.　　　　　[5] Enn. III. 6, 7.

[6] Enn. II. 4, 10: ἀοριστία τῆς ψυχῆς. Cf. Enn. I. 8, 9.

[7] Enn. III. 6, 7.

[8] *Adonais*, xxxix.—an exact expression of the idea of Plotinus.

of its own that it can say of things[1]. In that it can take no
permanent hold of any good, it may be called evil[2]. Fleeing
every attempt of perception to grasp it, it is equally receptive
in appearance of the contraries which it is equally unable to
retain.

3. *Cosmology and Theodicy.*

The theory of matter set forth, though turned to new metaphysical account, is fundamentally that of Aristotle. As with
Aristotle, Matter is the presupposition of physics, being viewed
as the indestructible "subject" of forms, enduring through all
changes in potency of further change; but Plotinus is careful
to point out that the world of natural things derives none of
its reality from the recipient. The formal reason (λόγος) that
makes matter appear as extended, does not "unfold" it to
extension—for this was not implicit in it—but, like that also
which makes it appear as coloured, gives it something that
was not there[3]. In that it confers no qualities whatever on
that which appears in it, matter is absolutely sterile[4]. The
forms manifested in nature are those already contained in
the intellect that is before it, which acquires them by turning
towards the Good. All differences of form, down to those of
the elements, are the product of Reason and not of Matter[5].

While working out his theory from a direct consideration
of the necessity that there should be something indestructible
beneath the transformations of body, Plotinus tries to prove
it not inconsistent with what is known as Plato's "theory of
matter" in the *Timaeus*. The phrases in which the "recipient"
is spoken of as a "room" and a "seat" are interpreted meta-
phorically. Here Plotinus is evidently arguing against commentators in his own time who took the "Platonic matter" to
be empty space[6]. This has now become the generally accepted
interpretation; opinions differing only as to whether the space
or matter in which the ideas manifest themselves is to be re-

---

[1] Enn. III. 6, 15.
[2] Enn. III. 6, 11.
[3] Enn. II. 4, 9.
[4] Enn. III. 6, 19.
[5] Enn. VI. 7, 11.
[6] See especially Enn. II. 4, 11: ὅθεν τινὲς ταὐτὸν τῷ κενῷ τὴν ὕλην εἰρήκασι.

garded as objective extension or as a subjective form[1]. Plotinus himself approaches the latter view when he consents to
call matter a "phantasm of mass" ($\phi\acute{a}\nu\tau a\sigma\mu a$ $\delta\grave{e}$ $\check{o}\gamma\kappa o\upsilon$ $\lambda\acute{e}\gamma\omega$),
though still regarding it as unextended ($\grave{a}\mu\acute{e}\gamma\epsilon\theta\epsilon\varsigma$). His account
of the mental process by which the nature opposed to that of
the ideas is known ($\nu\acute{o}\theta\omega$ $\lambda o\gamma\iota\sigma\mu\hat{\omega}$) quite agrees with Plato's.

On another point of Platonic interpretation, Plotinus and
all his successors take the view which modern criticism seems
now to find the most satisfactory. Plausible as was the reading
of the *Timaeus* which would regard it as teaching an origin of
the world from an absolute beginning of time, this was never,
even at the earliest period, really prevalent in the school of
Plato. During the Platonising movement that preceded Plotinus, the usual interpretation had been to regard what is said
about the making of the world from pre-existent elements as
mythological. The visible universe, said the earliest like the
latest interpreters, is described by Plato as "generated" because it depends on an unchanging principle while itself perpetually subject to mutation; not because it is supposed to
have been called into being at a particular moment. That this
was all along the authorised interpretation may be seen even
from Plutarch[2], who, in defending the opposite thesis, evidently feels that he is arguing against the opinion predominant among contemporary Platonists[3]. Thus Plotinus, when

---

[1] The first is Zeller's view, in which he is followed by Siebeck and by
Baeumker (*Das Problem der Materie in der griechischen Philosophie*, 1890),
who have skilfully defended it against objections. Mr Archer-Hind, in his
edition of the *Timaeus*, takes the view that the Platonic matter is space as a
subjective form. This would bring it very close to the Kantian doctrine. The
more usual view would in effect make it an anticipation of Descartes' attempt
in the *Principia Philosophiae* to construct body out of pure extension. There
is certainly a striking resemblance in general conception between Plato's and
Descartes' corpuscular theory: it has been noted by Mr Benn (*The Greek
Philosophers*, 1st ed., vol. ii. pp. 388–389). (In the first edition, I omitted to
make this reference, having forgotten the passage and rediscovered the
coincidence.)

[2] Περὶ τῆς ἐν Τιμαίῳ ψυχογονίας.

[3] It may be noted that the "Platonic matter," according to Plutarch, is
simply body or "corporeal substance." ἡ μὲν οὖν σώματος οὐσία τῆς λεγομένης
ὑπ' αὐτοῦ πανδεχοῦς φύσεως ἕδρας τε καὶ τιθήνης τῶν γενητῶν οὐχ ἑτέρα τίς ἐστιν
(c. 5 *fin.*).

he says that there never was a time when this whole was not, nor was there ever matter unformed, is not introducing a novelty. And on this point we do not hear that opposition to his doctrine arose from any quarter. His difference with Longinus was on the question whether the divine mind eternally contains the ideas in itself or contemplates them eternally as objective existences; not as to whether ideas and unordered matter once stood apart and were then brought together by an act or process of creative volition. The duration of the universe without temporal beginning or end was the accepted doctrine of Hellenic Platonism.

In accordance with this general view, however, it is possible, as Plotinus recognises[1], to hold either that the universe is permanent only as a whole, while *all* its parts perish as individual bodies (κατὰ τὸ τόδε) and are renewed only in type (κατὰ τὸ εἶδος), or that some of the bodies in the universe—namely, those that fill the spaces from the sphere of the moon outwards —are always numerically identical. If the former view is the true one, then the heavenly bodies differ from the rest only by lasting a longer time. About the latter view there would be no trouble if we were to accept Aristotle's doctrine that their substance is a fifth element, not subject like the rest to alteration. For those who allow that they consist of the elements of which living bodies on earth are constituted, the difficulty is that they must be by nature dissoluble. This Plato himself conceded to Heraclitus. As in his physics generally, so here, Plotinus argues in a rather tentative way. He suggests as the true solution, that the heaven with all its parts consists of a purer kind of fire, which we may call "light," moving if at all with a circular motion, losing nothing by efflux, and consequently in no need, like mortal bodies, of nourishment from without. This material light, being a kind of body, must of course be distinguished from light as an outflowing energy[2] Radiant light, as we have seen[3], is for Plotinus an activity carrying with it no loss either of substance or of efficiency;

[1] Enn. II. 1, 1.
[2] Enn. II. 1, 7: τὸ ὁμώνυμον αὐτῷ φῶς, ὃ δή φαμεν καὶ ἀσώματον εἶναι.
[3] Cf. Enn. IV. 5.

whence it furnished an analogy closer than is possible on any modern theory for the metaphysical doctrine of emanation.

For the rest, this picture of the physical universe does not essentially differ from Aristotle's. The whole forms a single system, with the fixed stars and the seven planets (including the sun and moon) revolving round the spherical earth in combinations of perfect circles. Like the stars, the earth too has a divinity of its own[1]. The space which the universe fills is finite. Body is not atomic in constitution but continuous. The complex movements of the whole system recur in astronomical cycles. In order to solve difficulties connected with the infinite duration of a world in constant change, Plotinus sometimes takes up the Stoical theory that in the recurrent periods the sequence of events is exactly repeated. This he does especially where the question presents itself, how that infinity in the world of sense is possible which is required by his doctrine that there are "ideas of particulars." Individual differences, he allows, must according to this view be infinite, seeing that there is no limit to the duration of the world either in the past or in the future. The difficulty would be met by supposing that differences finite in number recur exactly in succeeding cycles. Thus, in any one cycle no two individuals are without all formal difference, and yet the number of "forms" is limited[2]. This solution, however, seems to be offered with no great confidence. The point about which Plotinus is quite clear is that individual as well as specific differences have their rational determination in the ideal world. From this he deduces that, in any one period of the cosmos at least, there are no two individuals that differ only numerically, without a trace of inward distinction[3]. About infinity in the ideal world or in the soul there is no difficulty[4]. The conception of an actual quantitative infinite is not merely difficult, but impossible.

Yet, while repeatedly laying down this position, Plotinus allows that space and number as prefigured in eternal intellect

---

[1] Enn. iv. 4, 22–27.   [2] Enn. v. 7, 2.   [3] Enn. v. 7, 3.
[4] Enn. v. 7, 1: τὴν δὲ ἐν τῷ νοητῷ ἀπειρίαν οὐ δεῖ δεδιέναι· πᾶσα γὰρ ἐν ἀμερεῖ. As regards the soul and its λόγοι, cf. c. 3.

have an infinitude of their own. We may say that number is
infinite, though infinity is repugnant to number (τὸ ἄπειρον
μάχεται τῷ ἀριθμῷ), as we speak of an infinite line; not that
there is any such (οὐχ ὅτι ἔστι τις τοιαύτη), but that we can
go in thought beyond the greatest existing. This means that
in intellect the rational law of linear magnitude does not carry
with it the thought of a limit[1]. Similarly, number in intellect
is unmeasured. No actual number can be assigned that goes
beyond what is already involved in the idea of number. Intellectual being is beyond measure because it is itself the
measure. The limited and measured is that which is prevented
from running to infinity in its other sense of indeterminateness[2]. Thus limited and measured is the visible cosmos.

To time is allowed an explicit infinity that is denied to
space. It is the "image of eternity," reflecting the infinite
already existent whole of being by the continual going to
infinity of successive realisations[3]. Time belongs to apartness
of life (διάστασις οὖν ζωῆς χρόνον εἶχε). The Soul of the Whole
generates time and not eternity, because the things it produces
are not imperishable. It is not itself in time; nor are individual
souls themselves, but only their affections and deeds[4], which
are really those of the composite nature. Thus the past which
is the object of memory is in things done; in the soul itself
there is nothing past[5]. Of Zeus, whether regarded as Demiurgus or as Soul of the World, we must deny even the "before
and after" implied in memory[6]. That which guides the whole
(τὸ ἡγούμενον τοῦ παντός) knows the future as present (κατὰ
τὸ ἑστάναι), and has therefore no need of memory and discursive reason to infer it from the past[7]. These faculties belong to acquired intellect, and, as we shall see, are dismissed

---

[1] Enn. VI. 6, 17: ἢ τὸ ἄπειρον ἄλλον τρόπον, οὐχ ὡς ἀδιεξίτητον· ἀλλὰ πῶς
ἄπειρος; ἢ ἐν τῷ λόγῳ τῆς αὐτογραμμῆς οὐκ ἔνι προσνοούμενον πέρας.

[2] Enn. VI. 6, 18.   [3] Enn. III. 7, 11.

[4] Enn. IV. 4, 15.

[5] Enn. IV. 4, 16: ἀλλὰ πάντες οἱ λόγοι ἅμα, ὥσπερ εἴρηται...τὸ δὲ τόδε μετὰ
τόδε ἐν τοῖς πράγμασιν οὐ δυναμένοις ἅμα πάντα.

[6] Enn. IV. 4, 10.

[7] Enn. IV. 4, 12. Hence, adds Plotinus, the creative power (τὸ ποιοῦν) is not
subject to labour and difficulty, as was in the imagination of those who
thought the regulation of the whole would be a troublesome business.

even by the individual soul when it has reascended to intuitive
knowledge.

If things eternal were altogether alien to us, we could not
speak of them with intelligence. We also then must participate
in eternity[1]. How the soul's essence can be in eternity while
the composite nature consisting of soul and body is in time,
can only be understood when the definition of time has been
more strictly investigated. To define it in relation to physical
movement does not express its essential character. The means
by which we learn to know time is no doubt observation of
motion, and especially of the revolutions of the heavenly
bodies. Yet while ordered external motion more than anything else shows time forth to mental conception, it does not
make time be. When the motion of the whole is measured in
terms of time, which itself is fixed according to certain intervals marked out in the space through which the motions
proceed, this is an "accidental" relation. The parts of time,
invisible and inapprehensible in themselves, must have remained unknown till thus measured, but time itself is prior
to the measurement of its parts. We must bring it back
finally to a movement of the soul, though the soul could
hardly have known it to any purpose without the movement
of the heaven. Time is not, however, in the merely individual
soul, but in all souls so far as they are one. Therefore there
is one uniform time, and not a multitude of disparate times;
as in another relation there is one eternity in which all participate[2]. Thus the one soul, in which individual souls are
metaphysically contained, participates in eternity and produces time, which is the form of a soul living in apparent
detachment from its higher cause.

Unity in the soul of the whole, here so strongly insisted on,
does not with Plotinus exclude the reality of particular souls.
We have seen that he regards individuality as determined by
differences in the Ideas, and not by the metaphysically unreal

---

[1] Enn. III. 7, 7: δεῖ ἄρα καὶ ἡμῖν μετεῖναι τοῦ αἰῶνος.

[2] Enn. III. 7, 13: ἆρ᾽ οὖν καὶ ἐν ἡμῖν [ὁ] χρόνος; ἢ ἐν ψυχῇ τῇ τοιαύτῃ πάσῃ καὶ
ὁμοειδῶς ἐν πᾶσι καὶ αἱ πᾶσαι μία. διὸ οὐ διασπασθήσεται ὁ χρόνος· ἐπεὶ οὐδ᾽ ὁ
αἰὼν ὁ κατ᾽ ἄλλο ἐν τοῖς ὁμοειδέσι πᾶσιν.

modes of pluralising ascribed to Matter. What comes from
matter is separateness of external manifestation, and muta-
bility in the realisations attained; not inner diversity, which
pre-exists in the world of being. This view he turns against
the fatalism that would make the agency of the individual
soul count for nothing in the sum of things. He is without the
least hesitation a determinist. Within the universal order, he
premises, the uncaused (τὸ ἀναίτιον) is not to be received,
whether under the form of "empty declinations," or of a
sudden movement of bodies without preceding movement, or
of a capricious impulse of soul not assignable to any motive[1].
But to say that everything in each is determined by one soul
that runs through all, is, by an excess of necessity, to take
away necessity itself and the causal order; for in this case it
would not be true that all comes to pass by causes, but all
things would be one, without distinction between that which
causes and that which is caused; "so that neither we are we
nor is anything our work[2]." Each must be each, and actions
and thoughts must belong to us as our own[3]. This is the truth
that physical, and especially astrological, fatalism denies. To
preserve the causal order without exception while at the same
time allowing that we ourselves are something, we must introduce the soul as another principle into the contexture of
things,—and not only the soul of the whole, but along with it
the soul of each[4]. Being in a contexture, and not by itself, it
is not wholly master, and so far fate or destiny (εἱμαρμένη)
regarded as external, has a real existence. Thus all things

---

[1] Enn. III. 1, 1: ἢ γὰρ τὸ βουλητόν—τοῦτο δὲ ἢ ἔξω ἢ εἴσω—ἢ τὸ ἐπιθυμητὸν
ἐκίνησεν· ἤ, εἰ μηδὲν ὀρεκτὸν ἐκίνησεν, οὐδ' ἂν ὅλως ἐκινήθη. The principle of
psychological determinism could not be more clearly put. In view of this, it
is not a little surprising that Zeller should vaguely class Plotinus and his
successors as champions of "free-will." On the other hand Jules Simon, who
quite recognises the determinism of the school, misstates the doctrine of
Plotinus as regards the nature of the individual when he says (Histoire de
l'École d'Alexandrie, t. i. pp. 570–1) that that which is not of the essence of
each soul, and must consequently perish, is, according to Plotinus, its individuality, and that this comes from matter.

[2] Enn. III. 1, 4.

[3] Cf. Enn. III. 4, 6: οὐ γὰρ ὁμοίως ἐν τοῖς αὐτοῖς πᾶς κινεῖται ἢ βούλεται η
ἐνεργεῖ.

[4] Enn. III. 1, 8.

come to pass according to causes; but some by the soul, and
some through the other causes among which it is placed. Of
its not thinking and acting rationally (τοῦ μὴ φρονεῖν) other
things are the causes. Rational action has its cause within;
being only not hindered from without[1].

Virtue therefore is free; and the more completely free the
more the soul is purified from mixture. To the bad, who do
most things according to the imaginations excited by bodily
affections, we must assign neither a power of their own nor
a proper volition[2]. How then can punishment be just? The
answer is that the composite nature, which sins, is also that
which pays the penalty of sin[3]. The involuntariness of sin
(ὅτι ἁμαρτία ἀκούσιον) does not prevent the deed being from
the doer[4]. Some men indeed come into being as if by a witch-
craft of external things, and are little or nothing of themselves: others preserve the original nature of the soul's essence.
For it is not to be thought that the soul alone of all things is
without such a nature[5]. In preserving or recovering this lie
virtue and freedom.

A more elaborate treatment of the problem of theodicy here
raised is contained in three books that belong to Plotinus's
last period[6]. This problem he does not minimise. Although,
in metaphysical reality, the world has not come to be by a
process of contrivance resembling human art, yet, he says, if
reasoning had made it, it would have no reason to be ashamed
of its work[7]. This whole, with everything in it, is as it would
be if providentially ordered by the rational choice of the
Maker[8].

If, indeed, the world had come into existence a certain time
ago, and before was not, then the providence which regulates

---

[1] Enn. III. 1, 10.

[2] Enn. VI. 8, 3: οὔτε τὸ ἐπ αὐτοῖς οὔτε τὸ ἑκούσιον δώσομεν.

[3] Enn. I. 1, 12.　　　　　　　　[4] Enn. III. 2, 10.

[5] Enn. II. 3, 15: οὐ γὰρ δὴ νομιστέον τοιοῦτον εἶναι ψυχήν, οἷον, ὅ τι ἂν ἔξωθεν
πάθῃ, ταύτην φύσιν ἴσχειν μόνην τῶν πάντων οἰκείαν φύσιν οὐκ ἔχουσαν.

[6] Enn. III. 2, III. 3, I. 8.

[7] Enn. III. 2, 3: οὐδ' εἰ λογισμὸς εἴη ὁ ποιήσας, αἰσχύνεῖται τῷ ποιηθέντι.

[8] Enn. VI. 8, 17.

it would be like that of rational beings within the world; it would be a certain foresight and reasoning of God how this whole should come to exist, and how it should be in the best manner possible. Since, however, the world is without beginning and end, the providence that governs the whole consists in its being in accordance with mind, which is before it not in time but as its cause and model so to speak.

From mind proceeds a rational law which imposes harmony on the cosmos. This law, however, cannot be unmixed intellect like the first. The condition of there being a world below the purely intelligible order—and there must be such a world, that every possible degree of perfection may be realised—is mutual hindrance and separation of parts. The unjust dealings of men with one another arise from an aspiration after the good along with a want of power to attain it. Evil is a defection ($\check{\epsilon}\lambda\lambda\epsilon\iota\psi\iota\varsigma$) of good; and, in a universe of separated existences, absence of good in one place follows with necessity from its presence in another. Therefore evils cannot be destroyed from the world. What are commonly called evils, as poverty and disease, Plotinus continues to assert with the Stoical tradition, are nothing to those who possess true good, which is virtue; and they are not useless to the order of the whole. Yet, he proceeds, it may still be argued that the distribution of what the Stoics after all allow to be things "agreeable" and "not agreeable" to nature, is unfair. That the bad should be lords and rulers of cities, and that men of worth should be slaves, is not fitting, even though lordship and slavery are nothing as regards the possession of real good. And with a perfect providence every detail must be as it ought to be. We are not to evade the difficulty by saying that providence does not extend to earth, or that through chance and necessity it is not strong enough to sway things here. The earth too is as one of the stars ($\dot{\omega}\varsigma$ $\check{\epsilon}\nu$ $\tau\iota$ $\tau\hat{\omega}\nu$ $\check{\alpha}\sigma\tau\rho\omega\nu$)[1]. If, however, we bear in mind that we are to look for the greatest possible perfection that can belong to a world of mixture, not for that which can belong only to the intelligible order, the argument may be met in full. Among men

[1] Enn. III. 2, 8.

there are higher and lower and intermediate natures,—the last being the most numerous. Those that are so degenerate as to come within the neighbourhood of irrational animals do violence to the intermediate natures. These are better than those that maltreat them, and yet are conquered by the worse in so far as they themselves are worse in relation to the particular kind of contest to be undergone. If they are content to be fatted sheep, they should not complain of becoming a prey to the wolves. And, Plotinus adds parenthetically, the spoilers too pay the penalty; first in being wolves and wretched men, and then in having a worse fate after death, according to their acquired character. For the complete order of justice has regard to the series of past and future lives, not to each present life by itself. But to take things as seen in one life: always the mundane order demands certain means if we are to attain the end. Those who have done nothing worthy of happiness cannot reasonably expect to be happy. The law is, for example, that out of wars we are to come safe by proving our courage, not by prayer. Were the opposite the case,— could peace be preserved amid every kind of folly and cowardice,—then indeed would providence be neglectful. When the bad rule, it is by the unmanliness of those that are ruled; and it is just that it should be so. Yet, such as man is, holding a middle rank, providence does not suffer him to be destroyed, but he is borne up ever toward the higher; the divine element giving virtue the mastery in the long run. The human race participates, if not to the height, in wisdom and mind, and art and justice, and man is a beautiful creation so far as he can be consistently with his place in the universe. Reason (ὁ λόγος) made things in their different orders, not because it envied a greater good to those that are lower placed, but because the law itself of intelligential existence carries with it variety (οὐ φθόνῳ, ἀλλὰ λόγῳ ποικιλίαν νοερὰν ἔχοντι). Thus in a drama all the personages cannot be heroes. And reason does not take the souls from outside itself and fit them into the poem by constraining a portion of them from their own nature for the worse. The souls are as it were parts of reason itself, and it fits them in not by making them worse,

but by bringing them to the place suitable to their nature.
If then, it may be asked, we are not to explain evil by external
constraint, but reason is the principle and is all, what is the
rational necessity of the truceless war among animals and
men? First, destructions of animals are necessary because,
in a world composed of changing existences, they could not
be born imperishable. Thus, if they were not destroyed by
one another they would no less perish. Transference of the
animating principle from body to body, which is promoted
by their devouring each other, is better than that they should
not have been at all. The ordered battles men fight as if
dancing the Pyrrhic dance, show that what we take for the
serious affairs of mankind are but child's play, and declare
that death is nothing terrible[1]. It is not the inward soul but
the outward shadow of a man that groans and laments over
the things of life. But how then, the philosopher proceeds,
can there be any such thing as wickedness if this is the true
account? The answer which he ventures[2] is in effect that of
maleficent natures the Reason in the world might say: "These
too have their part in me, as I too in these." This reason (οὗτος
ὁ λόγος) is not unmixed mind (ἄκρατος νοῦς). Its essence is to
consist of the contraries that were in need of strife with one
another so that thus a world of birth might hold together (τὴν
σύστασιν αὐτῷ καὶ οἷον οὐσίαν τῆς τοιαύτης ἐναντιώσεως
φερούσης). In the universal drama the good and the bad must
perform the opposite parts assigned them. But from this does
it not follow that all is pardonable[3]? No, answers Plotinus,
for the reason which is the creative word of the drama fixes
the place both of pardon and of its opposite, and it does not
assign to men as their part that they should have nothing but
forgiveness for the bad[4]. In the consequences of evil for the

---

[1] Enn. III. 2, 15: ὥσπερ δὲ ἐπὶ τῶν θεάτρων ταῖς σκηναῖς, οὕτω χρὴ καὶ τοὺς
φόνους θεᾶσθαι καὶ πάντας θανάτους καὶ πόλεων ἁλώσεις καὶ ἁρπαγάς, μεταθέσεις
πάντα καὶ μετασχηματίσεις καὶ θρήνων καὶ οἰμωγῶν ὑποκρίσεις.

[2] Enn. III. 2, 16: τετολμήσθω γάρ· τάχα δ' ἂν καὶ τύχοιμεν.

[3] "Tout comprendre est tout pardonner."

[4] Enn. III. 2, 17: ἀλλ' ἴσως συγγνώμη τοῖς κακοῖς· εἰ μὴ καὶ τὸ τῆς συγγνώμης
καὶ μὴ ὁ λόγος ποιεῖ· ποιεῖ δὲ ὁ λόγος μηδὲ συγγνώμονας ἐπὶ τοῖς τοιούτοις
εἶναι.

whole there is nevertheless a rational order, and an order out
of which good may come¹.

Still, that good may come of evil is not the deepest ground
of its existence. Some one might argue that evil, while it is
actual, was not necessary. In that case, even if good comes of
it, the justification of providence must fail. The reply has
been given already in outline. The necessity of evil results
from matter. Matter is necessary because, the principle of
things having infinite productive power, that power must
manifest itself in every possible degree: there must therefore
be a last term, τὸ ἔσχατον, which can produce nothing beyond
itself. "This is matter, having nothing any longer of its own;
and this is the necessity of evil²." If it is argued that moral
evil in us, coming as it does from association with the body,
is to be ascribed rather to form than to matter, since bodies
derive their distinctive character from form, the reply is that
it is not in so far as the forms are pure that they are the source
of ignorance and bad desires, but in so far as they are mixed
with matter (λόγοι ἔνυλοι). The fall of the soul is its approach
to matter, and it is made weak because its energies are im-
peded by the presence of matter, which does not allow all its
powers to arrive at their realisation³. Yet without this principle of indeterminateness that vitiates the pure forms,
causing them to miss their true boundary by excess or defect,
there would be for us neither good nor any object of desire.
There would be neither striving after one thing nor turning
away from another nor yet thought. "For our striving is
after good and our turning away is from evil, and thought
with a purpose is of good and evil, and this is a good⁴."

The last sentence contains one of the two or three very

¹ Enn. III. 2, 18: οἷον ἐκ μοιχείας καὶ αἰχμαλώτου ἀγωγῆς παῖδες κατὰ φύσιν
βελτίους καὶ ἄνδρες, εἰ τύχοι, καὶ πόλεις ἄλλαι ἀμείνους τῶν πεπορθημένων ὑπὸ
ἀνδρῶν πονηρῶν. From a passage like this may we not infer that Plotinus was
able to see the barbarian inroads without despairing of the future?

² Enn. I. 8, 7.

³ Enn. I. 8, 14: ὕλη τοίνυν καὶ ἀσθενείας ψυχῇ αἰτία καὶ κακίας αἰτία. πρότερον
ἄρα κακὴ αὐτὴ καὶ πρῶτον κακόν.

⁴ Enn. I. 8, 15: ἡ γὰρ ὄρεξις ἀγαθοῦ, ἡ δὲ ἔκκλισις κακοῦ, ἡ δὲ νόησις καὶ ἡ
φρόνησις ἀγαθοῦ καὶ κακοῦ, καὶ αὕτη ἔν τι τῶν ἀγαθῶν.

slight possible allusions in the whole of the Enneads to orthodox Christianity. With Christian Gnosticism Plotinus deals
expressly in a book which Porphyry has placed at the end of
the second Ennead[1]. A separate exposition of it may be given
here, both because it is in some ways specially interesting, and
because it brings together Plotinus's theory of the physical
order of the world and of its divine government. Any ob-
scurity that there is in it comes from the allusive mode of
dealing with the Gnostic theories, of which no exposition is
given apart from the refutation. The main points of the
speculations opposed are, however, sufficiently clear.

After a preliminary outline of his own metaphysico-theo-
logical doctrine, in which he dwells on the sufficiency of three
principles in the intelligible world, as against the long series
of "aeons" introduced by the Platonising Gnostics[2], Plotinus
begins by asking them to assign the cause of the "fall" (σφάλ-
μα) which they attribute to the soul of the world. When did
this fall take place? If from eternity, the soul remains fallen.
If the fall had a beginning, why at that particular moment and
not earlier? Evidently, to undergo this lapse, the soul must
have forgotten the things in the intelligible world; but if so,
how did it create without ideas? To say that it created in
order to be honoured is a ridiculous metaphor taken from
statuaries on earth[3]. Then, as to its future destruction of the
world, if it repented of its creation, what is it waiting for? If
it has not yet repented, it is not likely to repent now that it
has become more accustomed to that which it made, and more
attached to it by length of time. Those who hold that, because
there are many hardships in the world, it has therefore come
into existence for ill, must think that it ought to be identical
with the intelligible world, and not merely an image of it.
Taken as what it is, there could be no fairer image. And why
this refusal to the heavenly bodies of all participation in the

---

[1] Enn. II. 9. Πρὸς τοὺς κακὸν τὸν δημιουργὸν τοῦ κόσμου καὶ τὸν κόσμον κακὸν
εἶναι λέγοντας, or Πρὸς τοὺς γνωστικούς.

[2] Cf. Enn. II. 9, 6: τὰς δὲ ἄλλας ὑποστάσεις τί χρὴ λέγειν ἃς εἰσάγουσι,
παροικήσεις καὶ ἀντιτύπους καὶ μετανοίας;

[3] Enn. II. 9, 4: τί γὰρ ἂν ἑαυτῇ καὶ ἐλογίζετο γενέσθαι ἐκ τοῦ κοσμοποιῆσαι;
γελοῖον γὰρ τὸ ἵνα τιμῷτο, καὶ μεταφερόντων ἀπὸ τῶν ἀγαλματοποιῶν τῶν ἐνταῦθα.

intelligible,—especially by men who complain of the disorder in terrestrial things? Then they introduce another soul, which they make to be compacted of the material elements, as if that was possible for a soul[1]. Not honouring this earth, they say that there is a "new earth" to which they are to go, made in the pattern of a world,—and yet they hate "the world." Whence this pattern if not from the creative power which they say has lapsed? Much in their teaching Plotinus never-theless acknowledges to be true. The immortality of the soul, the intelligible world, the first God, the doctrine that the soul ought to flee association with the body, the theory of its separation, the flight from the realm of birth to that of being, all these are doctrines to be found in Plato; and they do well in proclaiming them. On the part of Plato's disciples, there is no disposition to grudge them the right to declare also the points wherein they differ. They ought, however, to try to prove what they have to say of their own on its merits, putting their opinions with good feeling and like philosophers; not with contumely towards "the Greeks," and with assertions that they themselves are better men. As a matter of fact, they have only made incongruous additions to that which was better in the form given to it by the ancients[2]; introducing all sorts of births and destructions, and finding fault with the universe, and blaming the soul of the whole for its communion with the body, and casting reproach upon the ruler of this whole, and identifying the Demiurgus with the Soul of the World[3], and attributing the same affections to that which rules the whole as to particular things.

That it is not so good for *our* soul to be in communion with the body as to be separate, others have said before; but the case is different with the soul of the whole, which rules the frame of the world unimpeded, whereas ours is fettered by

[1] Enn. II. 9, 5: πῶς γὰρ ἂν ζωὴν ἡντινοῦν ἔχοι ἡ ἐκ τῶν στοιχείων σύστασις;

[2] Enn. II. 9, 6: ἐπεὶ τά γε εἰρημένα τοῖς παλαιοῖς περὶ τῶν νοητῶν πολλῷ ἀμείνω καὶ πεπαιδευμένως εἴρηται καὶ τοῖς μὴ ἐξαπατωμένοις τὴν ἐπιθέουσαν εἰς ἀνθρώπους ἀπάτην ῥᾳδίως γνωσθήσεται.

[3] Enn. II. 9, 6: καὶ εἰς ταὐτὸν ἄγοντες τὸν δημιουργὸν τῇ ψυχῇ. Both Vacherot and Jules Simon find this identification in the system of Plotinus himself. The error is corrected by Zeller, iii. 2, p. 633, n. 3.

the body. The question wherefore the creative power made a world is the same as the question wherefore there is a soul and wherefore the Demiurgus made it. It involves the error, first, of supposing a beginning of that which is for ever; in the next place, those who put it think that the cause of the creation was a turning from something to something else. The ground of that creative action which is from eternity, is not really in discursive thought and contrivance, but in the necessity that intelligible things should not be the ultimate product of the power that manifests itself in them. And if this whole is such as to permit us while we are in it to have wisdom, and being here to live in accordance with things yonder, how does it not bear witness that it has its attachment there?

In the distribution of riches and poverty and such things, the man of elevated character (ὁ σπουδαῖος) does not look for equality, nor does he think that the possessors of wealth and power have any real advantage. How if the things done and suffered in life are an exercise to try who will come out victorious in the struggle? Is there not a beauty in such an order[1]? If you are treated with injustice, is that so great a matter to your immortal being? Should you be slain, you have your wish, since you escape from the world. Do you find fault with civic life? You are not compelled to take part in it. Yet in the State, over and above legal justice with its punishments, there is honour for virtue, and vice meets with its appropriate dishonour. In one life, no doubt the fulfilment is incomplete, but it is completed in the succession of lives; the gods giving to each the lot that is consequent on former existences. Good men should try to rise to such height of goodness as their nature allows, but should think that others also have their place with God, and not dream that after God they themselves are alone in their goodness, and that other men and the whole visible world are without all part in the divine. It is easy, however, to persuade unintelligent men

---

[1] Enn. II. 9, 9: εἰ δὲ γυμνάσιον εἴη νικώντων καὶ ἡττωμένων, πῶς οὐ καὶ ταύτῃ καλῶς ἔχει;

who have no real knowledge what goodness is, that they alone are good and the sons of God[1].

Having remarked on some of the inconsistencies in the mythological cosmogonies of the Gnostics, Plotinus returns again to the point that the causation of natural things should not be compared to the devices of an artist, the arts being posterior to nature and the world[2]. We must not blame the universe because all is not equally good. That is as if one were to call the power of growth evil because it is not perception, or the perceptive faculty because it is not reason. There are necessarily degrees in things.

The practice of exorcisms and incantations by the Gnostics is especially attacked. They compose charms, says Plotinus, addressed not only to the soul of the world but to still higher powers, as if incorporeal things could be acted on by the sounds of the voice modulated according to some cunningly devised rules of art. Claiming as they do to have power against diseases, they would say rightly if, with the philosophers, they said that the means of keeping clear of them is temperance and a regular mode of life. They ascribe them, however, to the entrance of demons into the body, and profess to expel them by forms of words. Thus they become of great repute with the many, who stand in awe of magical powers; but they will not persuade rational men that diseases have not their physical cause in "changes externally or internally initiated[3]." If the demon can enter without a cause, why is the disease not always present? If there is a physical cause, that is sufficient without the demon. To say that, as soon as the cause comes to exist, the demonic agency, being ready, straightway takes up its position beside it, is ludicrous.

Next the antinomian tendency of the Gnostic sects is

---

[1] Near the end of c. 9, a comparison is borrowed from Plato, *Rep.* iv. 426: η οἴει οἷόν τ' εἶναι ἀνδρὶ μὴ ἐπισταμένῳ μετρεῖν, ἑτέρων τοιούτων πολλῶν λεγόντων ὅτι τετράπηχύς ἐστιν, αὐτὸν ταῦτα μὴ ἡγεῖσθαι περὶ αὐτοῦ;

[2] Enn. II. 9, 12: φυσικώτερον γὰρ πάντως, ἀλλ' οὐχ ὡς αἱ τέχναι ἐποίει· ὕστεραι γὰρ τῆς φύσεως καὶ τοῦ κόσμου αἱ τέχναι.

[3] Enn. II. 9, 14: τοὺς μέντοι εὖ φρονοῦντας οὐκ ἂν πείθοιεν, ὡς οὐχ αἱ νόσοι τὰς αἰτίας ἔχουσιν ἢ καμάτοις ἢ πλησμοναῖς ἢ ἐνδείαις ἢ σήψεσι καὶ ὅλως μεταβολαῖς ἢ ἔξωθεν τὴν ἀρχὴν ἢ ἔνδοθεν λαβούσαις.

touched upon. This way of thinking, the philosopher proceeds, with its positive blame of providence going beyond
even the Epicurean denial, and dishonouring all the laws of
our mundane life, takes away temperance, and the justice
implanted in moral habits and perfected by reason and practice, and in general all human excellence. For those who hold
such opinions, if their own nature is not better than their
teaching, nothing is left but to follow pleasure and self-
interest; nothing thought excellent here being in their view
good, but only some object of pursuit in the future. Those
who have no part in virtue, have nothing by which they can
be set in motion towards the world beyond. To say, "Look
to God," is of no use unless you teach men how to look. This
was taught in the moral discourses of the ancients, which the
present doctrine entirely neglects. It is virtue carried to the
end and fixed in the soul with moral wisdom that points to
God. Without true virtue, God is but a name[1].

The concluding chapters are directed against the refusal to
recognise in sensible things any resemblance to intelligible
beauty. How, Plotinus asks the Gnostic pessimists, can this
world be cut off from its intelligible cause? If that cause is
absent from the world, then it must also be absent from you;
for the providence that is over the parts must first be over the
whole. What man is there who can perceive the intelligible
harmony of music and is not moved when he hears that which
is in sensible sounds? Or who is there that is skilled in
geometry and numbers and does not take pleasure in seeing
the orderly and proportionate with his eyes? And is there
any one who, perceiving all the sensible beauty of the world,
has no feeling of anything beyond it? Then he did not
apprehend sensible things with his mind. Nothing can be
really fair outside and foul within. Those who are called
beautiful and internally are ugly, either have a false exterior
beauty also, or their ugliness is adventitious, their nature
being originally beautiful. For the hindrances here are many
to arriving at the end. Since this reason of shortcoming does
not apply to the whole visible world, which contains all, that

[1] Enn. II. 9, 15: ἄνευ δὲ ἀρετῆς ἀληθινῆς θεὸς λεγόμενος ὄνομά ἐστιν.

must necessarily be beautiful. Nor does admiration of the
beauty by which the physical universe participates in good
tend to bind us more to the body. Rather, it gives us reasons
for living well the life that is in the body. By taking all strokes
from without as far as possible with equanimity, we can make
our souls resemble, as nearly as may be, the soul of the whole
and of the stars. It is therefore in our power, while not finding
fault with our temporary dwelling-place, not to be too fond of
the body, and to become pure, and to despise death, and to
know the better and follow it, and to regard without envy
those higher mundane souls that can and do pursue the same
intelligible objects, and pursue them eternally[1].

4. *Aesthetics.*

The passages devoted by Plotinus to aesthetics are not
lengthy, but among ancient writings that touch upon the
general theory of beauty and the psychology of art, they are
of exceptional value. In his early book "On the Beautiful[2],"
where he closely follows Plato, he at the same time indicates
more than one new point of view. A brief summary will make
this clear.

Beauty, he first argues, cannot depend wholly on symmetry,
for single colours and sounds are beautiful. The same face too,
though its symmetry remains, may seem at one time beautiful,
at another not. And, when we go beyond sensible beauty, how
do action and knowledge and virtue, in their different kinds,

---

[1] Philo also, it may be noted here, accepted the opinion attributing life and
mind to the stars. In his optimism of course the Jewish philosopher agrees
with Plato and Plotinus. The Gnostics seem to have taken up from the
popular astrology the notion that the planets exercise malignant influences.
Plotinus has some ironical remarks on the terror they express of the immense
and fiery bodies of the spheres. Against the astrological polytheism which
regarded the planetary gods as rulers of the world, he himself protests in a
book where he examines sceptically and with destructive effect the claims of
astrology. See Enn. II. 3, 6: ὅλως δὲ μηδενὶ ἑνὶ τὸ κύριον τῆς διοικήσεως διδόναι,
τούτοις δὲ τὰ πάντα διδόναι, ὥσπερ οὐκ ἐπιστατοῦντος ἑνός, ἀφ' οὗ διηρτῆσθαι τὸ
πᾶν ἑκάστῳ διδόντος κατὰ φύσιν τὸ αὑτοῦ περαίνειν καὶ ἐνεργεῖν τὰ αὑτοῦ συντε-
ταγμένον αὖ μετ' αὐτοῦ, λύοντός ἐστι καὶ ἀγνοοῦντος κόσμου φύσιν ἀρχὴν ἔχοντος
καὶ αἰτίαν πρώτην ἐπὶ πάντα ἰοῦσαν.

[2] Enn. I. 6. Περὶ τοῦ καλοῦ.

become beautiful by symmetry? For, though the soul in which they inhere has a multiplicity of parts, they cannot display a true symmetry like that of magnitudes and numbers[1].

The explanation of delight in sensible beauty, so far as it can be explained, is that when the soul perceives something akin to its own nature it feels joy in it; and this it does when indeterminate matter is brought under a form proceeding from the real being of things. Thus beauty may attach itself to the parts of anything as well as to the whole. The external form is the indivisible internal form divided in appearance by material mass. Perception seizes the unity and presents it to the kindred soul. An example of this relation is that among the elements of body fire is especially beautiful because it is the formative element[2].

The beauty of action and knowledge and virtue, though not seized by sense-perception, is like sensible beauty in that it cannot be explained to those who have not felt it. It is itself in the soul. What then is it that those who love beauty of soul take delight in when they become aware of it either in others or in themselves? To know this, we must set its opposite, ugliness, beside beauty, and compare them. Ugliness we find in a disorderly soul, and this disorderliness we can only understand as superinduced by matter. If beauty is ever to be regained in such a soul, it must be by purification from the admixture. The ugliness is in fact the admixture of disorderly passions derived from too close association with the body, and it is the soul itself in its unmixed nature that is beautiful. All virtue is purification. Now the soul, as it becomes pure of regard for outward and inferior things, is borne upward to intellect. In intellect accordingly is the native and not alien beauty of the soul; because only when thus borne upward is it in truth soul and nothing else. Thus beauty is being, which is one with intellect, and the nature other than being is the ugly. The good and the beautiful are therefore to be looked for together, as are the ugly and the

---

[1] Enn. I. 6, 1: οὔτε γὰρ ὡς μεγέθη οὔτε ὡς ἀριθμοὶ σύμμετρα καίτοι πλειόνων μερῶν τῆς ψυχῆς ὄντων.

[2] Here the theoretical explanation is to be found in the Stoic physics.

evil. The first principle (τὸ πρῶτον) is Beauty itself (καλλονή),
as it is the Good (τἀγαθόν). Intellect is the beautiful (τὸ καλόν).
Soul is beautiful through intellect. All other things are
beautiful through the formative soul.

A return must therefore be made again to the principle
after which every soul aspires, to the Idea of the Good in
itself and of Beauty in itself. This is to be reached by closing
the eyes to common sights and arousing another power of
vision which all have but few make use of[1]. For such vision
you must prepare yourself first by looking upon things done
beautifully by other souls. Thus you will be enabled to see
the beauty of the soul itself. But to see this, you must refer
it to your own soul. If there is any difficulty here, then your
task must be to shape your soul into accord with ideal beauty
as a sculptor shapes a statue. For only by such inward reference is the beauty to be seen that belongs to souls[2].

At the end of this book, Plotinus suggests a distinction
afterwards developed. If, he says, we speak broadly and without exact discrimination, then the first principle, which pro-
jects or radiates beauty from itself, may be called beautiful.
If we distinguish more accurately, we shall assign to the Ideas
"intelligible beauty"; the Good which is beyond, we shall
regard as the spring and principle of beauty[3]. Elsewhere he
gives a psychological reason why beauty is in the second place.
Those who apprehend the beautiful catch sight of it in a
glimpse, and while they are as it were in a state of knowledge
and awake. The good is always present, though unseen,—
even to those that are asleep,—and it does not astound them
once they see it, nor is any pain mixed with the recognition
of it. Love of the beautiful gives pain as well as pleasure,

---

[1] Enn. I. 6, 8. No vehicle of land or sea is of avail, ἀλλὰ ταῦτα πάντα
ἀφεῖναι δεῖ καὶ μὴ βλέπειν, ἀλλ' οἷον μύσαντα ὄψιν ἄλλην ἀλλάξασθαι καὶ ἀνεγεῖραι,
ἣν ἔχει μὲν πᾶς, χρῶνται δὲ ὀλίγοι.

[2] Enn. I. 6, 9: τὸ γὰρ ὁρῶν πρὸς τὸ ὁρώμενον συγγενὲς καὶ ὅμοιον ποιησάμενον
δεῖ ἐπιβάλλειν τῇ θέᾳ. οὐ γὰρ ἂν πώποτε εἶδεν ὀφθαλμὸς ἥλιον ἡλιοειδὴς μὴ
γεγενημένος, οὐδὲ τὸ καλὸν ἂν ἴδοι ψυχὴ μὴ καλὴ γενομένη.

[3] Enn. I. 6, 9: ὥστε ὁλοσχερεῖ μὲν λόγῳ τὸ πρῶτον καλόν · διαιρῶν δὲ τὰ νοητὰ
τὸ μὲν νοητὸν καλὸν τὸν τῶν εἰδῶν φήσει τόπον, τὸ δ' ἀγαθὸν τὸ ἐπέκεινα καὶ πηγὴν
καὶ ἀρχὴν τοῦ καλοῦ.

because it is at once a momentary reminiscence and an aspiration after what cannot be retained[1]. In another place[2],
the higher kind of beauty that transcends the rules of art is
declared to be a direct impress of the good beyond intelligence.
It is this, says Plotinus, that adds to the mere symmetry of
beauty, which may still be seen in one dead, the living grace
that sets the soul actively in motion. By this also the more
lifelike statues are more beautiful even when they are less proportionate. The irregularity that comes from indeterminate
matter is at the opposite extreme, and is ugliness. Mere size
is never beautiful. If bulk is the matter of beauty ($\tau\grave{o}$ $\mu\acute{e}\gamma a$
$\H{v}\lambda\eta$ $\tau o\hat{v}$ $\kappa a\lambda o\hat{v}$), this means that it is that on which form is to
be impressed. The larger anything is, the more it is in need
of beautiful order. Without order, greater size only means
greater ugliness[3].

Discussing, in a separate book[4], Intellectual or Intelligible
Beauty, Plotinus begins by observing that the beauty of a
statue comes not from the matter of the unshapen stone, but
from the form conferred by art ($\pi a\rho\grave{a}$ $\tau o\hat{v}$ $\epsilon\H{i}\delta ov\varsigma$, $\grave{o}$ $\epsilon\nu\hat{\eta}\kappa\epsilon\nu$ $\acute{\eta}$
$\tau\acute{e}\chi\nu\eta$). If any one thinks meanly of the arts because they
imitate nature[5], first it must be pointed out that the natures of
the things imitated are themselves imitations of ideal being,
which precedes them in the logical order of causation. And
the arts do not simply imitate the thing seen, but run back to
the rational laws whence its nature is. Besides, they create
much from themselves ($\pi o\lambda\lambda\grave{a}$ $\pi a\rho$' $a\mathring{v}\tau\hat{\omega}\nu$ $\pi o\iota o\hat{v}\sigma\iota$), filling up
deficiencies in the visible model. Thus Phidias did not shape
his Zeus after anything in perception, but from his own
apprehension of the God as he might appear if he had the
will to manifest himself to our eyes.

The arts themselves—which as creative ideas are in the
soul of the artist—have a beauty surpassing that of the works

---

[1] Enn. v. 5, 12: $\kappa a\grave{\iota}$ $\H{e}\sigma\tau\iota$ $\delta\grave{e}$ $\tau\grave{o}$ $\mu\grave{e}\nu$ $\H{\eta}\pi\iota o\nu$ $\kappa a\grave{\iota}$ $\pi\rho o\sigma\eta\nu\grave{e}\varsigma$ $\kappa a\grave{\iota}$ $\mathring{a}\beta\rho\acute{o}\tau\epsilon\rho o\nu$ $\kappa a\acute{\iota}$, $\mathring{\omega}\varsigma$
$\mathring{e}\theta\acute{e}\lambda\epsilon\iota$ $\tau\iota\varsigma$, $\pi a\rho\grave{o}\nu$ $a\mathring{v}\tau\hat{\omega}$· $\tau\grave{o}$ $\delta\grave{e}$ $\theta\acute{a}\mu\beta o\varsigma$ $\H{e}\chi\epsilon\iota$ $\kappa a\grave{\iota}$ $\H{e}\kappa\pi\lambda\eta\xi\iota\nu$ $\kappa a\grave{\iota}$ $\sigma v\mu\mu\iota\gamma\hat{\eta}$ $\tau\hat{\omega}$ $\mathring{a}\lambda\gamma\acute{v}\nu o\nu\tau\iota$
$\tau\grave{\eta}\nu$ $\mathring{\eta}\delta o\nu\acute{\eta}\nu$.
[2] Enn. vi. 7, 22.   [3] Enn. vi. 6, 1.
[4] Enn. v. 8. $\Pi\epsilon\rho\grave{\iota}$ $\tau o\hat{v}$ $\nu o\eta\tau o\hat{v}$ $\kappa\acute{a}\lambda\lambda ov\varsigma$.
[5] The argument here is no doubt, as Professor Bosanquet remarks in his
History of Aesthetic, tacitly directed against Plato himself.

that proceed from them; these being necessarily, from the
separateness of manifestation which takes the place of the
original unity, weakened resemblances of the mental conception that remains. Thus we are brought back to the thought
that if we would recognise true beauty, whether seen in nature
or in art, we must look within[1]. The proper abode of beauty
is the intellectual being to which the soul attains only by
inward vision. Above it is the good beyond knowledge, from
which it is infused. Below it is the beauty found dispersed
in visible things, by which the soul, if not altogether depraved
from its original nature, is awakened to the Beauty of the
Ideas.

5. Ethics.

The good which is beyond beauty is also beyond moral
virtue, as we saw at an earlier stage of the exposition. The
attainment of it belongs to the mystical consummation of
Plotinus's philosophy, and not properly to its ethical any
more than to its aesthetical part. At the same time, it is not
regarded as attainable without previous discipline both in
practical moral virtue and in the pursuit of intellectual wisdom. The mere discipline is not sufficient by itself to assure
the attainment of the end; but it is, to begin with, the only
path to follow.

In treating of virtue on its practical side, Plotinus differs
from his Stoical predecessors chiefly in the stress he lays on
the interpretation even of civic virtue as a preliminary means
of purifying the soul from admixture with body. The one
point where he decidedly goes beyond them in the way of
precept is his prohibition of suicide[2] except in the rarest of
cases[3]. Here he returns in the letter of the prohibition to the
view of earlier moralists. The philosopher must no longer say
to his disciples, as during the period of the Stoic preaching,
that if they are in any way dissatisfied with life "the door is
open." A moralist under the Empire cannot, on the other
hand, take the ground of Aristotle, that suicide is an injury

---

[1] Enn. v. 8, 2.   [2] Enn. i. 9.

[3] Cf. Enn. i. 4, 7: ἀλλ' εἰ αἰχμάλωτος ἄγοιτο, πάρ τοί ἐστιν ὁδὸς ἐξιέναι, εἰ μὴ
εἴη εὐδαιμονεῖν.

to the State. No public interest was so obviously affected by the loss of a single unit as to make this ground of appeal clearly rational. The argument Plotinus makes use of is substantially that which Plato borrowed from the Pythagoreans. To take a violent mode of departing from the present life will not purify the soul from the passions that cling to the composite being, and so will not completely separate it and set it free from metempsychosis. Through not submitting to its appointed discipline, it may even have to endure a worse lot in its next life[1]. So long as there is a possibility of making progress here, it is better to remain.

The view that in moral action the inward disposition is the essential thing, is to be found already, as a clearly formulated principle, in Aristotle. The Stoics had persistently enforced it; and now in Plotinus it leads to a still higher degree of detachment, culminating as we shall see in mysticism. Porphyry made the gradation of the virtues by his master somewhat more explicit; and Iamblichus was, as Vacherot has remarked[2], more moderate and practical in his ethical doctrine; but invariably the attitude of the school is one of extreme inwardness. Not only is the inner spring that by which moral action is to be tested; the all-important point in relation both to conduct and insight is to look to the true nature of the soul and, keeping this in view, to rid it of its excrescences. First in the order of moral progress are the "political" virtues, which make the soul orderly in the world of mixture. After these come the "cathartic" virtues, which prepare it to ascend to the ideal world. Positive virtue is attained simply by the soul's turning back to the reality it finds when with purged sight it looks within; and it may find this reality as soon as the negative "purification" has been accomplished[3].

The perfect life of the sage is not in community but in detachment. If he undertakes practical activity, it must be from some plain obligation, and the attitude of detachment

---

[1] Enn. I. 9: καὶ εἰ εἱμαρμένος χρόνος ὁ δοθεὶς ἑκάστῳ, πρὸ τούτου οὐκ εὐτυχές, εἰ μή, ὥσπερ φαμέν, ἀναγκαῖον.

[2] *Histoire Critique de l'École d'Alexandrie*, t. ii. p. 62.

[3] Enn. I. 2, 4.

ought still to be maintained internally. Neither with Plotinus
nor with any of his successors is there the least doubt that the
contemplative life is in itself superior to the life of action.
Here they are Aristotelian. The chance that the philosopher
as such may be called on to reform practical life seems to them
much more remote than it did to Plato. Yet, in reference to
politics, as Zeller points out[1], a certain predilection may be
noticed for the "Platonic aristocracy." It may be observed
also that Plotinus by implication condemns Asiatic monarchy
as unjust and contrary to nature[2]. And the view is met with
incidentally that practical wisdom is the result of deliberation
in common; each by himself being too weak to achieve it.
Thus, in the single resolution arrived at by the joint effort of
all, political assemblies imitate the unity that is in the world[3].

That genuine freedom or self-dependence belongs properly
to the contemplative and not to the active life Plotinus main-
tains in one place[4] by the following argument. If virtue itself
were given the choice whether there should be wars so that it
might exercise courage, and injustice so that it might define
and set in order what is just, and poverty so that it might display liberality, or that all things should go well and it should
be at peace, it would choose peace. A physician like Hippocrates, for example, might choose, if it were within his choice,
that no one should need his art. Before there can be practical
virtue, there must be external objects which come from fortune and are not chosen by us. What is to be referred to virtue
itself and not to anything external, is the trained aptitude of
intelligence and the disposition of will prior to the occasion of
making a choice. Thus all that can be said to be primarily
willed apart from any relation forced upon us to external
things, is unimpeded theoretical activity of mind.

In another book, the philosopher sets himself to defend in
play the paradox that all outgoing activity is ultimately for

---

[1] iii. 2, p. 605.   [2] Enn. v. 5, 3.

[3] Enn. vi. 5, 10: μιμοῦνται δὲ καὶ ἐκκλησίαι καὶ πᾶσα σύνοδος ὡς εἰς ἓν τῷ
φρονεῖν ἰόντων ͵καὶ χωρὶς ἕκαστος εἰς τὸ φρονεῖν ἀσθενής, συμβάλλων δὲ εἰς ἓν πᾶς
ἐν τῇ συνόδῳ καὶ τῇ ὡς ἀληθῶς συνέσει τὸ φρονεῖν ἐγέννησε καὶ εὗρε.

[4] Enn. vi. 8, 5.

the sake of contemplation[1]. Production (ποίησις) and action (πρᾶξις) mean everywhere either an inability of contemplation to grasp its object adequately without going forth of itself, or a secondary resultant (παρακολούθημα) not willed but naturally issuing from that which remains in its own higher reality. Thus external action with its results, whether in the works of man or of nature, is an enfeebled product of contemplation. To those even who act, contemplation is the end; since they act so that they may possess a good and know that they possess it, and the knowledge of its possession is only in the soul. Practice, therefore, as it issues from theory, returns to it[2]. At the end of the book Plotinus, passing beyond the half-serious view hitherto developed, indicates that the first principle of all is prior even to contemplation. Here occurs the comparison of it to the spring of life in the root of an immense tree. This produces all the manifold life of the tree without becoming itself manifold[3]. It is the good which has no need even of mind, while mind contemplates and aspires after it.

The doubt for Plotinus is not whether the contemplative life is higher than the life of action, but whether it can properly be described as consisting in volition. Volition, he holds, is hardly the right term to apply to pure intellect and the life in accordance with it. Still less is it applicable to the One before intellect. Yet, as he also insists, to speak of the first principle as not-will and not-thought and not-knowledge would be even more misleading than the application to it of the positive terms. What is denied of the primal things is not denied in the sense that they are in want of it, but in the sense that they have no need of it, since they are beyond it. On the other hand, when the individual nature takes upon itself, as appears, one addition after another, it is in truth becoming more and

[1] Enn. III. 8, 1: παίζοντες δὴ τὴν πρώτην πρὶν ἐπιχειρεῖν σπουδάζειν εἰ λέγοιμεν πάντα θεωρίας ἐφίεσθαι καὶ εἰς τέλος τοῦτο βλέπειν,...ἆρ' ἄν τις ἀνάσχοιτο τὸ παράδοξον τοῦ λόγου;

[2] Enn. III. 8, 6: ἀνέκαμψεν οὖν πάλιν ἡ πρᾶξις εἰς θεωρίαν. Cf. c. 8: πάρεργον θεωρίας τὰ πάντα.

[3] Enn. III. 8, 10: αὕτη τοίνυν παρέσχε μὲν τὴν πᾶσαν ζωὴν τῷ φυτῷ τὴν πολλήν, ἔμεινε δὲ αὐτὴ οὐ πολλὴ οὖσα, ἀλλ' ἀρχὴ τῆς πολλῆς.

more deprived of reality[1]. To recover the reality that is all, it must dismiss the apparent additions—which, if they indeed affected the being that remains, would be diminutions—and return to itself. Of such additions are practical activities. In the world of mixture they are necessary, but they must be treated as such, not thought of as conferring something more upon the soul than it has in itself. Only by rising above them in self-knowledge can the soul become liberated. Otherwise, it remains attached to its material vehicle, and changes from body to body as from one sleep to another. "True waking is a true rising up from the body, not with a body[2]." This cannot be completely attained by practical virtue, which belongs to the composite nature and not to the separable soul; as the poet indicates in the Odyssey when he places the shade of Hercules in Hades but "himself among the gods." The hero has been thought worthy to ascend to Olympus for his noble deeds, but, as his virtue was practical and not theoretical, he has not wholly ascended, but something of him also remains below[3]. The man of practical virtue, as the Homeric account is interpreted elsewhere[4], will retain some memory of the actions he performed on earth, though he will forget what is bad or trivial; the man of theoretic virtue, possessing now intuitive knowledge, will dismiss all memories whatever[5]. Memory, however, seems to be thought of not as actually perishing, but as recoverable should the soul redescend to relation with the material universe.

Here Plotinus is expressing himself, after Plato, in terms of metempsychosis. As in the Platonic representation of the future life, intermissions are supposed during which the purified soul gets temporary respite from occupation with a body. Plotinus, however, as we have seen, does not treat that which is distinctively called the Platonic "reminiscence" as more than a myth or a metaphor. When the soul, even here, is energising in accordance with pure intellect, it is not "remembering." Memory is of past experience, and is relative to time and its

---

[1] Enn. VI. 5, 12: οὐ γὰρ ἐκ τοῦ ὄντος ἦν ἡ προσθήκη—οὐδὲν γὰρ ἐκείνῳ προσθήσεις—ἀλλὰ τοῦ μὴ ὄντος.
[2] Enn. III. 6, 6.   [3] Enn. I. 1, 12.   [4] Enn. IV. 3, 32.   [5] Enn. IV. 4, 1.

divisions. The energy of pure intellect is not in relation to time, but views things in the logical order of concepts. Hence it is that the better soul strives to bring the many to one by getting rid of the indefinite multiplicity of detail; and so commits much to oblivion.

Consistently with this general view, Plotinus holds that the happiness of the sage receives no increase by continuance of time[1]. We cannot make a greater sum by adding what no longer exists to what now is. Time can be measured by addition of parts that are not, because time itself, the "image of eternity," belongs to things that become and are not. Happiness belongs to the life of being, and this is incommensurable with the parts of time. Is one to be supposed happier for remembering the pleasure of eating a dainty yesterday or, say, ten years ago; or, if the question is of insight instead of pleasure, through the memory of having had insight last year? To remember things that went well in the past belongs to one who has them not in the present and, because now he has them not, seeks to recall those that have been. To the argument that time is necessary for the performance of fair deeds, the reply is, first, that it is possible to be happy—and not less but more so—outside the life of action. In the next place, happiness comes not from the actual performance of the deeds, but from the disposition with which they are done. The man of right disposition will find happiness in disinterested appreciation, for example, of patriotic deeds which he has not himself had the opportunity of performing. Hence (as the Stoics also held against Aristotle) length of life is not necessary for its moral perfection[2].

Several points of the ethics of Plotinus are brought together in a book giving a philosophical interpretation of the fancy that to each person is allotted his particular genius or "daemon[3]." Plotinus's interpretation is that the daemon of

---

[1] Enn. I. 5. Εἰ ἐν παρατάσει χρόνου τὸ εὐδαιμονεῖν.

[2] Enn. I. 5, 10: τὸ δὲ ἐν ταῖς πράξεσι τὸ εὐδαιμονεῖν τίθεσθαι ἐν τοῖς ἔξω τῆς ἀρετῆς καὶ τῆς ψυχῆς ἐστι τιθέντος· ἡ γὰρ ἐνέργεια τῆς ψυχῆς ἐν τῷ φρονῆσαι καὶ ἐν ἑαυτῇ ὡδὶ ἐνεργῆσαι. καὶ τοῦτο τὸ εὐδαιμόνως.

[3] Enn. III. 4. Περὶ τοῦ εἰληχότος ἡμᾶς δαίμονος.

each of us is the power next above that in accordance with
which his actual life is led. For those who live the common
life according to sense-perception, it is reason; for those who
live the life of reason, it is the power above that. How then,
he asks, with reference to the "lots" in the *Republic*, if each
while "there" chooses his tutelary daemon and his life "here,"
are we masters of anything in our actions? The explanation
he suggests is, that by its mythical choice once for all "there,"
is signified the soul's will and disposition in general everywhere[1]. Continuing in terms of the Platonic imaginations on
the destiny of souls, he observes that since each soul, as a
microcosm, contains within itself a representation not only of
the whole intelligible world, but also of the soul which guides
the visible universe[2], it may find itself, after departure from
the body, in the sun or one of the planets or in the sphere of
the fixed stars, according as it has energised with the power
related to this or that part of the whole. Those souls that
have overpassed the "daemonic nature" are at this stage of
their mutation outside all destiny of birth and beyond the
limits of the visible heaven.

[1] Enn. III. 4, 5: ἀλλ᾿ εἰ ἐκεῖ αἱρεῖται τὸν δαίμονα καὶ τὸν βίον, πῶς ἔτι τινὸς
κύριοι; ἢ καὶ ἡ αἵρεσις ἐκεῖ ἡ λεγομένη τὴν τῆς ψυχῆς προαίρεσιν καὶ διάθεσιν καθόλου καὶ πανταχοῦ αἰνίττεται. In Enn. II. 3, 15, the "lots" are interpreted as
meaning all the external circumstances of the soul at birth taken together.

[2] Enn. III. 4, 6: χρὴ γὰρ οἴεσθαι καὶ κόσμον εἶναι ἐν τῇ ψυχῇ ἡμῶν μὴ μόνον
νοητόν, ἀλλὰ καὶ ψυχῆς τῆς κόσμου ὁμοειδῆ διάθεσιν.

CHAPTER VI

THE MYSTICISM OF PLOTINUS

THE aim of philosophic thought, for Plotinus as for Plato, is pure truth expressed with the utmost exactitude. And, much as he abounds in metaphor, he knows how to keep his intellectual conceptions clear of mixture with their imaginative illustration. On the interpretation of myths, whether poetic or philosophic, he is as explicit as intelligent readers could desire. After allegorising the myth of Pandora and of Prometheus, for example, he remarks that the meaning of the story itself may be as any one likes, but that the particular interpretation has been given because it makes plain the philosophic theory of creation and agrees with what is set forth[1]. Again, in interpreting the Platonic myth of Eros, he calls to mind that myths, if they are to be such, must separate in time things not temporally apart, and divide from one another things that are in reality together; seeing that even rational accounts have to resort to the same modes of separation and division[2]. This relation between science and myth remained substantially the same for his successors. Some of them might devote greater attention to mythology, and indulge more seriously in fancies that a deep philosophic wisdom was embodied in it by the ancient "theologians"; but the theoretical distinction between truth of science and its clothing in imaginative form is made, if anything, sharper. The distinction comes to be used—as it is already to some extent by Plotinus—to explain the physical cosmogonies of early philosophers without supposing that they meant to teach an actual emergence of the world from some primordial

[1] Enn. IV. 3, 14: ταῦτα μὲν οὖν ὅπῃ τις δοξάζει, ἀλλ' ὅτι ἐμφαίνει τὰ τῆς εἰς τὸν κόσμον δόσεως, καὶ προσᾴδει τοῖς λεγομένοις.

[2] Enn. III. 5, 9: δεῖ δὲ τοὺς μύθους, εἴπερ τοῦτο ἔσονται, καὶ μερίζειν χρόνοις ἃ λέγουσι, καὶ διαιρεῖν ἀπ' ἀλλήλων πολλὰ τῶν ὄντων ὁμοῦ μὲν ὄντα, τάξει δὲ ἢ δυνάμεσι διεστῶτα, ὅπου καὶ οἱ λόγοι καὶ γενέσεις τῶν ἀγεννήτων ποιοῦσι, καὶ τὰ ὁμοῦ ὄντα καὶ αὐτοὶ διαιροῦσι, καὶ διδάξαντες ὡς δύνανται τῷ νοήσαντι ἤδη συγχωροῦσι συναιρεῖν.

element or chaotic aggregate and its return to this. What the
oldest philosophers had in view, according to the Neo-Platonist system of interpretation, was only to render their logical
analysis of the world into its permanent constituents easier to
grasp. As the Neo-Platonist doctrine itself was thought out
wholly on the line of the philosophical tradition, its relation
to "positive religion" is quite the opposite of subservience.
The myths are completely plastic in the hands of the philosophers. Of their original meaning, no doubt they have a less
keen sense than Plato, who saw the real hostility of a naturalistic "theogony" like that of Hesiod to his own type of
thought; but this only shows how dominant the philosophical
point of view has become. Plato could not yet treat the myths
of Greek religion so arbitrarily as would have been necessary
for his purpose, or did not think it worth while. For the Neo-
Platonists the poetic mythology has become like their own
"matter," absolutely powerless to modify the essence of
thought, but equally ready to take on an elusive reflexion of
every idea in turn. Not in this quarter, therefore, need we
look for any derogation from the scientific character of Neo-
Platonic thought.

If Plotinus accepted Hellenic religion as the basis of culture,
the reason was because he saw in it no obstacle to the adequate
expression of philosophic truth; which, moving freely on its
own plane, could turn the images of mythology themselves to
the account of metaphysics and ethics. Some members of the
school, as we know, were given to devotional practices and to
theurgy; but in all this the master did not personally join.
On one occasion indeed, he seemed to his disciples to speak too
loftily on the subject, though, as Porphyry tells us, they did
not venture to ask his meaning. Amelius had become diligent
in sacrificing and in attending the feasts of the gods, and
wished to take Plotinus with him. He declined, saying, "It
is for them to come to me, not for me to go to them[1]." The
explanation is no doubt to be found in the contrast between
the common religious need for a social form of worship and
the subjective intensity of the mystic. That this was in the

---

[1] Porph. *V. Plot.* 10: ἐκείνους δεῖ πρὸς ἐμὲ ἔρχεσθαι, οὐκ ἐμὲ πρὸς ἐκείνους.

temperament of Plotinus is evident all through the Enneads.
His religious attitude invariably is that the soul, having duly
prepared itself, must wait for the divinity to appear. External
excitement is the very reverse of the method he points out:
he insists above all on internal quietude. Porphyry also has
something to tell us on the subject. Four times while he was
with him, he relates, Plotinus attained the end of union with
the God who is over all, without form, above intellect and all
the intelligible. Porphyry himself attained this union once, in
his sixty-eighth year[1]. The mystical "ecstasy" was not found
by the later teachers of the school easier to attain, but more
difficult; and the tendency became more and more to regard it
as all but unattainable on earth. Are we to hold that it was
the beginning of Plotinus's whole philosophy; that a peculiar
subjective experience was therefore the source of the Neo-
Platonic doctrines? This will hardly seem probable after the
account that has been given of Plotinus's reasoned system;
and, in fact, the possibility of the experience is inferred from
the system, not the propositions of the system from the
experience. It is described as a culminating point, to be
reached after long discipline; and it can only be known from
itself, not from any description. Not being properly a kind
of cognition, it can become the ground of no inference. Now,
since the philosophy of Plotinus undoubtedly claims to be a
kind of knowledge, it must have its evidence for learners in
something that comes within the forms of thought. While he
was personally a mystic, his theory of knowledge could not
be mystical without contradicting the mysticism itself.

In modern phraseology, it was a form of Rationalism. Cognition at its highest degree of certainty, as Plotinus under-
stands it, may best be compared to Spinoza's "knowledge
of the third kind," or "scientia intuitiva[2]." Exactly as with
Spinoza, the inferior degrees that lead up to it are: first, the
"opinion" that is sufficient for practical life; second, the discursive "reason" that thinks out one thing adequately from
another, but does it only through a process, not grasping the
relation at once in its totality. The difference is that Plotinus

---

[1] *V. Plot.* 23.   [2] *Eth.* ii. Prop. 40, Schol. 2. Cf. Enn. VI. 7, 2.

conceives the highest kind of knowledge not as mathematical
in form but as "dialectical." By "dialectic" he means, not a
purely formal method, a mere "organon," but a method of
which the use, when once attained, gives along with the form
of thought its content, which is true being[1]. Before the learner
can reach this stage, he must be disciplined in the other
branches of liberal science. As with Plato, dialectic is the
crown of a philosophical education. Nor does Plotinus altogether neglect the logical topics he regards as subsidiary to
this. At the beginning of the sixth Ennead is placed a considerable treatise[2] in which he criticises first the Stoic and
then the Aristotelian categories, and goes on to expound a
scheme of his own. This scheme, as Zeller remarks, has not
the same importance for his system as those of Aristotle and
of the Stoics for theirs. Porphyry, in his larger commentary
on the *Categories*, defended Aristotle's treatment against the
objections of Plotinus, and thenceforth the Aristotelian categories maintained their authority in the school[3]. On the other
hand, it must be observed that this affects only a subsidiary
part of Plotinus's theory of knowledge. His general view regarding the supremacy of dialectic as conceived by Plato, was
also that of his successors. In subordination to this, Aristotle's
list of the most general forms of assertion about being held
its own against the newer scheme of Plotinus. By the
Athenian successors of Plotinus more definitely than by himself, Aristotle came to be regarded as furnishing the needful
preliminary training for the study of Plato[4].

The philosophic wisdom of which dialectic is the method,
Plotinus expressly declares[5], cannot be achieved without first
going through the process of learning to know by experience.
Knowledge and virtue at lower stages can exist, though not
in perfection, without philosophy; but except by starting from

---

[1] Enn. I. 3. Περὶ διαλεκτικῆς.

[2] Enn. VI. 1–3. Περὶ τῶν γενῶν τοῦ ὄντος.   [3] Zeller, iii. 2, pp. 523–4.

[4] The doctrine of categories elaborated by Plotinus being for the most part
in no organic relation to his general system, it did not seem necessary to
give a detailed exposition of it. Its abandonment by the Neo-Platonic school,
besides, makes it historically less important.

[5] Enn. I. 3, 6.

these, the height of theoretic philosophy is unattainable. Even
when that height is attained, and being is known in intuitive
thought, there is something remaining still. The One and
Good, which is the first principle of things, is beyond thought.
If it is to be apprehended at all, and not simply inferred as
the metaphysical unity on which all things necessarily depend,
there must be some peculiar mode of apprehending it. Here
Plotinus definitely enters upon the mystical phase of his
doctrine. The One is to be seen with "the eyes of the soul,"
now closed to other sights. It becomes impossible, as he
recognises, to use terms quite consistently, and he cannot
altogether dispense with those that signify cognition; but it is
always to be understood that they are not used in their strict
sense. That which apprehends the One is intellect—or the
soul when it has become pure intellect; so that the principle
above intelligence has sometimes to be spoken of as an "intelligible," and as that which mind, when it "turns back,"
thinks before it thinks itself. For by this reflexive process—in
the logical order of causes—mind comes to be, and its essence
is to think. On the other hand, the One does not "think";
its possession of itself is too complete for the need to exist
even of intuitive thought. Accordingly, since it can only be
apprehended by the identification with it of that which apprehends, mind, to apprehend it, must dismiss even the activity
of thought, and become passive. At last, unexpectedly, the
vision of the One dawns on the purified intellectual soul. The
vision is "ineffable"; for while it can only be indicated in
words that belong to being, its object is beyond being. All
that can be done is to describe the process through which it
comes to pass, and, with the help of inadequate metaphors,
to make it recognisable by those who may also attain it
themselves.

Since that which is sought is one, he who would have the
vision of it must have gone back to the principle of unity in
himself; must have become one instead of many[1]. To see it,
we must entrust our soul to intellect, and must quit sense and
phantasy and opinion, and pay no regard to that which comes

[1] Enn. VI. 9, 3.

from them to the soul. The One is an object of apprehension
(σύνεσις) not by knowledge, like the other intelligibles, but
by a presence which is more than knowledge. If we are to
apprehend it, we must depart in no way from being one, but
must stand away from knowledge and knowables, with their
still remaining plurality. That which is the object of the
vision is apart from no one, but is of all; yet so as being
present not to be present except to those that are able and
have prepared themselves to see it¹. As was said of matter,
that it must be without the qualities of all things if it is to
receive the impressions of all, so and much more so, the soul
must become unformed (ἀνείδεος) if it is to contain nothing to
hinder its being filled and shone upon by the first nature².
The vision is not properly a vision, for the seer no longer
distinguishes himself from that which is seen—if indeed we
are to speak of them as two and not as one³—but as it were
having become another and not himself, is one with that other
as the centre of the soul touching the centre of all⁴. While
here, the soul cannot retain the vision; but it can retreat to it
in alternation with the life of knowledge and virtue which is
the preparation for it. "And this is the life of gods and of
godlike and happy men, a deliverance from the other things
here, a life untroubled by the pleasures here, a flight of the
alone to the alone."

These are the concluding words of the Enneads in Porphyry's redaction. In another book, which comes earlier but
was written later⁵, Plotinus describes more psychologically
the method of preparation for the vision. The process, which
may begin at any point, even with the lowest part of the soul,

---

¹ Enn. VI. 9, 4: οὐ γὰρ δὴ ἄπεστιν οὐδενὸς ἐκεῖνο καὶ πάντων δέ, ὥστε παρὸν μὴ
παρεῖναι ἀλλ᾽ ἢ τοῖς δέχεσθαι δυναμένοις καὶ παρεσκευασμένοις. Cf. c. 7: οὐ γὰρ
κεῖταί που ἐρημῶσαν αὐτοῦ τὰ ἄλλα, ἀλλ᾽ ἔστι τῷ δυναμένῳ θιγεῖν ἐκεῖνο παρόν, τῷ
δ᾽ ἀδυνατοῦντι οὐ πάρεστιν.

² Enn. VI. 9, 7: εἰ μέλλει μηδὲν ἐμπόδιον ἐγκαθήμενον ἔσεσθαι πρὸς πλήρωσιν
καὶ ἔλλαμψιν αὐτῇ τῆς φύσεως τῆς πρώτης.

³ "An audacious saying," adds Plotinus.

⁴ Enn. VI. 9, 10. Cf. c. 11: τὸ δὲ ἴσως ἦν οὐ θέαμα, ἀλλὰ ἄλλος τρόπος τοῦ
ἰδεῖν, ἔκστασις καὶ ἅπλωσις καὶ ἐπίδοσις αὐτοῦ καὶ ἔφεσις πρὸς ἀφὴν καὶ στάσις.

⁵ Enn. v. 3.

consists in stripping off everything extraneous till the principle is reached. First the body is to be taken away as not
belonging to the true nature of the self; then the soul that
shapes the body; then sense-perception with appetites and
emotions. What now remains is the image of pure intellect[1].
Even when intellect itself is reached by the soul turning to it,
there still remains, it must be repeated, the duality and even
plurality implied in synthetic cognition of self as mind[2]. Mind
is self-sufficing, because it has all that it needs for self-knowledge; but it needs to think itself. The principle, which gives
mind its being and makes it self-sufficing, is beyond even this
need; and the true end for the soul is, by the light it sees by,
to touch and gaze upon that light. How is this to be done?
Take away all[3].

All other things, as Plotinus says elsewhere, in comparison
with the principle have no reality, and nothing that can be
affirmed of them can be affirmed of it. It has neither shape
nor form, and is not to be sought with mortal eyes. For those
things which, as perceptible by sense, are thought most of all
to be, in reality most of all are not. To think the things of
sense to be most real is as if men sleeping away all their lives
should put trust in what they saw in their dreams, and, if one
were to wake them up, should distrust what they saw with
open eyes and go off to sleep again[4]. Men have forgotten what
even from the beginning until now they desire and aspire
after. "For all things strive after that and aspire after it by
necessity of nature, as if having a divination that without it
they cannot be[5]."

Much as all this may resemble Oriental mysticism, it does
not seem to have come from any direct contact with the East.
Zeller indeed finds in the idea of a mental state beyond
cognition a decisive break with the whole direction of classical

[1] This is related to intellect itself as the moon to the sun. Cf. Enn. v. 6, 4.
[2] Enn. v. 3, 13: κινδυνεύει γὰρ ὅλως τὸ νοεῖν πολλῶν εἰς αὐτὸ συνελθόντων συναίσθησις εἶναι τοῦ ὅλου, ὅταν αὐτό τι ἑαυτὸ νοῇ· ὃ δὴ κυρίως ἐστὶ νοεῖν.
[3] Enn. v. 3, 17: καὶ τοῦτο τὸ τέλος τἀληθινὸν ψυχῇ, ἐφάψασθαι φωτὸς ἐκείνου καὶ αὐτῷ αὐτὸ θεάσασθαι, οὐκ ἄλλῳ φωτί, ἀλλ' αὐτῷ, δι' οὗ καὶ ὁρᾷ....πῶς ἂν οὖν τοῦτο γένοιτο; ἄφελε πάντα.
[4] Enn. v. 5, 11.   [5] Enn. v. 5, 12.

thought, and makes Philo here the sole predecessor of Plotinus[1]. But, we may ask, whence came the notion to Philo himself? The combination of the most complete "immanence" in one sense with absolute transcendence of Deity in another, does not seem native to Jewish religion, any more than the asceticism for which, in the Essenes, Zeller finds it necessary to recur to a Greek origin. Once get rid of the presupposition that Neo-Platonism sprang from a new contact with Eastern theosophy, and the solution is clear. To Philo and to Plotinus alike, the direct suggestion for the doctrine of "ecstasy" came from Plato. The germinal idea that there is a mode of apprehension above that of perfectly sane and sober mind appears already in more than one Platonic dialogue. During the period of almost exclusively ethical thinking, between Aristotle and revived Pythagoreanism and Platonism, hints of the kind naturally found little response. After the revival of speculative thought, it is not surprising that they should have appealed to thinkers of widely different surroundings. The astonishing thing would have been if in all the study then given to Plato they had been entirely overlooked. That neither Philo nor Plotinus overlooked them may be seen from the references and quotations given by Zeller himself[2]. What is more, Plotinus definitely contrasts intellect soberly contemplating the intelligible with intellect rapt into enthusiasm and borne above it; and explains the Platonic imagery of "insanity" and "intoxication" as referring to the latter state. Mind is still sane while contemplating intellectual beauty, and is seized upon by the "divine madness" only in rising above beauty to its cause beyond[3]. That Plotinus derived from Plato his conception of the Good beyond being is generally admitted. It is equally clear that for the theory of

---

[1] iii. 2, pp. 448, 611.

[2] See, for Philo, iii. 2, p. 415, n. 5; for Plotinus, p. 615, n. 3. Cf. Porph. V. Plot. 23.

[3] Enn. VI. 7, 35: καὶ τὸν νοῦν τοίνυν [δεῖ] τὴν μὲν ἔχειν δύναμιν εἰς τὸ νοεῖν, ᾗ τὰ ἐν αὑτῷ βλέπει, τὴν δέ, ᾗ τὰ ἐπέκεινα αὑτοῦ ἐπιβολῇ τινι καὶ παραδοχῇ, καθ' ἣν καὶ πρότερον ἑώρα μόνον καὶ ὁρῶν ὕστερον καὶ νοῦν ἔσχε καὶ ἕν ἐστι· καὶ ἔστιν ἐκείνη μὲν ἡ θέα νοῦ ἔμφρονος, αὕτη δὲ νοῦς ἐρῶν. ὅταν [γὰρ] ἄφρων γένηται μεθυσθεὶς τοῦ νέκταρος, τότε ἐρῶν γίνεται ἁπλωθεὶς εἰς εὐπάθειαν τῷ κόρῳ.

its apprehension also there presented itself a Platonic point of view. Thus even the mystical consummation of his philosophy may be traced to a Hellenic source.

Plato's own imagery, and in connexion with it his occasional mention of "bacchants" and "initiates," may of course have been suggested by forms of worship that were already coloured by contact with the East; but this does not affect the character of the Neo-Platonic school as in its own age essentially a classical revival. It was not inhospitable to Oriental cults, being indeed vaguely conscious of an affinity to those that were associated, in the higher order of their devotees, with a contemplative asceticism; and, as willingly as Plato, it found adumbrations of philosophic truth in religious mysteries. These, however, as we have seen, in no case determined the doctrine, which was the outcome of a long intellectual tradition worked upon by thinkers of original power. The system left by Plotinus was further elaborated by the best minds of his own period; and, during the century after his death, we find it making its way over all the Graeco-Roman world. Defeated in the practical struggle, it became, all the more, the accepted philosophy of the surviving Greek schools; to take up at last its abode at Athens with the acknowledged successors of Plato. These stages will be described in the chapters that follow.

CHAPTER VII

THE DIFFUSION OF NEO-PLATONISM

1. *Porphyry.*

Both for his own and for succeeding times, the name of Porphyry stands out conspicuous among the disciples of Plotinus. Eunapius, writing towards the end of the fourth century, observes that Plotinus is now more in the hands of educated readers than Plato himself; and that, if there is any popular knowledge of philosophy, it consists in some acquaintance with his doctrines. He then proceeds to give credit for this to the interpretations of Porphyry. And thus, he says, the honour was distributed from the first. Universally the doctrine was ascribed to Plotinus; while Porphyry gained fame by his clearness of exposition—"as if some Hermaic chain had been let down to men[1]." He then goes on to celebrate Porphyry's knowledge of all liberal science (οὐδὲν παιδείας εἶδος παραλελοιπώς); of which we have independent evidence in his extant works and in the titles of those that are lost. Eunapius's biography seems to have been mostly compiled— not always with perfect accuracy—from the information given by Porphyry himself in his Life of Plotinus.

Porphyry was born in 233 and died later than 301. He was a Tyrian by birth. His name was originally "Malchus," the root of which, in the Semitic languages, means "a king." At the suggestion of his teachers he Hellenised it first into "Basileus" and then into "Porphyrius" (from the colour of regal garments). After having studied under Longinus at Athens, he visited Rome, and there, as we have seen, became a disciple of Plotinus from the year 263. His journey to Sicily, with its cause, has been already mentioned. Afterwards he

---

[1] Eunap. *Vitae* (Porphyrius): ὁ μὲν γὰρ Πλωτῖνος τῷ τε τῆς ψυχῆς οὐρανίῳ καὶ τῷ λοξῷ καὶ αἰνιγματώδει τῶν λόγων, βαρὺς ἐδόκει καὶ δυσήκοος· ὁ δὲ Πορφύριος, ὥσπερ Ἑρμαϊκή τις σειρὰ καὶ πρὸς ἀνθρώπους ἐπινεύουσα, διὰ ποικίλης παιδείας πάντα εἰς τὸ εὔγνωστον καὶ καθαρὸν ἐξήγγελλεν.

returned to Rome; and it was in Rome, according to Eunapius, that he gained reputation by his expositions of Plotinus.
Late in life he married the widow—named Marcella—of a
friend; for the sake of bringing up her children, as we learn
both from Eunapius and from Porphyry's letter to her which
is extant. She was subjected to some kind of persecution by
her neighbours, who, Jules Simon conjectures[1], may have
been Christians, and may have sought to detach her from
philosophy. The letter is an exhortation to perseverance in
philosophical principles, and is full of the characteristic ethical
inwardness of Neo-Platonism[2]. That Porphyry engaged in
controversy with Christianity, now on the verge of triumph,
is well known; and with him, as with Julian, the effect is a just
perceptible reaction of Christian modes of thought or speech.
As theological virtues he commends "faith, truth, love, hope";
adding only truth to the Christian three[3].

A distinctive character of his treatise against the Christians
seems to have been its occupation with questions of historical
criticism. Very little of it has been preserved even in fragmen-
tary form, the set replies of apologists, as well as the treatise
itself, being lost; but the view he took about the Book of
Daniel is on record. According to Jerome, he maintained that
it was written in the time of Antiochus Epiphanes; so that the
historical events supposed to have been predicted were really
events that had taken place before the time of the writer.
This, Jerome says, proves the strength of the case in favour
of its genuinely prophetic character; for if events subsequent
to the time of Daniel had not been very clearly prefigured,
Porphyry would not have found it necessary to argue against
the ascription to him of the authorship[4].

---

[1] *Histoire de l'École d'Alexandrie*, t. ii. pp. 98–9.

[2] See for example *Epistola ad Marcellam*, c. 9: πῶς οὖν οὐκ ἄτοπον τὴν
πεπεισμένην ἐν σοὶ εἶναι καὶ τὸ σῴζον καὶ τὸ σῳζόμενον καὶ τό γε ἀπολλύον καὶ
<τὸ> ἀπολλύμενον τόν τε πλοῦτον καὶ τὴν πενίαν τόν τε πατέρα καὶ τὸν ἄνδρα καὶ
τὸν τῶν ὄντων ἀγαθῶν καθηγεμόνα, κεχηνέναι πρὸς τὴν τοῦ ὑφηγητοῦ σκιάν, ὡς δὴ
τὸν ὄντως ὑφηγητὴν μὴ ἐντὸς ἔχουσαν μηδὲ παρὰ σαυτῇ πάντα τὸν πλοῦτον;

[3] *Ad Marcellam*, 24: τέσσαρα στοιχεῖα μάλιστα κεκρατύνθω περὶ θεοῦ· πίστις,
ἀλήθεια, ἔρως, ἐλπίς.

[4] Cf. Jules Simon, *Histoire de l'École d'Alexandrie*, t. ii. p. 181. "L'on peu

In the time of Plotinus, Porphyry recounts, there were members of various sects, both Christians and others, who put forth apocalypses such as those attributed to Zoroaster and Zostrianus, by which they "deceived many, themselves also deceived." Amelius wrote against the book of "Zostrianus"; Porphyry himself against that of "Zoroaster," showing it to be spurious and recent and forged by the authors of the sect in order to give currency to the opinion that their own doctrines were those of the ancient Zoroaster[1]. The spirit of critical inquiry thus aroused in Porphyry seems to have led him more and more to take the sceptical view about all claims to particular revelations from the gods, including the "theurgic" manifestations to which attention was paid by some members of the Neo-Platonic school. It was probably at a late period of his life that he wrote the letter to the Egyptian priest Anebo, to which an unknown member of the school of Iamblichus replied, under the name of "Abammon," in the famous book *De Mysteriis*.

One little book of Porphyry, entitled *De Antro Nympharum*, is an interesting example of the mode of interpreting poetic mythology current in the school. Porphyry there sets out to show that Homer, in his description of the Grotto of the Nymphs at Ithaca[2], probably did not give an account of an actual cavern to be found in the island—for topographers make no mention of any that resembles the description—but deposited in allegorical form an ancient "theological wisdom" identical with true philosophy. If there really is such a cavern, then those who wrought it had the hidden meaning, which in that case was only transmitted by the poet. This meaning Porphyry educes with an ingenuity that has an attractiveness of its own. It must be noted, however, that the philosophers do not add, and do not think they are adding, anything to the

juger," says the historian on the preceding page, "par l'indignation même que cet ouvrage excita dans l'Église, de l'importance et de la gravité des attaques qu'il contenait."

[1] *Vita Plotini*, 16: νόθον τε καὶ νέον τὸ βιβλίον παραδεικνὺς πεπλασμένον τε ὑπὸ τῶν τὴν αἵρεσιν συστησαμένων εἰς δόξαν τοῦ εἶναι τοῦ παλαιοῦ Ζωροάστρου τὰ δόγματα, ἃ αὐτοὶ εἵλοντο πρεσβεύειν.

[2] *Od.* xiii. 102–112.

content or even to the authority of their doctrine. All such interpretations are in the interest of the old mythologists and no longer of the philosophers, who are not now putting themselves under the protection of the legends, but on the contrary are seeking if possible to save them.

Of all Porphyry's writings, that which had the most far-reaching influence on culture was his short introduction to the Aristotelian *Categories*. Coming down to the Middle Ages in the Latin translation of Boethius, it sufficed, by a few words at the opening, to set going the whole discussion on "universals" with which early Scholasticism was preoccupied. This of course was not due to any special originality, but to its summing up clearly and briefly the points of the rival theories maintained by Platonists, Peripatetics and Stoics. Porphyry's logical works generally were expository, and well adapted for use in the schools through keeping the subject clear of metaphysics[1]. Besides devoting much labour to commenting on Aristotle, he wrote a History of Philosophy, to which his extant Life of Pythagoras probably belonged; psychological works from which many passages are cited by Stobaeus; and mathematical works referred to by Proclus. Among his occasional writings of a more original kind, the most extensive now remaining is the *De Abstinentia* (Περὶ ἀποχῆς ἐμψύχων), a treatise against the eating of animal food. His expositions of Plotinus, already referred to, are still represented in the *Sententiae* (Ἀφορμαὶ πρὸς τὰ νοητά[2]).

In what is recorded of Porphyry's metaphysical doctrines, a tendency is found to greater elaboration of the triadic method of grouping, carried out still more systematically by later Neo-Platonism. The real importance of the writings in which he set forth the doctrine of his school was due, however, as his contemporaries recognised, to the insight with which he penetrated to his master's essential thought and to his lucidity in expounding it. Some illustration of this may be furnished from the *Sententiae*. Then, as an example of his more personal work, an exposition may be given of the *De Abstinentia*. The

---

[1] Cf. Zeller, iii. 2, pp. 640–3.
[2] Prefixed to the Didot edition of Plotinus (1855).

treatise has, besides, a more general interest in the specimens
it offers of the ethical questions raised and discussed in later
antiquity, not in a spirit of scholastic casuistry but with a
genuine desire for their solution in the light of reflective
conscience.

Preoccupation with ethics may be noticed in the *Sententiae*,
which contain a more systematic classification of the virtues
than Plotinus had explicitly given. Porphyry classifies them
into Political, Cathartic, Theoretic and Paradigmatic. The
virtues of the first class set the soul free from excess of
passionate attachment to the body, and produce moderation;
those of the second class liberate it altogether from this
attachment, so that it can now turn to its true good. The
third class comprises the virtues of the soul energising intellectually; the fourth, those that are in intellect itself, to which
the soul looks up as patterns. *Our* care must be chiefly about
the virtues of the second class, seeing that they are to be
acquired in this life. Through them is the ascent to the contemplative virtues of soul and to those that are their models in
pure intellect. The condition of purification is self-knowledge[1].

When the soul knows itself, it knows itself as other than
the corporeal nature to which it is bound. The error to which
we are especially liable is ascription of the properties of body
to incorporeal being. The body of the world is everywhere
spatially, its parts being spread out so that they can be discriminated by the intervals between them. To God, Mind and
Soul, local situation does not apply. One part of intelligible
being is not here and another there. Where it is, it is as a
whole. The union of an incorporeal nature with a body is
altogether peculiar[2]. It is present indivisibly, and as numerically one, to the multitude of parts, each and all. What

---

[1] *Sententiae*, 34.

[2] *Sententiae*, 35: οὔτε οὖν κρᾶσις, ἢ μῖξις, ἢ σύνοδος, ἢ παράθεσις· ἀλλ' ἕτερος
τρόπος. Cf. 6: οὐ τὸ ποιοῦν εἰς ἄλλο πελάσει καὶ ἀφῇ ποιεῖ ἃ ποιεῖ· ἀλλὰ καὶ τὰ
πελάσει καὶ ἀφῇ τι ποιοῦντα, κατὰ συμβεβηκὸς τῇ πελάσει χρῆται. On this Ritter
and Preller remark (524 a), "Favet theurgicis hoc placitum." Here is a good
illustration of the readiness which historians have often displayed to see
the "theurgical" in preference to the scientific side of the Neo-Platonists.
Whether by itself or taken along with the context, what the passage suggests

appears to be added—as locality or relation—in departing from incorporeal being, is really taken away. Not to know being and not to know oneself, have the same source, namely, an addition of what is not, constituting a diminution of being which is all,—and which, except in appearance, cannot be diminished. Recovery of yourself by knowledge is recovery of being which was never absent,—which is as inseparable from you in essence as you are from yourself[1].

This is of course the doctrine of Plotinus taken at its centre. With equal exactitude Porphyry reproduces his conception of being as differentiated intrinsically and not by participation in anything external[2]. Plurality of souls is prior to plurality of bodies, and is not incompatible with the continued unity of all souls in one. They exist without diremption, yet unconfused, like the many parts of knowledge in a single soul[3]. Time accompanies the cognitive process in soul, as eternity accompanies the timeless cognition of intellect. In such process, however, the earlier thought does not go out to give place to the later. It appears to have gone out, but it remains; and what appears to have come in is from the movement of the soul returning on itself[4].

Thus closely does the disciple follow the master into the psychological subtleties[5] by which he anticipated the modern

is a kind of Occasionalist phenomenism. All changes, even in bodies, have their true cause in immaterial being. Material approach or contact is not an efficient cause, but accompanies as its "accident" the real order of metaphysical causation.

[1] *Sententiae*, 41: ὃ δὴ οὕτω σου ἐστὶν ἀναπόσπαστον κατ᾽ οὐσίαν, ὡς σὺ σαυτοῦ.

[2] *Sententiae*, 38: οὐ γὰρ ἔξωθεν ἐπίκτητος, οὐδὲ ἐπεισοδιώδης αὐτοῦ ἡ ἑτερότης, οὐδὲ ἄλλου μεθέξει, ἀλλ᾽ ἑαυτῷ πολλά.

[3] *Sententiae*, 39: διέστησαν γάρ, οὐκ ἀποκοπεῖσαι, οὐδὲ ἀποκερματίσασαι εἰς ἑαυτὰς τὴν ὅλην· καὶ πάρεισιν ἀλλήλαις, οὐ συγκεχυμέναι, οὐδὲ σωρὸν ποιοῦσαι τὴν ὅλην·...ὥσπερ οὐδὲ αἱ ἐπιστῆμαι συνεχύθησαν αἱ πολλαὶ ἐν ψυχῇ μιᾷ....καὶ αἱ πᾶσαι, μία· καὶ πάλιν ἡ ὅλη ἄλλη παρὰ πάσας.

[4] *Sententiae*, 44: ψυχὴ δὲ μεταβαίνει ἀπ᾽ ἄλλου εἰς ἄλλο, ἐπαμείβουσα τὰ νοήματα· οὐκ ἐξισταμένων τῶν προτέρων, οὐδὲ ποθὲν ἄλλοθεν ἐπεισιόντων τῶν δευτέρων· ἀλλὰ τὰ μὲν ὥσπερ ἀπελήλυθε, καίπερ μένοντα ἐν αὐτῇ· τὰ δ᾽ ὥσπερ ἀλλαχόθεν ἔπεισιν. ἀφίκατο δ᾽ οὐκ ἀλλαχόθεν, ἀλλ᾽ αὐτῆς καὶ αὐτόθεν εἰς ἑαυτὴν κινουμένης, καὶ τὸ ὄμμα φερούσης εἰς ἃ ἔχει κατὰ μέρος. πηγῇ γὰρ ἔοικεν οὐκ ἀπορρύτῳ, ἀλλὰ κύκλῳ εἰς ἑαυτὴν ἀναβλυζούσῃ ἃ ἔχει.

[5] To ignore the subtleties of the school is especially misleading in the case

position that, as the idea of extension is not extended, so the succession of thoughts does not suffice to give the thought of succession. After the illustration offered of his penetrating clearness of exposition, we may go on to a work which shows him in a more distinctive light.

Plotinus, though personally an ascetic, laid no stress in his writings on particular ascetic practices. His precepts reduce themselves in effect to a general recommendation to thin down the material vehicle so that the soul may be borne quietly upon it[1]. There is no suggestion in the Enneads that the perfection of philosophic life requires abstinence from animal food. Not infrequently, however, both earlier and later, this abstinence was practised as a strict duty by those who traced their philosophic ancestry to Pythagoras. Now the Neo-Platonists, on the practical side, continued the movement of religious and moral reform represented by teachers like Apollonius of Tyana[2]. Thus many of them refrained on principle from flesh-eating. Among these was Porphyry. The occasion of his treatise was that Castricius Firmus, one of the disciples of Plotinus, having begun to practise abstinence from flesh, had returned to the ordinary custom. He could easily defend himself on theoretical grounds; for Peripatetics, Stoics and Epicureans had all their systematic refutation of the Pythagorean abstinence. To the arguments current in the schools, accordingly, Porphyry first sets himself to reply.

The contention of the Stoics and Peripatetics was that the

---

of a doctrine like that of "ecstasy." Jules Simon (*Histoire de l'École d'Alex-andrie*, t. ii. p. 156), referring to a passage of the *Sententiae* (26), says that, for Porphyry, "ecstasy is a sleep." What Porphyry really says is that, while we have to speak of the existence beyond mind in terms of thought, we can only contemplate it in a state that is not thought; as sleep has to be spoken of in terms of waking life, but can only be known through sleeping. Ecstasy, that is to say, is compared to sleep because it also has to be appre-hended by its like, and because language, by which alone we can try to com-municate our apprehension to others, has been framed for a different realm of experience; not at all because it is a kind of sleep.

[1] Enn. III. 6, 5.

[2] Eunapius, in the introduction to his *Lives*, says of Apollonius that he is not to be counted as a mere philosopher, but rather as something between the gods and man (οὐκέτι φιλόσοφος· ἀλλ' ἦν τι θεῶν τε καὶ ἀνθρώπου μέσον).

idea of justice is applicable only to rational beings; to extend
it beyond them to irrational beings, as those do who refuse to
kill animals for food, is to subvert its nature and to destroy the
possibility of that in it which is practicable. The Epicurean
argument which Porphyry cites is founded on a conjectural
account of the origin of laws. The primitive legislator perceived some utility, and other men, who had not perceived it
at first, as soon as their attention was drawn willingly attached
to its violation a social prohibition and a penalty. It is for
reasons of utility that there are laws against homicide but not
against the slaughter of animals. If indeed a contract could
have been made, not only among men but also between men
and animals, to refrain from killing one another at random, it
would have been well that justice should be so far extended,
for thus safety would have been promoted; but it is impossible
for animals that do not understand discourse to share in law.
To the general argument Porphyry in the first book replies
provisionally that he does not recommend this abstinence to
all men—not for example to those who have to do with the
mechanical arts, nor to athletes, nor to soldiers, nor to men
of affairs—but only to those who live the life of philosophy.
Legislators make laws not with a view to the theoretic life, but
to a kind of average life. Thus we cannot adopt their conces-
sions as rules for a life that is to be better than written law.
The asceticism of the philosopher consists in a withdrawal
from the things of ordinary life, if possible without trial of
them. No one can dwell at once with the things of sense and
the things of the mind[1]. The life of the body generally, and
such matters as diet in particular, cannot safely be left un-
regulated by reason. The more completely they are put in
order once for all, the less attention they will occupy, and
the freer the mind will be for its own life. The Epicureans
have to some extent recognised this in advising abstinence
from flesh, if not on the ground of justice yet as a means of
reducing needs and so making life simpler.

---

[1] *De Abst.* i. 42. The theories of some of the Gnostics are alluded to. τὸ
δὲ οἴεσθαι κατὰ τὴν αἴσθησιν παθαινόμενον πρὸς τοῖς νοητοῖς ἐνεργεῖν πολλοὺς καὶ
τῶν βαρβάρων ἐξετραχήλισεν.

From the practical side the objection was raised that to reject the flesh of animals as food is inconsistent with the custom of offering them as sacrifices to the gods. Porphyry replies by an unsparing attack on the custom. This fills the second book. An account of the origin of animal sacrifices is quoted from Theophrastus, who with reason, Porphyry says, forbids those who would be truly pious to sacrifice living things[1]. Offerings of fruits and corn and flowers and spices came earliest. The custom of sacrificing animals was not earlier than the use of them for food, which began, together with cannibalism, in a dearth of fruits. Living things then came to be sacrificed because men had been accustomed to make first offerings to the gods of all that they used[2]. Responses of oracles and sayings from the poets are quoted to show that the least costly sacrifices with purity of mind are the most pleasing to the gods. Porphyry disclaims any intention of overthrowing established customs; but remarks that the laws of the actual State allow private persons to offer the plainest sacrifices, and such as consist of things without life. To make an offering to the gods of food from which we ourselves abstain would undoubtedly be unholy; but we are not required to do it. We too must sacrifice, but in accordance with the nature of the different powers. To the God over all, as a certain wise man[3] said, we must neither offer nor even name anything material. Our offering must be contemplation without even inward discourse. To all the gods, the special thank-offering of the philosopher will be fair thoughts regarding them. Some of those who are devoted to philosophy, Porphyry allows, hesitate here, and make too much of externals. We will not quarrel with them, lest we too should be over-precise on such a matter, but will add contemplation, as our own offering, to their observance of pious tradition.

---

[1] De Abst. ii. 11: εἰκότως ὁ Θεόφραστος ἀπαγορεύει μὴ θύειν τὰ ἔμψυχα τοὺς τῷ ὄντι εὐσεβεῖν ἐθέλοντας.

[2] This is a generalised account. Here and elsewhere in the De Abstinentia there is much curious lore about the origin both of flesh-eating and of animal sacrifices.

[3] Apollonius of Tyana, as is mentioned in a note in Nauck's edition (Porphyrii Opuscula Selecta).

He who cares about piety knows that to the gods none but
bloodless sacrifices are to be offered. Sacrifices of another kind
are offered only to the daemons—which name Plato applied
without distinction to the multitude of invisible powers below
the stars. On the subject of daemons, Porphyry then proceeds
to give an account of the views popularly expounded by some
of the Platonists (ἃ τῶν Πλατωνικῶν τινὲς ἐδημοσίευσαν[1]).
One of the worst injuries done by the bad among the daemons
is to persuade us that those beings are the causes of earthly
ills who are really the causes of quite the opposite. After this,
they turn us to entreaties and sacrifices to the beneficent gods
as if they were angry[2]. They inflame the desires of men with
love of riches and power and pleasure, whence spring factions
and wars. And, what is most terrible, they reach the point of
persuading them that all this has been stirred up by the
highest God. Nor are the philosophers altogether blameless.
For some of them have not kept far enough apart from the
ideas of the multitude, who, hearing from those that appeared
wise things in harmony with their own opinions, were still
further encouraged in unworthy thoughts about the gods.

If cities must propitiate such powers, that is nothing to us
(οὐδὲν πρὸς ἡμᾶς). For by these wealth and external and
bodily things are thought to be goods and deprivation of
them an evil, and they have little care about the soul. The
same position must be taken as regards divination by the
entrails of victims. This, it may be said, will be done away
with if we refrain from killing and eating animals. Why not,
then, kill men also for the purpose? It is said that better
premonitions are to be got in that way, and many of the
barbarians really practise this mode of divination. As a
matter of fact, whether the victim is human or is an irrational
animal, thus to gain knowledge of the future belongs to injustice and greed[3].

---

[1] De Abst. ii. 37–43.
[2] De Abst. ii. 40: τρέπουσίν τε μετὰ τοῦτο ἐπὶ λιτανείας ἡμᾶς καὶ θυσίας τῶν
ἀγαθοεργῶν θεῶν ὡς ὠργισμένων.
[3] De Abst. ii. 51: ἀλλ᾽ ὥσπερ ἀδικίας καὶ πλεονεξίας ἦν τὸ ἕνεκα μαντείας
ἀναιρεῖν τὸν ὁμόφυλον, οὕτω καὶ τὸ ἄλογον ζῷον σφάττειν μαντείας ἕνεκα ἄδικον.

Here Porphyry recounts a number of cases of human sacrifice in former times, and their commutation into animal or symbolical sacrifices; appealing to historical authority for the statement that it was not until the time of Hadrian that all survivals of such rites throughout the Empire were practically abolished[1]. Before concluding the book, he observes that even the unperverted ideas of the multitude make some approach to right opinion about the gods; and illustrates the remark by passages from comic poets ridiculing the notion that divine powers are pleased with such things as are usually offered to them. Then he points to the swarm of evils brought in by those who introduced costly sacrifices[2]. To think that the gods delight in this kind of expenditure must have a specially bad influence on the minds of youth, teaching them to neglect conduct; whereas to think that they have regard above all to the disposition must tend to make them pious and just. The philosopher, in Plato's view, ought not to accommodate himself to bad customs, but to try to win men to the better; if he cannot, let him go the right way himself, caring neither for dangers nor abuse from the many. And surely if Syrians and Hebrews and Phoenicians and Egyptians could resist even to the death kings that strove to make them depart from their national laws in the matter of food, we ought not to transgress the laws of nature and divine precepts for the fear of men.

In the third book, Porphyry undertakes to show that animals, in so far as they have perception and memory, have some share in reason, and therefore are not beyond the range of justice. Defining uttered discourse, not according to the doctrine of any particular school but in the perfectly general sense of "a voice significant through the tongue of internal affections in the soul," we shall find that animals capable of uttering sounds have a kind of discourse among themselves. And before utterance, why should we not suppose the thought

---

[1] De Abst. ii. 56: καταλυθῆναι δὲ τὰς ἀνθρωποθυσίας σχεδὸν τὰς παρὰ πᾶσιν φησὶ Πάλλας ὁ ἄριστα τὰ περὶ τῶν τοῦ Μίθρα συναγαγὼν μυστηρίων ἐφ' Ἀδριανοῦ τοῦ αὐτοκράτορος.

[2] De Abst. ii. 60: ἀγνοοῦσιν δὲ οἱ τὴν πολυτέλειαν εἰσαγαγόντες εἰς τὰς θυσίας, ὅπως ἅμα ταύτῃ ἐσμὸν κακῶν εἰσήγαγον, δεισιδαιμονίαν, τρυφήν, ὑπόληψιν τοῦ δεκάζειν δύνασθαι τὸ θεῖον καὶ θυσίαις ἀκεῖσθαι τὴν ἀδικίαν.

of the affection to have been there[1]? Even if we pass over some of the stories about men that are said to have understood the tongues of animals, enough is recorded to show that the voices of birds and beasts, if intently listened to, are not wholly unintelligible. Voiceless animals too, such as fishes, come to understand the voices of men; which they could not do without some mental resemblance. To the truth of Aristotle's assertion that animals learn much both from one another and from men, every trainer can bear witness. Those who will not see all these evidences of their intelligence take the part of calumniating the creatures they mean to treat ruthlessly[2]. Animals are subject not only to the same bodily diseases as men but to the same affections of the soul. Some have even acuter senses. That animals do indeed possess internal reason is shown by the knowledge they display of their own strength and weakness and by the provisions they make for their life. To say that all this belongs to them "by nature" amounts to saying that by nature they are rational[3]. We too arrive at reason because it is our nature; and animals, as has been said, learn by being taught, as we do. They have vices of their own, though these are lighter than those of men; and the virtues of the social animals are undeniable, however difficult their mental processes may be for us to follow.

Against the external teleology of Chrysippus, according to which all other animals were created for the use of man, Porphyry cites the argument of Carneades, that where there is a natural end for any being, the attainment of the end must be marked by some profit to that being, and not to some other. If we were to follow the teleological method of the Stoics, we could not well escape the admission that it is we who have been produced for the sake of the most destructive brutes; for

---

[1] *De Abst.* iii. 3: τί δὲ οὐχὶ καὶ ἃ πάσχει τι, πρότερον καὶ πρὶν εἰπεῖν ὃ μέλλει, διενοήθη;

[2] *De Abst.* iii. 6: ἀλλ' ὁ μὲν εὐγνώμων καὶ ἐκ τούτων μεταδίδωσι συνέσεως τοῖς ζῴοις, ὁ δὲ ἀγνώμων καὶ ἀνιστόρητος αὐτῶν φέρεται συνεργῶν αὐτοῦ τῇ εἰς αὐτὰ πλεονεξίᾳ. καὶ πῶς γὰρ οὐκ ἔμελλεν κακολογήσειν καὶ διαβαλεῖν ἃ κατακόπτειν ὡς λίθον προῄρηται;

[3] *De Abst.* iii. 10: ὁ δὲ φύσει λέγων αὐτοῖς προσεῖναι ταῦτα ἀγνοεῖ λέγων ὅτι φύσει ἐστὶ λογικά.

while they are of no use to us, they sometimes make their prey
of men. This they do driven by hunger, whereas we in our
sports and public games kill in wantonness[1]. Returning to the
question about the reason of animals, Porphyry argues, after
Plutarch, that to an animal that could not reason at all, its
senses would be of no use towards action for ends. Inferiority
in reasoning power is not the same as total deprivation of it.
We do not say that we are entirely without the faculty of
vision because the hawk has sharper sight. If normally
animals had not reason, how could they go mad, as some do?
Porphyry next cites from Theophrastus an argument for a
relation of kinship not only among all men, but between men
and all animals[2]. In the bodies and souls of both, we find the
same principles. For our bodies consist not only of the same
primary elements but of the same tissues—"skin, flesh, and
the kind of humours natural to animals." Likewise the souls
of animals resemble those of men by their desires and impulses, by their reasonings, and above all by their sense-perceptions. The difference, in the case of souls as of bodies, is
in degree of fineness. Therefore, in abstaining from the flesh
of animals, Porphyry concludes, we are more just in that we
avoid harming what is of kindred nature; and, from thus
extending justice, we shall be less prone to injure our fellow-
men. We cannot indeed live in need of nothing, like the
divinity; but we can at least make ourselves more like God
by reducing our wants. Let us then imitate the "golden
race," for which the fruits of the earth sufficed.

[1] De Abst. iii. 20. Here follow some pages adapted from Plutarch's De
Sollertia Animalium, cc. 2–5, beginning: ἐξ ὧν δὴ καὶ τὸ μὲν φονικὸν καὶ θηριῶδες
ἡμῶν ἐπερρώσθη καὶ τὸ πρὸς οἶκτον ἀπαθές, τοῦ δ' ἡμέρου τὸ πλεῖστον ἀπήμβλυναν οἱ
πρῶτοι τοῦτο τολμήσαντες. οἱ δὲ Πυθαγόρειοι τὴν πρὸς τὰ θηρία πραότητα μελέτην
ἐποιήσαντο τοῦ φιλανθρώπου καὶ φιλοικτίρμονος. In view of modern discussions on
teleology and evolution, a passage that occurs later may be found interesting.
Having enumerated the devices of animals that live in the water for catching
prey and escaping from enemies, one of the spokesmen in the dialogue argues
that the struggle is nature's means of promoting animal intelligence. De
Sollertia Animalium, 27 (979 A): καὶ τὸν κύκλον τοῦτον καὶ τὴν περίοδον ταῖς κατ'
ἀλλήλων διώξεσι καὶ φυγαῖς γύμνασμα καὶ μελέτην ἡ φύσις αὐτοῖς ἐναγώνιον
πεποίηκε δεινότητος καὶ συνέσεως.

[2] De Abst. iii. 25.

The fourth book, which is incomplete, accumulates testimonies to show that abstinence from flesh is not a mere eccentric precept of Pythagoras and Empedocles, but has been practised by primitive and uncorrupted races, by communities of ascetics like the Essenes, and by the Egyptian and other priesthoods, some of whom have abstained from all kinds of animal food, some from particular kinds. Then, after giving an account of the Brahmans and of the Buddhist monks (who are evidently meant by the Σαμαναῖοι) on the authority of Bardesanes (perhaps the Gnostic), who derived his information from an Indian embassy to the imperial court early in the third century, Porphyry returns to the general ascetic argument for abstinence. One who would philosophise ought not to live like the mass of mankind, but ought rather to observe such rules as are prescribed to priests, who take upon themselves the obligation of a holier kind of life[1].

This is the strain in which the work breaks off, but it will be observed that on the whole the point of view is as much humanitarian as ascetic. Transmigration of human souls into the bodies of animals Porphyry explicitly denied. Here he mentions it only as a topic of ridicule used against Pythagoras. The stories of men who have been transformed into animals, he interprets as a mythical indication that the souls of animals have something in common with our own. The way in which the whole subject is discussed reveals a degree of reflectiveness with regard to it in the ancient schools which has scarcely been reached again by civilised Europe till quite modern times. And perhaps, for those who wish to preserve the mean, no more judicious solution will be found than Plutarch came upon incidentally in his Life of Cato the Censor; where he contends that, while justice in the proper sense is applicable only among men, irrational animals also may claim a share of benevolence[2].

---

[1] De Abst. iv. 18.

[2] Vitae, Cato Major, 5: καίτοι τὴν χρηστότητα τῆς δικαιοσύνης πλατύτερον τόπον ὁρῶμεν ἐπιλαμβάνουσαν· νόμῳ μὲν γὰρ καὶ τῷ δικαίῳ πρὸς ἀνθρώπους μόνον χρῆσθαι πεφύκαμεν, πρὸς εὐεργεσίας δὲ καὶ χάριτας ἔστιν ὅτε καὶ μέχρι τῶν ἀλόγων ζῴων ὥσπερ ἐκ πηγῆς πλουσίας ἀπορρεῖ τῆς ἡμερότητος.

2.   *Iamblichus.*

Iamblichus, who was regarded as the next after Porphyry
in the Neo-Platonic succession[1], had been his pupil at Rome.
He was a native of Chalcis in Coele-Syria, and his own later
activity as a teacher was in Syria. He died in the reign of
Constantine, about 330. Eunapius describes him as socially
accessible and genial, and as living on familiar terms with his
numerous disciples. Though he is often described as having
given to the Neo-Platonic school a decisive impulse in the
direction of theurgy, the one well-authenticated anecdote on
the subject in his biography does not lend any particular
support to this view. A rumour had gone abroad that sometimes during his devotions he was raised in the air and under-
went a transfiguration. His disciples, fearing that they were
being excluded from some secret, took occasion to ask him if
it was so. Though not much given to laughter, he laughed
upon this inquiry, and said that the story was prettily invented but was not true[2]. Eunapius was told this by his
teacher Chrysanthius; and Chrysanthius had it from Aedesius,
who bore a part in the conversation. The biographer certainly
goes on to relate some marvels on hearsay, but he mentions
distinctly that none of the disciples of Iamblichus wrote them
down. He records them, as he says himself, with a certain
hesitation; but he did not think himself justified in omitting
what was told him by trustworthy witnesses.

The literary style of Iamblichus, Eunapius allows, has not
the beauty and lucidity of Porphyry's. Not that it altogether
fails of clearness, nor that it is grammatically incorrect; but it
does not draw the reader on. As Plato said of Xenocrates, he
had not sacrificed to the Hermaic Graces. An interesting
account is given of the way in which he was stirred up to
reflection on political topics by Alypius, an acute dialectician
of Alexandria. A public disputation having been arranged

---

[1] See Julian, Or. VII. 222 B, where Plotinus, Porphyry and Iamblichus are
mentioned in order as carrying on the tradition of Plato.

[2] Eunap. *Vitae* (Iamblichus): ὁ μὲν ἀπατήσας ὑμᾶς οὐκ ἦν ἄχαρις, ταῦτα δὲ
οὐχ οὕτως ἔχει.

between them, Alypius put to him a question from which he
at first turned away with disdain. The query was: "Whether
a rich man is necessarily either unjust or the heir of one who
has been unjust[1]." According to the traditional philosophic
view that poverty and wealth, in comparison with the goods of
the mind, are alike indifferent, the question seemed frivolous;
but further thought modified the impression, and Iamblichus
became an admirer of Alypius and afterwards wrote his life.
The composition, Eunapius thought, was not successful; and
this he ascribes to the author's want of aptitude for political
discussion and of real interest in it. It conveyed a sense of
Iamblichus's admiration for Alypius, but did not succeed in
giving the reader any clear idea as to what he had said or
done.

Eunapius himself was not by special training a philosopher,
but a rhetorician. He was an adherent of the party attached
to the old religion. Commonly, he is described as an indiscriminate panegyrist of all the philosophers of his party; but,
as we see, he was not wanting in candour. While looking
back with reverence to Iamblichus as the intellectual chief
of the men whose doctrines he followed, he does not in the
least understate his defects of style. And on no one does he
lavish more praise than on his Athenian teacher in rhetoric,
Prohaeresius, who was a Christian. Iamblichus was one of
those who are placed higher by their own age than by later
times. His reputation had probably reached its greatest
height about the time of Julian, who spoke of him as not
inferior in genius to Plato[2]. Still, he remains a considerable

---

[1] 'Εἰπέ μοι, φιλόσοφε,' πρὸς αὐτὸν ἔφη, 'ὁ πλούσιος ἢ ἄδικος ἢ ἀδίκου κληρονόμος,
ναὶ ἢ οὔ; τούτων γὰρ μέσον οὐδέν.'

[2] Or. IV. 146 A. To save their genuineness, the letters of Julian "to
Iamblichus the philosopher" are as a rule assumed to have been written to
a nephew of Iamblichus, known from the correspondence of Libanius. Zeller
(iii. 2, p. 679, n. 2) points to circumstances which show that they must have
purported to be written to the elder Iamblichus, who died near the time when
Julian was born (331). He therefore follows Dodwell ("A Discourse concerning the Time of Pythagoras," cited by Fabricius, *Bibliotheca Graeca*) in
regarding them as spurious. Dodwell gives what seems a decisive reason for
rejecting them, namely, that Sopater, who was executed under Constantine,
s referred to as alive.

philosopher. He modified the doctrine of Plotinus more deeply
than Porphyry; and the changes he made in it were taken up
and continued when it came to be systematised by the
Athenian school. If he does not write so well as Porphyry or
Proclus, he succeeds in conveying his meaning. And, while
professedly expounding the tradition of a school, and freely
borrowing from his predecessors, he always has a distinctive
drift of his own.

The surviving works of Iamblichus belonged to a larger
treatise in which the Pythagorean philosophy was regarded as
the original source of the tradition he expounds. The whole
treatise was entitled Συναγωγὴ τῶν Πυθαγορείων δογμάτων.
Of the separate works, the first in order is a Life of Pythagoras.
The second is mainly ethical in content, and is a general exhortation to the study of philosophy (Λόγος προτρεπτικὸς ἐπὶ
φιλοσοφίαν). The remaining three are mathematical[1]. The
best notion of the individual tone of Iamblichus's thought
will be given by an abstract of the second book—the *Protrepticus*. But first a word must be said on the kind of modification he made in the doctrine of Plotinus.

From the references in later writers, it is known that he
attempted a more systematic analysis of the stages of emanation by resolving them into subordinate triads. As there are
traces of this already in Porphyry, and as Proclus carried the
method much further, the interest of Iamblichus here is that
he illustrates the continuous effort of the school towards completeness and consistency. He dwelt with special emphasis on
the position that the causal process from higher to lower is
logical, and not in time; and thought it not without danger to
suppose a temporal production of the world even as a mere
hypothesis. More explicitly than Plotinus or Porphyry, he
insisted that no individual soul can remain permanently in
the intelligible world any more than in Tartarus. It is the
nature of every particular soul to descend periodically and to

---

[1] The genuineness of one of these (Τὰ θεολογούμενα τῆς ἀριθμητικῆς) has
been contested. The other two bear the titles Περὶ τῆς κοινῆς μαθηματικῆς
ἐπιστήμης and Περὶ τῆς Νικομάχου ἀριθμητικῆς εἰσαγωγῆς. See, on the former,
Appendix III.

reascend in accordance with a law of universal necessity. The
point where he was most original was, however, his affirmation, as against Plotinus, that when the soul "descends" it
descends wholly. The whole soul, and not merely a kind of
effluence of it, is in relation with this world so long as it is here
at all. There is no "pure soul" that remains exempt from
error while the "composite nature" is at fault. If the will
sins, how can the soul be without sin[1]? This correction in
what seemed Plotinus's over-exalted view was almost universally allowed, and was definitively taken up by Proclus.
It certainly does not bear out the notion that Iamblichus
was a thinker who deserted all sobriety in order to turn a
philosophic school into an association of theosophic adepts.

The *Protrepticus* is in considerable part made up of excerpts
from Plato, Aristotle, and Neo-Pythagorean writings, but it is
at the same time consistently directed to the end of showing
the importance of theoretical knowledge both for itself and in
relation to practice. Contemplation is put first; but, of all the
school, Iamblichus dwells most on the bearing of knowledge
upon practical utilities. At the beginning he brings out the
point that general scientific discipline must be communicated
before philosophy, "as the less before the greater mysteries[2]."
We are to regard the constancy of the stellar movements, so
that we may be prepared to adapt ourselves to the necessary
course of things. From scientific knowledge we are to rise to
wisdom (σοφία) as knowledge of first principles, and finally as
theology. We need knowledge to make use of "goods," which
without the wisdom to use them are not goods, or rather are
evils. Things in use (τὰ χρήματα) have reference to the body,
and the body is to be attended to for the sake of the soul and
its ruling powers. Each of us is the soul, and knowledge of the
soul is knowledge of oneself. The physician as such does not
know himself. Those who practise arts connected not with the
body directly but with things that are for the body, are still

---

[1] Procl. *in Tim.* 341 D; ed. Diehl iii. 334 (R. P. 528). εἰ δὲ ἡ προαίρεσις
ἁμαρτάνει, πῶς ἀναμάρτητος ἡ ψυχή;

[2] *Protrepticus*, c. 2, ed. H. Pistelli, p. 10: ὡς πρὸ τῶν μεγάλων μυστηρίων τὰ
μικρὰ παραδοτέον, καὶ πρὸ φιλοσοφίας παιδείαν.

more remote from self-knowledge, and their arts are rightly called mechanical. We must exercise the divinest part of the soul by the appropriate motions. Now to what is divine in us the movements of the whole are akin[1]. In the part of the soul that has rational discourse is the intellectual principle, which is the best that belongs to the soul. For the sake of this, and of the thoughts with which it energises, all else exists.

While without philosophy practical life cannot be well regulated, the theoretic life is yet not finally for the sake of practice. Rather, mind itself and the divine are the ultimate end, the mark at once of the intellectual eye and of love. It is by the power of living the life of theory that we differ from other animals. Of reason and prudence there are in them also some small gleams, but they have no part in theoretic wisdom; whereas in accuracy of perception and vigour of impulse many of them surpass man. Since, however, we are discoursing with men and not with gods, we must mingle exhortations bearing on civic and practical life. Now philosophy alone, in relation to the other kinds of knowledge, can judge and direct. And philosophical knowledge is not only possible but is in one way more attainable than other knowledge, because it is of first principles, which are better known by nature and are more determinate. It is of the highest degree of utility, because it definitely makes its object the insight by which the wise man judges and the reason which proceeds from insight and is expressed in law. And that it is not inaccessible is shown by the eagerness with which students devote themselves to it. Unlike other scientific pursuits, it demands no special appliances or conditions of time and place.

After further elaborating this argument, Iamblichus proceeds to infer from "common notions" that insight ($\phi\rho\acute{o}\nu\eta\sigma\iota\varsigma$) is most to be chosen for itself, and not for the sake of other things. Suppose a man to have everything else and to suffer from a malady in the part of him that has insight, life would not be for him a gift to choose, for none of its other goods

---

[1] *Protr.* 5, p. 31: τῷ δ' ἐν ἡμῖν θείῳ ξυγγενεῖς εἰσι κινήσεις αἱ τοῦ παντὸς διανοήσεις καὶ περιφοραί.

would be of any use to him[1]. Insight, therefore, cannot be a
mere means to gaining other things. The way too in which
death is shunned proves the soul's love of knowledge; for it
flees what it does not know, the dark and the unapparent, and
by nature pursues what is plain to sight and knowable[2]. And
although, as they that declare the mysteries say, our souls are
bound to our bodies to pay the penalty of some antenatal
offence, yet, in so far as human life has the power of sharing
in divine and immortal intellect, man appears as a god in
relation to the other things that are on earth.

Iamblichus next argues on Aristotelian grounds that man
has a natural end, and that this end is that which in the
genetic order, fulfilling itself as this does continuously, is the
latest to be perfected[3]. Now in human development mental
insight is that which is last attained. This then is the final
good of man. For we must at length stop at something that
is good in itself. Otherwise, by viewing each thing in turn as
a means to some extraneous end, we commit ourselves to a
process to infinity. Yet, though insight is not properly a
utility, but a good to be chosen for itself, it also furnishes the
greatest utilities to human life, as may be seen from the arts.
Just as the physician needs a knowledge of nature, so the
lawgiver and the moralist need theoretical knowledge, though
of another kind, if they are to regulate the social life of man.
The relation of this knowledge to the whole of life is like that
of sight to physical action. In itself it simply judges and
shows, but without it we could do nothing or very little.

Those who enjoy the pleasure of insight enjoy most the
perfection of life in itself; an enjoyment which is to be distinguished from incidental pleasures, received while living but
not springing essentially from the proper activity of life. The
difficulty of living the theoretic life here, comes from the

---

[1] *Protr.* 8, p. 45: εἰ γὰρ καὶ πάντα τις ἔχοι, διεφθαρμένος δὲ εἴη καὶ νοσῶν τῷ
φρονοῦντι, οὐχ αἱρετὸς ὁ βίος· οὐδὲν γὰρ ὄφελος οὐδὲ τῶν ἄλλων ἀγαθῶν.

[2] *Protr.* 8, p. 46: καὶ τὸ φεύγειν δὲ τὸν θάνατον τοὺς πολλοὺς δείκνυσι τὴν
φιλομάθειαν τῆς ψυχῆς. φεύγει γὰρ ἃ μὴ γιγνώσκει, τὸ σκοτῶδες καὶ τὸ μὴ δῆλον,
φύσει δὲ διώκει τὸ φανερὸν καὶ τὸ γνωστόν.

[3] *Protr.* 9, p. 51: τέλος δὲ κατὰ φύσιν τοῦτό ἐστιν ὃ κατὰ τὴν γένεσιν πέφυκεν
ὕστατον ἐπιτελεῖσθαι περαινομένης τῆς γενέσεως συνεχῶς.

conditions of human nature; for now we have to be constantly
doing things that have relation to needs. This is most of all
the lot of those deemed happiest by the many. If, however,
we prepare ourselves by philosophising, we may hope, having
returned whence we came, to live in untroubled contemplation
of divine truth. Thus Iamblichus is led from the Aristotelian
ideal of the contemplative life to the thought of the *Phaedo*,
that philosophising is a kind of dying; death being nothing
but the separation of the soul from the body to live a life by
itself. Our soul can never perceive truth in its purity till it is
released. To prepare it for such knowledge, and to approach
that knowledge as near as possible while we live, we must
purify the soul from all that comes to it from the body,—
from common desires and fears, care about needs, and the
hindrances thrown in the way by external sense. The genuine
virtues of courage, temperance and justice proceed from the
insight reached by philosophic purification; the virtues that
result from a balancing of pleasures and pains are a mere
adumbration of virtue. When a distinction is drawn between
the lot in Hades of the uninitiated and of the initiated, we
may understand by the truly initiated ('ναρθηκοφόροι μὲν
πολλοί, βάκχοι δέ τε παῦροι') no other than those who have
become purified through philosophy. Those who do not arrive
in Hades as purified souls, quickly become subject to rebirth
in new bodies. Therefore, since the soul is immortal, there is
for it no escape from ills and no safety except to acquire as
much goodness and insight as possible.

The character of the philosopher is next set forth by an ex-
cerpt of the celebrated passage in the *Theaetetus*. An account
of the ideal philosophic education is adapted from the seventh
book of the *Republic*. The Platonic view is enforced that the
special function of philosophy is to remove from the soul the
accretion that comes to it from birth, and to purify that
energy of it to which the power of reason belongs[1]. The argument of the *Gorgias* is then taken up, that the intemperate
soul, which would be ever getting and spending, is like a

---

[1] *Protr.* 16, p. 83: τὸ γὰρ περιαιρεῖν τὴν γένεσιν ἀπὸ τῆς ψυχῆς καὶ ἐκκαθαίρειν
τὴν λογίζεσθαι δυναμένην αὐτῆς ἐνέργειαν μάλιστα αὐτῇ προσήκει.

"leaky vessel," while orderliness in the soul resembles health
in the body. After some further development of this topic,
Iamblichus returns to the point that philosophy is the most
directive of all the arts (ἡγεμονικωτάτη πασῶν τῶν τεχνῶν).
Hence most pains ought to be spent in learning it. An art of
dealing with words, indeed, might be learned in a short time,
so that the disciple should be no worse than the teacher; but
the excellence that comes from practice is only to be acquired
by much time and diligence. The envy of men, too, attaches
itself to rapid acquisitions of every kind; praise is more
readily accorded to those that have taken long to acquire.
Further, every acquirement ought to be used for a good end.
He that aims at all virtue is best when he is useful to most[1].
Now that which is most useful to mankind is justice. But
for any one to know the right distribution of things and to
be a worker with the true law of human life, he must have
acquired the directive knowledge that can only be given by
philosophy.

Iamblichus then goes on to argue that even if one were to
arise exempt from wounds and disease and pain, and gigantic
of stature, and adamantine of body and soul, he could in the
long run secure his own preservation only by aiding justice.
An evil so monstrous as tyranny arises from nothing but lawlessness. Some wrongly deem that men are not themselves the
causes of their being deprived of freedom, but are forcibly
deprived of it by the tyrant. To think that a king or tyrant
arises from anything but lawlessness and greed is folly[2]. When
law and justice have departed from the multitude, then, since
human life cannot go on without them, the care of them has
to pass over to one. The one man whom some suppose able by
his single power to dissolve justice and the law that exists for
the common good of all, is of flesh like the rest and not of
adamant. It is not in his power to strip men of them against
their will. On the contrary, he survives by restoring them

---

[1] *Protr.* 20, p. 97: τόν τε αὖ ἀρετῆς ὀρεγόμενον τῆς συμπάσης σκεπτέον εἶναι, ἐκ
τίνος ἂν λόγου ἢ ἔργου ἄριστος εἴη· τοιοῦτος δ' ἂν εἴη ὁ πλείστοις ὠφέλιμος ὤν.

[2] *Protr.* 20, p. 103: ὅστις γὰρ ἡγεῖται βασιλέα ἢ τύραννον ἐξ ἄλλου τινὸς
γίγνεσθαι ἢ ἐξ ἀνομίας τε καὶ πλεονεξίας, μωρός ἐστιν.

when they have failed. Lawlessness then being the cause of such great evils, and order being so great a good, there is no means of attaining happiness but to make law preside over one's own life.

The *Protrepticus* concludes with an interpretation of thirty-nine Pythagorean "symbols," or short precepts which are taken as cryptic expressions of philosophic truths. In their literal meaning, Iamblichus says, they would be nonsensical; but, according to the "reserve" (ἐχεμυθία) inculcated by Pythagoras on his disciples, not all of them were intended to be understood easily by those who run (τοῖς ἁπλῶς ἀκούουσιν ἐξ ἐπιδρομῆς τε ἐντυγχάνουσιν). Iamblichus proposes to give the solutions of them all, without making an exception of those that fell under the Pythagorean reserve.

The interpretations contain many points of interest. If the precepts were ever literal "taboos," not a trace of this character is retained. The last given, which was generally understood to command abstinence from animal food, is interpreted simply as inculcating justice with fit regard for what is of kindred nature and sympathetic treatment of the life that is like our own[1]. The absence of any reference to the literal meaning seems to indicate that Iamblichus did not follow Porphyry on this point. In interpreting the "symbols" relating to theology, if the whole of what he says is fairly considered, he seems to give them a turn against credulity; his last word being that that which is to be believed is that which is demonstrable. One of them runs, "Mistrust nothing marvellous about the gods, nor about the divine opinions." After pointing out generally the weakness of man's faculties, which should prevent him from judging rashly as to what is possible to the gods, Iamblichus goes on to explain more particularly that by "the divine opinions" (τὰ θεῖα δόγματα) are meant those of the Pythagorean philosophy, and that they are proved by cogent demonstration to be necessarily true[2].

[1] *Protr.* 21, p. 125: τὸ δὲ 'ἐμψύχων ἀπέχου' ἐπὶ δικαιοσύνην προτρέπει καὶ πᾶσαν τὴν τοῦ συγγενοῦς τιμὴν καὶ τὴν τῆς ὁμοίας ζωῆς ἀποδοχὴν καὶ πρὸς ἕτερα τοιαῦτα πλείονα.

[2] *Protr.* 21, pp. 110–111.

The precept therefore means: Acquire mathematical knowledge, so that you may understand the nature of demonstrative evidence, and then there will be no room for mistrust.
That is also what is meant in reference to the gods[1]. The
truth about the whole, Iamblichus says in another place, is
concealed and hard to get hold of, but is to be sought and
tracked out by man through philosophy, which, receiving
some small sparks from nature, kindles them into a flame
and makes them more active by the sciences that proceed from
herself[2]. Many of the sayings are interpreted as commending
the method of philosophising from intelligible principles setting forth the nature of the stable and incorporeal reality.
The "Italic" philosophy—which had long since come to be
regarded as a doctrine of incorporeal being—is to be preferred
before the Ionic[3]. The precept, not to carve the image of a god
on a ring ('θεοῦ τύπον μὴ ἐπίγλυφε δακτυλίῳ') is interpreted
to mean, "Think of the gods as incorporeal[4]." The model of
method for the discovery of truth about divine things is, as
has been said, that of mathematics. Thus the precept 'ἐν
ὁδῷ μὴ σχίζε' is turned against the method of search by a
series of dichotomies, and in favour of a process which leads
directly to truth without ambiguity because each step of the
way is demonstratively certain as soon as it is taken[5]. The
special bearing of the Pythagorean philosophy, with its appeal
to equality and proportion, on the virtue of justice (τὴν
τελειοτάτην ἀρετήν) is dwelt on[6]. Then, in nearing the end,

[1] This extended interpretation, with its preface about the inadequacy of
human judgments on divine things, comes out of its proper place. The
"symbol," which is the twenty-fifth, is also explained in due order (p. 121),
and there the preface is omitted and the whole runs thus: Τὸ δὲ 'περὶ θεῶν
μηδὲν θαυμαστὸν ἀπίστει μηδὲ περὶ θείων δογμάτων' προτρέπει μετιέναι καὶ κτᾶσθαι
ἐκεῖνα τὰ μαθήματα, δι' ἃ οὐκ ἀπιστήσεις οὐκέτι περὶ θεῶν καὶ περὶ θείων δογμάτων
ἔχων τὰ μαθήματα καὶ τὰς ἐπιστημονικὰς ἀποδείξεις.

[2] Protr. 21, p. 116: ἐπεὶ γὰρ ἀπόκρυφος φύσει ἡ περὶ τοῦ παντὸς ἀλήθεια, καὶ
δυσθήρατος ἱκανῶς· ζητητέα δὲ ὅμως ἀνθρώπῳ καὶ ἐξιχνευτέα μάλιστα διὰ φιλοσοφίας. διὰ γὰρ ἄλλου τινὸς ἐπιτηδεύματος οὕτως ἀδύνατον· αὐτη δὲ μικρά τινα
ἐναύσματα παρὰ τῆς φύσεως λαμβάνουσα καὶ ὡσανεὶ ἐφοδιαζομένη ζωπυρεῖ τε αὐτὰ
καὶ μεγεθύνει καὶ ἐνεργέστερα διὰ τῶν παρ' αὐτῆς μαθημάτων ἀπεργάζεται.

[3] Protr. 21, p. 125: προτίμα τὴν Ἰταλικὴν φιλοσοφίαν τὴν τὰ ἀσώματα καθ'
αὑτὰ θεωροῦσαν τῆς Ἰωνικῆς τῆς τὰ σώματα προηγουμένως ἐπισκοπουμένης.

[4] Protr. 21, p. 120.   [5] Protr. 21, pp. 118–119.   [6] Protr. 21, p. 114.

Iamblichus points out as one incitement to philosophise, that of all kinds of knowledge philosophy alone has no touch of envy or of joy in others' ill, since it shows that men are all akin and of like affections and subject in common to unforeseen changes of fortune. Whence it promotes human sympathy and mutual love[1].

3. *The School of Iamblichus.*

After the death of Iamblichus, his school dispersed itself over the whole Roman Empire[2]. His most brilliant disciple was Sopater, a man of ambitious temperament, who, as Eunapius expresses it, thought to change the purpose of Constantine by reason. He did in fact succeed in gaining a high position at Court; but in the struggle of intrigue his enemies at last got the better of him, and he was condemned by the Christian emperor to be executed, apparently on a charge of magic. According to Eunapius, he was accused of binding the winds so as to prevent the arrival of the ships on which Constantinople depended for its supply of corn[3].

Both now and for some time later, philosophers and others who were not even nominal adherents of Christianity could be employed by Christian rulers. Eustathius, another of Iamblichus's disciples, was sent by Constantius on an embassy to Persia. Themistius, who was an Aristotelian, held offices at a later period. The Christians themselves, long after the death of Julian, were still for the most part obliged to resort to the philosophical schools for their scientific culture[4]. The contest in the world, however, was now effectively decided, and the cause represented by the philosophers was plainly seen to be the losing one. Of its fortunes, and of the personalities of its adherents, we get a faithful picture from Eunapius, whose life of Aedesius is especially interesting for the passages showing the feelings with which the triumph of the Church was regarded. Aedesius was the successor of Iamblichus at

---

[1] *Protr.* 21, p. 123.

[2] Eunap. *Vitae* (Iamblichus): ἄλλοι μὲν γὰρ ἀλλαχοῦ τῶν εἰρημένων ὁμιλητῶν διεκρίθησαν εἰς ἄπασαν τὴν Ῥωμαϊκὴν ἐπικράτειαν.

[3] Eunap. *Vitae* (Aedesius).   [4] Zeller, iii. 2, p. 739.

Pergamum in Mysia. The biographer, it may be noted, distinctly tells us that he had no reputation for theurgy. The
marvels he connects with his name relate to the clairvoyance
of Sosipatra, the wife of Eustathius. Aedesius educated the
sons of Eustathius and Sosipatra; hence the connexion. One
of them, Antoninus, took up his abode at the Canopic mouth
of the Nile, whither came the youth eager for philosophical
knowledge. To him again, as to Aedesius, no theurgical accomplishments are ascribed; a possible reason in both cases,
Eunapius suggests, being concealment on account of the
hostility of the new rulers of the world. Those who put before him logical problems were immediately satisfied; those
who threw out anything about "diviner" inquiries found him
irresponsive as a statue. He probably did not himself regard
it as supernatural prescience when he uttered the prophecy,
afterwards held for an oracle, that soon "a fabulous and
formless darkness shall tyrannise over the fairest things on
earth" (καί τι μυθῶδες καὶ ἀειδὲς σκότος τυραννήσει τὰ ἐπὶ
γῆς κάλλιστα)[1]. The accession of Julian to the empire created
no illusion in the most clear-sighted of the philosophers. Chrysanthius, one of his instructors in the Neo-Platonic philosophy,
was pressingly invited by him to come and join him in the
restoration of Hellenism. Deterred, the biographer says, by
unfavourable omens, he declined. The Emperor nevertheless conferred on him, in association with his wife Melite,
the high-priesthood of Lydia[2]. This he accepted: but, fore-
warned of the failure of Julian's attempt to revive the ancient
worship, he altered as little as possible during his tenure of

---

[1] Cf. Gibbon on the "Final Destruction of Paganism," where the prediction
is quoted in a note. (Decline and Fall of the Roman Empire, ed. J. B. Bury,
vol. iii. p. 208.) In the chapter referred to, however, Gibbon antedated the
disappearance of pagan rites; as may be seen from the lives of philosophers
later than Eunapius's period. With the impression made on the biographer,
it is interesting to compare his contemporary St Jerome's description, cited
by Grote at the end of the preface to his Plato, of the desertion of the philosophic schools. Who now, asks the Christian Father, reads Plato or Aristotle?
"Rusticanos vero et piscatores nostros totus orbis loquitur, universus mundus
sonat."

[2] Eunap. Vitae (Maximus). Melite was a kinswoman of Eunapius, and
Chrysanthius became his teacher in philosophy.

office; so that there was hardly any disturbance there when
the state of things was again reversed; whereas elsewhere the
upheavals and depressions were violent. This was at the time
looked upon as an example of his unerring foresight, derived
from the knowledge of divine things communicated by his
Pythagorean masters[1]. It was added, that he knew how to
make use of his gift of prevision; this, no doubt, in contrast
with Maximus[2].

Maximus and Chrysanthius were fellow-pupils of Aedesius,
and were united in their devotion to theurgy. When Julian
was first attracted to the philosophic teachers of his time, the
aged Aedesius had commended him to his disciples Eusebius
and Chrysanthius, who were present, and Priscus and Maximus, who were then absent from Pergamum. Eusebius, whose
special interest was in logical studies, spoke with disparage-
ment of theurgy, but Julian's curiosity was excited by what he
heard. To satisfy it, he visited Maximus at Ephesus, at whose
suggestion he sent for Chrysanthius also. Under Maximus and
Chrysanthius he continued his philosophical studies. It may
have been his interest in theurgy that led him to seek initiation, during his visit to Greece, in the Eleusinian mysteries;
though his argument afterwards for being initiated was merely
compliance with ancient usage; he treats it as a matter of
course that such ceremonies can make no difference to the
soul's lot[3]. When he had become Emperor, he invited Maximus
with Chrysanthius, and afterwards Priscus, to Court. Unlike
Chrysanthius, Maximus, when he found the omens unfavourable, persisted till he got favourable ones. In power, as
Eunapius frankly acknowledges, he displayed a want of
moderation which led to his being treated afterwards with
great severity. He was put to death under Valens, as the

---

[1] Eunap. *Vitae* (Chrysanthius): ὁρᾶν γοῦν ἄν τις αὐτὸν ἔφησε μᾶλλον τὰ
ἐσόμενα ἢ προλέγειν τὰ μέλλοντα, οὕτως ἅπαντα διήθρει καὶ συνελάμβανεν, ὡσανεὶ
παρών τε καὶ συνὼν τοῖς θεοῖς.

[2] *Ib.*: ἐθαυμάσθη γοῦν ἐπὶ τούτοις, ὡς οὐ μόνον δεινὸς τὰ μέλλοντα προνοεῖν,
ἀλλὰ καὶ τοῖς γνωσθεῖσι χρήσασθαι.

[3] Or. VII. 239 BC: τούτοις μέν, οἷς ἀξίως τοῦ μυηθῆναι βεβίωται, καὶ μὴ
μυηθεῖσιν οἱ θεοὶ τὰς ἀμοιβὰς ἀκεραίους φυλάττουσι, τοῖς δὲ μοχθηροῖς οὐδέν ἐστι
πλέον κἂν εἴσω τῶν ἱερῶν εἰσφρήσωσι περιβόλων.

penalty of having been consulted regarding divinations about
the Emperor's successor. Priscus, we learn[1], had been from
his youth up a person of rather ostentatious gravity and reserve. He was, however, no pretender, but maintained the
philosophic character consistently during the reign of Julian;
nor was he afterwards accused of any abuse of power. He
died at the time when the Goths were ravaging Greece (396–8).
Preserving always his grave demeanour, says Eunapius, and
laughing at the weakness of mankind, he perished along with
the sanctuaries of Hellas, having lived to be over ninety,
while many cast away their lives through grief or were killed
by the barbarians. During the events that followed Julian's
reign (361–363), the biographer was himself a youth[2]. He was
born probably in 346 or 347, and died later than 414.

Of the literary activity of the school during the period from
the death of Iamblichus to the end of the fourth century,
there is not much to say. Many of the philosophers seem to
have confined themselves to oral exposition. Chrysanthius
wrote much, but none of his works have come down to us.
We have reports of the opinions of Theodore of Asine[3], an
immediate disciple both of Porphyry and of Iamblichus. His
writing seems to have taken the form chiefly of commentaries.
Proclus had a high opinion of him and frequently cites him.
We learn that with Plotinus he maintained the passionlessness
and uninterrupted activity of the higher part of the soul; and
that he defended Plato's position on the equality of the sexes.
Dexippus, another disciple of Iamblichus, wrote, in the form of
a dialogue with a pupil, a work on the Aristotelian Categories
which survives[4]. The book *De Mysteriis*, long attributed to
Iamblichus himself, is now considered only as illustrating the
general direction of his school[5]. Its most distinctive feature is
insistence on the necessity and value of ceremonial religion for

---

[1] Eunap. *Vitae* (Priscus).

[2] Eunap. *Vitae* (Maximus): καὶ ὁ ταῦτα γράφων ἐπαιδεύετο κατ' ἐκείνους τοὺς
χρόνους παῖς ὢν καὶ εἰς ἐφήβους ἄρτι τελῶν.

[3] Zeller, iii. 2, pp. 724 ff.

[4] Zeller, iii. 2, p. 737, n. 1.

[5] An edition of it was published at Oxford by Gale in 1678, with Latin
version and notes and a reconstruction of Porphyry's letter to Anebo, to which

the mass of mankind, and indeed for all but an inappreciable minority. It is admittedly well-written, as is also the little book of Sallust *De Diis et Mundo*[1]. This Sallust, as Zeller[2] proved against doubts that had been raised, was certainly the friend of Julian known from the Emperor's Orations and from references in the historians; and the book may have been put forth with a popular aim as a defence of the old religious system now restored and to be justified in the light of philosophy. A noteworthy point in it is the apology for animal sacrifices. As in the *De Mysteriis*, the higher place of philosophy is saved by the position that the incorporeal gods are in no way affected by prayer or sacrifice or by any kind of ceremony, and are moved by no passions. The forms of traditional religion, it is nevertheless maintained, are subjectively useful to men, and its modes of speech admit of a rational interpretation. The book ends by affirming the position of the *Republic*, that virtue would be sufficient for happiness even if there were no rewards reserved for it in another life.

it is a reply. The later edition by Parthey (Berlin, 1857) is based on Gale's. English readers will find an exact account of the sceptical queries of Porphyry, and of the solutions given by the author, in Maurice's *Moral and Metaphysical Philosophy*, vol. i.

[1] Edited by Orelli, with Latin version and notes, in 1821, and included in Mullach's *Fragmenta Philosophorum Graecorum*, vol. iii. (1881).

[2] iii. 2, p. 734.

CHAPTER VIII

THE POLEMIC AGAINST CHRISTIANITY

In taking up the defence of the old against the new religious institutions of the Roman Empire, the Neo-Platonists were simply continuing the attitude of earlier philosophical culture. From the time when the new religious phenomenon was first consciously recognised—that is to say, from about the beginning of the second century—it had aroused an instinctive antagonism among men who were as far from believing the pagan myths as the Christians themselves. The outlines of the apology for paganism, so far as it can be recovered, remain from first to last without essential modification. Celsus, writing in the second century, conceives the problem to be that of reconciling philosophical theism with diversities of national worship. It may be solved, in his view, by supposing the supreme Deity to have allotted different regions to subordinate divine powers, who may either be called gods, as by the Greeks, or angels, as by the Jews. Then, to show that the Christians have no philosophical advantage, he points to the declarations of Greek thinkers that there is one supreme God, and that the Deity has no visible form. On the other side, he insists on the resemblances between Hebrew and Greek legends. Greek mythology, he remarks, has in common with Christianity its stories of incarnations. In other religions also resurrections are spoken of. Such are those of Zamolxis in Scythia and of Rhampsinitus among the Egyptians. Among the Greeks too there are cases in which mortal men have been represented as raised to divinity. Noah's flood may have been borrowed from Deucalion's, and the idea of Satan from the Greek Titanomachies. The more intelligent Jews and Christians are ashamed of much in Biblical history, and try to explain it allegorically. What is supposed to be distinctive of Christian ethics has been put better, because more temperately, by the Greek philosophers.

Plato holds much the same view about the difficulty there is for a rich man to enter into the kingdom of heaven. He declares likewise that evil is never to be returned for evil. The reproach of idolatry against the non-Judaic religions is a calumny. Statues are not regarded as deities, but only as aids to devotion. To the highest God, as all agree, only the worship of the mind ought to be offered. But why should not hymns be addressed to beneficent visible powers like the sun, or to mental attributes such as Wisdom, represented by Athena? Piety is more complete when it has regard to all the varied manifestations of divinity in the world[1].

On their side, the Christians were quite willing to appeal to philosophers and poets who had had ideas of a purer religion than that of the multitude. All such ideas, they maintained, were borrowed from the Hebrew Scriptures. Philo had previously taken that view; and Numenius, among men who attached themselves to the Hellenic tradition, was at least thought to have been ready to allow something of the same kind. Theodoret, early in the fifth century, is sarcastic upon the ignorance displayed by the pagans of his time, who are not aware of the fact, to be learned from their own sages, that the Greeks owed most of their knowledge of the sciences and arts to the "barbarians[2]." As against unmodified Judaism, the Christians could find support for some of their own positions in the appeal to religious reformers like Apollonius of Tyana; who, condemning blood-offerings as he did on more radical grounds than themselves, was yet put forward by the apologists of paganism as a half-divine personage. So far did this go that Hierocles, the Proconsul of Bithynia who wrote against the Christians in the time of Diocletian, gave his ecclesiastical antagonist Eusebius occasion to treat the part of his book that dealt with Apollonius as the only part worth replying to. And Porphyry, in whom the Christians saw their most dangerous adversary, himself made a distinct claim to

---

[1] See Keim's reconstruction of the arguments of Celsus from Origen's reply (*Celsus' Wahres Wort*, 1873).

[2] See p. 89 of Neumann's prolegomena to his reconstruction of Julian's work against the Christians, to be spoken of later.

what we should now call religious as distinguished from philosophical liberty in the matter of food and of sacrificing. Nor
was any objection usually raised by the authorities to re-
forming sects that aimed at personal holiness. The Roman
Government even looked upon it as part of its own function
to repress savage rites, such as human sacrifices. Whence
then sprang the repugnance almost uniformly to be observed
in the statesmen, philosophers and men of letters who were
brought into contact with the new religion? For they were
quite prepared to appreciate a monotheistic worship, and to
welcome anything that afforded a real prospect of moral reform.

We might be tempted to find the cause in the want of
culture among ordinary Christians. Julian, for example, who
detested the "uneducated Cynics" of his time, can think of
nothing worse to say of them than that they resemble the
Christian monks (ἀποτακτισταί)[1]. The only difference is that
the Cynics do not make a business of gathering alms; and perhaps this is only because they can find no plausible pretext.
It is those, he adds, who have shown no capacity for rhetorical
or philosophical culture that rush straight to the profession of
Cynicism[2]. Yet, he goes on to admit, there is really, as the
Cynics claimed on their own behalf, a "shorter path" to philosophic virtue than the normal one of intellectual discipline.
The shorter path is, however, the more difficult; requiring
greater and not less vigour of mind and firmness of will. Of
those who took it were the elder Cynics like Diogenes. The
true as distinguished from the false Cynic remained, in fact,
for Julian as for Epictetus, a hero among philosophers. This
was part of the Stoical tradition continued into Neo-Platonism. And, as we know, it was a commonplace with philosophic preachers to make light of mental accomplishments as
compared with moral strength. Besides, the Christians had
among them men of rhetorical training who were not without

---

[1] Or. VII. 224 A–C.

[2] Or. VII. 225 B: τῶν ῥητορικῶν οἱ δυσμαθέστατοι καὶ οὐδ' ὑπ' αὐτοῦ τοῦ βασιλέως
Ἑρμοῦ τὴν γλῶτταν ἐκκαθαρθῆναι δυνάμενοι, φρενωθῆναι δὲ οὐδὲ πρὸς αὐτῆς τῆς
Ἀθηνᾶς σὺν τῷ Ἑρμῇ,…ὁρμῶσιν ἐπὶ τὸν Κυνισμόν.

knowledge of philosophy. The antagonism therefore cannot
be accounted for altogether on this line.

The truth is that the Graeco-Roman world had a perception,
vague at first but gradually becoming clearer, of what was to
be meant by Christian theocracy. When Tacitus spoke of the
"exitiabilis superstitio," he had doubtless come face to face,
as Pro-consul of Asia, with nascent Catholicism. In the fourth
century, the new types of the fanatical monk and the domi-
neering ecclesiastic were definitely in the world, and we may
see by the expressions of Eunapius the intense antipathy they
aroused[1]. Already in the second century, Celsus, while he
treated the Gnostic sects, with their claims to a higher "knowledge," as having a perfect right to the Christian name, was
evidently much more struck by the idea of a common creed
which was to be humbly accepted. This was the distinctive
idea of that which he recognises as the "great Church" among
the Christians. It is remarkable that, in dealing with the
claims of Christianity generally, and not with the strange
tenets of some speculative sects, the defender of the established order in the Roman State treats philosophy as the true
wisdom by which everything is to be tested, and reproaches
the revolutionary innovators on the ground that they say to
their dupes, "Do not examine." Celsus was probably a
Roman official; and he may have seen already some of the
political aims of the new society. For of course the word
"catholic" as applied to the Church was not intended to
remain without a very tangible meaning. The Christian apologists of the second century are already looking forward to
spiritual control over the public force of the Empire[2]. A verse
of the New Testament by which the claim was held to be made
is pointed to by Julian in arguing that the Christians are not
legitimate successors of the Israelites. Christ, according to
the view of the Church, was the prophet that Moses foretold,

---

[1] Eunap. *Vitae* (Aedesius): εἶτα ἐπεισῆγον τοῖς ἱεροῖς τόποις τοὺς καλουμένους
μοναχούς, ἀνθρώπους μὲν κατὰ τὸ εἶδος, ὁ δὲ βίος αὐτοῖς συώδης,...τυραννικὴν γὰρ
εἶχεν ἐξουσίαν τότε πᾶς ἄνθρωπος μέλαιναν φορῶν ἐσθῆτα καὶ δημοσίᾳ βουλόμενος
ἀσχημονεῖν.

[2] See Renan, *Marc-Aurèle*. The alternative imposed by the Church on the
Empire was, Renan says, to persecute or to become a theocracy.

of whom it was said, "that every soul, which will not hear
that prophet, shall be destroyed from among the people"
(Acts iii. 23). The Church possessed the teachings of Christ,
and was a living body with the right to declare them authori-
tatively. The true religion was not now, as under an earlier
dispensation, for one chosen race, but for the whole world.
Hence the whole world was bound to hear and to obey it.
The reply of Julian was that the application of the prediction
supposed to have been made was false. Moses never had the
least idea that his legislation was to be abrogated, but intended it for all time. The prophet he meant was simply a
prophet that should renew his own teaching of the law. The
law was for the Jews only, and the Christians had no claim to
represent them. The Jewish religion had its proper place as
one national religion among others. It was open even to those
who were not born under it to adopt it as their own if they
chose; but they should have submitted to all its obligations.
The care of the Jews about religious observances, and their
readiness to face persecution on behalf of them, are contrasted
by the Emperor in one place with the laxity and indifference
of the Greeks. They are in part pious, he says, worshipping as
they do the God who rules the visible world, whom we also
serve under other names. In this only are they in error, that
they arrogate to themselves alone the worship of the one true
God, and think that to us, "the nations," have been assigned
none but gods whom they themselves do not deign to regard
at all[1].

Julian, we see, had no hostility to Hebrew religion as such.
On the contrary, he agrees with Porphyry in showing special
friendliness to it in so far as its monotheism may be taken to
coincide with that of philosophy. The problem presented to
the Empire by Judaism, so difficult at an earlier period, had
now become manageable through the ending of all political
aspirations on the part of the Jewish community. The question as to the respective merits of Hebrew and Greek religion,
if no new question had arisen, would soon have been reduced

---

[1] Ep. 63 (ed. Hertlein). ἀλαζονείᾳ βαρβαρικῇ, adds Julian, πρὸς ταυτηνὶ τὴν
ἀπόνοιαν ἐπαρθέντες.

to a topic of the schools. The system, at once philosophical
and political, of the classical world in its dealings with religion,
was not of course "religious liberty" in its modern sense. In
a congeries of local worships, mostly without definite creeds,
the question of toleration for dissentients had scarcely arisen.
The position reached by the representatives of ancient thought,
and allowed in practice, was that the national religions might
all be preserved, not only as useful, but as adumbrations of
divine truth. To express that truth adequately is the business
of philosophy and not of popular religion. Philosophy is to be
perfectly free. This is laid down explicitly by Julian[1]. Thus,
according to the system, philosophy is cosmopolitan and is an
unfettered inquiry into truth. Religion is local and is bound
to the performance of customary rites. Those who are in quest
of a deeper knowledge will not think of changing their ancestral religion, but will turn to some philosophical teacher. At
the same time, the religions are to be moralised[2]. Priests are
to be men of exemplary life, and are to be treated with high
respect. The harmony of the whole system had of course been
broken through by Christianity, which, after the period of
attempted repression by force, had now been for more than a
generation the religion of the Empire. Julian's solution of the
problem, renewed by his reversal of the policy of his uncle,
was to grant a formal toleration to all[3]. Both sides are for-
bidden to use violence, which is entirely out of place where
opinions are concerned[4]. Nevertheless, for dignities, "the

---

[1] Or. v. 170 BC. For those of ordinary capacity (τοῖς ἰδιώταις) the utility of
divine myths is sufficiently conveyed through symbols without rational understanding. For those of exceptional intelligence (τοῖς περιττοῖς) there can be
no utility without investigation into truth of reason, continued to the end,
οὐκ αἰδοῖ καὶ πίστει μᾶλλον ἀλλοτρίας δόξης ἢ τῇ σφετέρᾳ κατὰ νοῦν ἐνεργείᾳ.

[2] See Ep. 49. The progress of Hellenism is not sufficient without moral
reform. The example set by the Christians of philanthropy to strangers, and
by the Jews of supporting their own poor, ought to be followed by the Greeks.
Anciently, continues Julian, this belonged to the Hellenic tradition, as is
shown by the words of Eumaeus in the Odyssey (xiv. 56).

[3] The earliest edicts of Constantine had simply proclaimed a toleration of
Christianity; but these, it was well understood, were a mere preliminary to
its acceptance as the State religion. Julian stripped the Church of the
privileges, over and above toleration, which it had acquired in the meantime.

[4] Ep. 52, 438 B: λόγῳ δὲ πείθεσθαι χρὴ καὶ διδάσκεσθαι τοὺς ἀνθρώπους, οὐ

pious"—that is to say, the adherents of the old religions—
are to be preferred[1]. Christians are not allowed to be public
teachers of Grecian letters; the reason assigned being that the
Greek poets, historians and orators treat the gods with honour,
whereas the Christians speak dishonourably of them. It is unworthy of an educated or of a good man to teach one thing
and to think another. Let them either change their views
about the theology of the Greeks or confine themselves to the
exposition of their own[2].

By this policy there is no reason to think that the Emperor
was putting back a process by which captive Greece might
again have led the conqueror captive. The Church absolutely
needed the elements of culture if it was to rule the world; and
it could find them only in the classical tradition. It was now
in more or less conscious possession of its own system, which
was precisely the antithesis of the system which Julian desired
to restore. A religion had been revealed which claimed to be
true for all. Philosophy, so far as it was serviceable, could be
treated as a preparation for it or as an instrument in defining
its doctrines, but could have no independent standing-ground.
Letters, in the hands of ecclesiastics, could furnish the grammatical and rhetorical training without which the reign of a
"spiritual power" would have been impossible. The new
system, however, was as yet far from being fully at work.
Christian pupils, we must remember, continued to frequent
the pagan schools much later. Thus there was evidently no
insuperable prejudice by which they would have been universally excluded from a liberal education not subjugated to ecclesiastical authority. If then by any possibility the advance
of the theocratic idea could have been checked, it is clear that
the Emperor took exactly the right measures. The classical
authors were to be seen, so far as public authority could secure
it, under the light of the tradition to which they themselves

πληγαῖς οὐδὲ ὕβρεσιν οὐδὲ αἰκισμῷ τοῦ σώματος. αὖθις δὲ καὶ πολλάκις παραινῶ
τοῖς ἐπὶ τὴν ἀληθῆ θεοσέβειαν ὁρμωμένοις μηδὲν ἀδικεῖν τῶν Γαλιλαίων τὰ πλήθη,
μηδὲ ἐπιτίθεσθαι μηδὲ ὑβρίζειν εἰς αὐτούς.

[1] Ep. 7, 376 c: προτιμᾶσθαι μέντοι τοὺς θεοσεβεῖς καὶ πάνυ φημὶ δεῖν.

[2] Ep. 42.

belonged. Pupils were not to be systematically taught in the
schools of the Empire that the pagan gods were "evil demons,"
and that the heroes and sages of antiquity were among the
damned. And, hopeless as the defeated party henceforth was
of a change of fortune, Julian's memory furnished a rallying-
point for those who now devoted themselves to the preservation of the older culture interpreted by itself. Marinus, in
writing the biography of Proclus, dates his death "in the
124th year from the reign of Julian." Thus the actual effect
of his resistance to that system of ecclesiastical rule which
afterwards, to those who again knew the civic type of life,
appeared as a "Kingdom of Darkness," may have been to
prolong the evening twilight.

All who have studied the career of Julian recognise that his
great aim was to preserve "Hellenism," by which he meant
Hellenic civilisation. Of this the ancient religion was for him
the symbol. The myths about the gods are not to be taken
literally. The marriage of Hyperion and Thea, for example, is
a poetic fable[1]. What the poets say, along with the divine
element in it, has also much that is human[2]. Pure truth,
unmixed with fable, is to be found in the philosophers, and
especially in Plato[3]. On the Jewish religion, the Emperor's
position sometimes appears ambiguous. He easily finds, in the
Old Testament, passages from which to argue that the God of
Israel is simply a tribal god like those of the nations. His
serious opinion, however, seems to have been that the Hebrew
prophets had arrived at an expression, less pure indeed than
that of the Greek philosophers, but quite real, of the unity of

---

[1] Or. IV. 136 C: μὴ δὲ συνδυασμὸν μηδὲ γάμους ὑπολαμβάνωμεν, ἄπιστα καὶ
παράδοξα τῆς ποιητικῆς μούσης ἀθύρματα.

[2] Ib. 137 C: ἀλλὰ τὰ μὲν τῶν ποιητῶν χαίρειν ἐάσωμεν· ἔχει γὰρ μετὰ τοῦ θείου
πολὺ καὶ τὸ ἀνθρώπινον.

[3] Julian, however, like the Neo-Platonists generally, is unwilling to allow
that Plato could ever have intended to treat the poetic legends with dis-
respect. In Or. VII. 237 BC, he cites as an example of εὐλάβεια περὶ τὰ τῶν θεῶν
ὀνόματα, the well-known passage in the Timaeus, 40 D, about the gods that
have left descendants among us, whom we cannot refuse to believe when they
tell us of their own ancestors. This, he says, might have been ironical (as
evidently many took it to be) if put in the mouth of Socrates; but Timaeus,
to whom it is actually assigned, had no reputation for irony.

divine government[1]. In one passage—than which no better
could be found to illustrate the antithesis between "Hebra-
ism" and "Hellenism"—he compares them to men seeing a
great light as through a mist, and unable to describe what
they see except by imagery drawn from the destructive force
of fire[2]. While himself regarding the divinity as invisible and
incorporeal, he treats as prejudice their denunciations of the
making of statues. The kind of truth he would recognise in
popular polytheism he finds not altogether inconsistent with
the Hebrew Scriptures, which speak of the angels of nations.
National deities, whether to be called angels or gods, are interpreted as a kind of genius of each race. The various natural
aptitudes of peoples suppose a variety in the divine cause, and
this can be expressed as a distribution made by the supreme
God to subordinate powers[3]. That is the position taken up by
Julian in his book against the Christians—which is at the
same time a defence of Hellenism. From the fragments contained in Cyril's reply—of which perhaps half survives—it has
been beautifully reconstructed by C. J. Neumann[4]. A summary of the general argument will serve better than anything
else to make clear the spiritual difference that separated from
their Christian contemporaries the men who had received their
bent in the philosophic schools.

Evidently neither Julian's work nor any other was felt to
be so peculiarly damaging as Porphyry's. By a decree of the
Council of Ephesus (431) and by a law of Theodosius II. (448),
Porphyry's books, though not those of Celsus, Hierocles or
Julian, were sentenced to be burned. In the changed form of
the law in Justinian's code, the books written by any one else
to the same purpose (κατὰ τῆς εὐσεβοῦς τῶν Χριστιανῶν

---

[1] Cf. Ep. 25.

[2] *Fragmentum Epistolae*, 296 A : οἷον φῶς μέγα δι᾽ ὁμίχλης οἱ ἄνθρωποι βλέποντες
οὐ καθαρῶς οὐδὲ εἰλικρινῶς, αὐτὸ δὲ ἐκεῖνο νενομικότες οὐχὶ φῶς καθαρόν, ἀλλὰ πῦρ,
καὶ τῶν περὶ αὐτὸ πάντων ὄντες ἀθέατοι βοῶσι μέγα · Φρίττετε, φοβεῖσθε, πῦρ, φλόξ,
θάνατος, μάχαιρα, ῥομφαία, πολλοῖς ὀνόμασι μίαν ἐξηγούμενοι τὴν βλαπτικὴν τοῦ
πυρὸς δύναμιν.

[3] This idea, which we meet with also in Celsus, appears to have been
suggested by a passage in the *Critias*, where such a distribution is described.
Cf. Procl. *in Remp.*, ed. Kroll, i. 17.

[4] *Iuliani Imperatoris Librorum contra Christianos quae supersunt* (1880).

θρησκείας) are brought under the decree, but not by name[1]. The difference between Julian's line of attack and Porphyry's, so far as it can be made out, is that Julian, while much that he too says has an interest from its bearing on questions of Biblical criticism, pays no special attention to the analysis of documents. He takes for granted the traditional ascriptions of the Canonical books, and uniformly quotes the Septuagint. Porphyry is said to have known the Hebrew original. We have already met with his view on the Book of Daniel; and so characteristic was his inquiry into questions of authorship and chronology, that Neumann is inclined to refer to him an assertion of the late and non-Mosaic origin of the Pentateuch, quoted by Macarius Magnes about the end of the fourth century from an unknown philosopher[2]. What line was taken either by Julian or by Porphyry on the primitive teaching of Christianity itself, hardly anything remains to show. Of Porphyry, as was said, all the express refutations have disappeared; and of the later books of Cyril's reply to Julian there are left only a few fragments. We learn from one of these[3] that the Catholic saint, with his expert's knowledge of the text, pointed out that the saying "Father, forgive them" in Luke xxiii. 34 is spurious. "The Apostate" had apparently quoted it against anticipations of the mediaeval treatment of the Jews. On the cult of martyrs, the Bishop of Alexandria's reply is not without point, as Julian would have been the first to allow[4]. The Greeks themselves, he says[5], go in procession to the tombs and celebrate the praises of those who fought for Greece; yet they do not worship them as gods. No more do we offer to our martyrs the worship due to God, nor do we pray to them. Moreover, the gods of the Gentiles were men who were born and died, and the tombs of some of them remain. Connected with this recurrence to the "Euhemerism"

---

[1] Neumann, *Prolegomena*, pp. 8–9.

[2] Neumann, *Prolegomena*, p. 20: Μωυσέως οὐδὲν ἀποσώζεται. συγγράμματα γὰρ πάντα συνεμπεπρῆσθαι τῷ ναῷ λέγεται. ὅσα δ᾽ ἐπ᾽ ὀνόματι Μωυσέως ἐγράφη μετὰ ταῦτα, μετὰ χίλια καὶ ἑκατὸν καὶ ὀγδοήκοντα ἔτη τῆς Μωυσέως τελευτῆς ὑπὸ ῞Εσδρα καὶ τῶν ἀμφ᾽ αὐτὸν συνεγράφη.

[3] Neumann, pp. 69, 130–1.

[4] Cf. Ep. 78.   [5] Neumann, pp. 85–6.

which the Christian Fathers sometimes borrowed from Greek speculators on the origin of religion, is a quotation from Porphyry's Life of Pythagoras; introduced, Neumann conjectures (p. 80), to prove that the Greeks had no right to be incredulous about the declaration (1 Peter iii. 19, 20) that Christ preached to the spirits in prison; since Pythagoras is represented as having descended into the Idaean cave (here apparently identified with the underworld) where the tomb of Jupiter was.

On the relation of Christianity to its Hebrew origins, and on these as compared with the poetry and philosophy of Greece, a coherent account of Julian's view can be put together. He seems to have begun by speaking of the intuitive knowledge men have of God. To such knowledge, he says,—perhaps with an allusion to the elements of Gnostic pessimism that had found their way into orthodox Christianity,—has usually been attached the conviction that the heavens, as distinguished from the earth, are a diviner part of the universe, though it is not meant by this that the earth is excluded from divine care. He entirely repudiates the fables about Cronos swallowing his children, and about the incestuous marriages of Zeus, and so forth. But, he proceeds, the story of the Garden of Eden is equally mythical. Unless it has some secret meaning, it is full of blasphemy, since it represents God as forbidding to his creatures that knowledge of good and evil which alone is the bond of human intelligence, and as envious of their possible immortality. In what do stories like that of the talking serpent—according to the account, the real benefactor of the human race—differ from those invented by the Greeks? Compare the Mosaic with the Platonic cosmogony, and its speculative weakness becomes plain. In the language of the Book of Genesis there is no accurate definition. Some things, we are told, God commanded to come into being; others he "made"; others he separated out. As to the Spirit ($\pi\nu\epsilon\hat{\upsilon}\mu a$) of God, there is no clear determination whether it was made, or came to be, or is eternal without generation. According to Moses, if we are to argue from what he says explicitly[1], God is

---

[1] Angels, Julian contends elsewhere, are the equivalents, in the Hebrew

not the creator of anything incorporeal, but is only a shaper of underlying matter. According to Plato, on the other hand, the intelligible and invisible gods of which the visible sun and moon and stars are images, proceed from the Demiurgus, as does also the rational soul of man. Who then speaks better and more worthily of God, the "idolater" Plato, or he of whom the Scripture says that God spoke with him mouth to mouth?

Contrast now the opinions of the Hebrews and of the Greeks about the relations of the Creator to the various races of mankind. According to Moses and all who have followed the Hebrew tradition, the Creator of the world chose the Hebrews for his own people, and cared for them only. Moses has nothing to say about the divine government of other nations, unless one should concede that he assigns to them the sun and moon for deities (Deut. iv. 19). Paul changes in an elusive manner[1]; but if, as he says sometimes (Rom. iii. 29), God is not the God of the Jews only, why did he neglect so long all but one small nation settled less than two thousand years ago in a portion of Palestine? Our teachers say that their creator is the common father and king of all, and that the peoples are distributed by him to presiding deities, each of whom rules over his allotted nation or city. In the Father, all things are perfect and all things are one; in the divided portions, one power is predominant here, another there. Thus Ares is said to rule over warlike nations, Athena over those that are warlike with wisdom, and so forth. Let the appeal be to the facts. Do not these differences in the characters of nations exist? And it cannot be said that the differences in the parts are uncaused without denying that providence governs the whole. Human laws are not the cause of them, for it is by the natural characters of men that the laws peculiar to each people are determined. Legislators by the lead they give can do little in

Scriptures, of the gods of polytheism. No doubt Moses held that they were produced by divine power, and were not independently existing beings; but, pre-eminent as their rank in the universe must be, he has no account to give of them in his cosmogony, where we should have expected to find one.

[1] The words are given from Cyril by Neumann (p. 177, 11): ὥσπερ οἱ πολύποδες πρὸς τὰς πέτρας.

comparison with nature and custom. Take the case of the
Western races. Though they have been so long under Roman
rule, you find extremely few among them showing aptitude
for philosophy or geometry or any of the sciences. The
cleverest appreciate only debate and oratory, and concern
themselves with no other branch of knowledge. So strong is
nature.

The cause assigned by Moses for the diversity of languages
is altogether mythical. And yet those who demand that the
Greeks should believe the story of the tower of Babel, themselves disbelieve what Homer tells about the Aloadae, how
they thought to pile three mountains on one another, $\ddot{\iota}\nu'$ οὐρανὸς
ἀμβατὸς εἴη[1]. One story is neither more nor less fabulous than
the other. While Moses thus tries to account for the varieties
of human speech, neither he nor any of his successors has a
clear cause to assign for the diversity of manners and customs
and constitutions, which is greater than that of languages.
What need to go through the particulars: the freedom-loving
and insubordinate ways of the German tribes; the submissive-
ness and tameness of the Syrians and Persians and Parthians,
and, in a word, of all the barbarians towards the East and the
South?

How can a God who takes no providential care for human
interests like those of legal and political order, and who has
sent no teachers or legislators except to the Hebrews, claim
reverence or gratitude from those whose good, both mental
and physical, he has thus left to chance? But let us see
whether the Creator of the world—be he the same as the God
of the Hebrews or not—has so neglected all other men.

First, however, the point must be insisted on, that it is not
sufficient in assigning the cause of a thing to say that God
commanded it. The natures of the things that come into
existence must be in conformity with the commands of God.
If fire is to be borne upwards and earth downwards, fire must
be light and earth heavy. Similarly, if there are to be differences of speech and political constitution, they must be in

[1] *Od.* xi. 316.

accordance with pre-existing differences of nature. Any one who will look may see how much Germans. and Scythians differ in body from Libyans and Aethiopians. Is this also a mere command? Do not air too and geographical situation act together with the gods to produce a certain complexion? In reality, the commands of God are either the natures of things or accordant with the natures of things. To suppose these natural diversities all ordered under a divine government appropriate to each, is to have a better opinion of the God announced by Moses, if he is indeed the Lord of all, than that of Hebrew and Christian exclusiveness.

Julian now turns to the detailed comparison. The admired decalogue, he observes, contains no commandments not recognised by all nations, except to have no other gods and to keep the Sabbath Day. For the transgression of the rest, penalties are imposed everywhere, sometimes harsher, sometimes milder, sometimes much the same as those of the Mosaic law. The commandment to worship no other gods has joined with it the slander that God is jealous. The philosophers tell us to imitate the gods as far as possible; and they say that we can imitate them by contemplating the things that exist and so making ourselves free from passion. But what is the imitation of God celebrated among the Hebrews? Wrath and anger and savage zeal. Take the instance of Phinehas (Num. xxv. 11), who is represented as turning aside God's wrath by being jealous along with him.

In proof that God did not care only for the Hebrews, consider the various gifts bestowed on other peoples. Were the beginnings of knowledge given to the chosen race? The theory of celestial phenomena was brought to completion by the Greeks after the first observations had been made in Babylon. The science of geometry, taking its origin from the art of mensuration in Egypt, grew to its present magnitude. The study of numbers, beginning from the Phoenician merchants, at length assumed the form of scientific knowledge among the Greeks, who, combining this science with the others, discovered the laws of musical intervals.

Shall I, the Emperor continues, mention the names of

illustrious Greeks as they occur, or bring them under the
various heads,—philosophers, generals, artificers, lawgivers?
The hardest and cruellest of the generals will be found dealing
more leniently with those who have committed the greatest
crimes than Moses with perfectly unoffending people. Other
nations have not wanted legislators in sacred things. The
Romans, for example, have their Numa, who also delivered
his laws under divine inspiration. The spirit from the gods,
Julian allows in a digression, comes seldom and to few among
men. Hebrew prophecy has ceased; none remains among the
Egyptians; the indigenous oracles of Greece have yielded to
the revolutions of time and are silent. You, he says, turning
to the Christians, had no cause to desert us and go over to the
Hebrews for any greater gifts they have to boast of from God;
and yet, having done so, you would have done well to adhere
to their discipline with exactitude. You would not then have
worshipped, not merely one, but many dead men. You would
have been under a harsh law with much of the barbarous in it,
instead of our mild and humane laws, and would have been
worse in most things though better as regards religious purity
(ἀγνότεροι δὲ καὶ καθαρώτεροι τὰς ἁγιστείας). But now you do
not even know whether Jesus spoke of purity. You emulate
the angry spirit and bitterness of the Jews, overturning temples and altars and slaughtering not only those who remain
true to their paternal religion but also the heretics among
yourselves[1]. These things, however, belong to you and not to
your teachers. Nowhere did Jesus leave you such commands
or Paul.

---

[1] Cf. Ep. 52, where Julian recalls several massacres of "the so-called
heretics" (τῶν λεγομένων αἱρετικῶν) in the reign of his predecessor Constantius.
Those who are called clerics, he says, are not content with impunity for their
past misdeeds; but craving the lordship they had before, when they could
deliver judgments and write wills and appropriate the portions of others, they
pull every string of disorder and add fuel to the flames (πάντα κινοῦσιν ἀκοσμίας
κάλων καὶ τὸ λεγόμενον πῦρ ἐπὶ πῦρ ὀχετεύουσι). At the opening of the epistle, he
professes to find that he was mistaken in the thought that "the rulers of the
Galilaeans" would regard him more favourably than his Arian predecessor,
under whom they were banished and imprisoned and had their goods con-
fiscated; whereas he himself has repealed their sentences and restored to them
their own.

To return: the gods gave Rome the empire; to the Jews they granted only for a short time to be free; for the most part, they made them alien sojourners and subject to other nations. In war, in civil government, in the fine and useful arts, in the liberal sciences, there is hardly a name to be mentioned among the Hebrews. Solomon, who is celebrated among them for his wisdom, served other gods, deceived by his wife (ὑπὸ τῆς γυναικός), they say. This, if it were so, would not be a mark of wisdom; but may he not have paid due honour to the religions of the rest of the world by his own judgment and by the instruction of the God who manifested himself to him? For envy and jealousy are so far from angels and gods that they do not extend even to the best men, but belong only to the demons.

If the reading of your own scriptures is sufficient for you, why do you nibble at Greek learning? Why, having gone over to the Hebrews, do you depart further from what their prophets declare than from our own manners? The Jewish ritual is very exact, and requires a sacerdotal life and profession to fulfil it. The lawgiver bids you serve only one God, but he adds that you shall "not revile the gods" (Exod. xxii. 28). The brutality of those who came after thought that not serving them ought to be accompanied by blaspheming them. This you have taken from the Jews. From us you have taken the permission to eat of everything. That the earliest Christian converts were much the same as those of to-day is proved by what Paul says of them (1 Cor. vi. 9–11). Baptism, of which the Apostle speaks as the remedy, will not even wash off diseases and disfigurements from the body. Will it then remove every kind of transgression out of the soul?

The Christians, however, say that, while they differ from the present Jews, they are in strictness Israelites according to the prophets, and agree with Moses and those who followed him. They say, for example, that Moses foretold Christ. But Moses repeatedly declares that one God only is to be honoured. It is true that he mentions angels, and admits many gods in this sense; but he allows no second God comparable with the first. The sayings usually quoted by the Christians from Moses and

Isaiah have no application to the son of Mary[1]. Moses speaks
of angels as the sons of God (Gen. vi. 2); Israel is called the
firstborn son of God (Exod. iv. 22), and many sons of God
(*i.e.* angels) are recognised as having the nations for their
portion; but nothing is said of a Firstborn Son of God, or
θεὸς λόγος, in the sense of the Christian doctrine.

At this point comes a disquisition on the agreement, in all
but a few things, of Hebrew and of Greek religion. According
to Cyril, Julian argued that Moses commanded an offering, in
the form of the scapegoat (Levit. xvi. 8), to unclean demons
(μιαροῖς καὶ ἀποτροπαίοις δαίμοσι). In not following the
general custom of sacrificing, the Christians stand apart from
the Jews as well as from all other nations. But the Jews, they
will say, do not sacrifice. The reason, however, is that they do
not think it lawful for them to sacrifice except at Jerusalem,
and that they have been deprived of their temple. And they
still keep up customs which are in effect sacrificial, and abstain
from some kinds of meat. All this the Christians neglect.
That the law in these matters was at some future time to be
annulled, there is not the slightest suggestion in the books of
Moses. On the contrary, the legislator distinctly declares that
it is to be perpetual.

That Jesus is God neither Paul nor Matthew nor Luke nor
Mark ventured to assert. The assertion was first made—not
quite distinctly, though there is no doubt about the meaning—
by the worthy John, who perceived that a great multitude in
many of the Grecian and Italian cities was taken hold of by
this malady[2], and who had heard, as may be supposed, that
the tombs of Peter and Paul were secretly objects of adoration

---

[1] A more exact discussion of them was left over for the second part, to
which Cyril's reply has not been preserved. The point is made in passing
that anything which may be said of a ruler from Judah (Gen. xlix. 10) can
have no reference to Jesus, since, according to the Christians, he was not the
son of Joseph but of the Holy Spirit. Besides, the genealogies of Matthew
and Luke, tracing the descent of Joseph from Judah, are discrepant.

[2] What Julian has in view here is not any and every form of apotheosis,
but, as the context shows, the devotion to corpses and relics, which seemed
to him to distinguish the Christians from Jews and Greeks alike. In Ep. 49
he even commends their care about tombs.

at Rome. In their adoration of tombs and sepulchres, the Christians do not listen to the words of Jesus of Nazareth, who said they were full of all uncleanness (Matth. xxiii. 27). Whence this comes, the prophet Isaiah shall say. It is the old superstition of those who "remain among the graves, and lodge in the monuments" (Is. lxv. 4), for the purpose of divining by dreams. This art the apostles most likely practised after their master's end, and handed it down to their successors.

And you, Julian proceeds, who practise things which God abominated from the beginning through Moses and the prophets, yet refuse to offer sacrifices. Thence he returns to the point that, if the Christians would be true Israelites, they ought to follow the Jewish customs, and that these on the whole agree more with the customs of "the Gentiles" than with their own. Approval of animal sacrifices is clearly implied in the account of the offerings of Cain and Abel. Circumcision, which was enjoined on Abraham and his seed for ever, the Christians do not practise, though Christ said that he was not come to destroy the law. "We circumcise our hearts," they say. By all means, replies Julian, for none among you is an evildoer, none is wicked; thus you circumcise your hearts. Abraham, he goes on to interpret the account in Genesis xv., practised divination from shooting-stars (v. 5), and augury from the flight of birds (v. 11). The merit of his faith therefore consisted not in believing without but with a sign of the truth of the promise made to him. Faith without truth is foolishness.

Incomplete as the reconstruction necessarily remains, there is enough to show the general line the Emperor took. It was to deny any ground, in the Old Testament as it stood, for the idea of Christianity as a universalised Judaism. All else is incidental to this. If then no religion was meant to be universal, but Judaism, in so far as it excludes other religions, is only for Jews, the idea of Christian theocracy loses its credentials. Divine government is not through a special society teaching an authoritative doctrine, but through the order of the visible universe and all the variety of civic and national institutions in the world. The underlying harmony of these is to be sought out by free examination, which is philosophy. Of philosophy, accordingly, and not of polytheism as such, Julian was the champion. And if the system he opposed did not succeed in finally subjugating the philosophy and culture for which he cared, that was due not to any modification in the aims and ideals of its chiefs, but to the revival of forces which in their turn broke the unity of the cosmopolitan Church as the Church had broken the unity of the Roman State.

CHAPTER IX

THE ATHENIAN SCHOOL

1. *The Academy becomes Neo-Platonic.*

About the opening of the fifth century, the chair of Plato was occupied by Plutarch, an Athenian by birth and the first distinguished representative at Athens of Neo-Platonism. By what particular way the Neo-Platonic doctrine had reached Athens is unknown; but Plutarch and the "Platonic successors" (Διάδοχοι Πλατωνικοί) who followed him, connected themselves directly with the school of Iamblichus, and through Iamblichus with Porphyry and Plotinus. Their entrance on the new line of thought was to be the beginning of a revival of philosophical and scientific activity which continued till the succession was closed by the edict of Justinian in 529. Strictly, it may be said to have continued a little longer; for the latest works of the school at Athens were written some years after that date. From that year, however, no other teacher was allowed to profess Hellenic philosophy publicly; so that it may with sufficient accuracy be taken as fixing the end of the Academy, and with it of the ancient schools.

Approximately coincident with the first phase of the revival at Athens, was the brilliant episode of the school at Alexandria, where Neo-Platonism was now taught by Hypatia as its authorised exponent. Of her writings nothing remains, though the titles of some mathematical ones are preserved. What is known is that she followed the tradition of Iamblichus, whose doctrines appear in the works of her pupil and correspondent Synesius. Her fate in 415 at the hands of the Alexandrian monks, under the patriarchate of Cyril (as recorded by the ecclesiastical historian Socrates), was not followed immediately by the cessation of the Alexandrian chair of philosophy, which indeed continued to have occupants longer than any other. Between 415 and 450, Hierocles, the author of the

commentary on the Pythagorean *Golden Verses*, still professed
Neo-Platonism. He was a pupil of Plutarch at Athens, but
took up the office of teacher at Alexandria, of which he was
a native. He too was an adherent of the old religion; and, for
something he had said that was thought disrespectful towards
the new, he was sentenced by a Christian magistrate of Constantinople to be scourged[1]. Several more names of Alexandrian commentators are recorded; ending with Olympiodorus
in the latter part of the sixth century[2]. All these names, however,—beginning with Hierocles,—belong in reality to the
Athenian succession[3].

Plutarch died at an advanced age in 431. His successor
was Syrianus of Alexandria, who had been his pupil and for
some time his associate in the chair. Among the opinions of
Plutarch, it is recorded that with Iamblichus he extends immortality to the irrational part of the soul, whereas Proclus
and Porphyry limit it to the rational part[4]. A psychological
position afterwards developed by Proclus may be noted in his
mode of defining the place of imagination (φαντασία) between

---

[1] See the note, pp. 9–10, in Gaisford's edition of the Commentary on the
Golden Verses, appended as a second volume to his edition of the Eclogues of
Stobaeus (Oxford, 1850).

[2] See Zeller, iii. 2, p. 852, n. 1, where it is shown that Olympiodorus the
commentator on Plato is identical with the Olympiodorus who wrote (later
than 564) the commentary on Aristotle's Meteorology. Olympiodorus the
Aristotelian teacher of Proclus at Alexandria is of course much earlier.

[3] In one of his commentaries, Olympiodorus remarks that the succession
still continues in spite of the many confiscations (καὶ ταῦτα πολλῶν δημεύσεων
γινομένων). This, according to Zeller, refers to the succession at Alexandria,
not at Athens; but all the Alexandrian teachers of this last period received
their philosophical inspiration, directly or indirectly, from the occupants of
the chair at Athens, and in that way come within the Athenian school.

[4] See the quotation from Olympiodorus given by Zeller, ii. 1, p. 1008, n. 4,
where the views of different philosophers on this subject are compactly stated.
For its convenience as a conspectus, it may be given here; though qualifica-
tions are needed when we come to the subtleties, as will be seen in the case of
Proclus. Olympiodor. *in Phaed.* p. 98 Finckh: ὅτι οἱ μὲν ἀπὸ τῆς λογικῆς
ψυχῆς ἄχρι τῆς ἐμψύχου ἕξεως ἀπαθανατίζουσιν, ὡς Νουμήνιος· οἱ δὲ μέχρι τῆς
φύσεως, ὡς Πλωτῖνος ἔνι ὅπου· οἱ δὲ μέχρι τῆς ἀλογίας, ὡς τῶν μὲν παλαιῶν
Ξενοκράτης καὶ Σπεύσιππος, τῶν δὲ νεωτέρων Ἰάμβλιχος καὶ Πλούταρχος· οἱ δὲ
μέχρι μόνης τῆς λογικῆς, ὡς Πρόκλος καὶ Πορφύριος· οἱ δὲ μέχρι μόνου τοῦ νοῦ,
φθείρουσι γὰρ τὴν δόξαν, ὡς πολλοὶ τῶν Περιπατητικῶν· οἱ δὲ μέχρι τῆς ὅλης
ψυχῆς, φθείρουσι γὰρ τὰς μερικὰς εἰς τὴν ὅλην.

thought and perception[1]. By Plutarch first, and then by
Syrianus, the use of Aristotle as an introduction to Plato, with
insistence on their agreements rather than on their differences,
was made systematic in the school. Most of its activity henceforth takes the form of exceedingly elaborate critical commentaries[2]. It is not that originality or the recognition of it altogether ceases. When any philosopher introduces a distinctly
new point of view, it is mentioned in his honour by his successors. In the main, however, the effort was towards systematising what had been done. This was the work specially
reserved for the untiring activity of Proclus.

2. *Proclus.*

We now come to the last great name among the Neo-
Platonists. After Plotinus, Proclus was undoubtedly the most
original thinker, as well as the ablest systematiser, of the
school. His abilities were early recognised, and the story of
an omen that occurred on his arrival at Athens was treasured
up. He had lingered outside and arrived at the Acropolis a
little late, as his biographer records[3]; and the porter said to
him, "If you had not come, I should have shut the gates."
His life was written by his successor in the Academic chair,
some time before the decree of Justinian; so that this anecdote
has the interest of showing what the feeling already was in the
school about its prospects for the future.

Proclus (or Proculus) was born at Constantinople in 410, but
was of a Lycian family. His father was a jurist; and he himself studied at Alexandria first rhetoric and Roman law, afterwards mathematics and philosophy. Under Olympiodorus, his

---

[1] Philop. de An. (Zeller, iii. 2, p. 751, n. 2). τῶν μὲν αἰσθητῶν τὸ διῃρημένον
εἰς ἓν συναθροίζει, τὸ δὲ τῶν θείων ἁπλοῦν καὶ ὡς ἄν τις εἴποι ἑνικὸν εἰς τύπους
τινὰς καὶ μορφὰς διαφόρους ἀναμάττεται.

[2] Plutarch wrote an important commentary on Aristotle's *De Anima*.
Between the commentary of Alexander of Aphrodisias (fl. 200) and that of
Plutarch, says Zeller (iii. 2, p. 749, n. 4), none is on record except the para-
phrase of Themistius. Syrianus, besides many other commentaries, wrote
one on the *Metaphysics*. The portions formerly published are referred to by
Vacherot, *Histoire Critique de l'École d'Alexandrie*, t. ii. livre iii. ch. 1, and
Zeller, iii. 2, p. 761, n. 2. A complete edition by W. Kroll appeared in 1902.

[3] Marinus, *Vita Procli*, c. 10.

Alexandrian teacher, he rapidly acquired proficiency in the Aristotelian logic. Becoming dissatisfied with the philosophical teaching at Alexandria, he went to Athens when he was not quite twenty. There he was instructed both by Syrianus and by Plutarch, who, notwithstanding his great age, was willing to continue his teaching for the sake of a pupil of such promise. At that time Proclus abstained severely from animal food, and Plutarch advised him to eat a little flesh, but without avail; Syrianus for his part approving of this rigour[1]. His abstinence remained all but complete throughout his life. When he deviated from it, it was only to avoid the appearance of singularity[2]. By his twenty-eighth year he had written his commentary on the *Timaeus*, in addition to many other treatises. According to Marinus, he exercised influence on public affairs; but he was once obliged to leave Athens for a year. The school secretly adhered to the ancient religion, the practice of which was of course now illegal. His year's exile Proclus spent in acquiring a more exact knowledge of the ancient religious rites of Lycia[3]. Marinus describes him as an illustration of the happiness of the sage in the type of perfection conceived of by Aristotle—for he enjoyed external good fortune and lived to the full period of human life—and as a model of the ascetic virtues in the ideal form set forth by Plotinus. He was of a temper at once hasty and placable; and examples are given of his practical sympathy with his friends[4]. Besides his originality and critical spirit in philosophy, his proficiency in theurgy is celebrated[5], and various marvels are related of him. He died at Athens in 485[6].

The saying of Proclus has often been quoted from his biography, that the philosopher ought not to observe the religious customs of one city or country only, but to be the common

---

[1] Marinus, *Vita Procli*, c. 12.

[2] *Ibid.*, 19: εἰ δέ ποτε καιρός τις ἰσχυρότερος ἐπὶ τὴν τούτων (sc. τῶν ἐμψύχων) χρῆσιν ἐκάλει, μόνον ἀπεγεύετο, καὶ τοῦτο ὁσίας χάριν.

[3] *Ibid.*, 15.   [4] *Ibid.*, 17.   [5] *Ibid.*, 28.

[6] The dates of his birth and death are fixed by the statement of Marinus (c. 36) that he died, at the age of 75, "in the 124th year from the reign of Julian." This, as Zeller shows (iii. 2, p. 776, n. 1), must be referred to the beginning and not to the end of Julian's reign.

hierophant of the whole world. The closeness, however, with which he anticipated in idea Comte's Religion of Humanity, does not seem to have been noticed. First, we are told that he practised the ceremonial abstinences prescribed for the sacred days of all religions, adding certain special days fixed by the appearance of the moon[1]. In a later chapter, Marinus tells us about his cult of the dead. Every year, on certain days, he visited the tombs of the Attic heroes, then of the philosophers, then of his friends and connexions generally. After performing the customary rites, he went away to the Academy; where he poured libations first to the souls of his kindred and race, then to those of all philosophers, finally to those of all men. The last observance corresponds precisely to the Positivist "Day of All the Dead," and indeed is described by Marinus almost in the identical words[2].

A saying quoted with not less frequency than that referred to above, is the declaration of Proclus that if it were in his power he would withdraw from the knowledge of men for the present all ancient books except the *Timaeus* and the Sacred Oracles[3]. The reason he gave was that persons coming to them without preparation are injured; but the manner in which the aspiration was soon to be fulfilled in the Western world[4] suggests that the philosopher had a deeper reason. May he not have seen the necessity of a break in culture if a new line of intellectual development was ever to be struck

---

[1] Marinus, 19: καὶ ἰδικώτερον δέ τινας ἐνήστευσεν ἡμέρας ἐξ ἐπιφανείας. The note in Cousin's edition (*Procli Opera Inedita*, Paris, 1864) seems to give the right interpretation: "'Εξ ἐπιφανείας, *ex apparentia*, scilicet *lunae*, ut monet Fabricius et indicant quae sequuntur." Zeller (iii. 2, p. 784, n. 5) refers the observance to special revelations from the gods to Proclus himself.

[2] *Ibid.*, 36: καὶ ἐπὶ πᾶσι τούτοις ὁ εὐαγέστατος τρίτον ἄλλον περιγράψας τόπον, πάσαις ἐν αὐτῷ ταῖς τῶν ἀποιχομένων ἀνθρώπων ψυχαῖς ἀφωσιοῦτο.

[3] *Ibid.*, 38: εἰώθει δὲ πολλάκις καὶ τοῦτο λέγειν, ὅτι ' Κύριος εἰ ἦν, μόνα ἂν τῶν ἀρχαίων ἀπάντων βιβλίων ἐποίουν φέρεσθαι τὰ Λόγια καὶ τὸν Τίμαιον, τὰ δὲ ἄλλα ἠφάνιζον ἐκ τῶν νῦν ἀνθρώπων.'

[4] Corresponding to the Oracles, which Proclus would have kept still current, were of course in the West the Hebrew and Christian Scriptures and the Fathers. Of these he was not thinking; but, curiously, along with the few compendia of logic and "the liberal arts" which furnished almost the sole elements of European culture for centuries, there was preserved a fragment of the *Timaeus* in Latin translation.

out? He and his school, indeed, devoted themselves to the task, not of effacing accumulated knowledge for a time, but of storing it up. Still, in the latter part of the period, they must have been consciously preserving it for a dimly foreseen future rather than for the next age. Whatever may have been the intention of the utterance, it did as a matter of fact prefigure the conditions under which a new culture was to be evolved in the West.

That the Neo-Platonists had in some respects more of Hellenic moderation than Plato has been indicated already; and this may be noted especially in the case of Proclus, who on occasion protests against what is overstrained in the Platonic ethics. His biographer takes care to show that he possessed and exercised the political as a basis for the "cathartic" virtues[1]. And while ascetic and contemplative virtue, in his view as in that of all the school, is higher than practical virtue, its conditions, he points out, are not to be imposed on the active life. Thus he is able to defend Homer's manner of describing his heroes. The soul of Achilles in Hades is rightly represented as still desiring association with the body, because that is the condition for the display of practical virtue. Men living the practical life could not live it strenuously if they were not intensely moved by feelings that have reference to particular persons and things. The heroic character, therefore, while it is apt for great deeds, is also subject to grief. Plato himself would have to be expelled from his own ideal State for the variety of his dramatic imitations. Only in societies falling short of that severe simplicity could lifelike representations of buffoons and men of inferior moral type, such as we meet with in Plato, be allowed. Besides, he varies from one dialogue to another in the opinions he seems to be conveying, and so himself departs from his ideal. Where Plato then is admitted, there is no reason why Homer too should not be admitted[2].

---

[1] Marinus, 14–17.

[2] The defence of Homer is to be found in the Commentary on the *Republic*. Cf. Zeller, iii. 2, p. 818, n. 4, for references to the portion of it cited. Zeller, however, represents as a concession what is really a contention.

A large part of the activity of Proclus was given to commenting directly on Plato; but he also wrote mathematical works[1], philosophical expositions of a more independent kind, and Hymns to the Gods[2], in which the mythological personages are invoked as representatives of the powers by which the contemplative devotee rises from the realm of birth and change to that of immutable being. Of the philosophical works that do not take the form of commentaries on particular treatises, we possess an extensive one entitled *Platonic Theology*; three shorter ones on Providence, Fate, and Evils, preserved only in a Latin translation made in the thirteenth century by William of Morbeka, Archbishop of Corinth; and the *Theological Elements* (Στοιχείωσις Θεολογική). All these have been published[3]. Of the last, an attempt will be made to set forth the substance. In its groundwork, it is an extremely condensed exposition of the Plotinian doctrine; but it also contains the most important modifications made in Neo-Platonism by Proclus himself. The whole is in the form of dialectical demonstration, and may perhaps best be compared, as regards method, with Spinoza's expositions of Cartesianism. An abstract of so condensed a treatise cannot of course do justice to its argumentative force, since much must necessarily be omitted that belongs to the logical development; but some idea may be given of the genuine individual power of Proclus as a thinker. A "scholastic" turn of expression, remarked on by the historians, will easily be observed; but Proclus is not a Scholastic in the sense that he in principle takes any doctrine whatever simply as given from without.

---

[1] See, on one of these, Appendix III. A short treatise on Astronomy (Ὑποτύπωσις τῶν ἀστρονομικῶν ὑποθέσεων) and one on Physics (Στοιχείωσις φυσική) have been published, with German translation, in the Teubner Series; the first in 1909, the second in 1912.

[2] Seven of these have been preserved. See the end of Cousin's collection. Like Porphyry's *De Antro Nympharum*, they have a charm of their own for those who are, in Aristotle's phrase, φιλόμυθοι.

[3] The *Platonic Theology* does not seem to have been reprinted since 1618, when it appeared along with a Latin translation by Aemilius Portus. An English translation, by Thomas Taylor, was published in 1816. The next three works are placed at the beginning of Cousin's collection. The Στοιχείωσις is printed after the *Sententiae* of Porphyry in the Didot edition of Plotinus.

As a commentator, no doubt his aim is to explain Plato; and here the critics cannot fairly complain when he says that his object is only to set forth what the master taught. Indeed the complaint that he is a "scholastic" in this sense is neutralised by the opposite objection that his *Platonic Theology* contains more of Neo-Platonism than of Plato. And one point of his teaching—not comprised in the treatise now to be expounded—seems to have been generally misunderstood. In more than one place[1] he describes belief (πίστις) as higher than knowledge (γνῶσις), because only by belief is that Good to be reached which is the supreme end of aspiration. This has been supposed to be part of a falling away from pure philosophy, though Zeller allows that, after all, the ultimate aim of Proclus "goes as much beyond positive religion as beyond methodical knowing[2]." And in fact the notion of "belief," as Proclus formulates it, instead of being a resignation of the aims of earlier philosophy, seems rather to be a rendering into more precise subjective terms of Plato's meaning in the passage of the *Republic* where Socrates gives up the attempt at an adequate account of the Idea of the Good[3]. As Plotinus had adopted for the highest point of his ontological system the Platonic position that the Good is beyond even Being[4], so Proclus formulated a definite principle of cognition agreeing with what Plato indicates as the attitude of the mind when it at last descries the object of its search. At the extreme of pure intellect—at the point, as we might say, which terminates the highest segment of the line representing the kinds of cognition with their objects—is a mode of apprehension which is not even "dialectical," because it is at the very origin of dialectic. And to call this "belief" is to prepare a return from the mysticism of Plotinus—which Proclus, however, does not give up—to the conception of a mental state which, while not strictly cognitive, is a common instead of a peculiar experience. The contradiction between this view and that which makes belief as "opinion" lower

---

[1] Cf. R. P. 543; Zeller, iii. 2, p. 820.
[2] iii. 2, p. 823.   [3] *Rep.* vi. 506.
[4] *Rep.* vi. 509.

than knowledge is only apparent[1]. A view of the kind has become more familiar since. Put in the most general terms it is this: that while belief in its sense of opinion is below scientific knowledge, belief as the apprehension of metaphysical principles is above it; because scientific knowledge, if not attached to some metaphysical principle, vanishes under analysis into mere relations of illusory appearances.

The method of discriminating subordinate triads within each successive stage of emanation, which is regarded as characteristic of Proclus, had been more and more elaborated during the whole interval from Plotinus. The increasing use of it by Porphyry, by Iamblichus, and by their disciple Theodore of Asine, is noted by the historians. Suggestions of the later developments are to be met with in Plotinus himself, who, for example, treats being, though in its essence identical with intellect, as prior if distinguished from it, and goes on further to distinguish life, as a third component of primal Being, from being in the special sense and from intellect[2]. This is not indeed the order assigned to the same components by Proclus, who puts life, instead of intellect, in the second place; but the germ of the division is there. A doctrine in which he seems to have been quite original is that of the "divine henads[3]," to which we shall come in expounding the *Elements*. For the rest, the originality of many things in the treatise, as well as its general agreement with Plotinus, will become evident as we proceed.

Every multitude, the treatise begins, participates in a manner in the One. For if in a multitude there were no unity, it would consist either of parts which are nothings, or of parts which are themselves multitudes to infinity. From

---

[1] Pico della Mirandola seized the general thought of Proclus on this point, and applied it specially to philosophical theology. See the "Fifty-five Conclusions according to Proclus" appended to the edition of the *Platonic Theology* already referred to. The words of Pico's forty-fourth proposition are these: "Sicut fides, quae est credulitas, est infra intellectum; ita fides, quae est vere fides, est supersubstantialiter supra scientiam et intellectum, nos Deo immediate conjungens."

[2] Enn. VI. 6, 3: τὸ ὂν πρῶτον δεῖ λαβεῖν πρῶτον ὄν, εἶτα νοῦν, εἶτα τὸ ζῷον.

[3] Cf. Zeller, iii. 2, p. 793.

this starting-point we are led to the position that every multitude, being at the same time one and not one, derives its real
existence from the One in itself (τὸ αὐτοέν).

The producing (τὸ παράγον), or that which is productive
of another (τὸ παρακτικὸν ἄλλου), is better than the nature
of that which is produced (κρεῖττον τῆς τοῦ παραγομένου
φύσεως).

The first Good is that after which all beings strive, and is
therefore before all beings. To add to it anything else is to
lessen it by the addition, making it some particular good
instead of the Good simply.

If there is to be knowledge, there must be an order of
causation, and there must be a first in this order. Causes
cannot go in a circle: if they did, the same things would be
prior and posterior, better and worse. Nor can they go in an
infinite series: to refer back one cause to another without a
final term would make knowledge impossible[1].

Principle and primal cause of all being is the Good. For all
things aspire to it; but if there were anything before it in the
order of causes, that and not the Good would be the end of
their aspiration. The One simply, and the Good simply, are
the same. To be made one is to be preserved in being—which
is a good to particular things; and to cease to be one is to be
deprived of being.

In order that the derivation of motion may not go on in a
circle or to infinity, there must be an unmoved, which is the
first mover; and a self-moved, which is the first moved; as
well as that which is moved by another. The self-moved is
the mean which joins the extremes[2].

Whatever can turn back upon itself, the whole to the whole,
is incorporeal. For this turning back is impossible for body,
because of the division of its parts, which lie outside one an-

---

[1] Στοιχ. Θεολ. 11. The order meant here is of course logical, not chronological. All existing things depend on an actual first cause of their being.
ἔστιν αἰτία πρώτη τῶν ὄντων, ἀφ' ἧς οἷον ἐκ ῥίζης πρόεισιν ἕκαστα, τὰ μὲν ἐγγὺς
ὄντα ἐκείνης, τὰ δὲ πορρώτερον.

[2] Στοιχ. Θεολ. 14. Here again the order is purely logical. There is no
notion of a first impulse given to a world that has a chronological beginning.

other in space[1]. That which can thus turn back upon itself, has an essence separable from all body. For if it is inseparable in essence, it must still more be inseparable in act; were it separable only in act, its act would go beyond its essence. That is, it would do what, by definition, is not in its power to do. But body does not actually turn back upon itself. Whatever does thus turn back is therefore separable in essence as in act.

"Beyond all bodies is the essence of soul, and beyond all souls the intellectual nature, and beyond all intellectual existences the One[2]." Intellect is unmoved and the giver of motion, soul self-moving, body moved by another. If the living body moves itself, it is by participation in soul. Similarly, the soul through intellect participates in perpetual thought (μετέχει τοῦ ἀεὶ νοεῖν). For if in soul there were perpetual thinking primarily, this would be inherent in all souls, like self-motion. Since not all souls, as such, have this power, there must be before soul the primarily intelligent (τὸ πρώτως νοητικόν). Again, before intellect there must be the One. For intellect, though unmoved, is not one without duality, since it thinks itself; and all things whatsoever participate in the One, but not all things in intellect.

To every particular causal chain (σειρὰ καὶ τάξις), there is a unity (μονάς) which is the cause of all that is ordered under it. Thus after the primal One there are henads (ἐνάδες); and after the first intellect, minds (νόες); and after the first soul, souls; and after the whole of nature, natures.

First in order is always that which cannot be participated in (τὸ ἀμέθεκτον),—the "one before all" as distinguished from the one in all. This generates the things that are participated in. Inferior to these again are the things that participate, as those that are participated in are inferior to the first.

The perfect in its kind (τὸ τέλειον), since in so far as it is perfect it imitates the cause of all, proceeds to the production

---

[1] Στοιχ. Θεολ. 15: οὐδὲν ἄρα σῶμα πρὸς ἑαυτὸ πέφυκεν ἐπιστρέφειν, ὡς ὅλον ἐπεστράφθαι πρὸς ὅλον. εἴ τι ἄρα πρὸς ἑαυτὸ ἐπιστρεπτικόν ἐστιν, ἀσώματόν ἐστι καὶ ἀμερές.

[2] Στοιχ. Θεολ. 20: πάντων σωμάτων ἐπέκεινά ἐστιν ἡ ψυχῆς οὐσία, καὶ πασῶν ψυχῶν ἐπέκεινα ἡ νοερὰ φύσις, καὶ πασῶν τῶν νοερῶν ὑποστάσεων ἐπέκεινα τὸ ἕν.

of as many things as it can; as the Good causes the existence
of everything. The more or the less perfect anything is, of the
more or the fewer things is it the cause, as being nearer to or
more remote from the cause of all. That which is furthest from
the principle is unproductive and the cause of nothing.

The productive cause of other things remains in itself while
producing[1]. That which produces is productive of the things
that are second to it, by the perfection and superabundance of
its power. For if it gave being to other things through defect
and weakness, they would receive their existence through its
alteration; but it remains as it is[2].

Every productive cause brings into existence things like
itself before things unlike. Equals it cannot produce, since it
is necessarily better than its effects. The progression from the
cause to its effects is accomplished by resemblance of the
things that are second in order to those that are first[3]. Being
similar to that which produces it, the immediate product is
in a manner at once the same with and other than its cause.
It remains therefore and goes forth at the same time, and
neither element of the process is apart from the other. Every
product turns back and tries to reach its cause; for everything
strives after the Good, which is the source of its being; and
the mode of attaining the Good for each thing is through its
own proximate cause. The return is accomplished by the resemblance the things that return bear to that which they
return to[4]; for the aim of the return is union, and it is always
resemblance that unites. The progression and the return
form a circular activity. There are lesser and greater circles
according as the return is to things immediately above or to

---

[1] Στοιχ. Θεολ. 26: εἰ γὰρ μιμεῖται τὸ ἕν, ἐκεῖνο δὲ ἀκινήτως ὑφίστησι τὰ μετ'
αὐτό, καὶ πᾶν τὸ παράγον ὡσαύτως ἔχει τὴν τοῦ παράγειν αἰτίαν.

[2] Στοιχ. Θεολ. 27: οὐ γὰρ ἀπομερισμός ἐστι τοῦ παράγοντος τὸ παραγόμενον ·
οὐδὲ γὰρ γενέσει τοῦτο προσῆκεν, οὐδὲ τοῖς γεννητικοῖς αἰτίοις· οὐδὲ μετάβασις· οὐ
γὰρ ὕλη γίνεται τοῦ προϊόντος· μένει γάρ, οἷον ἔστι. καὶ τὸ παραγόμενον ἄλλο παρ'
αὐτό ἐστιν.

[3] Στοιχ. Θεολ. 29: πᾶσα πρόοδος δι' ὁμοιότητος ἀποτελεῖται τῶν δευτέρων πρὸς
τὰ πρῶτα.

[4] Στοιχ. Θεολ. 32: πᾶσα ἐπιστροφὴ δι' ὁμοιότητος ἀποτελεῖται τῶν ἐπιστρεφο-
μένων, πρὸς ὃ ἐπιστοέφεται.

those that are higher. In the great circle to and from the principle of all, all things are involved[1].

Accordingly, everything that is caused remains in its own cause, and goes forth from it, and returns to it[2]. The remaining (μονή) signifies its community with its cause; the going forth, its distinction from it (ἅμα γὰρ διακρίσει πρόοδος); the return, its innate endeavour after its own good, from which its particular being is. Of the things multiplied in progressive production, the first are more perfect than the second, these than the next, and so forth; for the "progressions" from cause to effect are remissions of being (ὑφέσεις) of the second as compared with the first. In the order of return, on the contrary, the things that are most imperfect come first, the most perfect last. Every process of return to a remoter cause is through the same intermediate stages as the corresponding causal progression. First in the order of return are the things that have received from their cause only being (τὸ εἶναι); next, those that have received life with being; last, those that have received also the power of cognition. The endeavour (ὄρεξις) of the first to return is a mere fitness for participation in causes[3]; the endeavour of the second is "vital," and is a motion to the better; that of the third is identical with conscious knowledge of the goodness of their causes (κατὰ τὴν γνῶσιν, συναίσθησις οὖσα τῆς τῶν αἰτίων ἀγαθότητος).

Between the One without duality, and things that proceed from causes other than themselves, is the self-subsistent (τὸ αὐθυπόστατον), or that which is the cause of itself. That which is in itself, not as in place, but as the effect in the cause, is self-subsistent. The self-subsistent has the power of turning back upon itself[4]. If it did not thus return, it would not

---

[1] Στοιχ. Θεολ. 33: πᾶν τὸ προϊὸν ἀπό τινος καὶ ἐπιστρέφον, κυκλικὴν ἔχει τὴν ἐνέργειαν....μείζους δὲ κύκλοι καὶ ἐλάττους τῶν μὲν ἐπιστροφῶν πρὸς τὰ ὑπερκείμενα συνεχῶς γινομένων, τῶν δὲ πρὸς τὰ ἀνωτέρω, καὶ μέχρι τῶν πάντων ἀρχῆς. ἀπὸ γὰρ ἐκείνης πάντα, καὶ πρὸς ἐκείνην.

[2] Στοιχ. Θεολ. 35: πᾶν τὸ αἰτιατὸν καὶ μένει ἐν τῇ αὐτοῦ αἰτίᾳ, καὶ πρόεισιν ἀπ' αὐτῆς, καὶ ἐπιστρέφει πρὸς αὐτήν.

[3] Στοιχ. Θεολ. 39: οὐσιώδη ποιεῖται τὴν ἐπιστροφήν. That is to say, they tend to be embodied in some definite form, which is their "essence."

[4] Στοιχ. Θεολ. 42: εἰ γὰρ ἀφ' ἑαυτοῦ πρόεισι, καὶ τὴν ἐπιστροφὴν ποιήσεται πρὸς

strive after nor attain its own good, and so would not be self-sufficing and perfect; but this belongs to the self-subsistent if to anything. Conversely, that which has the power of turning back upon itself is self-subsistent. For thus to return, and to attain the end, is to find the source of its perfection, and therefore of its being, within itself. The self-subsistent is ungenerated. For generation is the way from imperfection to the opposite perfection[1]; but that which produces itself is ever perfect, and needs not completion from another, like things that have birth. The self-subsistent is incorruptible, for it never departs from the cause of its preservation, which is itself. It is indivisible and simple. For if divisible, it cannot turn back, the whole to the whole; and if composite, it must be in need of its own elements, of which it consists, and hence not self-sufficing.

After some propositions on the everlasting or imperishable (ἀΐδιον) and the eternal (αἰώνιον), and on eternity and time, not specially distinctive of his system, Proclus goes on to a characteristic doctrine of his own, according to which the higher cause—which is also the more general—continues its activity beyond that of the causes that follow it. Thus the causal efficacy of the One extends as far as to Matter, in the production of which the intermediate causes, from intelligible being downwards, have no share.

That which is produced by the things second in order, the series of propositions begins[2], is produced in a higher degree by the things that are first in order and of more causal efficacy; for the things that are second in order are themselves produced by the first, and derive their whole essence and causal efficacy from them. Thus intellect is the cause of all that soul is the cause of; and, where soul has ceased to energise, the intellect that produces it still continues its causal activity. For the inanimate, in so far as it participates in form, has part in

ἑαυτό. ἀφ' οὗ γὰρ ἡ πρόοδος ἑκάστοις, εἰς τοῦτο καὶ ἡ τῇ προόδῳ σύστοιχος ἐπιστροφή.

[1] Στοιχ. Θεολ. 45: καὶ γὰρ ἡ γένεσις ὁδός ἐστιν ἐκ τοῦ ἀτελοῦς εἰς τὸ ἐναντίον τέλειον.

[2] Στοιχ. Θεολ. 56.

intellect and the creative action of intellect[1]. Further, the
Good is the cause of all that intellect is the cause of; but not
conversely. For privations of form are from the Good, since
all is thence, but intellect, being form, is not the ground of
privation[2].

The product of more causes is more composite ($\sigma\upsilon\nu\theta\epsilon\tau\acute{\omega}\tau\epsilon\rho\rho\nu$)
than the product of fewer. For if every cause gives something
to that which proceeds from it, more causes must confer more
elements and fewer fewer. Now where there are more elements
of the composition, the resultant is said to be more composite;
where there are fewer, less. Hence the simple in essence is
either superior to things composite or inferior. For if the extremes of being are produced by fewer concurrent causes and
the means by more, the means must be composite while the
extremes on both sides are simpler. But that the extremes are
produced by fewer causes is evident, since the superior causes
both begin to act before the inferior, and in their activity
stretch out beyond the point where the activity of the latter
ceases through remission of power ($\delta\iota$' $\acute{\upsilon}\phi\epsilon\sigma\iota\nu$ $\delta\upsilon\nu\acute{\alpha}\mu\epsilon\omega\varsigma$).
Therefore the last of things, like the first, is most simple,
because it proceeds only from the first; but, of these two
simplicities, one is above all composition, the other below it.

Of things that have plurality, that which is nearer the One
is less in quantity than the more distant, greater in potency[3].
Consequently there are more corporeal natures than souls,
more of these than of minds, more minds than divine henads.

The more universal ($\acute{o}\lambda\iota\kappa\acute{\omega}\tau\epsilon\rho\sigma\nu$) precedes in its causal
action the more particular ($\mu\epsilon\rho\iota\kappa\acute{\omega}\tau\epsilon\rho\sigma\nu$) and continues after
it. Thus "being" comes before "living being" ($\zeta\hat{\omega}\sigma\nu$), and
"living being" before "man," in the causal order as in the
order of generality. Again, at a point below the agency of the
rational power, where there is no longer "man," there is still
a breathing and sentient living being; and where there is no

---

[1] $\Sigma\tau o\iota\chi$. $\Theta\epsilon o\lambda$. 57: $\kappa\alpha\grave{\iota}$ $\gamma\grave{\alpha}\rho$ $\tau\grave{o}$ $\check{\alpha}\psi\upsilon\chi o\nu$, $\kappa\alpha\theta\acute{o}\sigma o\nu$ $\epsilon\check{\iota}\delta o\upsilon\varsigma$ $\mu\epsilon\tau\acute{\epsilon}\sigma\chi\epsilon$, $\nu o\hat{\upsilon}$ $\mu\epsilon\tau\acute{\epsilon}\chi\epsilon\iota$ $\kappa\alpha\grave{\iota}$
$\tau\hat{\eta}\varsigma$ $\tau o\hat{\upsilon}$ $\nu o\hat{\upsilon}$ $\pi o\iota\acute{\eta}\sigma\epsilon\omega\varsigma$.

[2] $\Sigma\tau o\iota\chi$. $\Theta\epsilon o\lambda$. 57: $\nu o\hat{\upsilon}\varsigma$ $\delta\grave{\epsilon}$ $\sigma\tau\epsilon\rho\acute{\eta}\sigma\epsilon\omega\varsigma$ $\acute{\upsilon}\pi o\sigma\tau\acute{\alpha}\tau\eta\varsigma$ $o\grave{\upsilon}\kappa$ $\acute{\epsilon}\sigma\tau\acute{\iota}\nu$, $\epsilon\check{\iota}\delta o\varsigma$ $\acute{\omega}\nu$.

[3] $\Sigma\tau o\iota\chi$. $\Theta\epsilon o\lambda$. 62: $\acute{o}\mu o\iota o\nu$ $\gamma\grave{\alpha}\rho$ $\tau\hat{\omega}$ $\acute{\epsilon}\nu\grave{\iota}$ $\mu\hat{\alpha}\lambda\lambda o\nu$ $\tau\grave{o}$ $\acute{\epsilon}\gamma\gamma\acute{\upsilon}\tau\epsilon\rho o\nu$ · $\tau\grave{o}$ $\delta\grave{\epsilon}$ $\acute{\epsilon}\nu$ $\pi\acute{\alpha}\nu\tau\omega\nu$ $\mathring{\eta}\nu$
$\acute{\upsilon}\pi o\sigma\tau\alpha\tau\iota\kappa\grave{o}\nu$ $\acute{\alpha}\pi\lambda\eta\theta\acute{\upsilon}\nu\tau\omega\varsigma$.

longer life there is still being. That which comes from the
more universal causes is the bearer of that which is communicated in the remitting stages of the progression. Matter,
which is at the extreme bound, has its subsistence only from
the most universal cause, namely, the One. Being the subject
of all things, it proceeded from the cause of all[1]. Body in
itself, while it is below participation in soul, participates in a
manner in being. As the subject of animation (ὑποκείμενον
τῆς ψυχώσεως), it has its subsistence from that which is more
universal than soul.

Omitting some auxiliary propositions, we may go on to the
doctrine of infinity as formulated by Proclus. In passing, it
may be noted that he explicitly demonstrates the proposition
that that which can know itself has the power of turning back
upon itself. The reason assigned is that in the act of self-
knowledge that which knows and that which is known are one.
And what is true of the act is true also of the essence[2]. That
only the incorporeal has the power of thus turning back upon
itself was proved at an earlier stage.

Infinity in the sense in which it really exists, with Proclus
as with Plotinus, means infinite power or potency. That
which ever is, is infinite in potency; for if its power of being
(ἡ κατὰ τὸ εἶναι δύναμις) were finite, its being would some
time fail[3]. That which ever becomes, has an infinite power of
becoming. For if the power is finite, it must cease in infinite
time; and, the power ceasing, the process must cease. The
real infinity of that which truly is, is neither of multitude nor
of magnitude, but of potency alone[4]. For self-subsistent being
(τὸ αὐθυποστάτως ὄν) is indivisible and simple, and is in
potency infinite as having most the form of unity (ἐνοειδέσ-
τατον); since the greatest causal power belongs to that which
is nearest the One. The infinite in magnitude or multitude,

---

[1] Στοιχ. Θεολ. 72: ἡ μὲν γὰρ ὕλη, ὑποκείμενον οὖσα πάντων, ἐκ τοῦ πάντων
αἰτίου προῆλθε.

[2] Στοιχ. Θεολ. 83: πᾶν γὰρ τὸ τῷ ἐνεργεῖν πρὸς ἑαυτὸ ἐπιστρεπτικὸν καὶ οὐσίαν
ἔχει πρὸς ἑαυτὴν συννεύουσαν, καὶ ἐν ἑαυτῇ οὖσαν.

[3] Στοιχ. Θεολ. 84.

[4] Στοιχ. Θεολ. 86: πᾶν τὸ ὄντως ὂν τῷ ὄντι ἄπειρόν ἐστι, οὔτε κατὰ τὸ πλῆθος
οὔτε κατὰ τὸ μέγεθος, ἀλλὰ κατὰ τὴν δύναμιν μόνην.

on the other hand, is at once most divided and weakest. Indivisible power is infinite and undivided in the same relation (κατὰ ταὐτόν); the divided powers are in a manner finite (πεπερασμέναι πως) by reason of their division. From this sense of the finite, as limited power, is to be distinguished its sense as determinate number, by which it comes nearest to indivisible unity.

That which is infinite, is infinite neither to the things above it nor to itself, but to the things that are inferior. To these, there is that in it which can by no means be grasped; it has what exceeds all the unfolding of its powers: but by itself, and still more by the things above it, it is held and defined as a whole[1].

We have already met with the position that in a complete causal series the first term is "imparticipable" (ἀμέθεκτον). This means that in no way do the things it produces share it among them. The cause, thus imparticipable or transcendent, remains by itself in detachment from every succeeding stage. In drawing out the consequences of this position, Proclus introduces those intermediate terms which are held to be characteristic of his system. Within the Being or Intellect of the Plotinian Trinity, he constitutes the subordinate triad of being, life and mind. To these discriminated stages he applies his theory that causes descend in efficacy as they descend in generality. The series of things in which mind is immanent is preceded by imparticipable mind; similarly life and being precede the things that participate in them; but of these being is before life, life before mind[2]. In the order of dependence, the cause of more things precedes the cause of fewer. Now all things have being that have life, and all things have life that have mind, but not conversely. Hence in the causal order being must come first, then life, then mind. All are in

---

[1] Στοιχ. Θεολ. 93: ἑαυτὸ δὲ συνέχον καὶ ὁρίζον οὐκ ἂν ἑαυτῷ ἄπειρον ὑπάρχοι, οὐδὲ πολλῷ μᾶλλον τοῖς ὑπερκειμένοις, μοῖραν ἔχον τῆς ἐν ἐκείνοις ἀπειρίας· ἀπειρό- τεραι γὰρ αἱ τῶν ὁλικωτέρων δυνάμεις, ὁλικώτεραι οὖσαι καὶ ἐγγυτέρω τεταγμέναι τῆς πρωτίστης ἀπειρίας.

[2] Στοιχ. Θεολ. 101: πάντων τῶν νοῦ μετεχόντων ἡγεῖται ὁ ἀμέθεκτος νοῦς, καὶ τῶν τῆς ζωῆς ἡ ζωή, καὶ τῶν τοῦ ὄντος τὸ ὄν· αὐτῶν δὲ τούτων τὸ μὲν ὂν πρὸ τῆς ζωῆς, ἡ δὲ ζωὴ πρὸ τοῦ νοῦ.

all; but in each each is present in the manner appropriate to the subsistence of that in which it inheres[1].

All that is immortal is imperishable, but not all that is imperishable is immortal. For that which ever participates in life participates also in being, but not conversely. As being is to life, so is the imperishable, or that which cannot cease to be, to the immortal, or that which cannot cease to live[2]. Since that which is altogether in time is in every respect unlike that which is altogether eternal, there must be something between them; for the causal progression is always through similars[3]. This mean must be eternal in essence, temporal in act. Generation, which has its essence in time, is attached causally to that which on one side shares in being and on the other in birth, participating at once in eternity and in time; this, to that which is altogether eternal; and that which is altogether eternal to being before eternity (εἰς τὸ ὄν, τὸ προαιώνιον)[4].

The highest terms of each causal chain (σειρά), and only those, are connected with the unitary principle of the chain next above. Thus only the highest minds are directly attached to a divine unity; only the most intellectual souls participate in mind; and only the most perfect corporeal natures have a soul present to them[5]. Above all divine unities is the One, which is God; as it must be, since it is the Good; for that beyond which there is nothing, and after which all things strive, is God[6]. But that there must also be many divine unities is evident, since every cause which is a principle takes the lead in a series of multiplied existences descending from itself by degrees of likeness. The self-complete unities (αὐτο-τελεῖς ἑνάδες) or "divine henads," are "the gods," and every

---

[1] Στοιχ. Θεολ. 103: πάντα ἐν πᾶσιν· οἰκείως δὲ ἐν ἑκάστῳ. As for example, ἐν τῇ ζωῇ κατὰ μέθεξιν μὲν τὸ εἶναι, κατ' αἰτίαν δὲ τὸ νοεῖν· ἀλλὰ ζωτικῶς ἑκάτερον· κατὰ τοῦτο γὰρ ἡ ὕπαρξις.

[2] Στοιχ. Θεολ. 105.

[3] Στοιχ. Θεολ. 106: αἱ πρόοδοι πᾶσαι διὰ τῶν ὁμοίων.   [4] Στοιχ. Θεολ. 107.

[5] Στοιχ. Θεολ. 111. Cf. 112: πάσης τάξεως τὰ πρώτιστα μορφὴν ἔχει τῶν πρὸ αὐτῶν.

[6] Στοιχ. Θεολ. 113: οὗ γὰρ μηδέν ἐστιν ἐπέκεινα, καὶ οὗ πάντα ἐφίεται, θεὸς τοῦτο.

god is above being and life and mind[1]. In all there is participation, except in the One[2].

Much has been written upon the question, what the henads of Proclus really mean. Usually the doctrine is treated as an attempt to find a more definite place for polytheism than was marked out in the system of Plotinus. This explanation, however, is obviously inadequate, and there have not been wanting attempts to find in it a more philosophical meaning. Now so far as the origin of the doctrine is concerned, it seems to be a perfectly consequent development from Plotinus. Proclus seeks the cause of plurality in things at a higher stage than the intelligible world, in which Plotinus had been content to find its beginning. Before being and mind are produced, the One acts as it were through many points of origin; from each of these start many minds; each of which again is the principle of further differences. As the primal unity is called θεός, the derivative unities are in correspondence called θεοί. Thus the doctrine is pure deductive metaphysics. There is hardly any indication that in thinking it out Proclus had in view special laws of nature or groups of natural facts[3]. Though not otherwise closely resembling Spinoza's doctrine of the "infinite attributes," it resembles it in this, that it is a metaphysical deduction intended to give logical completeness, where intuitive completeness becomes impossible, to a system of pure conceptual truth.

From the divine henads, according to Proclus, the providential order of the world directly descends. This position he supports by a fanciful etymology[4], but deduces essentially from the priority of goodness as characterising the divinity[5].

---

[1] Στοιχ. Θεολ. 115: πᾶς θεὸς ὑπερούσιός ἐστι καὶ ὑπέρζωος καὶ ὑπέρνους.

[2] Στοιχ. Θεολ. 116: πᾶς θεὸς μεθεκτός ἐστι, πλὴν τοῦ ἑνός....εἰ γὰρ ἔστιν ἄλλη μετὰ τὸ πρῶτον ἀμέθεκτος ἑνάς, τί διοίσει τοῦ ἑνός;

[3] A slight development on this line is to be met with in §§ 151–8, but not such as to affect the general aspect of the doctrine.

[4] Στοιχ. Θεολ. 120: ἐν θεοῖς ἡ πρόνοια πρώτως·...ἡ δὲ πρόνοια (ὡς τοὔνομα ἐμφαίνει) ἐνέργειά ἐστι πρὸ νοῦ. τῷ εἶναι ἄρα θεοὶ καὶ τῷ ἀγαθότητες εἶναι πάντων προνοοῦσι, πάντα τῆς πρὸ νοῦ πληροῦντες ἀγαθότητος.

[5] Στοιχ. Θεολ. 121: πᾶν τὸ θεῖον ὕπαρξιν μὲν ἔχει τὴν ἀγαθότητα, δύναμιν δὲ ἑνιαίαν καὶ γνῶσιν κρύφιον, ἄληπτον πᾶσιν ὁμοῦ τοῖς δευτέροις....ἀλλ' ἡ ὕπαρξις τῷ ἀρίστῳ χαρακτηρίζεται, καὶ ἡ ὑπόστασις κατὰ τὸ ἄριστον· τοῦτο δὲ ἡ ἀγαθότης.

After goodness come power and knowledge. The divine knowledge is above intellect; and the providential government of
the world is not by a reasoning process (οὐ κατὰ λογισμόν). By
nothing that comes after it can the divinity in itself either be
expressed or known. Since, however, it is knowable as henads
from the things that participate in them, only the primal One
is entirely unknowable, as not being participated in[1]. The
divinity knows indivisibly the things that are divided, and
without time the things that are in time, and the things that
are not necessary with necessity, and the things that are
mutable immutably; and, in sum, all things better than according to their own order. Its knowledge of the multiple and
of things subject to passion is unitary and without passivity.
On the other hand, that which is below has to receive the
impassible with passive affection, and the timeless under the
form of time[2].

The order of the divine henads is graduated; some being
more universal, some more particular. The causal efficacy of
the former is greater; of the latter, less. The more particular
divine henads are generated from the more universal, neither
by division of these nor by alteration, nor yet by manifold
relationships, but by the production of secondary progressions
through superabundance of power[3]. The divine henad first
communicates its power to mind; through mind, it is present
to soul; and through soul it gives a resonance of its own
peculiar nature even to body. Thus body becomes not only
animate and intelligential, but also divine, receiving life and
motion from soul, indissoluble permanence from mind, divine
union from the henad participated in[4]. Not all the other
henads together are equal to the primal One[5]. There are as
many kinds of beings that participate in the divine henads as
there are henads participated in. The more universal henads
are participated in by the more universal kinds of beings; the
more particular by the more particular. Thus the order of

---

[1] Στοιχ. Θεολ. 123: μόνον τὸ πρῶτον παντελῶς ἄγνωστον, ἅτε ἀμέθεκτον ὅν.

[2] Στοιχ. Θεολ. 124.   [3] Στοιχ. Θεολ. 126.   [4] Στοιχ. Θεολ. 129.

[5] Στοιχ. Θεολ. 133: οὐ γὰρ αἱ πᾶσαι τῶν θεῶν ὑπάρξεις παρισοῦνται τῷ ἑνί·
τοσαύτην ἐκεῖνο πρὸς τὸ πλῆθος τῶν θεῶν ἔλαχεν ὑπερβολήν.

beings is in precise accordance with the order of the henads. Each being has for its cause not only the henad in which it participates, but, along with that, the primal One[1].

All the powers of the divinity penetrate even to the terrestrial regions, being excluded by no limits of space from presence to all that is ready for participation[2]. Beside that providence of the gods which is outside and above the order over which it is exercised, there is another, imitating it within the order and exercised over the things that are at a lower stage of remission by those that are higher in the causal series[3]. The gods are present in the same manner to all things, but not all things are present in the same manner to the gods. It is unfitness of the things participating that causes obscuration of the divine presence. Total deprivation of it would mean their complete disappearance into not-being. At each stage of remission, the divinity is present, not only in the manner peculiar to each causal order, but in the manner appropriate to the particular stage. The progressions have the form of a circle; the end being made like the beginning through the return of all things within the order to its principle[4].

The whole multitude of the divine henads is finite in number. It is indeed more definitely limited than any other multitude, as being nearest to the One. Infinite multitude, on the other hand, is most remote from the One[5]. There is at the same time, as has been shown, a sense in which all divine things are infinite. That is to say, they are infinite in potency, and incomprehensible to what is below them[6].

The henads participated in by being which is prior to intellect are intelligible (νοηταί); those that are participated in by intellect itself are intelligential (νοεραί), as producing

---

[1] Στοιχ. Θεολ. 137: πᾶσα ἑνὰς συνυφίστησι τῷ ἑνὶ τὸ μετέχον αὐτῆς ὄν.

[2] Στοιχ. Θεολ. 140.   [3] Στοιχ. Θεολ. 141.

[4] Στοιχ. Θεολ. 146. Cf. 148: πᾶσα θεία τάξις ἑαυτῇ συνήνωται τριχῶς· ἀπό τε τῆς ἀκρότητος τῆς ἑαυτῆς καὶ ἀπὸ τῆς μεσότητος, καὶ ἀπὸ τοῦ τέλους....καὶ οὕτως ὁ σύμπας διάκοσμος εἷς ἐστι διὰ τῆς ἑνοποιοῦ τῶν πρώτων δυνάμεως, διὰ τῆς ἐν τ μεσότητι συνοχῆς, διὰ τῆς τοῦ τέλους εἰς τὴν ἀρχὴν τῶν προόδων ἐπιστροφῆς.

[5] Στοιχ. Θεολ. 149.

[6] Στοιχ. Θεολ. 150: ἡ δὲ ἀπειρία κατὰ τὴν δύναμιν ἐκείνοις· τὸ δὲ ἄπειρον ἀπερίληπτον, οἷς ἐστιν ἄπειρον.

intelligence¹; those that are participated in by soul are supramundane (ὑπερκόσμιοι). As soul is attached to intellect, and
intellect turns back upon intelligible being; so the supramundane gods depend on the intelligential, as those again on the
intelligible gods². Something also of visible bodies being from
the gods, there are also "mundane henads" (ἐγκόσμιοι ἑνάδες).
These are mediated by mind and soul; which, according as
they are more separable from the world and its divided contents, have more resemblance to the imparticipable³.

Having dealt so far with the ontology of intellect, Proclus
goes on to formulate the characters of intellectual knowledge.
Intellect has itself for the object of its thought⁴. Mind in act
knows that it thinks; and it does not belong to one mind to
think an object and to another to think the thought of the
object⁵. The thought, the knowledge of the thought, and the
cognisance of itself as thinking, are simultaneous activities of
one subject. It is the character of mind to think all things
together. Imparticipable mind thinks all of them together
simply; each mind that follows thinks them all still together,
but under the form of the singular⁶. That mind is incorporeal
is shown by its turning back upon itself⁷. In accordance with
its being, it contains all things intellectually, both those before
it and those after it; the former by participation, the latter by
containing their causes intellectually⁸.

Mind constitutes what is after it by thinking; and its crea-

---

¹ Στοιχ. Θεολ. 163: οὐχ οὕτω νοεραί, ὡς ἐν νῷ ὑφεστηκυῖαι, ἀλλ' ὡς κατ' αἰτίαν
τοῦ νοῦ προϋπάρχουσαι, καὶ ἀπογεννήσασαι τὸν νοῦν.

² Στοιχ. Θεολ. 164: ὡς οὖν ψυχὴ πᾶσα εἰς νοῦν ἀνήρτηται, καὶ νοῦς εἰς τὸ νοητὸν
ἐπέστραπται, οὕτω δὴ καὶ οἱ ὑπερκόσμιοι θεοὶ τῶν νοερῶν ἐξέχονται, καθάπερ δὴ
καὶ οὗτοι τῶν νοητῶν.

³ Στοιχ. Θεολ. 166.

⁴ Στοιχ. Θεολ. 167.

⁵ Στοιχ. Θεολ. 168: πᾶς νοῦς κατ' ἐνέργειαν οἶδεν, ὅτι νοεῖ, καὶ οὐκ ἄλλου μὲν
ἴδιον τὶ νοεῖν, ἄλλου δὲ τὸ νοεῖν, ὅτι νοεῖ.

⁶ Στοιχ. Θεολ. 170: πᾶς νοῦς πάντα ἅμα νοεῖ· ἀλλ' ὁ μὲν ἀμέθεκτος ἁπλῶς
πάντα, τῶν δὲ μετ' ἐκεῖνον ἕκαστος καθ' ἓν ἅπαντα. Cf. 180.

⁷ Στοιχ. Θεολ. 171: ὅτι μὲν οὖν ἀσώματος ὁ νοῦς, ἡ πρὸς ἑαυτὸν ἐπιστροφὴ
δηλοῖ· τῶν γὰρ σωμάτων οὐδὲν πρὸς ἑαυτὸ ἐπιστρέφεται.

⁸ Στοιχ. Θεολ. 173: τὸ δὲ εἶναι αὐτοῦ νοερόν, καὶ τὰ αἴτια ἄρα νοερῶς ἔχει τῶν
πάντων· ὥστε πάντα νοερῶς ἔχει πᾶς νοῦς, καὶ τὰ πρὸ αὐτοῦ, καὶ τὰ μετ' αὐτόν· ὡς
οὖν τὰ νοητὰ νοερῶς ἔχει πᾶς νοῦς, οὕτω καὶ τὰ αἰσθητὰ νοερῶς.

tion is in thinking, and its thought in creating[1]. It is first participated in by the things which, although their thought is according to the temporal and not according to the eternal order, which is timeless, yet have the power of thinking and actually think during the whole of time. That such existences should be interposed before particular souls, is required by the graduated mediation characteristic of every causal progression[2]. Soul that is sometimes thinking and sometimes not, cannot participate without mediation in eternal mind.

The intellectual forms in mind are both in one another and each for itself without either spatial interval or confusion. This Proclus demonstrates from the nature of indivisible essence. If any one needs an analogy as well as a demonstration, then, he says, there is the case of the various theorems existing in one soul. The soul draws forth the propositions that constitute its knowledge, not by pulling them apart from one another, but by making separately clear to itself implicit distinctions that already exist[3]. The minds that contain more universal forms are superior in causal efficacy to those that contain more particular forms. The first by forms that are quantitatively less produce more effects; the second fewer by forms that are quantitatively more. From the second proceed the finer differences of kinds[4]. The products of intellectual forms are imperishable. Kinds that are only for a time do not subsist from a formal or ideal cause of their own; nor have perishable things, as such, a pre-existent intellectual form[5]. The number of minds is finite[6]. Every mind is a whole; and each is at once united with other minds and discriminated

---

[1] Στοιχ. Θεολ. 174: πᾶς νοῦς τῷ νοεῖν ὑφίστησι τὰ μετ' αὐτόν, καὶ ἡ ποίησις ἐν τῷ νοεῖν, καὶ ἡ νόησις ἐν τῷ ποιεῖν.

[2] Στοιχ. Θεολ. 175: οὐδαμοῦ γὰρ αἱ πρόοδοι γίνονται ἀμέσως, ἀλλὰ διὰ τῶν συγγενῶν καὶ ὁμοίων, κατά τε τὰς ὑποστάσεις καὶ τὰς τῶν ἐνεργειῶν τελειότητας.

[3] Στοιχ. Θεολ. 176: πάντα γὰρ εἰλικρινῶς ἡ ψυχὴ προάγει, καὶ χωρὶς ἕκαστον, μηδὲν ἐφέλκουσα ἀπὸ τῶν λοιπῶν, ἃ (εἰ μὴ διεκέκριτο ἀεὶ κατὰ τὴν ἕξιν) οὐδ' ἂν ἡ ἐνέργεια διέκρινε τῆς ψυχῆς.

[4] Στοιχ. Θεολ. 177: ὅθεν οἱ δεύτεροι νόες ταῖς τῶν εἰδῶν μερικωτέραις διακρίσεσιν ἐπιδιαρθροῦσί πως καὶ λεπτουργοῦσι τὰς τῶν πρώτων εἰδοποιίας.

[5] Στοιχ. Θεολ. 178: πᾶν νοερὸν εἶδος ἀϊδίων ἐστὶν ὑποστατικόν....οὔτε ἄρα τὰ γένη τὰ κατά τινα χρόνον ἀπ' αἰτίας ὑφέστηκεν εἰδητικῆς, οὔτε τὰ φθαρτά, ᾗ φθαρτά, εἶδος ἔχει νοερὸν προϋπάρχον.   [6] Στοιχ. Θεολ. 179.

from them. Imparticipable mind is a whole simply, since it has in itself all the parts under the form of the whole; of the partial minds each contains the whole as in a part[1].

The mean between divine imparticipable mind and mind participated in and intelligential but not divine, is divine mind participated in. In this participate divine souls. Of souls there are three kinds: first, those that are divine; second, those that are not divine but that always participate in intelligible mind; third, those that change between mind and deprivation of it. Every soul is an incorporeal essence and separable from the body[2]. For since it knows that which is above it, namely, mind and intellectual things in their purity, much more is it the nature of the soul to know *itself*. Now that which knows itself turns back upon itself. And that which turns back upon itself is neither body nor inseparable from body; for the mere turning back upon itself, of which body is incapable, necessitates separability. Every soul is indestructible and incorruptible. For everything that can in any way be dissolved and destroyed is either corporeal and composite or has its existence in a subject. That which is dissolved undergoes corruption as consisting of a multitude of divisible parts; that of which it is the nature to exist in another, being separated from its subject vanishes into not-being. But the soul comes under neither of these determinations; existent as it is in the act of turning back upon itself. Hence it is indestructible and incorruptible.

Proclus now goes on to define more exactly the characters of the soul in relation to things prior and posterior to it. It is self-subsistent and is the principle of life to itself and to all that participates in it. As it is a mean between things primarily indivisible and those that have the divisibility belonging to body, so also it is a mean between things wholly eternal and those that are wholly temporal. Eternal in essence and temporal in act, it is the first of things that have part in the world of generation. In the logical order of causes, it

---

[1] Στοιχ. Θεολ. 180: ἀλλ' ὁ μὲν ἀμέθεκτος νοῦς ἁπλῶς ὅλος, ὡς τὰ μέρη πάντα ὁλικῶς ἔχων ἐν ἑαυτῷ, τῶν δὲ μερικῶν ἕκαστος ὡς ἐν μέρει τὸ ὅλον ἔχει. Cf. 170.

[2] Στοιχ. Θεολ. 186.

comes next after mind, and contains all the intellectual forms
that mind possesses primarily. These it has by participation,
and as products of the things before it. Things perceptible
it anticipates in their pre-formed models (παραδειγματικῶς).
Thus it holds the reasons of things material immaterially, and
of corporeal things incorporeally, and of things apart in space
without spatially separating them. Things intelligible, on the
other hand, it receives in their expression by images (εἰκονικῶς); divisibly the forms of those that are undivided, by
multiplication the forms of those that are unitary, by self-
motion the forms of those that are unmoved[1].

Every soul participated in has for its first organ an imperishable body, ungenerated and incorruptible. For if every
soul is imperishable in essence and primarily animates something corporeal, then, since its being is immutable, it animates
it always. If that which has soul has it always, it also participates ever in the life of soul[2]. But that which is ever
living ever is, that is to say, is imperishable[3].

All that participates in time yet is perpetually moved, is
measured by circuits. For since things are determinate both in
multitude and in magnitude, transition cannot go on through
different collocations to infinity. On the other hand, the transitions of that which is ever moved can have no term. They
must therefore go from the same to the same; the time of the
circuit furnishing the measure of the motion. Every mundane
soul, since it passes without limit through transitions of which
time is the measure, has circuits of its proper life, and restitu-
tions to its former position[4]. While other souls have some
particular time for the measure of their circuit, the circuit of

---

[1] Στοιχ. Θεολ. 195. Cf. Arist. *De An.* iii. 8, 431 b 21: ἡ ψυχὴ τὰ ὄντα πώς
ἐστι πάντα.

[2] Στοιχ. Θεολ. 196: εἰ δὲ τοῦτο τὸ ψυχούμενον ἀεὶ ψυχοῦται, καὶ ἀεὶ μετέχει
ζωῆς.

[3] The chief propositions on the imperishable vehicle of the soul are to be
found near the end of the treatise (207–10). The substance of them is that,
in the descent and reascent of the particular soul, extraneous material
clothings are in turn put upon the vehicle and stripped off from it; the
vehicle itself remaining impassible.

[4] Στοιχ. Θεολ. 199: πᾶσα ψυχὴ ἐγκόσμιος περιόδοις χρῆται τῆς οἰκείας ζωῆς
καὶ ἀποκαταστάσεσιν....πᾶσα γὰρ περίοδος τῶν ἀϊδίων ἀποκαταστατική ἐστι.

the first soul measured by time coincides with the whole of time[1].

With greater distance of souls from the One there goes, according to the general principle already set forth, increase of number and diminution of causal efficacy[2]. Every particular soul may descend to birth infinite times and reascend from birth to being. For it now follows after the divine and now falls away; and such alternation must evidently be recurrent. The soul cannot be an infinite time among the gods, and then the whole succeeding time among bodies; for that which has no temporal beginning can never have an end, and that which has no end necessarily has no beginning[3].

Every particular soul, descending to birth, descends as a whole. It does not partly remain above and partly descend. For if part of the soul remains in the intelligible world, it must either think ever without transition, or by a transitive process. But if without transition, then it thinks as pure intellect, and not as a part of the soul; and so must be the soul immediately participating in mind, that is, the general soul. If it thinks by a transitive process, then, out of that which is always thinking and that which sometimes thinks one essence is composed. But this also is impossible. Besides, it is absurd that the highest part of the soul, being, as it is if it does not descend, ever perfect, should not rule the other powers and make them also perfect. Every particular soul therefore descends as a whole[4].

3. *The End of the Platonic Succession.*

Of the successors to Plato's chair after Proclus, the most noteworthy was Damascius, the last of all. A native of Damascus, he had studied at Alexandria and at Athens. Among his teachers was Marinus, the immediate successor and the biographer of Proclus. The skill in dialectic for which he was celebrated, he himself attributed to the instructions

---

[1] Στοιχ. Θεολ. 200.   [2] Στοιχ. Θεολ. 203.

[3] Στοιχ. Θεολ. 206: λείπεται ἄρα περιόδους ἑκάστην ποιεῖσθαι ἀνόδων τε ἐκ τῆς γενέσεως καὶ τῶν εἰς γένεσιν καθόδων, καὶ τοῦτο ἄπαυστον εἶναι διὰ τὸν ἄπειρον χρόνον. ἑκάστη ἄρα ψυχὴ μερικὴ κατιέναι τε ἐπ' ἄπειρον δύναται καὶ ἀνιέναι. καὶ τοῦτο οὐ μὴ παύσεται περὶ ἀπάσας τὸ πάθημα γενόμενον.   [4] Στοιχ. Θεολ. 211.

of Isidore, his predecessor in the chair, whose biography he
wrote[1]. In an extensive work on First Principles ('Απορίαι
καὶ λύσεις περὶ τῶν πρώτων ἀρχῶν)[2], he maintained with the
utmost elaboration that the principle of things is unknowable.
This we have met with as a general position in Proclus[3]; and
it is already laid down distinctly by Plotinus, who says for
example that we can learn by intellect *that* the One is, but not
what it is. Even to call it the One is rather to deny of it
plurality than to assert any truth regarding it that can be
grasped by the intelligence[4]. Still, with Plotinus and Proclus,
this is more a recognition of the inadequacy of all forms of
thought to convey true knowledge of the principle which is the
source of thought, than a doctrine standing out by itself as the
last word of their philosophy. Damascius on the other hand
seems to exhaust human language in the effort to make plain
how absolutely unknowable the principle is[5]. Thus his doctrine has the effect of a new departure, and presents itself as
the most definitely agnostic phase of ancient metaphysics.
Zeller treats this renunciation of all knowledge of the principle
as a symptom of the exhaustion of Greek philosophy; a view
which perhaps, at certain points of time, would not have
allowed us to hope much more from modern philosophy. The
ancient schools, however, did not die till a final blow was
struck at them on behalf of the spiritual authority that now
ruled the world.

It may be read in Gibbon how the Emperor Justinian (527
–565), while he directed the codification of the Roman law,
succeeded in effacing in considerable measure the record of
stages of jurisprudence less conformable to the later imperial

---

[1] The fragments of this, preserved by Photius, are printed in the appendix
to the Didot edition of Diogenes Laertius.

[2] About half of this work was edited by Kopp in 1826; the whole by Ruelle
in 1889. In 1898 was published a complete French translation by M. Chaignet
in three volumes. [3] Στοιχ. Θεολ. 123.

[4] Enn. v. 5, 6: τὸ δὲ οἷον σημαίνοι ἂν τὸ οὐχ οἷον· οὐ γὰρ ἔνι οὐδὲ τὸ οἷον, ὅτῳ
μηδὲ τὸ τί....τάχα δὲ καὶ τὸ ἓν ὄνομα τοῦτο ἄρσιν ἔχει πρὸς τὰ πολλά, ὅθεν καὶ
'Απόλλωνα οἱ Πυθαγορικοὶ συμβολικῶς πρὸς ἀλλήλους ἐσήμαινον ἀποφάσει τῶν
πολλῶν.

[5] Cf. R. P. 545: καὶ τί πέρας ἔσται τοῦ λόγου πλὴν σιγῆς ἀμηχάνου καὶ ὁμο-
λογίας τοῦ μηδὲν γινώσκειν ὧν μηδὲ θέμις, ἀδυνάτων ὄντων εἰς γνῶσιν ἐλθεῖν;

absolutism. To make that absolutism unbroken even in name, he afterwards suppressed the Roman Consulship, which had gone on till his time. Before the completion of his Code—the great positive achievement to which he owes his fame—he had already promulgated a decree for securing uniformity in the spiritual sphere. So far, in spite of the formal prohibition of the ancient religion, the philosophers at Athens had retained some freedom to oppose Christian positions on speculative questions. This seems clear from the fact that Proclus had been able to issue a tractate in which he set forth the arguments for the perpetuity of the world against the Christian doctrine of creation[1]. Justinian, who was desirous of a reputation for strictness of orthodoxy, resolved that even this freedom should cease; and in 529 he enacted that henceforth no one should teach the ancient philosophy. In the previous year, when there was a "great persecution of the Greeks" (that is, of all who showed attachment to the ancient religion), it had been made a law that those who "Hellenised" should be incapable of holding offices. Suppression of the philosophical lectures was accompanied by confiscation of the endowments of the school. And these were private endowments; the public payments to the occupants of the chairs having long ceased[2]. The liberty of philosophising was now everywhere brought within the limits prescribed by the Christian Church. Not till the dawn of modern Europe was a larger freedom to be reassumed; and not even then without peril.

The narrative of the historian Agathias (fl. 570) is well known, how Damascius, Simplicius, Eulalius, Priscianus, Hermias, Diogenes and Isidorus departed from Athens for Persia, having been invited by King Chosroes (Khosru Nushirvan), and hoping to find in the East an ideal kingdom and a philosophic king[3]. Though Chosroes himself was not without a real interest in philosophy, as he showed by the translations he caused to be made of Platonic and Aristotelian writings, their

---

[1] A reply to the Ἐπιχειρήματα κατὰ Χριστιανῶν of Proclus was written by Joannes Philoponus, in the form of a lengthy work (included in the Teubner Series, 1899) bearing the title De Aeternitate Mundi.

[2] See, for the evidence as to the exact circumstances of the suppression, Zeller, iii. 2, pp. 849–50, with notes. Cf. R. P. 547 c.   [3] R. P. 547.

expectations were thoroughly disappointed. They found that the genuine unmodified East was worse than the Roman Empire in its decline. At length they entreated to return to their own country under any conditions; and Chosroes, though pressing them to stay, not only allowed them to go, but in a special clause of a treaty of peace with Justinian, stipulated that they should not be constrained to forsake their own opinions, but should retain their freedom while they lived. This was in 533. The date of their voluntary exile was probably 532.

After their return, as has been already indicated, the philosophers devoted themselves to the writing of learned commentaries. The most illustrious of the commentators was Simplicius, whose works on Aristotle's *Categories*, *Physics*, *De Caelo* and *De Anima*, and on the *Encheiridion* of Epictetus, are extant. Even this last period was not marked by complete inability to enter on a new path. What the speculative exhaustion animadverted on by Zeller really led to was a return to the most positive kind of knowledge that then seemed attainable. Aristotle now came to be studied with renewed zeal; and it was in fact by a tradition from the very close of antiquity that he afterwards acquired his predominant authority, first among the Arabians and then among the schoolmen of the West[1]. The last Neo-Platonists thus had the merit of comprehending his unapproached greatness as the master in antiquity of all human and natural knowledge. If to some extent they were wrong in trying to prove his thoroughgoing agreement with Plato, their view was at any rate nearer the mark than that which makes the two philosophers types of opposition. The most recent students of Plato would perfectly agree with one at least of the distinctions by which Simplicius reconciles apparently conflicting positions. When Plato, he says, describes the world as having come to be, he means that it proceeds from a higher cause; when Aristotle describes it as not having become, he means that it has no beginning in time[2]. Apart from learned research, subtleties may still be found in the commentators that had never before been ex-

---

[1] Cf. Renan, *Averroès et l'Averroïsme*, pp. 92–3.
[2] Zeller, iii. 2, p. 846. Cf. Archer-Hind, *The Timaeus of Plato*.

pressed with such precision. For the rest, they are themselves
as conscious of the decline as their modern critics. What they
actually did was in truth all that was possible, and the very
thing that was needed, in their own age.

To the latest period, as was said at the beginning of the
chapter, belong the names of several Alexandrian teachers.
Among these are Hermias, the pupil of Syrianus; Ammonius,
the son of Hermias and the pupil of Proclus[1]; Asclepiodotus,
a physician, who, according to Damascius, surpassed all his
contemporaries in knowledge of mathematics and natural
science; and Olympiodorus, a pupil of Ammonius and the
last teacher of the Platonic philosophy whose name has been
preserved. Commentaries by Hermias and Ammonius, as well
as by Olympiodorus, are still extant.

An exhaustive history of Neo-Platonism would find in the
writings of the Athenian school materials especially abundant.
Much has been printed, though many works still remain un-
published. In the present chapter, only a very general account
is attempted[2]. The object, here as elsewhere, has been to bring
out the essential originality of the Neo-Platonic movement;
not to trace minutely the various currents that contributed to
its formation and those into which it afterwards diverged as it
passed into later systems of culture. To follow, "per incertam
lunam sub luce maligna," the exact ways by which it modified
the culture of mediæval Europe, would be a work of research
for a separate volume. The general direction, however, and its
principal stages, are sufficiently clear; and some attempt will
be made in the next chapter to trace first the continued
influence of Neo-Platonism in the Middle Ages, and then its
renewed influence at the Renaissance and in modern times.
For the earliest period—for the unmistakably "dark ages" of
the West—the transmission was in great part through Christian
writers, who, living at the close of the ancient world, had received
instruction as pupils in the still surviving philosophic schools.

---

[1] Joannes Philoponus (fl. 530), the Christian commentator on Aristotle,
had Ammonius for his teacher, and quotes him as "the philosopher." See
Zeller, iii. 2, p. 829, n. 4.

[2] This is now supplemented by an account of the Commentaries of Proclus;
for which see the end of the volume.

CHAPTER X

THE INFLUENCE OF NEO-PLATONISM

THE influence of Neo-Platonism on the official Christian philosophy of the succeeding period was mainly in the department of psychology. Biblical psychology by itself did not of course fix any determinate scientific view. Its literal interpretation might seem, if anything, favourable to a kind of materialism combined with supernaturalism, like that of Tertullian. Even the Pauline conception of "spirit," regarded at once as an infusion of Deity and as the highest part of the human soul, lent itself quite easily to a doctrine like that of the Stoics, which identified the divine principle in the world with the corporeal element most remote by its lightness and mobility from gross matter. For a system, however, that was to claim on behalf of its supernatural dogmas a certain justification by human reason as a preliminary condition to their full reception by faith, the idea of purely immaterial soul and mind was evidently better adapted. This conception, taken over for the practical purposes of the Church in the scientific form given to it by the Neo-Platonists, has accordingly maintained its ground ever since. The occasional attempts in modern times by sincerely orthodox Christians to fall back upon an exclusive belief in the resurrection of the body, interpreted in a materialistic sense, as against the heathen doctrine of the natural immortality of the soul, have never gained any appreciable following. At the end of the ancient world Platonic idealism, so far as it was compatible with the dualism necessitated by certain portions of the dogmatic system, was decisively adopted. In the East, Greek ecclesiastical writers such as Nemesius (fl. 450), who had derived their culture from Neo-Platonism, transmitted its refutations of materialism to the next age. In the West, St Augustine, who, as is known, was profoundly influenced by Platonism, and who had read Plotinus in a Latin translation, performed the same philosophical service. The great positive result was to familiarise the European mind with the elements of certain metaphysical conceptions elaborated by the latest school of independent philosophy. When the time came for renewed independence, long practice with abstractions had made it easier than it had ever hitherto been—difficult as it still was—to set out in the pursuit of philosophic truth from a primarily subjective point of view.

It was long, however, before Western Europe could even begin to fashion for itself new instruments by provisionally working within the prescribed circle of revealed dogma and subordinated philosophy. The very beginning of Scholasticism is divided by a gulf of more than three centuries from the end of Neo-Platonism; and not for about two centuries more did this lead to any continuous intellectual movement. In the meantime, the elements of culture that remained had been transmitted by Neo-Platonists or writers influenced by them. An especially important position in this respect is held by Boethius, who was born at Rome about 480, was Consul in 510, and was executed by order of Theodoric in 524. In philosophy Boethius represents an eclectic Neo-Platonism turned to ethical account. His translation of Porphyry's logical work has already been mentioned. He also devoted works of his own to the exposition of Aristotle's logic. It was when he had fallen into disgrace with Theodoric that he wrote the *De Consolatione Philosophiae*; and the remarkable fact has often been noticed that, although certainly a nominal Christian, he turned in adversity wholly to heathen philosophy, not making the slightest allusion anywhere to the Christian revelation. The vogue of the *De Consolatione* in the Middle Ages is equally noteworthy. Rulers like Alfred, eagerly desirous of spreading all the light that was accessible, seem to have been drawn by a secret instinct to the work of a man of kindred race, who, though at the extreme bound, had still been in living contact with the indigenous culture of the old European world. Another work much read in the same period was the commentary of Macrobius (fl. 400) on the *Somnium Scipionis* extracted from Cicero's *De Republica*. Macrobius seems not to have

been even a nominal Christian. He quotes Neo-Platonist
writers, and, by the impress he has received from their type
of thinking, furnishes evidence of the knowledge there was of
them in the West.

In the East some influence on theological metaphysics was
exercised by Synesius, the friend of Hypatia. Having become
a Christian, Synesius unwillingly allowed himself to be made
Bishop of Ptolemais (about 410); seeking to reserve the philosophical liberty to treat portions of popular Christianity as
mythical, but not quite convinced that this was compatible
with the episcopal office. A deeper influence of the same kind,
extending to the West, came from the works of the writer
known under the name of that "Dionysius the Areopagite"
who is mentioned among the converts of St Paul at Athens
(Acts xvii. 34). As no incontestable reference to those works
is found till the sixth century, and as they are characterised by
ideas distinctive of the school of Proclus, it is now held that
they proceeded from some Christian Platonist trained in the
Athenian school. It is possible indeed that the real Dionysius
had been a hearer of Proclus himself. We learn from Marinus[1]
that not all who attended his lectures were his philosophical
disciples. The influence of the series of works, in so far as
they were accepted officially, was to fix the "angelology" of
the Church in a learned form. They also gave a powerful
impulse to Christian mysticism, and, through Scotus Erigena,
set going the pantheistic speculations which, as soon as
thought once more awoke, began to trouble the faith.

When, about the middle of the ninth century, there emerges
the isolated figure of John Scotus Erigena, we may say, far as
we still are from anything that can be called sunrise, that

> now at last the sacred influence
> Of light appears, and from the walls of Heaven
> Shoots far into the bosom of dim Night
> A glimmering dawn.

He has been regarded both as a belated Neo-Platonist and
as the first of the Scholastics. In reality he cannot be classed
as a Neo-Platonist, for his whole effort was directed towards

---

[1] *Vita Procli*, 38.

rationalising that system of dogmatic belief which the Neo-Platonists had opposed from the profoundest intellectual and ethical antipathy. On the other hand, he was deeply influenced by the forms of Neo-Platonic thought transmitted through Dionysius, whose works he translated into Latin; and his own speculations soon excited the suspicion of ecclesiastical authority. His greatest work, the *De Divisione Naturae*, was in 1225 condemned by Pope Honorius. III to be burned. Scotus had, however, begun the characteristic movement of Christian Scholasticism. And Dionysius, who could not well be anathematised consistently with the accredited view about the authorship of his writings—who indeed was canonised, and came to be identified with St Denys of France—had been made current in Latin just at the moment when the knowledge of Greek had all but vanished from the West.

The first period of Scholasticism presents a great gap between Scotus and the next considerable thinkers, who do not appear before the latter part of the eleventh century. Towards the end of the twelfth century, the second period begins through the influx of new Aristotelian writings and of the commentaries upon them by the Arabians. The Arabians themselves, on settling down after their conquest of Western Asia, had found Aristotle already translated into Syriac. Translations were made from Syriac into Arabic. These translations and the Arabian commentaries on them were now translated into Latin, sometimes through Hebrew; the Jews being at this time again the great intermediaries between Asia and Europe. Not long after, translations were made directly from the Greek texts preserved at Constantinople. Thus Western Europe acquired the complete body of Aristotle's logical writings, of which it had hitherto only possessed a part; and, for the first time since its faint reawakening to intellectual life, it was put in possession of the works dealing with the content as well as the form of philosophy. After prohibiting more than once the reading of the newly recovered writings, and in particular of the *Physics* and *Metaphysics*, the ecclesiastical chiefs at length authorised them; having come to see in the theism of Aristotle, which they were now able to discriminate from the pantheism of pseudo-Aristotelian writings, a preparation for the faith. It is from this period that the predominating sciéntific authority of Aristotle in the Christian schools must be dated. Taken over as a tradition from the Arabians, it had been by them received from the latest commentators of the Athenian school of Neo-Platonism.

The Arabian philosophy, highly interesting in itself, is still more interesting to us for its effect on the intellectual life of Europe. Aristotelian in basis, it was Neo-Platonic in super-structure. Its distinctive doctrine of an impersonal immor-tality of the general human intellect is, however, as contrasted both with Aristotelianism and with Neo-Platonism, essentially original. This originality it does not owe to Mohammedanism. Its affinity is rather with Persian and Indian mysticism. Not that Mohammedanism wanted a speculative life of its own; but that which is known to history as "Arabian philosophy" did not belong to that life[1]. The proper intellectual life of Islam was in "theology." From the sharp antagonism which sprang up between the Arabian philosophers and "theo-logians" seems to date the antithesis which became current especially in the Europe of the Renaissance. For the Greek philosophers, "theology" had meant first a poetic exposition of myths, but with the implication that they contained, either directly or when allegorised, some theory of the origin of things. Sometimes—as occasionally in Aristotle and oftener in the Neo-Platonists—it meant the highest, or metaphysical, part of philosophy. It was the doctrine of God as first prin-ciple of things, and was accordingly the expression of pure speculative reason. With Islam, as with Christianity, it might mean this; but it meant also a traditional creed imposed by the authority of Church and State. The creed contained many articles which philosophy might or might not arrive at by the free exercise of reason. To the Mohammedan "theologian," however, these were not points which it was permissible to question, except hypothetically, but principles to argue from. Hence the "philosophers," having made acquaintance with

[1] See Renan, *Averroès et l'Averroïsme*, ch. ii.

the intellectual liberty of Greece, which they were seeking to naturalise in Arabian science, were led to adopt the custom of describing distinctively as a "theologian" one who speculated under external authority and with a practical purpose. Of course the philosophers claimed to deal equally—or, rather, at a higher level—with divine objects of speculation; but, according to their own view, they were not bound by the definitions of the theologian. At the same time, they were to defer to theology in popular modes of speech, allowing a "theological" truth, or truth reduced to what the multitude could profit by, in distinction from "philosophical" or pure truth. The Jews and the Christians too, they allowed, were in possession of theological truth; each religion being good and sufficient in practice for the peoples with whom it was traditional. The reason of this procedure—which has no precise analogue either in ancient or in modern times—was that the Arabian Hellenising movement was pantheistic, while the three religions known to the philosophers all held to the personality of God. Hence the Arabian philosophy could not, like later Deism, find what it regarded as philosophic truth by denuding all three religions of their discrepant elements. Since they were expressed in rigorously defined creeds, it could not allegorise them as the ancient philosophers had allegorised polytheism. Nor was the method open to it of ostensibly founding a new sect. The dominant religions were theocratic, claiming the right, which was also the duty, of persecution. The consequence was, formulation of the strange doctrine known as that of the "double truth."

Under the dominion of Islam, the "philosophers," in spite of their distinction between the two kinds of truth, were treated by the "theologians" as a hostile sect and reduced to silence. Their distinction, however, penetrated to Christian Europe, where, though condemned by Church Councils, it long held its ground as a defence against accusations of heresy. The orthodox distinction between two spheres of truth, to be investigated by different methods but ultimately not in contradiction, may easily be put in its place. Hence a certain elusiveness which no doubt helped to give it vogue in a society not inwardly quite submissive to the authority of the Church even at the time when the theocracy had apparently crushed all secular and intellectual opposition. The profundity of the revolt is evident alike in the philosophical and in the religious movements that marked the close of the twelfth and the opening of the thirteenth century. The ideas that animated both movements were of singular audacity. In philosophy, the intellectual abstractions of Neo-Platonism, and in particular the abstraction of "matter," were made the ground for a revived naturalistic pantheism. Ideas of "absorption," or impersonal immortality, genuinely Eastern in spirit, may have appealed as speculations to the contemplative ascetics of Orientalised Europe. These were not the only ideas that came to the surface. In common with its dogmas, the Catholic hierarchy was threatened; and, to suppress the uprising, the City of Dis on earth was completed by the Dominican Inquisition. Yet philosophy, so far as it could be made subservient to orthodoxy, was to be a most important element in the training of the Dominicans themselves. From their Order proceeded Thomas Aquinas, the most systematic thinker of the Middle Ages, at whose hands scholastic Aristotelianism received its consummate perfection. Against older heresies, against "Averroism," against the pantheism of heterodox schoolmen, the Angelic Doctor furnished arguments acceptable to orthodoxy, marshalled in syllogistic array. For a short time, his system could intellectually satisfy minds of the highest power, skilled in all the learning of their age, if only they were in feeling at one with the dominant faith.

Over and above its indirect influence through the psychology of the Fathers, Neo-Platonic thought found direct admission into the orthodox no less than into the heterodox speculation of the Scholastic period. Aquinas quotes largely from Dionysius; and Dante was, as is well known, a student both of Aquinas and of Dionysius himself, whose classification of the "Heavenly Hierarchy" he regarded as a direct revelation communicated by St Paul to his Athenian proselyte. Thus, if we find Neo-Platonic ideas in Dante, there is no difficulty about their source. The line of derivation goes straight

back to the teaching of Proclus. We are not reduced to the
supposition of an indirect influence from Plotinus through
St Augustine. Incidental Neo-Platonic expressions in Dante
have not escaped notice[1]. More interesting, however, than
any detailed coincidence is the fundamental identity of the
poet's conception of the beatific vision with the vision of the
intelligible world as figured by Plotinus. Almost equally
prominent is the use he makes of the speculative conception
of emanation. That the higher cause remains in itself while
producing that which is next to it in order of being, is affirmed
by Dante in terms that might have come directly from Plotinus or Proclus[2]. And it is essentially by the idea of emanation that he explains and justifies the varying degrees of
perfection in created things.

The Neo-Platonism of the *Divina Commedia*, as might be
expected, is found almost exclusively in the *Paradiso*; though
one well-known passage in the *Purgatorio*, describing the mode
in which the disembodied soul shapes for itself a new material
envelope, bears obvious marks of the same influence. Here,
however, there is an important difference. Dante renders
everything in terms of extension, and never, like the Neo-
Platonists, arrives at the direct assertion, without symbol, of
pure immaterialism. This may be seen in the passage just
referred to, as compared with a passage from Porphyry's
exposition of Plotinus closely resembling it in thought. While
Dante represents the soul as having an actual path from one
point of space to another, Porphyry distinctly says that the
soul's essence has no locality, but only takes upon itself relations depending on conformity between its dispositions and

---

[1] Some of them are referred to by Bouillet in the notes to his French
translation of the Enneads (1857–61).

Here, for want of a more appropriate place, it may be mentioned that there
is no complete translation of the Enneads into English. The marvellous
industry of Thomas Taylor, "the Platonist," in translating Neo-Platonic
writings, did not carry him through the whole of Plotinus. The portions
translated by him have been reprinted for the Theosophical Society in Bohn's
Series.

[2] The general thought finds expression at the end of *Par.* xxix.

l' eterno Valor...
Uno manendo in sè come davanti

those of a particular body; the body, whether of grosser or of
finer matter, undergoing local movement in accordance with
its own nature and not with the nature of soul[1]. Again, the
point of exact coincidence between Dante and Plotinus in
what they say of the communications between souls that are
in the world of being, is that, for both alike, every soul
"there" knows the thought of every other without need of
speech. Plotinus, however, says explicitly that the indi-
vidualised intelligences within universal mind are together
yet discriminated without any reference to space. What
Dante says is that while the souls are not really in the planetary spheres, but only appear in them momentarily, they *are*
really above in the empyrean. Even in his representation of
the Deity, the Christian poet still retains his spatial symbolism.
God is seen as the minutest and intensest point of light, round
which the angels—who are the movers of the spheres—revolve
in their ninefold order. At the same time, the divine mind is
said to be the place of the *primum mobile*, thus enclosing the
whole universe[2]. Viewed in relation to the universe as distinguished from its cause, the angelic movers are in inverted
order, the outermost and not the innermost being now the
highest. Thus, by symbol, it is finally suggested that immaterial essence is beyond the distinction of the great and
the small in magnitude; but even at the end the symbolism
has not disappeared.

Like the completed theocratic organisation of society, the
Scholastic system which furnished its intellectual justification
was hardly finished before it began to break up from within.
St Thomas Aquinas was followed by John Duns Scotus, who,
while equally orthodox in belief, limited more the demonstra-

---

[1] Cf. *Purg.* xxv. 85–102 and *Sententiae*, 32. Porphyry is explaining the way
in which the soul may be said to descend to Hades. ἐπεὶ δὲ διήκει τὸ βαρὺ
πνεῦμα καὶ ἔνυγρον ἄχρι τῶν ὑπογείων τόπων, οὕτω καὶ αὕτη λέγεται χωρεῖν ὑπὸ
γῆν· οὐχ ὅτι ἡ αὐτὴ οὐσία μεταβαίνει τόπους, καὶ ἐν τόποις γίνεται· ἀλλ᾽ ὅτι τῶν
πεφυκότων σωμάτων τόπους μεταβαίνειν, καὶ εἰληχέναι τόπους, σχέσεις ἀναδέχεται,
δεχομένων αὐτὴν κατὰ τὰς ἐπιτηδειότητας τῶν τοιούτων σωμάτων ἐκ τῆς κατ᾽ αὐτὴν
ποιᾶς διαθέσεως.

[2]　　　　　E questo cielo non ha altro dove
　　　　　Che la mente divina.
　　　　　　　　　　　Par. xxvii. 109–110.

tive power of reason in relation to ecclesiastical dogma. Soon
after came William of Ockham, whose orthodoxy is to some
extent ambiguous. The criticisms of the Subtle and of the
Invincible Doctor had for their effect to show the illusoriness
of the systematic harmony which their great predecessor
seemed to have given once for all to the structure composed
of dominant Catholic theology and subordinated Aristotelian
philosophy. Duns Scotus was indirectly influenced by Neo-
Platonism, which came to him from the Jewish thinker Ibn
Gebirol, known to the schoolmen as Avicebron. This was the
source of his theory of a "first matter" which is a component
of intellectual as of corporeal substances. His view that the
"principle of individuation" is not matter but form, coincides
with that of Plotinus. Ockham was a thinker of a different
cast, representing, as against the Platonic Realism of Duns
Scotus, the most developed form of mediaeval Nominalism.
In their different ways, both developments contributed to
upset the balance of the Scholastic eirenicon between science
and faith. The rapidity with which the disintegration was
now going on may be judged from the fact that Ockham died
about 1349, that is, before the end of the half-century which
had seen the composition of the *Divina Commedia*.

The end of Scholasticism as a system appealing to the living
world is usually placed about the middle of the fifteenth century. From that time, it became first an obstruction in the
way of newer thought, and then a sectarian survival. The
six centuries of its effective life are those during which Greek
thought was wholly unknown in its sources to the West.
John Scotus Erigena was one of the very last who had some
knowledge of Greek before the study of it revived in the Italy
of Petrarch and Boccaccio. For the new positive beginning
of European culture, the classical revival, together with the
impulse towards physical research,—represented among the
schoolmen by Roger Bacon,—was the essential thing.

In the familiar story of the rise of Humanism, the point
that interests us here is that the first ancient system to be
appropriated in its content, and not simply studied as a
branch of erudition, was Platonism. And it was with the eyes

of the Neo-Platonists that the Florentine Academy read Plato himself. Marsilio Ficino, having translated Plato, turned next to Plotinus. His Latin translation of the Enneads appeared in 1492[1]. Platonism was now set by its new adherents against Aristotelianism, whether in the Scholastic form or as restored by some who had begun to study it with the aid of the Greek instead of the Arabian commentaries. The name of Aristotle became for a time to nearly all the innovators the synonym of intellectual oppression.

The Platonists of the early Renaissance were sincere Christians in their own manner. This was not the manner of the Middle Age. The definitely articulated system of ecclesiastical dogma had no real part in their intellectual life. They were Christians in a general way; in the details of their thinking they were Neo-Platonists. In relation to astrology and magic, indeed, they were Neo-Platonists of a less critical type than the ancient chiefs of the school. Belief in both magic and astrology, it is hardly necessary to say, had run down through the whole course of the intervening centuries; so that there was little as yet in the atmosphere of the modern time that could lead to a renewal of the sceptical and critical sifting begun by thinkers like Plotinus and Porphyry. The influence of Christianity shows itself in the special stress laid on the religious aspect of Neo-Platonism. An example of this is to be met with at the end of Marsilio Ficino's translation of Plotinus. In the arguments prefixed to the closing chapters, Ficino tries to make Plotinus say definitely that the union of the soul with God, once attained, is perpetual. He has himself a feeling that the attempt is not quite successful; and he rather contends that Plotinus was logically bound to make the affirmation than that it is there in his very words. As a matter of fact, Plotinus has nowhere definitely made it; and it seems inconsistent alike with his own position that differences of individuality proceed with necessity from eternal distinctions in the divine intellect, and with his hypothetical use of the Stoic doctrine that events recur in exactly repeated

---

[1] The Greek was printed for the first time in 1580, when it appeared along with the translation.

cycles. When he says that in the intelligible world, though not in earthly life, the vision is continuous, this does not by itself mean that the soul, when it has ascended, remains above without recurrent descents. It is true, nevertheless, that Plotinus and Porphyry did not so explicitly as their successors affirm that all particular souls are subject to perpetual vicissitude[1].

This point is of special interest because Ficino's interpretation may have helped to mislead Bruno, who, in a passage in the dedication of his *Eroici Furori* to Sir Philip Sidney, classes Plotinus, so far as this doctrine is concerned, with the "theologians." All the great philosophers except Plotinus, he says, have taught that the mutations in the destiny of souls are without term. On the other hand, all the great theologians except Origen have taught that the soul either attains final rest or is finally excluded from beatitude. The latter doctrine has a practical reference, and may be impressed on the many lest they should take things too lightly. The former is the expression of pure truth, and is to be taught to those who are capable of ruling themselves. Great as is for Plotinus the importance of the religious redemption to which his philosophy leads, the theoretic aspect of his system is here misapprehended. Nothing, however, could bring out more clearly than this pointed contrast, Bruno's own view. Coming near the end of Renaissance Platonism, as Ficino comes near its beginning, he marks the declared break with tradition and the effort after a completely independent philosophy.

Other elements as well as Neo-Platonism contributed to Bruno's doctrine; yet he too proceeds in his metaphysics from the Neo-Platonic school. In expression, he always falls back upon its terms. The system, indeed, undergoes profound modifications. Matter and Form, Nature and God, become antithetic names of a single reality, rather than extreme terms in a causal series descending from the highest to the

---

[1] Thus St Augustine could commend Porphyry for what he took to be the assertion that the soul, having once wholly ascended to the realm of being, can never redescend to birth. That any soul can remain perpetually lapsed is unquestionably contrary to the opinion both of Plotinus and of Porphyry. One of Porphyry's objections to Christianity was that it taught that doctrine.

lowest[1]. Side by side with the identity, however, the difference
is retained, in order to express the "circle" in phenomenal
things. In Bruno's cosmological view, modifications were of
course introduced by his acceptance and extension of the
Copernican astronomy. Yet he seeks to deduce this also from
propositions of the Neo-Platonic metaphysics. The Neo-Platonists held, as he did, that the Cause is infinite in potency,
and necessarily produces all that it can produce. The reason
why they did not infer that the extended universe is quantitatively infinite was that, like some moderns, they thought
actual quantitative infinity an impossible conception.

One of Bruno's most interesting points of contact with
Plotinus is in his theory of the beautiful. For this he may
have got the hint from the difference that had struck Plotinus
between the emotion that accompanies pursuit of knowledge
and beauty on the one hand, and mystical unification with the
good on the other. By this unification, however, Plotinus does
not mean moral virtue; so that when Bruno contrasts intellectual aspiration with a kind of stoical indifference to fortune,
and treats it as a "defect" in comparison, because there is in
the constantly baffled pursuit of absolute truth or beauty an
element of pain, he is not closely following Plotinus. Yet in
their account of the aspiration itself, the two thinkers agree.
The fluctuation and pain in the aesthetic or intellectual life
are insisted on by both. In Bruno indeed the thought is
immensely expanded from the hint of Plotinus; the *Eroici
Furori* being a whole series of imaginative symbols interpreted
as expressive of the same ardour "to the unknown God of
unachieved desire." There is here manifest a difference of
temperament. Bruno had more of the restlessness which
Plotinus finds in the soul of the artist and the theorist.
Plotinus, along with his philosophical enthusiasm, had more
of the detachment and repose of the religious mystic.

The most striking difference between the Platonism of the
Neo-Platonists and that of the Renaissance, is the stronger

---

[1] Identification of all in the unity of Substance is regarded by Vacherot as
characterising Bruno's thought, in contrast with the Neo-Platonic "emanation." See *Histoire Critique de l'École d'Alexandrie*, t. iii. p. 196.

accentuation by the latter of naturalistic pantheism. This, though not absent in Neo-Platonism itself, is subordinate. Plotinus, as we saw, regards the heavenly bodies as divine, and can on occasion speak like Bruno of the earth as one of the stars. This side of his doctrine, however, is less prominent than his conception of intellectual and superessential divinity. With Bruno the reverse is the case. And Campanella too seizes on the naturalistic side of the doctrine to confound the despisers of the visible world. Among his philosophical poems there is one in particular which conveys precisely the feeling of the book of Plotinus against the Gnostics.

> Deem you that only you have thought and sense,
>   While heaven and all its wonders, sun and earth,
>   Scorned in your dullness, lack intelligence?
> Fool! what produced you? These things gave you birth:
>   So have they mind and God[1].

This tone of feeling, characteristic of the Renaissance, passed away during the prevalence of the new "mechanical philosophy," to reappear later when the biological sciences were making towards theories of vital evolution. It is thus no accident that it should then have been rendered by Goethe, who combined with his poetic genius original insight in biology.

While the Platonising movement was going on, other ancient doctrines had been independently revived. For the growth of the physical sciences, now cultivated afresh after long neglect, the revival of Atomism was especially important. The one scientific doctrine of antiquity which Neo-Platonism had been unable to turn to account was seen by modern physicists to be exactly that of which they were in need. Thus whether, like Descartes and Hobbes, they held that the universe is a plenum, or, with Democritus himself, affirmed the real existence of

---

[1] Sonnet XIX. in Symonds's translation. The original of the passage may be given for comparison.

> Pensiti aver tu solo provvidenza,
>   E 'l ciel la terra e l' altre cose belle,
>   Le quali sprezzi tu, starsene senza?
> Sciocco, d' onde se' nato tu? da quelle,
>   Dunque ci è senno e Dio.

vacuum, all the physical thinkers of the seventeenth century thought of body, for the purposes of science, as corpuscular. Corpuscular physics was the common foundation of the "mechanical philosophy." Now it is worthy of note that the first distinctively Platonic revival, beyond the period we call the Renaissance, decisively adopted the corpuscular physics as not incompatible with "the true intellectual system of the universe." The Cambridge Platonists, as represented especially by Cudworth, did not, in their opposition to the naturalism of Hobbes, show any reactionary spirit in pure science; but were so much awake to the growing ideas of the time that, even before the great impression made by Newton's work, they were able to remedy for themselves the omission that had limited the scientific resources of their ancient predecessors. And More, in appending his philosophical poem on *The Infinity of Worlds* to that on *The Immortality of the Soul*, does not shrink from appealing to the authority of Democritus, Epicurus and Lucretius in favour of those infinite worlds in space which the Neo-Platonists had rejected. Neither on this question nor on the kindred one as to the manifestation of Deity in a phenomenal universe without past or future limit in time, does he commit himself to a final conclusion; but evidently, after at first rejecting both infinities as involving impossibilities of conception, he inclined to the affirmation of both.

The new metaphysical position that philosophy had in the meantime gained, was the subjective point of view fixed by Descartes as the principle of his "method for conducting the reason and seeking truth in the sciences." This, as has been indicated, was remotely Neo-Platonic in origin; for the Neo-Platonists had been the first to formulate accurately those conceptions of immaterial subject and of introspective consciousness which had acquired currency for the later world through the abstract language of the schools. Thus Descartes, with Scholasticism and Humanism behind him, could go in a summary way through the whole process, without immersing himself in one or the other as a form of erudition; and could then start, so far as the problem of knowledge is concerned, where the ancients had left off. Knowledge of that which is within, they had found, is in the end the most certain. The originality of Descartes consisted in taking it as the most certain in the beginning. Having fixed the point of view, he could then proceed, from a few simple positions ostensibly put forward without appeal to authority, to construct a new framework for the sciences of the inner and of the outer world.

Here was the beginning of idealism in its modern form. The other great innovation of the modern world in general principle, was the notion that there is a mode of systematic- ally appealing to experience as the test of scientific truth; that rational deduction, such as was still the main thing for Descartes, must be supplemented by, if not ultimately sub- ordinated to, the test of inductive verification. This, though not exclusively an English idea, has been mainly promoted by English thinkers, in its application first to the physical, and then, still more specially, to the mental sciences. In antiquity, experience had indeed been recognised as the beginning of knowledge in the genetic order. Its priority in this sense could be allowed by a school as rationalist as Neo-Platonism. It had not, however, even by the experiential schools, been rigorously defined as a test applicable to all true science. On this side Bacon and Locke, as on the other side Descartes, were the great philosophical initiators of the new time.

The essential innovations of modern thought, as we see, were innovations in method. They did not of themselves suggest any new answer to questions about ultimate reality or the destiny of the universe. It is not that such answers have been lacking; but they have always remained, in one way or another, new formulations of old ones. The hope cherished by Bacon and Descartes that the moderns might at length cut themselves loose from the past and, by an infallible method, discover all attainable truth, has long been seen to be vain. Not only individual genius, but historical study of past ideas and systems, have become of more and not of less importance. The most original and typical ontologies of modern times are those of Spinoza and Leibniz; and, much as they owe to the newer developments of science and theory of knowledge, both are expressed by means of metaphysical conceptions that had taken shape during the last period of ancient thought. Pantheism and Monadism are not merely implicit in the Neo-Platonic doctrine; they receive clear formulation as different aspects of it. If, as some modern critics think, the two conceptions are not ultimately irreconcilable, the best hints for a solution may probably still be found in Plotinus. No one has ever been more conscious than he of the difficulty presented by the problem of comprehending as portions of one philosophical truth the reality of universal and that of individual intellect.

Perhaps the strongest testimony to the intrinsic value of the later Greek thought is Berkeley's *Siris*. For if that thought had really become obsolete, Berkeley was in every way prepared to perceive it. He had pushed the Cartesian reform as far as it would go, by reducing what Descartes still thought of as real extended substance to a system of phenomena for consciousness. He had at the same time all the English regard for the test of experience, fortified by knowledge of what had been done in his own age in investigating nature. Thus, he had taken most decisively the two steps by which modern philosophy has made a definite advance. Besides, as a theologian, he might easily have assumed that anything there was of value in the work of thinkers who, living long after the opening of the Christian era, had been the most uncompromising antagonists of the Christian Church, must have been long superseded. His own early Nominalism, which, as may be seen in *Siris* itself, he had never abandoned, might also have been expected to prejudice him against Platonic Realism. Yet it is precisely in the Neo-Platonists that Berkeley, near the end of his philosophical career, found hints towards a tentative solution of ontological questions which he had at first thought to settle once for all by a resolutely logical carrying out of the principles of Descartes and Locke. It is true that in actual result *Siris* makes no advance on the original Neo-Platonic speculations, which are not really fused with Berkeley's own early doctrine, but are at most kept clear of contradiction with it. For all that, *Siris* furnishes the most decisive evidence of enduring vitality in a school of thought which, to Berkeley's age if to any since the classical revival, must have seemed entirely of the past.

Berkeley's work here seems in a manner comparable with that of the Platonising English poets from Spenser to Shelley. The influence of Platonism on literature is, however, too wide a subject to be treated episodically. The one remark may be made, that not till modern times did it really begin to influence poetic art. In antiquity it had its theories of art,—varying greatly, as we have seen, from Plato to Plotinus,—but artistic production was never inspired by it. If poetic thought, as some think, is an anticipation of the future, this influence on poetry may be taken as further evidence that the ideas of the philosophy itself are still unexhausted.

During the seventeenth and eighteenth centuries, the great controversies of metaphysics did not centre in Platonism. There is truth in the view that would make this first period of distinctively modern philosophy a kind of continuation of later Scholasticism, more than of the Renaissance which immediately preceded it. Its ostensible questions were about method. The usual division of its schools or phases by historians is into "Dogmatism" (by which is meant the rationalistic theory of certitude) and its opposite "Empiricism," followed by "Scepticism" and then by "Criticism." As these names show, it is concerned less with inquiry into the nature of reality than with the question how reality is to be known, or whether indeed knowledge of it is possible. And, with all its differences, the modern "Enlightenment" has this resemblance to Scholasticism, that a particular system of doctrine is always in the background, to which the controversy is tacitly referred. This system is in effect the special type of theism which the more rationalistic schoolmen undertook to prove as a preliminary to faith in the Catholic creed. Even in its non-Christian form, as with the "Deists," it is still of the Judaeo-Christian tradition. The assumption about the relation of God to the world is that the world was created by an act of will. Ordinary Rationalism is "dogmatic" by its assertion that "natural religion" of this type can be demonstrated. "Empiricism" usually holds that the same general positions can be established sufficiently on at least "probable" grounds. The Scepticism of Hume proceeds to show the failure of Empiricism—with which he sides philosophically as against Rationalism—to establish anything of the kind. Hume's philosophical questioning, while this was the practical refer-ence which aroused so much lively feeling in his own age, had of course a wider reach. Yet when Kant, stirred by the impulse received from Hume, took up again from a "Critical" point of view the whole problem as to the possibility of knowledge, he too thought with a reference to the same practical centre of the controversy. Having destroyed the Wolffian "Dogmatism," he still aimed at reconstructing from its theoretical ruin a generalised theology of essentially the same type. For Kant, as for the line of thinkers closed by him, there was only one ontology formally in question; and that was Christian theism, with or without the Christian revelation.

The German movement at the opening of the nineteenth century, if it did nothing else, considerably changed this aspect of things. In its aims, whatever may now be thought of its results, it was a return to ontology without presuppositions. The limited dogmatic system which was the centre of interest for the preceding period has for the newer speculation passed out of sight. Spinoza perhaps on the positive side exercises a predominant influence; but there are returns also to the thinkers of the Renaissance, to Neo-Platonism, and to the ancient systems of the East, now beginning to be known in Europe from translations of their actual documents. A kind of Neo-Christianity too appears, which again treats Christian dogma in the spirit of the Gnostics or of Scotus Erigena. And all this is complicated by the necessity imposed on every thinker of taking up a definite attitude to the Kantian criticism of knowledge. Among the systems of the time, that of Hegel in particular has frequently been compared to Neo-Platonism; but here the resemblance is by no means close. The character of Hegel's system seems to have been determined mainly by its relation to preceding German philosophy and to Spinoza. Both on Spinoza himself and on Leibniz, the influence of Neo-Platonism, direct or indirect, was much more definite, and points of comparison might be sought with more profit. In Hegel, as in the other philosophers of the period, the resemblance is partly of a quite general kind. They are again ontologists, interested in more possibilities than in the assertion or denial of the rudiments of a single creed. But, knowing the historical position of the Neo-Platonists, they find in them many thoughts that agree with their personal tendencies.

Up to this point the outline given of the course of later philosophy may, it seems to me, on the whole be regarded as abbreviated history. The next stage may perhaps be summed up as another return from ontology to questions about the possibility of knowledge, and to logical and methodological inquiries. To pursue further the attempt to characterise the successive stages of European thought would be to enter the region where no brief summary can fairly pretend to be a deposit of ascertained results. The best plan, from the point now reached, will be to try to state the law of philosophic development which the history of Neo-Platonism suggests; and then to make some attempt to learn what positive value the doctrine may still have for the modern world. This will be the subject of the concluding chapter.

CHAPTER XI

CONCLUSION

ONCE the Neo-Platonic period, instead of being left in shadow, is brought into clear historical light, the development of Greek philosophy from Thales to Proclus is seen to consist of two alternations from naturalism to idealism. The "physical" thinkers are followed by Socrates, Plato and Aristotle. Then, by a similar antithesis, the more developed naturalism of the Stoics and Epicureans is followed by the more developed idealism of the Neo-Platonists. The psychology of the Greeks has been brought by Prof. Siebeck under the order assigned by this law. Mr Benn has suggested the law as that of Greek philosophy in general, but without carrying it through in its application to the details[1]. When to the empirical formula the test of psychological deduction is applied, this seems to show that it must have a more general character—that it must be a law, not only of Greek thought, but of the thought of mankind. For evidently, as the objective and subjective points of view become distinguished, the mind must tend to view things first objectively, and then afterwards to make a reflective return on its own processes in knowing. Thus we ought to find universally that a phase of speculative naturalism—the expression of the objective point of view—is followed, when reflection begins to analyse things into appearances for mind, by a phase of idealism. Unfortunately, no exact verification of so extended a deduction can be made out. All that can be said is that the facts do not contradict it.

The law, in the most general terms, may be stated thus: Whenever there is a spontaneous development of philosophic thought beyond the stage of dependence on tradition, a

---

[1] Both historians call the later phase Spiritualism, but on etymological grounds Idealism is the preferable term. "Spirit" ($\pi\nu\epsilon\hat{\upsilon}\mu\alpha$), as Prof. Siebeck has shown in his detailed history, was not used by the Greek philosophers themselves as the name of an immaterial principle.

naturalistic phase comes first and an idealistic phase second. In no intrinsic development, whether of individuals or of peoples, is there a reversal of the order. One or other of the phases, however, may be practically suppressed. An individual mind, or the mind of a people, may stop at naturalism, or after the most evanescent phase of it may go straight on to pure idealism. Where both phases definitely appear, as in the case of Greece, we must expect returns of the first, making a repeated rhythm. Further, we must take account of foreign influences, which may modify the intrinsic development. Also, when both stages have been passed through, and are represented by their own teachers, revivals of either may appear at any moment. Thus in modern Europe we can hardly expect to trace through the whole development any law whatever. When thinkers began to break through the new tradition which had substituted itself for ancient mythology and philosophy alike, and had ruled through the Middle Ages, there was from the first a possibility, according to the temper of the individual mind, of reviving any phase of doctrine, naturalistic or idealistic, without respect to its order in the past. We may occasionally get a typical case of the law, as in the idealistic reaction of the Cambridge Platonists on the naturalism of Hobbes; but we cannot expect anything like this uniformly.

Two great ethnical anomalies are the precisely opposite cases of India (that is, of the Hindus) and of China. Nowhere in Asia of course has there been that self-conscious break with traditional authority which we find in ancient Greece and in modern Europe; in both of which cases, however, it must be remembered that the authoritative tradition has never ceased to exist, but has continued always, even in the most sceptical or rational periods, to possess more of direct popular power than philosophy. The philosophies of India and of China are not formally distinct from their religions, and have not found it necessary to repudiate any religious belief simply as such. Still, each has a very distinct character of its own. The official philosophy of China is as purely naturalistic as that of India is idealistic. And in both cases the learned doctrine succeeds in giving a general direction to the mind of the people without appealing to force. With the Hindus, naturalism seems to have been an almost entirely suppressed phase of development. The traces of it found in some of the philosophic systems may be remains of an abortive attempt at a naturalistic view of things in India itself, or may be the result of a foreign influence such as that of Greek Atomism. On the other hand, the Taoism and the Buddhism of China are admittedly much reduced from the elevation they had at first, and have become new elements in popular superstition instead of idealistic philosophies. Buddhism of course is Indian; and Taoism, in its original form perhaps the sole attempt at metaphysics by a native Chinese teacher, seems to have been an indeterminate pantheism, not strictly to be classed either as naturalistic or as idealistic. Both are officially in the shade as compared with Confucianism; and this, while agnostic with regard to metaphysics, is as a philosophy fundamentally naturalistic; adding to ancestral traditions about right conduct simply a very general idea of cosmic order as the theoretic basis for its ethical code.

India and China being thus taken to represent one-sided evolutions of the human mind, we shall see in ancient Greece the normal sequence under a comparatively simplified form. In modern Europe we shall see a complex balance of the two tendencies. Turning from the question of historical law to that of philosophical truth, we may conjecture that the reflective process must somehow mark an advance in insight; but that, if nothing is to be lost, it ought to resume in itself what has gone before. And, as a matter of fact, European idealists, both ancient and modern, have not been content unless they could incorporate objective science with their metaphysics.

Thus we arrive at a kind of "law of three states"—tradition or mythology, naturalism, idealism. In its last two terms, this law seems to be an inversion of the sequence Comte sought to establish from the "metaphysical" to the "positive" stage; naturalism being the philosophy underlying "positivism," while idealism is another name for "metaphysics." How then are we to explain Comte's own mental development? For he

undoubtedly held that he himself had passed from tradition
through "metaphysics" to "positivity." *Exceptio probat
regulam:* "the exception tests the rule[1]." In the first place,
what Comte regarded as his own metaphysical stage was not
metaphysics at all, but a very early mode of political thought
in which he accepted from eighteenth century teachers their
doctrine of abstract "natural rights." In the second place,
his mental history really had a kind of metaphysical phase;
but this came after his strictly "positive" or naturalistic
period. His later philosophy became subjective on two sides.
Having at first regarded mathematics as the sufficient formal
basis of all the sciences, he arrived later at the view that before
the philosophy of mathematics there ought to be set out a
more general statement of principles. That is to say, his intention was to fill up the place that belongs properly to logic,
which in its formal division is subjective. Again, in his later
scheme, after the highest of the sciences, which he called
"morality"—meaning really a psychology of the individual,
placed after and not before sociology—there came his "subjective synthesis." This was an adumbration of metaphysics
in the true sense of the term; so that his circle of the sciences,
beginning with formal principles of reasoning, would have
completed itself by running into subjectivity at the other
extreme. The apparently exceptional case of Comte therefore
turns out to be a real confirmation of the law.

However it may be with this proposed law of three states,
there can be no doubt that a very highly developed form of
idealism is represented by the Neo-Platonists. How does this
stand in relation to modern thought? An obvious position to
take up would be to allow the merit of Plotinus and his successors in scientifically elaborating the highest metaphysical
conceptions, but to dismiss all their detailed ontology as of
merely historic interest. Thus we should fall back upon a
position suggested by Plato in the *Philebus*; namely, that
though there may be very little "dialectical," or, as we should
now say, metaphysical knowledge, that little may be "pure[2]."

[1] See Prof. Carveth Read's *Logic*, 1st ed., p. 214; 4th ed., p. 274.
[2] *Phileb.* 58 c.

This, however, is too easy a way. The Neo-Platonic thought is, metaphysically, the maturest thought that the European world has seen. Our science, indeed, is more developed; and so also, with regard to some special problems, is our theory of knowledge. On the other hand, the modern time has nothing to show comparable to a continuous quest of truth about reality during a period of intellectual liberty that lasted for a thousand years. What it has to show, during a much shorter period of freedom, consists of isolated efforts, bounded by the national limitations of its philosophical schools. The essential ideas, therefore, of the ontology of Plotinus and Proclus may still be worth examining in no merely antiquarian spirit.

A method of examination that suggests itself is to try whether, after all, something of the nature of verification may not be possible in metaphysics. The great defect of idealistic philosophy has been that so little can be deduced from it. The facts of nature do not, indeed, contradict it, but they seem to offer no retrospective confirmation of it. Now this, to judge from the analogy of science, may be owing to the extreme generality with which modern idealism is accustomed to state its positions. It is as if in physics we were reduced to an affirmation of the permanence of "matter" defined in Aristotelian terminology. Let us try what can be made of an idealistic system that undertakes to tell us more than that reality is in some way to be expressed in terms of mind. Plotinus and Proclus, from their theory of being, make deductions that concern the order of phenomena. Since their time, great discoveries have been made in phenomenal science. Do these tend to confirm or to contradict the deductions made from their metaphysical principles by the ancient thinkers?

We must allow, of course, for the defective science of antiquity. The Neo-Platonists cannot be expected to hold any other than the Ptolemaic astronomy. They do not, however, profess to deduce the details of astronomy from their metaphysics. Just as with the moderns, much in the way of detail is regarded as given only by experience. That the universe has this precise constitution—if it has it—is known only as an empirical fact, not as a deduction from the nature of its cause. What the Neo-Platonists deduce metaphysically is not the geocentric system, but the stability of that system—or of any other—if it exists. Thus they do not agree with the Stoics; who, though taking the same view about the present constitution of the universe, held that the system of earth with surrounding planetary and stellar spheres is periodically resolved into the primeval fire and again reconstituted, the resolution being accompanied by an enormous expansion of bulk. All such ideas of an immense total change from a given state of things to its opposite, Plotinus and his successors reject. Any cycle that they can allow involves only changes of distribution in a universe ordered always after the same general fashion. They carry this even into their interpretation of early thinkers like Empedocles. According to Simplicius, the periods of concentration and diffusion which alternate in his cosmogony were by Empedocles himself only assumed hypothetically, and to facilitate scientific analysis and synthesis[1]. For universal intellect, as all the Neo-Platonists say, is ever-existent and produces the cosmic order necessarily; hence it does not sometimes act and sometimes remain inactive. Undeviating necessity, in its visible manifestation as in reality, belongs to the divinity above man as to the unconscious nature below him. Change of manifestation depending on apparently arbitrary choice between opposites belongs to man from his intermediate position. To attribute this to the divinity is mythological. There must therefore always be an ordered universe in which every form and grade of being is represented. The phenomenal world, flowing from intellectual being by a process that is necessary and as it were natural, is without temporal beginning or end. These propositions we are already familiar with; and these are the essence of the deduction. Thus if the universe—whatever its detailed constitution may be—does not always as a whole manifest a rational order, the metaphysical principle is fundamentally wrong. To prove scientifically that the world points to an absolute temporal beginning, or that it is running down

[1] *De Caelo* (R. P. 133 i.*).

to an absolute temporal end, or even that it is as a whole
alternately a chaos and a cosmos, would be a refutation of the
form of idealism held by Plotinus. How then does modern
science stand with regard to this position?

It may seem at first sight to contradict it. For does not
the theory of cosmic evolution suppose just such immense
periodic changes as were conceived by Empedocles, according
to the most obvious interpretation of his words? So far as the
solar system is concerned, no doubt it does; but the solar
system is only a part of the universe. And there seems to be
no scientific evidence for the theory that the universe as a
whole has periods of evolution and dissolution. Indeed, the
evidence points rather against this view. Astronomical ob-
servers find existent worlds in all stages. This suggests that,
to an observer on any planet, the stellar universe would always
present the same general aspect, though never absolute
identity of detail as compared with its aspect at any other
point of time. For every formed system that undergoes dissolution, some other is evolved from the nebulae which we
call relatively "primordial." Thus the total phenomenal
manifestation of being remains always the same. If this view
should gain strength with longer observation, then science
may return in the end to the Neo-Platonic cosmology on an
enlarged scale, and again conceive of the whole as one stable
order, subject to growth and decay only in its parts. At no
time, as the metaphysician will say, is the mind of the universe wholly latent. There is no priority of sense to intellect
in the whole. The apparent priority of matter, or of the
sentiency of which matter is the phenomenon, is simply an
imaginative representation of the evolutionary process in a
single system, regarded in isolation from the universe of
which it forms part.

That this view is demonstrated by science cannot of course
be said. The evidence, however, is quite consistent with it,
and seems to point to this rather than to any other of the
possible views. The question being not yet scientifically
settled, the idealism of Plotinus still offers itself, by the
cosmology in which it issues, for verification or disproof. And

14—2

empirical confirmation, if this were forthcoming, would be quite real as far as it goes, precisely because the metaphysical doctrine is not so very general as to be consistent with all possible facts. A scientific proof that the universe is running down to a state of unalterable fixation would refute it.

To the speculative doctrine of Plotinus no very great addition, as we have seen, was made before Proclus. The additions that Proclus was able to make have by historians as a rule been treated as useless complications,—multiplications of entities without necessity. Yet the power of Proclus as a thinker is not denied even by those who find little to admire in its results; and it had undergone assiduous training. He may be said to have known in detail the whole history of ancient thought, scientific as well as philosophical, at a time when it could still be known without any great recourse to fragments and conjecture. And he came at the end of a perfectly continuous movement. It is therefore of special interest to see how the metaphysical developments he arrived at appear in the light of discoveries made since the European community returned again to the systematic pursuit of knowledge.

What is noteworthy first of all is the way in which, following Aristotle, he has incorporated with the idea of the one stable universe that of an upward movement in the processes that belong to the realm of birth. As we have seen, he distinctly says that in the order of genesis the imperfect comes before the perfect. And this is not meant simply in reference to the individual organism, where it is merely a generalised statement of obvious facts, but is applied on occasion to the history of science. Now the technical terms by which he expresses the philosophical idea of emanation admit of transference to an evolutionary process in time through which its components may be supposed to become explicit. The πρόοδος and the ἐπιστροφή, or the going forth from the metaphysical principle and the return to it, are not of course themselves processes of the universe in time. Yet there is no reason why they should not have respectively their temporal manifestations in its parts, so long as neither type of manifestation is supposed to be chronologically prior or posterior in relation to the whole. When the terms are thus applied, they find accurate expression in the idea of an evolution, and not of a lapse manifested chronologically,—with which "emanation" is sometimes confounded. Primarily, it is the ἐπιστροφή, rather than the πρόοδος, that becomes manifest as the upward movement. Indeed the term corresponds pretty closely to "involution," which, as Spencer has said[1], would more truly express the nature of the movement than "evolution." This process is seen in history when thought, by some great discovery, returns to its principle. The antithetic movement, which may be regarded as the manifestation of the πρόοδος, is seen when, for example, a great discovery is carried, as time goes on, into more and more minute details, or is gradually turned to practical applications. Thus it corresponds to most of what in modern times is called "progress." A corollary drawn by Proclus from his system, it may be noted, also suggests itself from the point of view of modern evolution. The highest and the lowest things, Proclus concludes, are simple; "composition," or complexity, belongs to intermediate natures.

An even more remarkable point of contact between the metaphysics of Proclus and later science is that which presents itself when we bring together his doctrine of the "divine henads" and the larger conceptions of modern astronomy. This doctrine, as we saw, is with Proclus abstract metaphysics. The One, he reasons, must be mediated to the remoter things by many unities, to each of which its own causal "chain" is attached. Elaborate as the theory is, it had, when put forth, hardly any concrete application. If, however, we liberate the metaphysics from the merely empirical part of the cosmology, a large and important application becomes clear. The primal One, as we know, is by Neo-Platonism identified with the Platonic Idea of the Good. Now this, with Plato, corresponds in the intelligible world to the sun in the visible world, and is its cause. But if, as Proclus concluded, the One must be mediated to particular beings by many divine unities, what constitution should we naturally suppose the visible universe

[1] *First Principles*, 6th ed., p. 261.

to have? Evidently, to each "henad" would correspond a single world which is one of many, each with its own sun. Thus the metaphysical conception of Proclus exactly prefigures the post-Copernican astronomy, for which each of the fixed stars is the centre of a planetary "chain," and the source of life to the living beings that appear there in the order of birth[1].

From the infinite potency of the primal Cause, Bruno drew the inference that the universe must consist of actually innumerable worlds. If we take the Neo-Platonic doctrine, not in its most generalised form—in which, as soon as we go beyond a single world, it might seem to issue naturally in an assertion of the quantitative infinite—but with the additions made to it by Proclus, the plurality of worlds certainly becomes more scientifically thinkable. For the "henads"—composing, as Proclus says, the plurality nearest to absolute unity—are finite in number. Quantitative infinity he in common with all the school rejects[2]. A kind of infinity of space as a subjective form would have presented no difficulty. Indeed both the geometrical and the arithmetical infinite were allowed by Plotinus in something very like this sense. The difficulty was in the supposition that there are actually existent things in space which are infinite in number. The problem, of course, still remains as one of metaphysical inference. For there can be no astronomical proof either that the whole is finite or that it is infinite. An infinite *real* ethereal space, with a finite universe of gravitating matter—which seems to be the tacit supposition of those who argue from the fact of radiant heat that the sum of worlds is running down to an end—Bruno and his Neo-Platonic predecessors would alike have rejected.

[1] That the supreme unity, in distinction from the henads, has no central body to correspond with it, would have removed, not created, a difficulty. To Proclus, the representation of the transcendent idea of the good by a particular physical body in the universe was embarrassing (see *Comm. in Remp.*, ed. Kroll, i. 274–5; cf. *in Tim.* 170 E, ed. Diehl, ii. 102).

[2] He himself, however, regarded it as most plausible, if there are more worlds than one, that they should be infinite in number; for a finite number would seem accidental (*Comm. in Tim.* 133 c, ed. Diehl, i. 438). But clearly this objection applies also to his own henads.

The Neo-Platonic idealism, it ought now to be evident, was
far removed from the reproach of peculiar inability to bring
itself into relation with the things of time and space. If both
finally baffle the attempt at complete mental comprehension,
this, the philosophers would have said, is because they are
forms of becoming, and hence remain mixed with illusory
imagination. Contrasted with the eternity of intellect, that
which appears under those forms is in a sense unreal. The
whole philosophy of "genesis," however largely conceived,
becomes again what it was for Parmenides, to whom the
explanations of physics, though having truth as a coherent
order in the world of appearance, where

πᾶν πλέον ἐστὶν ὁμοῦ φάεος καὶ νυκτὸς ἀφάντου,
ἴσων ἀμφοτέρων[1],

are yet false as compared with the unmixed truth of being.
In whatever sense Parmenides conceived of being, the Neo-
Platonists, as we know, conceived of it in the manner of
idealism. Their idealistic ontology, not deprived of all its
detail but merely of its local and temporal features, would, if
accepted, clear up more things than the most ambitious of
modern systems. That it does not in the end profess to make
all things clear, should not be to a modern mind a reason for
contemning it, but should rather tell in its favour.

[1] Parmenides ap. Simplic. *Phys.* (Fr. 9, Diels).

APPENDIX

I. THE COMMUNISM OF PLATO

THE feature of Plato's *Republic* that has drawn most general attention both in ancient and in modern times is its communism. This communism, however, had no place in the doctrine of his philosophical successors. And his system is in one important point quite opposed to that which is usual in modern socialism with its effort after equality. Some unremembered anticipation of this may have been caricatured by Aristophanes in the *Ecclesiazusae*: but the artifices in the comedy for maintaining strict "democratic justice" are of course the very antithesis of the Platonic conception, the essence of which is to cultivate to the highest point, by separation of classes and by special training, every natural difference of faculty. Besides, the Platonic community of goods is applied only to the ruling philosophic class of guardians and to the military class of their auxiliaries. The industrial portion of the community is apparently left to the system of private property and commercial competition—though no doubt with just so much regulation from the guardians as is necessary to preserve the social health and keep down imposthumes. Now the interesting thing is that this offers something far more practicable than socialism of the modern industrial type.

That this is so may be seen by bringing the Platonic community of goods into comparison with Spencer's generalisations, in the third volume of his *Principles of Sociology*, on the origin of "Professional Institutions." Spencer shows that professional, as distinguished from industrial, institutions are all differentiated from the priesthood, which, along with the military class, forms the dominant part of the earliest specialised society. Now the remuneration of all professional classes is for a long time public. Like Plato's guardians, they receive support from the rest of the community, not so much for particular services as for constant readiness to perform certain kinds of service. And a sort of disinterested character long continues to be assumed in professional functions, so that the remuneration is formally a voluntary gift, and not the market price of the service immediately done. This is now looked upon as a "survival." The normal system is thought to be that in which every form of social activity is thrown into the competition of the market-place. Perhaps Spencer himself took this view. If, however, we follow out the clue supplied by his inductions, we are led to imagine a new transformation by which predominant industrialism might, having done its work, be displaced by a reform in the spirit though not according to the letter of the Platonic communism.

Industrial institutions, as Spencer says, are for the "sustentation" of life; professional institutions are for its "augmentation." Now, where there is to be augmentation, sustentation, and the activities subservient to it, must not be the direct aim of everyone in the community. Among Spencer's "professional" activities, for example, are science and philosophy. The beginnings of these, Aristotle had already said, appeared among the Egyptian priests because they had leisure to speculate. As Hobbes put it, "leisure is the mother of philosophy." The same thing is recognised in Comte's social reconstruction, where, though individual property is retained, commercial competition is allowed only in the industrial sphere; the class that corresponds to the higher class of Plato's guardians being supported publicly on condition of renouncing all claim to a private income. The difference of Comte's from Plato's scheme is that it is social and not directly political. Comte assigns no "secular power" to his ecclesiastical or philosophical class. What Spencer's inductive conclusions also suggest is a social rather than a political transformation, but one more generalised than Comte's. For the professional class, as conceived by Spencer, includes much more than the philosophic and scientific class. It is far too differentiated to be restored to anything like the homogeneity of an early priesthood. Hence it could not, as such, become a ruling class, either directly like Plato's guardians, or indirectly like the Comtean hierocracy.

The point of the reform that suggests itself is this: if the whole social organism is ever to be brought under an ethical ideal of the performance of social duties, transcending the conception of an unmitigated struggle for individual profit or subsistence, the class to begin with is the class which, by its origin, has already something of the disinterested character. The liberal professions must be, as it were, brought back to their original principles. The natural method of achieving this would be an extension of the system of public payment as opposed to quasi-commercial competition. Competition itself cannot be dispensed with; but it would then be in view of selection or promotion by qualified judges, and no longer with a view to individual payments from members of the general community taken at random. Payments would be graduated but fixed; not left to the chances of employment in each particular case. In short, the method would be that of the ecclesiastical and military professions, and of the Civil Service, generalised; though it would no doubt be necessary, as Comte admitted in the case of teachers, to leave just enough liberty of private practice to guard against the repression of originality.

To attempt such a reform from below, as is the idea of industrial socialism, is evidently chimerical. Industrial institutions have their first origin in the necessity of subsistence, not in an overflow of unconstrained energy; and, so far as they are developed from within, they owe their development to the keenest desire for gain. Hence they cannot but be the last to be effectively "moralised." This is just as fatal to Comte's proposal that the supreme secular power should be handed over to the "industrial chiefs" as it is to "social democracy." A purely industrial society could not supply enough disinterested elements for the work of general regulation. The conclusion seems to be that competition with a view to individual profit must, as Plato and Comte equally recognised, be left in the industrial sphere because in that sphere it supplies the only natural and adequate motive of exertion; but that, even there, it can only be carried on justly and humanely under political regulation by representatives of the whole community. To constitute a complete political society, it is generally allowed that there must be diversity of interests. If we allow that there must also be disinterested elements, then it is evident that these can only be fitly developed by the reduction of material motives, within a certain portion of the society, to their lowest possible limit. The Platonic communism was the first attempt to solve this problem systematically instead of leaving it to accident.

II. The Gnostics

While the generalised position about the Gnostics stated at the end of Chapter III is still quite in conformity with what is known, I have to correct the more special interpretations adopted in the Appendix as it appeared in the first edition. In the present outline of the views since arrived at, I have carried over particular points that can still be sustained; but the account of the relation of Gnosticism,—or, more accurately, of the gnosis,—to Christianity has had to be radically modified.

A critic in *The Guardian* who objected to the classification of Gnosticism as a development of Christianity was substantially right. It is true that the article of R. A. Lipsius in Ersch and Gruber's *Encyclopaedia*, to which I referred as the most accurate appreciation of Gnosticism known to me, represented an advance on the position of Matter, in his *Histoire Critique du Gnosticisme*, that it was an amalgam of Christianity with Greek philosophy and miscellaneous theogonies. Lipsius recognised that the gnosis was fundamentally Oriental, and here he was right; but his presupposition that it was a spontaneous development from Christian data was mistaken; and in tracing its non-Judaic and non-Christian elements to Phoenician and Syro-Chaldaic polytheism, he took too limited a view. The theory of its origins has since been revolutionised by studies like those of R. Reitzenstein on the ancient "mystery-religions" and the theosophic speculations that arose from their intermixture. As books of epoch-making importance, containing points of view that will necessitate the re-writing of the whole history of Gnosticism, I must mention especially Reitzenstein's *Poimandres* (1904) and *Die hellenistischen Mysterienreligionen* (1910).

The real origins of the gnosis, he finds, go back at least as far as to the period of the first Persian Empire. Of its various elements, he himself lays most stress on compositions which he attributes to Egyptian priests or prophets who wrote in Greek but had command of a genuine basis of native theology. Evidence for the existence of a varied literature of this kind is found in what are called the "magical papyri," which have come to light abundantly in recent years. Through its points of contact with these, the "Hermetic" literature, so much studied at the Renaissance, but since neglected as the product of a late "syncretism," again acquires special importance. In this, it now appears from comparative study, there is a nucleus that had taken form probably in the first years of the Christian era. It therefore derived at the start nothing from Christianity. Of influence from Christianity or from Neo-Platonism at a later time there is very little. Christianity, in Reitzenstein's view, though it gave practically nothing, received much from the gnosis that sprang out of the mystery-religions; but Neo-Platonism stood out, as is seen especially

in the treatise of Plotinus against the Gnostics, not distinctively against Christian positions incidentally touched, but
for methodical thought in opposition to the revelations of
prophets in general. Now the literary mode of those who
speak in the name of "thrice-great Hermes" is that of prophetic revealers. Some use of a terminology derived from the
philosophic schools is not to be denied to the writers of the
gnosis, Hermetic and other; but it was used to translate into
Hellenistic form ideas Eastern in their source. These, Reitzenstein is careful to point out, were in part Persian and in
part Chaldaean, and not exclusively Egyptian. That he
should himself see, above all, the Egyptian elements, he with
great impartiality ascribes to bias derived from his own
studies[1]. On the philosophic side, Reitzenstein finds that the
Stoic Posidonius (c. 130–46 B.C.) approximated most to the
Hellenistic theosophy, and had a powerful influence on the
development, in later antiquity, of religious philosophy and
philosophical religion. Still, whatever this may have been, it
remains clear, from Reitzenstein's own conclusions, that the
contact of philosophy and gnosis was mainly external. Each,
in taking over ideas or terms from the other, supplied the
order of connexion from its own tradition; and the traditions
were different.

For the gnosis was not primarily disinterested search for
truth, scientific or philosophical. The phrase was, in full,
"knowledge of God" ($\gamma\nu\tilde{\omega}\sigma\iota\varsigma$ $\theta\epsilon o\tilde{v}$), and this knowledge had
such objects as material prosperity or protection from
"demons." A safe passage into the invisible world, it was
thought, could be secured by means of sacred formulae like
those of the old Egyptian religion. Rebirth ($\pi\alpha\lambda\iota\gamma\gamma\epsilon\nu\epsilon\sigma\iota\alpha$)
was supposed to be conferred by rites of baptism (called in
the Epistle to Titus, iii. 5, the $\lambda o\nu\tau\rho\grave{o}\nu$ $\pi\alpha\lambda\iota\gamma\gamma\epsilon\nu\epsilon\sigma\iota\alpha\varsigma$). The
astrological fatalism that had come from Babylonia was felt
as an actual oppression, and deliverance from it was sought
through the aid of a higher power than the planetary spirits
(the $\kappa o\sigma\mu o\kappa\rho\acute{\alpha}\tau o\rho\epsilon\varsigma$ of the Pauline demonology). Here the

---

[1] The future historian of Gnosticism, however much the general position
may have been modified, will have to do justice to Matter's breadth of view.
In trying to bring everything under the formula of "eclecticism," which
dominated French philosophy in his time, he was all-inclusive in his attitude
to the sources. Among these, he did not fail to see the peculiar importance
of Egypt; and, in Book i. chap. 10 ("Origines Chrétiennes"), while treating
Christianity as "the most direct element of Gnosticism," he in effect proves
by examination of the New Testament that the gnosis was prior.

readiest illustrations occur in the New Testament: but it was the recipient, not the source, of the Gnostic ideas; which were not distinctively either Jewish or Christian, but belonged to a wider movement in which the Judaeo-Christian tradition was only one current.

The Egyptian gnosis had its revealer in the god Thoth, translated as Hermes, with the epithet "Trismegistus." Here, according to Reitzenstein, was the source, not indeed of the term Logos in Philo, but of its "hypostasis[1]." In reality, Philo's Λόγος was a god, identical originally with Thoth or Hermes, the Word of God or of the gods. Only from this implicit Egyptian element can his phraseology about the Logos be explained in its detail. His interpretations of Hebrew revelation by means of Greek philosophy are thus determined by an idea that came to him from his Alexandrian environment.

Another name of the revealing god in the Hellenistic Egyptian theology is Νοῦς, whence the "Hermetic religion" was sometimes called, in its own documents, "the religion of the mind." Of an origin not Egyptian, though the name is found in the Hermetic books, is the god Ἄνθρωπος. The relations of this conception to the phraseology of the New Testament Reitzenstein does not fail to notice. In all these cases, the Greek names, he holds, are not the expression of artificial deifications, but are renderings of the names of ancient deities known in the popular religions, and now regarded as revealing their true nature to chosen devotees.

How far these explanations will carry the theory of religious origins remains to be seen. Clearly they do not essentially affect the history of philosophy. For example, there may be something of Egyptian gnosis lurking behind Philo's explicit reasoning; but (with very imperfect knowledge) I am inclined to think that he will remain for the history of thought a kind of Jewish scholastic, mediating between philosophy and official religion[2]. Again, Ἄνθρωπος, the Heavenly Man, or the Idea of Man, is to be found, more or less prominently, in

---

[1] This expression is not taken over from Neo-Platonism, for which it means no more than "existence" and has no special technical significance. It was through application to the Persons of the Christian Trinity that it gave origin to the modern philosophical phrase, "to hypostasise," that is, to set up as a being marked off from other beings (cf. Vacherot as cited p. 34, n. 1).

[2] Thus, while drawing attention here to Reitzenstein's view, I have retained in Chapter IV the usual explanation of Philo's Logos from Greek philosophical sources.

Proclus, in John Scotus Erigena, in the Arabian philosophy,
in the *Homo Noumenon* of Kant, perhaps in Comte's Humanity. If, however, it came into the philosophical systems remotely from without, this is only a matter of minute historical
curiosity. The rational place and value of the idea can be
studied without reference to any source it may have had outside the philosophical tradition, or even outside the particular
system[1].

As regards philosophical terminology, one point remains
quite firmly established; the effect of the newer investigations
being only to show that that which was thought to be a distinctively Judaeo-Christian usage is more general, and belonged originally to the "heathen" gnosis. Siebeck, in his
Geschichte der Psychologie, has traced the modification in the
meaning of the word "spirit" ($\pi\nu\epsilon\hat{\nu}\mu\alpha$) to the influx of
Hebrew religious conceptions; and, though this is too limited
a view, his genealogy of the later philosophical notion (patristic
and scholastic) is essentially unaffected by the limitation.
He found that in the Pauline language $\pi\nu\epsilon\hat{\nu}\mu\alpha$ is the term for
the higher part of the soul, and $\pi\nu\epsilon\nu\mu\alpha\tau\iota\kappa o\iota$ for the illuminated.
The terms in this sense, we now know, were gnostic; and in-
deed Siebeck traced the usage in those historically known
Gnostics who claimed to be the successors of Paul. Our translation of the terms is "spirit" and "spiritual"; and this conveys their meaning, though with a metaphysical implication
brought in later than the gnostic period. For, in the tradition
of Greek science, $\pi\nu\epsilon\hat{\nu}\mu\alpha$ was never a name for the higher part
of the soul. This was called not spirit but mind ($\nu o\hat{\nu}s$), as in
Aristotle's psychology. Spirit, retaining its primary sense of
breath, was always a material principle. Sometimes, in terms
of a kind of materialism, it was identified with the soul ($\psi\nu\chi\dot{\eta}$);
sometimes it was conceived as a subtler fiery element between
gross matter and the pure soul; but it was never applied distinctively to the soul's higher part or aspect[2]. An early modern
usage continuous with this, is when "animal spirits" were
conceived as the soul's instrument for moving the limbs. For

----

[1] It was a shrewd remark of Jowett that every philosopher must be
interpreted by his own writings.

[2] In the *Axiochus*, 370 C, there seems to be a trace of influence from the
phraseology of the gnosis; though the turn given to the thought is Hellenic.
The great works and the speculative discoveries of man, it is said, would have
been impossible were there not some truly divine spirit in his soul ($\epsilon\iota$ $\mu\dot{\eta}$ $\tau\iota$
$\theta\epsilon\hat{\iota}o\nu$ $\check{o}\nu\tau\omega s$ $\dot{\epsilon}\nu\hat{\eta}\nu$ $\pi\nu\epsilon\hat{\nu}\mu\alpha$ $\tau\hat{\eta}$ $\psi\nu\chi\hat{\eta}$). Compare 371 A, where Socrates is made to
cite a revelation of the future life from a certain Gobryes, $\dot{\alpha}\nu\dot{\eta}\rho$ $\mu\dot{\alpha}\gamma os$.

the Gnostics, the questions answered by the different philo-sophical views scarcely existed. Their thought was meta-physically vaguer, and did not concern itself with such dis-tinctions of the schools. It was sufficient for them that "spirit" could be regarded as an emanation of deity, a kind of influx that raised the soul above the level of a mere ani-mating principle, and fitted it to become the recipient of a religious revelation. In the meantime, the Neo-Platonic move-ment had carried on the intellectual analysis and completely dematerialised the conceptions both of "soul" and "mind." The later patristic writers, therefore, proceeding from the religious usage of their own tradition, Judaeo-Christian and remotely gnostic, on the one side, and from the science of the Greek schools on the other, gave a purely immaterial sense to "soul" and "spirit"; identifying the $\pi\nu\epsilon\hat{\nu}\mu\alpha$ of their own tradition with $\nu o\hat{\nu}s$ as conceived by Neo-Platonism. This is the true source of the predominant meaning of "spirit" in those modern languages that possess equivalents for all the three terms. Soul, spirit and mind being all alike conceived as immaterial, "spirit" differs from "mind" only by a shade of connotation. In English at least, which has here a vocabu-lary precisely corresponding to the Greek, the stress is on emotion and will rather than on intellect, for which the term "mind" is the native equivalent. This implication of "spirit" comes from the gnostic and, more definitely, from the Judaeo-Christian side; while the immateriality comes from Neo-Pla-tonism, mediated by the later Fathers and by the Schoolmen.

Historically, as we see in this particular case, orthodox Christianity presents itself as in a manner a compromise be-tween Greek philosophy and Oriental gnosis. Yet in one respect the extremes have more in common than either of them has with the mean. While the Fathers of the Church were more Western than the Gnostics in their use of the methods elaborated in the philosophic schools, their notion of the "Catholic Church" separated them at once from those who appealed ultimately to rational tests and from those who claimed personal illumination by a revealing God. Philosophy and gnosis were alike expressions of intellectual or spiritual liberty. The system of compromise wrought out under the Catholic idea aimed at establishing one rule of faith for the many and the few, to be coercively enforced as soon as it had brought over the imperial despotism to its side. Thus its triumph involved the "heretical" communities of Gnostics and the independent philosophic schools in the same ruin.

Yet, as Matter showed in his History, persecution by the same power never brought them together. It is true that the later Neo-Platonists were not unfriendly to the idea of revelations and inspirations of prophets, and were fond of quoting Chaldaean and Zoroastrian Oracles; and it is true that the Eastern gnosis was influenced from a very early period by Plato; but the gnosis, if it may be called in its own manner a philosophy, was a philosophy of separate type. This separateness continued in the Middle Ages, when the reappearance of popular heresies related to Gnosticism, and the revived knowledge of ancient philosophy, leading to heterodoxy in the schools, though coincident in time, were on the whole as external to one another as the gnosis and the academical philosophy of antiquity.

The last revival of the gnosis, after it had been suppressed, along with the teaching of Hellenic philosophy, by the Orthodox Byzantine Emperors, seems to have been in the movement of the Albigenses of Languedoc, to whom it had been carried by the dispersed Manichaeans and "Paulicians" of the East. In the early years of the thirteenth century, it was trampled out in the Crusade organised against it by Pope Innocent III, and finally crushed in detail by the centralised Dominican Inquisition which became the perfected form of ecclesiastical discipline under the Papacy. Its only possible later survival seems to be, as I have conjectured, among the heterodox religious sects of modern Russia.

In the first edition, I indulged in the speculation that, starting again from thence, it may still have a future. The conclusion to which later investigation of origins has led seems to render this at least highly improbable. For it appears that, so far as there is a relation between the gnosis and orthodoxy, Christian or post-Christian Gnosticism is not the result of a vaporisation of historical faith, but, on the contrary, orthodox dogma is a concretion of the earlier gnosis. The movement in this direction having culminated in one rigorous and powerful type, it can hardly be repeated with a similarly successful result. Against a new divine story, there would not only be the old with its prestige, but the immense modern development of philosophy and criticism on the basis of verifiable science, with searchlights penetrating every corner of the world. Thus I find myself obliged to acquiesce in the view of Matter, that the last vestiges of Gnosticism as a living faith were destroyed in the mediaeval persecutions. Science and philosophy could reflourish, and could look forward to an ever-expanding life, when the Western theocracy had been broken by religious schism; but the wandering speculations of the Gnostics remain only interesting fragments, curiously suggestive sometimes by an audacity that goes beyond that of regular philosophising, but offering no outlook either for hope or fear that they should grow together into a new organised religion.

III. Iamblichus and Proclus on Mathematical Science

For the theory of knowledge, the views of the later Neo-Platonists on mathematics are still not without interest even to students of Kant. An outline of some of the positions taken up may be found in the book of Iamblichus on the Common Science of Mathematics[1], and in the two Prologues of Proclus to his Commentary on the first book of Euclid's *Elements*[2]. Of these Prologues, the first coincides in subject with the treatise of Iamblichus; dealing with that which is common to arithmetic and geometry, and prior to all special departments of mathematics. The second is an introduction to the general theory of geometry and to Euclid's *Elements* in particular, and gives in its course a brief chronicle of the history of the science to the time of Euclid. The first Prologue draws from the same sources as the work of Iamblichus, setting forth views that had gradually taken shape in the schools of Plato and Aristotle. In the case of one theory at least in the second, Proclus seems to lay claim to originality. In other cases, he mentions incidentally that he is only selecting a few things from what earlier writers have said. Iamblichus is professedly expounding the ideas of the "Pythagorean philosophy."

The starting-point with both writers is the position of Plato at the end of the sixth book of the *Republic*. The objects of mathematics and the faculty of understanding (διάνοια) that deals with them come between dialectic and its objects above, and sense-perception and its objects below. Being thus intermediate, are mathematical forms and the reasonings upon them derivatives of sense-perception, or are they generated by the soul? In the view most clearly brought out by Proclus, they result from the productive activity of the soul, but not without relation to a prior intellectual norm, conformity to

[1] *Iamblichi de Communi Mathematica Scientia Liber*, ed. N. Festa, 1891. (Teubner.)

[2] *Procli Diadochi in Primum Euclidis Elementorum Librum Commentarii*, ex rec. G. Friedlein, 1873. (Teubner.)

which is the criterion of their truth. What is distinctive of Proclus is the endeavour to determine exactly the character of this mental production. Iamblichus does not so specially discuss this, but lays stress on the peculiar fixity of relations among the objects of mathematics. Mathematical objects are not forms that can depart from their underlying matter, nor yet qualities, like the heat of fire, which though actually inseparable can be thought of as taken away. The forms that constitute number and extension have a coherence which does not admit of this kind of disaggregation, whether real or ideal.

According to the view made specially clear by Iamblichus, mathematical science does not take over its employment of division and definition and syllogism from dialectic. The mathematical processes to which these terms are applied are peculiar to mathematics. From itself it discovers and perfects and elaborates them; and it has tests of its own, and needs no other science towards the order of speculation proper to it. Its difference from dialectic is that it works with its own assumptions, and does not consider things "simply," without assumptions[1]. As Proclus also says, there is only one science without assumptions ($\dot{a}\nu\upsilon\pi\acute{o}\theta\epsilon\tau\sigma s$). No special science demonstrates its own principles or institutes an inquiry about them. Thus the investigator of nature ($\dot{o}$ $\phi\upsilon\sigma\iota\sigma\lambda\acute{o}\gamma\sigma s$) assumes that there is motion, and then sets out from that determinate principle; and so with all special inquirers and practitioners[2].

Both writers, while they make considerations about the practical utility of knowledge subordinate, yet repeatedly draw attention to the applications, direct and indirect, of mathematics to the arts of life. Proclus cites Archimedes as a conspicuous example of the power conferred by science when directed to practical invention. And science in general, as both he and Iamblichus insist, derives its necessity from the mathematical principles on which it depends. The perception of the peculiar scientific importance of mathematics, grounded in the necessity of its demonstrations, they ascribe to Pythagoras; who, as both declare in almost the same terms, brought it to the form of a liberal discipline. By this is meant that, instead of treating it as a collection of isolated pro-

---

[1] *De Comm. Math. Scientia*, pp. 89–90: ἀφ᾽ ἐαυτῆς οὖν εὑρίσκει τε αὐτὰ καὶ τελειοῖ καὶ ἐξεργάζεται, τά τε οἰκεῖα αὐτῇ καλῶς οἶδε δοκιμάζειν, καὶ οὐ δεῖται ἄλλης ἐπιστήμης πρὸς τὴν οἰκείαν θεωρίαν. οὐ γὰρ τὸ ἁπλῶς καθάπερ ἡ διαλεκτική, ἀλλὰ τὰ ὑφ᾽ ἑαυτὴν διαγινώσκει, οἰκείως τε αὐτὰ θεωρεῖ καθόσον αὐτῇ ὑπόκειται.

[2] *Prologus* II., p. 75.

positions, each discovered for itself, Pythagoras began to impress on it the systematically deductive character which it assumed among the Greeks. In the order of genetic development, men turn to knowledge for its own sake when the care about necessary things has ceased to be pressing[1].

The classification of the mathematical sciences given in the two treatises is the same. First in order comes the "common mathematical science" which sets forth the principles that form a bond of union between arithmetic and geometry. The special branches of mathematics are four: namely, arithmetic, geometry, music, and spherics (σφαιρική). Music is a derivative of arithmetic; containing the theory of complex relations of numbers as distinguished from the numbers themselves. Spherics is similarly related to geometry; dealing with abstract motion prior to the actual motion of bodies. To beginners it is more difficult than astronomy, which finds aid in the observation of moving bodies; but as pure theory it is prior[2]. Next come the various branches of mixed mathematics, such as mechanics, optics, astronomy, and generally the sciences that employ instruments for weighing, measuring and observing. These owe their less degree of precision and cogency to the mixture of sense-perception with pure mathematical demonstration. Last in the theoretic order come simple data of perception brought together as connected experience (ἐμπειρία).

The ground of this order is to be found in the rationalistic theory of knowledge common to the school. As Proclus remarks, the soul is not a tablet empty of words, but is ever written on and writing on itself—and moreover, he adds, written on by pure intellect which is prior to it in the order of being. Upon such a basis of psychology and consequent theory of knowledge, he goes on to put the specific question about geometrical demonstration and the activity of the soul in its production. How can geometry enable us to rise above

---

[1] Prologus I., p. 29: καὶ γὰρ πᾶσα ἡ γένεσις καὶ ἡ ἐν αὐτῇ στρεφομένη τῆς ψυχῆς ζωὴ πέφυκεν ἀπὸ τοῦ ἀτελοῦς εἰς τὸ τέλειον χωρεῖν. Cf. Στοιχ. Θεολ. 45.

[2] With the substitution of astronomy for "spherics," the four Pythagorean sciences of Iamblichus and Proclus form the "quadrivium," or second division of the "seven liberal arts," of mediaeval tradition. (The "trivium," according to the list usually given, comprises grammar, dialectic and rhetoric.) A more curious point of contact is the identity of the conception of "spherics"— simply as classification of science and apart from philosophical theory of knowledge—with Comte's "rational mechanics," regarded by him as the branch of mathematics immediately prior to astronomy, which is the first of the physical sciences.

matter to unextended thought, when it is occupied with extension, which is simply the result of the inability of matter to receive immaterial ideas otherwise than as spread out and apart from one another? And how can the διάνοια, proceeding as it does by unextended notions, yet be the source of the spatial constructions of geometry? The solution is that geometrical ideas, existing unextended in the διάνοια, are projected upon the "matter" furnished by the φαντασία. Hence the plurality and difference in the figures with which geometrical science works. The idea of the circle as understood (in the διάνοια) is one; as imagined (in the φαντασία) it is many; and it is some particular circle as imagined that geometry must always use in its constructions. At the same time, it is not the perceived circle (the circle in the αἴσθησις) that is the object of pure geometry. This, with its unsteadiness and inaccuracy, is the object only of applied geometry. The true geometrician, while necessarily working by the aid of imagination, strives towards the unextended unity of the understanding with its immaterial notions. Hence the disciplinary power of geometry as set forth by Plato[1]. According to this view, those are right who say that all geometrical propositions are in a sense theorems, since they are concerned with that which ever is and does not come into being; but those also are right who say that all are in a sense problems, for, in the way of theorems too, nothing can be discovered without a going forth of the understanding to the "intelligible matter" furnished by the imagination, and this process resembles genetic production[2]. The division once made, however, the theoretic character is seen not only to extend to all but to predominate in all.

[1] In his theory of "geometrical matter," Proclus remarks, he has taken the liberty of dissenting from Porphyry and most of the Platonic interpreters. See Prologus II., pp. 56–7: περὶ μὲν οὖν τῆς γεωμετρικῆς ὕλης τοσαῦτα ἔχομεν λέγειν οὐκ ἀγνοοῦντες, ὅσα καὶ ὁ φιλόσοφος Πορφύριος ἐν τοῖς συμμίκτοις γέγραφεν καὶ οἱ πλεῖστοι τῶν Πλατωνικῶν διατάττονται, συμφωνότερα δὲ εἶναι ταῦτα ταῖς γεωμετρικαῖς ἐφόδοις νομίζοντες καὶ τῷ Πλάτωνι διανοητὰ καλοῦντι τὰ ὑποκείμενα τῇ γεωμετρίᾳ. συνᾴδει γὰρ οὖν ταῦτα ἀλλήλοις, διότι τῶν γεωμετρικῶν εἰδῶν αἱ μὲν αἰτίαι, καθ᾽ ἃς καὶ ἡ διάνοια προβάλλει τὰς ἀποδείξεις, ἐν αὐτῇ προϋφεστήκασιν, αὐτὰ δὲ ἕκαστα τὰ διαιρούμενα καὶ συντιθέμενα σχήματα περὶ τὴν φαντασίαν προβέβληται.

[2] Prologus II., pp. 77–79.

THE COMMENTARIES
OF PROCLUS

THE COMMENTARIES OF PROCLUS

THE view usually taken of Proclus might be summed up in an epigram to the effect that philosophies die of too much method. This is, on the whole, the view of Zeller, who, while expressing the deepest admiration for the organising work of the last great Neo-Platonist, finds that work in detail un-inspiring because essentially deprived of philosophic freedom through its combination of formal deduction with subordina-tion to the authority of tradition. In fact, it seems to him a kind of scholastic theology, not indeed wholly anticipating the spirit of the Western schoolmen, for it was still Greek, but forming the appropriate transition from Greek antiquity to the Middle Ages.

There are obvious elements of truth in this view. Proclus is undoubtedly characterised by a finish of logical method in which he excelled all his predecessors. In Plotinus the in-tuitive reason predominates, in Proclus the discursive reason. On the formal side, this was the principle of Scholasticism, as authority was its principle on the material side. And Proclus, though free to reject the authority of his texts if reason is against them, does not in fact cut himself loose at any critical point from the meaning that he thinks can be educed from Plato. It is undeniable that in his age, for the philosophers of the Hellenic tradition, Homer and Plato had become a kind of sacred scriptures, with Orphic poems and Chaldaean oracles for apocryphal addenda. Yet the implied analogy is misleading. Although Neo-Platonism had in a manner in-corporated such distinctly religious movements of antiquity as Orphicism and Neo-Pythagoreanism, the philosophical in-terest remained dominant to the last. Proclus unquestionably regarded himself, in perfectly clear distinction at once from theologians like the Orphics and from men of science like Ptolemy, as a philosopher of the succession of Plato and

Plotinus[1]. Now in Scholasticism the philosophical interest
was never supreme. And, on the formal side, Proclus, with
all his method and system, remains much more literary, and
is never so bound to his texts, even in the minutest expositions,
that he cannot leave the track of direct deduction. He is also
much more in contact with actual science, mathematical,
astronomical and physical. It may be said with truth, however, that he fixed the philosophical method of the schoolmen,
and that this fixation was only reinforced by the later dominance of Aristotle. The method was that dialectical or discursive reasoning which goes back to Socrates and Plato as
its most accomplished representatives, and assumes its completed scientific form in the Aristotelian syllogism. To recognise this may help us to understand the relative justification
of the procedure both of the later Neo-Platonism and of
mediaeval Scholasticism.

If too much method is at last fatal to progress, too little
means intellectual anarchy. This became visible to Athenian
thinkers at the end of the first period of Greek philosophy
with its divergent development of conflicting principles. It
again became visible to the initiators of modern philosophy
after the chaotic mixture of old and new thought at the
Renaissance. Bacon and Descartes saw that, whether the
distinctive watchword was to be reason or experience, the
immediately pressing need was to determine the method of
seeking truth. The paths then struck out were certainly the
beginning of a new age of ordered progress. If we have since
been warned against a new anarchy, this is not any too
audacious flight of intellect, but the "dispersive specialism"
that never leaves the parts to deal with the whole. To
counteract this in its turn, perhaps the best remedy is the
study of some all-comprehensive system, modern or ancient,
positivist or idealist, the system of Comte or the system of
Proclus. Such study is not only astringent but also emanci-
pating. For the modern anarchy of endless specialism is an

---

[1] In one place, he comes very near to the actual name, Neo-Platonist. See
Comm. in Tim., ed. Diehl, ii. 88, 12: τῶν νεωτέρων οἱ ἀπὸ Πλωτίνου πάντες
Πλατωνικοί.

anarchy without liberty. It means that industrialism has led science captive. A renewed sense of wholeness is at the same time a renewed sense of freedom.

No more in the case of Proclus than of Comte or Hegel, however, is the interest merely that of systematic grasp. A sufficient idea of his schematism, I think, has been given by the exposition of his fundamental and probably quite early treatise, the Στοιχείωσις Θεολογική. What remains is to furnish evidence that he was not only a great systematiser but a deep-going original thinker. It was the fatality of being born in the fifth century that made him unable to bring out his most remarkable thoughts except by writing huge commentaries. For there is in fact more originality of detail in his commentaries on Plato than in his systematic treatises. Their distinctive interest is in the flashing out of new thoughts from the ancient setting, not in the light they throw on earlier thought, though this is of course not negligible. The age of erudition made subservient to the storing up of ancient science did not fully arrive till the sixth century, the time of the commentators like Simplicius, for whom the old world was visibly as dead as the new was unborn.

With the exposition in Chapter IX as a clue to the outlines of the system, the points to be brought out will take their places as parts of an organic structure. The Commentaries that I shall give an account of are now all accessible without going back to old editions not easily procurable. In my references, I shall follow the pagination of the most recent texts[1].

[1] I append a list of the editions used:

Procli Philosophi Platonici Opera Inedita, 2nd ed., Cousin. Paris, 1864. [This contains, besides the Life by Marinus, (1) the three works that exist only in the mediaeval Latin translation: *De Decem Dubitationibus circa Providentiam*; *De Providentia et Fato et eo quod in nobis*, ad Theodorum, Mechanicum; *De Malorum Subsistentia*; (2) the Commentary on the *First Alcibiades*; (3) the Commentary on the *Parmenides*; (4) the Hymns.]

Procli Diadochi in Platonis Rem Publicam Commentarii, ed. W. Kroll. 2 vols. Leipzig, 1899, 1901.

Procli Diadochi in Platonis Timaeum Commentaria, ed. E. Diehl. 3 vols. Leipzig, 1903, 1904, 1906.

Procli Diadochi in Platonis Cratylum Commentaria, ed. G. Pasquali. Leipzig, 1908. [Of this Commentary there remain only selections preserved in Scholia.]

The chronological order of the works of Proclus, through the existence of cross-references, cannot be treated as quite certain; but, of those to be dealt with circumstantially, I take the order to be: Commentaries on the *Timaeus*[1], *Parmenides*, *First Alcibiades*, *Republic*. This is of course an impossible order of exposition. The logical order, corresponding to that which was adopted in Chapter V for the system of Plotinus, is: *First Alcibiades*, *Parmenides*, *Timaeus*, *Republic*. We thus begin with psychology, the centre of the system; next we go on to theory of knowledge, ontology and cosmology; lastly to the aesthetic and practical aspects of philosophy. Of course, in following approximately the order of the commentaries, it will be impossible to keep these divisions of the subject-matter exact.

But first, by way of introduction, a few points may be brought together from the comparatively popular treatises on Theodicy which we possess in William of Morbeka's translation. From the Scholiast's notes of the Commentary on the *Cratylus*, one or two details of interest for the Neo-Platonic interpretation of mythology can be appropriately added. After these preliminaries, the way will be clear for the exposition of the larger works.

An important innovation on Plotinus in statement is the rejection of the position that Matter is evil. Evils are the result of conflict in the world of birth. This world involves destruction, decay and death; but it was necessary that such a world should exist for the perfection of the whole; and of its existence matter, or infinite possibility, was a necessary condition. Against making matter in itself evil, the doctrine of Plotinus himself is urged, that there cannot be two principles. It is allowed that there are apparent differences of doctrine in Plato[2]; but the *Philebus* is found to be decisive against making

---

[1] The Commentary on the *Timaeus* is known from the biography of Marinus to have been finished when Proclus was twenty-eight; but its extant form is no doubt a later edition. It was his own favourite among his commentaries.

[2] *De Malorum Subsistentia*, 233–234.

either body or matter evil[1]. Matter cannot be the cause of the
fall of souls, for it does not explain the different inclinations
of different souls. The cause of descent to birth pre-exists in
the soul itself as a certain necessity of alternation between the
life of intellect and the life of its irrational part[2]. There is no
principle of evil[3]. Evil is always incidental to the pursuit of
some good[4].

This is clearly an improvement on Plotinus in formal statement, conveying much better the essential optimism of his
doctrine; for his actual account of evils does not differ from
that of Proclus. Nor does his account of the origin of matter
essentially differ[5]. Matter, according to Plotinus, is directly
produced, just as in the theory of Proclus, by the infinity that
the One creates ($\pi o\iota\epsilon\hat{\iota}$). And Proclus agrees with Plotinus
that it may be called in a sense evil as the ultimate stage of
the descent of beings[6]. It is, however, also in a sense good as
being the condition for the kind of good that exists in our
world. Distinctively, it is to be called neither good nor evil,
but only necessary[7].

But what is the meaning of "creation" by the One? It
means, for both philosophers, essentially this: that without
unity in and over the system of things there would be no particular existence as an actually realised thing. It does not mean
that abstract unity, without the latent existence of a many

[1] *De Malorum Subsistentia*, 236, 9–12: "Neque ergo corpus malum, neque
materia: haec enim sunt Dei γεννήματα, hoc quidem ut mixtura, haec autem
ut infinitum."

[2] *Ibid.* 233, 21–26: "hoc erat ipsis malum qui ad deterius impetus et
appetitus, sed non materia…et propter debilitatem patiuntur quae oportet
tales pati male eligentes."

[3] *Ibid.* 250, 5–6: "Unam quidem itaque secundum se malorum causam
nullatenus ponendum."

[4] *Ibid.* 254, 16–17: "boni enim gratia omne quod fit, fit." Cf. *De Providentia et Fato*, 190, 31: "malum videtur bonum esse eligentibus ipsum."

[5] Zeller, iii. 2, p. 808, n. 3, finds a discrepancy; but the quotation he gives
from the *Platonic Theology* of Proclus is simply a paraphrase of Plotinus:
πρόεισιν οὖν καὶ ἡ ὕλη καὶ τὸ ὑποκείμενον τῶν σωμάτων ἄνωθεν ἀπὸ τῶν πρωτίστων
ἀρχῶν, αἳ δὴ διὰ περιουσίαν δυνάμεως ἀπογεννᾶν δύνανται καὶ τὸ ἔσχατον τῶν
ὄντων. For the view of Plotinus, compare p. 68, n. 3, above.

[6] *De Malorum Subsistentia*, 238. Compare the position of Plotinus as
stated above, p. 81.

[7] Cf. *in Remp.* i. 37–38.

as it were in its own right, calls it from nothing into being. The many real beings have their individual eternity. Their "freedom," that which depends on themselves and makes possible for them moral fall or ascent, is this ultimate existence of theirs. It could not indeed be anything actually without the One: the existence of an actual many without a common unity is unthinkable. And there is no bringing of chaos into order by a sort of accidental coming together of God and an independent Matter. Of all doctrines, the Neo-Platonists desire to be clear of this, precisely because it was defended by some who called themselves disciples of Plato. Hence the apparent stringency of their immaterialist monism. For a real understanding of their position, however, we must equally avoid attributing to them the ideas of volitional creation and of "pantheistic absorption." The many are never finally absorbed into the One; and therefore, on Neo-Platonic principles, there was never a time when they did not in some sense exist as a many. On this, Proclus is more explicit than Plotinus.

I have deviated a little from direct exposition of the treatises; but it will be seen that this anticipation of later discussions has an important bearing on the metaphysics implied in them. Proclus is, of course, quite Platonic when he places goodness above intellect, and describes the soul that has it as desiring to benefit all and to make them, as far as possible, like itself. But here he finds one source of danger, —a danger inherent in the order of the world. For if, in descending to communicate the good which it possesses to the common life, the soul loses the intellectual mode of being which is its own highest state, this is a loss to it and so far an evil[1]. He admits no intrinsically evil soul; though souls may need long discipline by punishment. The maleficent soul of which the existence is suggested by Plato in the *Laws*, he takes to be no unitary being at all, but those irrational elements in each soul which, when they become preponderant, cause it to sink[2]. Not that they are in themselves evil: the

[1] *De Malorum Subsistentia*, 220–221. Cf. *in Tim.* iii. 324–325.
[2] *De Malorum Subsistentia*, 247–250.

evil consists in the want of due relation between the rational and the irrational activities.

On the most obvious form of evil, the mutual destructions of men and animals, Plotinus, as we have seen, replies that they are necessary for the continued life of the universe and do not affect the reality of any soul. Men, in the gaiety with which they give their lives in battle, show that they have a divination of this truth[1]. His solution is in effect that of the celebrated passage in the Bhagavad-gita, where the god who accompanies the hero Arjuna explains to him that slaying or being slain is only illusory appearance[2]. Justice, he holds, is realised in the series of lives; but about the detail of this, if the general principle can be proved defensible, he is not curious. Here Proclus is not content with a merely general solution, but tries to furnish detailed answers to scepticism on the existence of a providential order. All the questions having been long debated, he had abundant speculative theodicy behind him[3]. So serious is he about the detail that he tries to determine what shadow of justice there may be in the lot of the lower animals[4]. Their lot, he seems to say, is partly in accordance with the qualities in them that resemble human virtues; but the effect of his reasonings on the subject is that, where there is not a rational soul, there is no permanent individuality[5]. Animal souls may perhaps be understood as differentiations of the general life of nature under ideas of species only. If this is so, then animal life is to be considered as a necessary part of our world, linked to the higher parts in an order intelligible from the point of view of

---

[1] See above, p. 80.

[2] Compare Sir Alfred Lyall's *Asiatic Studies*, Second Series (1899), ch. i. p. 20.

[3] This becomes evident from a study of Origen's treatise Περὶ ἀρχῶν (ed. Koetschau, 1913). Origen adapts to Biblical stories exactly those presuppositions of Platonising theodicy which Proclus applies to the stories in Homer.

[4] *De Decem Dubitationibus*, 118–125.

[5] Proclus often returns to the question about animal souls; but he always seems conscious of a final want of certainty in his own mind as to how far individuality is to be carried down the scale.

the whole, but not intelligible by itself[1]. Considered apart, it comes under the conception of Fate rather than of Providence.

This distinction, brought down the ages by Boethius[2], is drawn with great subtlety by Proclus. The causes which we know only as mechanical or external are unknown to us in their essence: hence the appearance of blind fate. In the system of the whole, that which appears to us as mechanical necessity really follows intellect. The way in which it follows may be partly understood by tracing the higher order of intellectual causation through the order intermediate between that and mechanism, *viz.*, the vitality of nature as an internal principle[3]. Determination in the apparatus of the mechanician is not primarily in an arrangement of wheels and pulleys and so forth, but depends on an incorporeal pre-conception of the arrangement, working through mental imagination and a living organism[4]. Proclus treats it as a paradox that a mechanical philosopher, who in his own investigations makes especial use of pure intellect, should think this explicable as the result of sense inseparable from body[5]. His tone towards Theodorus, to whom the treatise on Providence was addressed, is, it may be noted, far more amicable than that of Plato to the mechanicists of his time. He recognises at the beginning that these questions will always be discussed[6]. Theodorus, he puts it playfully, thinks to honour his own art by making the author of the universe a mechanician[7]. Mental determinations, however, are not really explicable as last re-

---

[1] In the Commentary on the *Parmenides* (735, 15–24), it is said that while justice takes part in ordering things without life, these do not themselves participate in the just: a stick or a stone cannot be called just or unjust. The absence here of any reference to irrational animals accentuates the uncertainty in the discussion of them elsewhere.

[2] See Prof. W. P. Ker's *Dark Ages*, pp. 108–109.

[3] *De Providentia et Fato*, 155.

[4] *Ibid.* 194, 34–38: "Neque enim tua fixio, tympanis et tornis utens et materiis corporalibus, in tua praecognitione corporaliter erat; sed illa quidem incorporabiliter phantasia et vitaliter habuit futuri rationem."

[5] *Ibid.* 178.

[6] *Ibid.* 146, 14–16: "Quaeris autem millesies dicta quidem et neque requiem habitura unquam secundum meam opinionem."

[7] *Ibid.* 148, 19–23.

sultants of an all-comprehending succession of mechanical causes. We know mind and soul from within as of an intrinsically different nature; and it is from these internally known intellectual and psychical causes that we must seek insight into the real order of the whole.

For Proclus this implies more than that mechanism has an inner or psychical side. It means also that the metaphysical universe of mental realities is wider than the physical universe. In the corporeal order, not only does appearance take the place for us of reality, but the reality that is manifested is itself a small part of the whole, not ultimately intelligible out of relation to the larger part. "Many things escape Fate; nothing escapes Providence[1]." Fate is the destiny undergone by particular beings without insight into its true causes. With complete knowledge of reality, fate itself would be seen as part of providence.

Thus it becomes a philosophical problem to understand as far as we may the scheme of cosmic justice. To solve the difficulty, why descendants suffer for the sins of their forefathers, Proclus brings in the idea of the solidarity of cities and races[2]. There is a vital influence along a certain line, sometimes producing close resemblance at long intervals. And souls are not associated with such and such races or cities by chance, but in accordance with their former deeds and their acquired characters[3]. This understood, the transmission of ancestral guilt or merit can be conceived as part of a system by which justice is realised for each individual also. This must not be tested simply by what appears externally. Some have deprived themselves of possessions for the love of virtue. How then can providence be blamed for treating the good as they treat themselves? Future fame is a compensation for present neglect[4]. Gifts of wealth and power, abused by the bad, bring punishment. And the bad are not outside the care of providence. If by such gifts they

---

[1] *De Providentia et Fato*, 149, 17–18.

[2] *De Decem Dubitationibus*, 136, 32–35: "Omnis civitas et omne genus unum quoddam animal est majori modo quam hominum unusquisque, et immortalius et sanctius."

[3] *Ibid.* 139, 3–6.   [4] *Ibid.* 117–118.

are apparently made worse and then punished for their deeds,
this is not only for some good to the whole, but for the good
of the offenders. Latent dispositions to vice often cannot be
cured unless they pass into act[1]. Only then can the repentance follow that is necessary for remedy. All souls are at some
time curable. It would be inconsistent with the order of the
universe that any being, among men or even demons, should
be always evil[2].

The ruthlessness of the processes by which the cosmic order
is sustained does not in the end trouble Proclus, as it did not
trouble Plotinus. The heroic race, he says in one passage, is
impelled by vehement phantasy and resolute will, not distinctively by reason; but this is its own nature, and is no more
evil in itself than the ferocity of a lion or a panther. Thus the
Whole makes use of heroes as instruments for correcting dis-
orders; just as it makes use of beasts for devouring men, and
of inanimate things for the purposes for which they are fitted[3].

I have given only a slight selection of topics from these
little treatises. Their perennial interest will probably always
gain for them some readers; and so, in the absence of the
originals, one example of the singular mode of translation
from Greek into Latin practised in the Middle Ages will be preserved in living memory. In the Commentary on the *Cratylus*,
one point which directly concerns mythology is of special
interest for its bearing on the same topics. Apparently
hostile chance or fortune is declared to be always finally
beneficent destiny[4]. The particular event that we class under
the head of chance may seem to go unguided; but in the total
order generalised as Fortune there is nothing irrational. All
is ordered, down to the destiny of the individual. Hence the
deification of Fortune is philosophically justified.

---

[1] *De Decem Dubitationibus*, 113, 18–21. Cf. *De Malorum Subsistentia*, 263,
7–11.

[2] *De Malorum Subsistentia*, 214–215.

[3] *Ibid.* 217, 3–7.

[4] 44, 8–13: μὴ δή τις τὴν τύχην ταύτην ἀλόγιστον αἰτίαν ἡγείσθω καὶ ἀόριστον
(τὸ γὰρ ἔργον αὐτῆς εἰς νοῦν βλέπει), ἀλλὰ θείαν ἢ δαιμονίαν δύναμιν, οὐδὲν ἀφεῖσαν
ἔρημον τῆς οἰκείας ἐπιστασίας, ἀλλὰ πάντα καὶ τὰ ἔσχατα τῶν ἐνεργημάτων ἡμῶν
κατευθύνουσαν πρὸς τὸ εὖ καὶ πρὸς τὴν τοῦ παντὸς τάξιν.

What most interested the Scholiast, and perhaps Proclus
himself, in the Dialogue, was not the mingled scientific sug-
gestiveness and irony of the discussion on language, but the
interpretation of mythology. On scandalous myths, the usual
view of the later Greek philosophy is stated, that the myth
should be referred to a true intellectual meaning as its inner
sense[1]. To the same god may be assigned different meanings
in varied references[2]. Among the connexions of ideas suggested, it is interesting to come upon an exact summary by
anticipation of Swinburne's *Last Oracle*. As the god that
furnishes forth from himself the light of the visible world is
called the Sun, so the god that furnishes forth from himself
truth is called Apollo[3].

This is a rapid indication of developments that fill a considerable space in the writings of Proclus. In general, where
these developments occur, I shall content myself with such
indications. I find the allegorical interpretations of the
myths agreeable to read; but, as no philosophical doctrine
is ever educed from a myth except through being first read
into it, little can be done with them for exposition. The serious
part of the detailed theology of Proclus was the idea, touched
on above, that the metaphysical is wider than the physical
universe; and that the beings of which it consists are not only
human minds, but include hierarchies of intelligences beyond
that of man. These take part in working out the providential
order. They are called gods, angels, daemons and so forth,
and are spoken of by the names of mythological personages;
but the stories about them are not taken to be even disguised
accounts of historical events; so that Greek polytheism has
in effect evaporated into philosophical fancies by which the
abstract thought of Neo-Platonism, in full consciousness of

[1] 55, 21–22: τὴν φαινομένην τερατολογίαν εἰς ἐπιστημονικὴν ἔννοιαν ἀναπέμπειν.
Cf. *in Remp.* i. 80–81. The myths objected to by Socrates in the *Republic* have
a mystical, not an educational aim; and it is only—so Proclus argues—to their
educational use that he objects.

[2] 56, 3–6. Cf. 62, 24–27: ἀλλὰ πάντων ὄντων ἐν πᾶσι καὶ ἑκάστου πάσας ἔχοντος
τὰς ἐνεργείας, ἄλλος κατ᾽ ἄλλην ἐξέχει καὶ κατὰ ταύτην χαρακτηρίζεται διαφερόντως.

[3] 78, 23–25: ὅτι ὥσπερ ὁ τὸ ἐγκόσμιον πᾶν φῶς ἀφ᾽ ἑαυτοῦ χορηγῶν "Ἡλιος
καλεῖται, οὕτως καὶ ὁ τὴν ἀλήθειαν ἀφ᾽ ἑαυτοῦ χορηγῶν Ἀπόλλων καλεῖται.

what it is doing, strives to complete itself imaginatively. What Proclus called theology is a system of metaphysics running out at intervals into these fancies.

ON THE *FIRST ALCIBIADES*[1]

THE circumstantial account of the commentaries must begin with one that takes for its text a Dialogue assigned in modern times to the "Platonic apocrypha." Of late the controversy about this small group of writings has been revived. An exposition of Proclus is of course not the place for entering into the controversy; but not to offer a personal opinion, even when it has no authority, might seem an evasion of a question naturally asked. My conjecture about the present dialogue is that it was an early exercise in the Academy found to be of exceptional merit and therefore, with a few others of the kind, added as an appendix to the actual dialogues of Plato. This, I think, is something like Jowett's explanation of the way in which the apocryphal dialogues came to be preserved; and his final literary judgment was passed after consideration of all that Grote could say against any discrimination between genuine and spurious writings not already fixed by the universal consent of antiquity. It remains to be seen whether the later defence, by undoubted experts, of the Epistles and other compositions generally rejected in recent times, will succeed where that of Grote failed in carrying with it the judgment of critical scholars.

The *First Alcibiades* Proclus thinks an especially good introduction at once to philosophy and to Plato, because it begins with the problem of knowing oneself. The aim of the Dialogue is perfectly general, not directed only to the individual mind of Alcibiades, but concerned with the theory of human knowledge; and with this primarily, not with any investigations beyond it or beside it[2]. For this is fundamental, the basis at once of the theory of our own being and of our ethical perfection[3]. We cannot hope to succeed in determining the

---

[1] 103 A–116 A.   [2] 292–293.   [3] 296.

nature of the known without first distinguishing the different kinds of knowledge[1].

All, says Proclus, is directed to the conclusion that man has his real existence in the soul[2]: the soul is the man. The ideal method is demonstration by irrefutable arguments[3]; but much, it is allowed, is actually knowable only by the kinds of experience of which opinion and perception are the criteria[4].

The theory of knowledge developed by Proclus, we shall see later, centres in discursive reason. Intuition, higher or lower, is to be tested by its coherence in a ratiocinative system. Here he introduces an idea, not much developed elsewhere, though it occurs in the *Platonic Theology*[5], that may have been suggested by the phrase πίστις ἀληθής in the poem of Parmenides. To "belief" distinctively is assigned the grasp of reality at its summit. The order of existences, the good, the wise, the beautiful (*Phaedrus*, 246 E), has corresponding to it the triad of mental virtues, faith, truth, love (πίστις καὶ ἀλήθεια καὶ ἔρως)[6].

Love is the principle at once of return to divine beauty and of the outgoing action by which this irradiates the world[7]. In its sense of benevolence, it has its part both in the energising of the world-process and in the descent of souls to birth. Some descend to raise others. Thus Socrates and Alcibiades tend to become for Proclus figures in an allegory. Socrates is the "good daemon" to whose guardianship Alcibiades is assigned[8]. Again, Socrates is the soul's intellect (νοῦς τῆς ψυχῆς) and Alcibiades the rational soul (λογικὴ ψυχή). There is a madness of love that is above the sobriety of prudence, as there is one that is below it[9]. Socrates, in being altogether exempt from passion, illustrates the providential direction of the lower by the higher order of causes. In this there is something divine or "daemonic" as contrasted with the providence exercised over more imperfect souls by others

---

[1] Cf. 394, 16–19: πῶς γὰρ οὐκ ἄτοπον τῇ φύσει τῶν γνωστῶν τὰς τῶν γνώσεων ἀφορίζειν διαφοράς, ἀλλὰ μὴ τοὐναντίον ταῖς τῶν γνώσεων διαιρεῖν;
[2] 308, 9.   [3] 309, 8–14.   [4] 312–313.
[5] See above, pp. 162–3.   [6] 356–357.   [7] 325, 10–20.   [8] 340.
[9] 352, 26–27: τῆς γὰρ μανίας ἡ μέν ἐστι σωφροσύνης κρείττων, ἡ δὲ ἀποπέπτωκεν ἀπ' αὐτῆς.

that have had to descend into the perturbations of life to become the agents of this care[1].

Proclus turns to a more generalised discussion of the
daemonic. The daemon or genius in each of us is not the
rational soul, though Plato (*Timaeus*, 90 ʌ) may have appeared to say so[2]. The view of Plotinus also must be rejected, that
the daemon is the power next above that with which the soul
energises in the present life[3]. In the view of Proclus as here
stated, it is the whole destiny, or providential direction, of the
individual life as a whole[4]. In Socrates himself, the daemon
was analogous to Apollo, the rational discourse (λόγος) to
Dionysus; the function of the daemon being to check the
exuberance of the Dionysiac impulsion[5].

Divine love is an action, not a passion[6]. The movement
whereby the higher seeks to perfect the lower concurs with
the movement of the lower seeking to be perfected, the former
being only slightly anticipatory; whence some have thought
that matter could organise itself[7]. Natural virtue, as Plotinus
said, adumbrates its own perfection[8].

The innate abilities of Alcibiades, brought into relation
with the choice made by the first soul in the myth of Er
(*Republic* x. 619 BC), suggest to Proclus a position developed
in more than one place in an especially interesting way. Souls
from heaven aspire to despotisms[9]. The life of ambition is
indeed higher than the common life, as was recognised by

---

[1] 372.

[2] 383, 26–31.

[3] See above, pp. 96–7.

[4] 386–387.

[5] 391.

[6] 417, 1: ὁ μὲν θεῖος ἔρως ἐνέργειά ἐστιν. Cf. Spinoza, *Eth.* v. Prop. 36:
"Mentis amor intellectualis erga Deum...actio est."
Another interesting point of contact between Spinoza and Neo-Platonism
occurs in the Appendix to the first Part of the *Ethics*. Spinoza, though not,
like Plotinus and Proclus, a teleologist, puts the necessity for lower grades of
being in precisely the same way: "Iis autem, qui quaerunt: cur Deus omnes
homines non ita creavit, ut solo rationis ductu gubernarentur? nihil aliud
respondeo, quam: quia eo non defuit materia ad omnia ex summo nimirum
ad infimum perfectionis gradum creanda."

[7] 422, 31–37.

[8] 429, 1–3: ἡ γὰρ φυσικὴ ἀρετὴ τοιάδε τίς ἐστι· καὶ γὰρ 'ὄμμα ἀτελὲς καὶ ἦθος
ἔχει,' κατὰ τὸν θεῖον Πλωτῖνον.

[9] 432. Cf. 403.

Plato (*Gorgias*, 523)[1]. It is, however, in the second place; as is seen in Alcibiades, who aims at honour and power before the good of his city. This is to seek a partial good in contest with others, instead of those goods of which no one has less because many share in them[2]. He thus shows himself inferior to Pericles, his kinsman and guardian, with whom among the rest he means to contend; for Pericles was accustomed to remind himself that he ruled over Greeks, over Athenians and over freemen. By this insatiability his life has the character of passion and not of reason[3]. Measureless ambition despises everything short of governing the whole world with absolute power in company with the gods, and, if not checked by knowledge, is capable of ruining mankind[4].

In the sequel to this discussion, we find a much-needed qualification of the modern maxim that knowledge is power. Power, indeed, cannot be acquired without knowledge; but there can be knowledge without power; for the addition of power depends on a concurrence of the whole and on presiding good fortune[5].

As God and Matter are alike in unlikeness, being without form and infinite and unknowable[6], so also those who know and those who do not know but are not aware of their ignorance are alike in not seeking or learning. Of those who have come to know either by their own discovery or by being taught, it is rightly said that there was a time within their memory when they did not know; and yet no time can be

---

[1] 433, 7–8: διὸ καὶ ὁ Πλάτων ἔσχατον χιτῶνα τῶν ψυχῶν ἀπεκάλει τὴν φιλοτιμίαν.

[2] 439, 1–5: τὰ μὲν γὰρ ἀμέριστα τῶν ἀγαθῶν ἅμα πλείοσι παρεῖναι δυνατὸν καὶ οὐδεὶς ἔλαττον ἔχει περὶ αὐτὰ διὰ τὴν ἄλλων κτῆσιν, τὰ δὲ μεριστὰ σὺν ἐλαττώσεσι τῶν ἄλλων παραγίνεται τοῖς ἔχουσιν. The ἀμέριστα are of course those goods of which it can be said "that to divide is not to take away."

[3] 439, 27–30: καθόλου γὰρ εἰπεῖν ἕκαστον τῶν παθῶν ἀπέραντόν ἐστι καὶ ἄμετρον, λόγῳ μὴ κρατούμενον· ὁ γὰρ λόγος πέρας ἐστί, τὸ δὲ πάθος ἄλογον καὶ ἀόριστον.

[4] 439–440.

[5] 446, 21–27: ἐπιστήμης μὲν γὰρ χωρὶς οὐκ ἄν τις τῆς δυνάμεως τύχοι· τῶν γὰρ ἀγαθῶν ἡ δύναμις, τὰ δὲ ἀγαθὰ μετ' ἐπιστήμης κτώμεθα· παρούσης δὲ ἐπιστήμης, θαυμαστὸν οὐδὲν μὴ παρεῖναι τὴν δύναμιν· δεῖ γὰρ καὶ τῆς τοῦ παντὸς συμπνοίας καὶ τῆς ἀγαθῆς τύχης τῆς τούτων προεστώσης.

[6] 473, 3–4: ὡς γὰρ ἡ ὕλη ἀνείδεος, καὶ ὁ θεός· καὶ δὴ καὶ ἄπειρον ἑκάτερον καὶ ἄγνωστον.

assigned to the learning of certain notions such as the equal and the just. These apparently antithetic positions, says Proclus, have no real incompatibility; for while such notions have in the soul a bare existence to which no beginning in time can be assigned, the articulate knowledge of them, whether by learning or by discovery, dates from remembered times[1].

Justice, Proclus finds, is discovered through the fact of injustice which leads to war. This is from the point of view of the statesman, as distinguished from the soldier and the general, whose business is specialised action. The true statesman first tries to persuade the enemy, and only recurs to force when persuasion has failed. Socrates, it is observed, makes clear to Alcibiades that injustice is a more generalised conception than deceiving or doing violence or taking away a person's goods. The Stoics, indeed, declared all these things always wrong; but the poets and philosophers of an earlier time were more in accordance with the common sense of mankind in regarding them as all justified in a variety of actual cases[2]. Justice and injustice, on the other hand, differ wholly, and are not capable of being good or bad according to circumstances.

The proper end of war is justice, not victory. Enemies are to be made better. Of peace the good that is the end is greater; namely, friendship and unity, the positive completion of all moral virtue, as was said by the Pythagoreans and Aristotle[3]. Later[4], Proclus makes a triad of the good, the

---

[1] 474, 12–28: διττή ἐστι τῶν ψυχῶν ἡ γνῶσις, ἡ μὲν ἀδιάρθρωτος καὶ κατ' ἔννοιαν ψιλήν, ἡ δὲ διηρθρωμένη καὶ ἐπιστημονικὴ καὶ ἀναμφισβήτητος....τῆς μὲν οὖν καθ' ὕπαρξιν ἐν ἡμῖν ἐστώσης τῶν εἰδῶν ἐννοίας χρόνος οὐκ ἔστι προηγούμενος· ἐξ ἀϊδίου γὰρ αὐτὴν εἰλήφαμεν· τῆς δὲ κατὰ προβολὴν καὶ διάρθρωσιν τῶν λόγων γνώσεως καὶ χρόνον ἔχομεν εἰπεῖν. οἶδα γὰρ ὅτι τὸ μὲν εἶδος τοῦ κύκλου τί ἐστιν ἔμαθον ἐν τῷδε τῷ χρόνῳ, τὸ δὲ εἶδος τῆς δικαιοσύνης ἐν ἄλλῳ, καὶ οὕτως ἐφ' ἑκάστου τῶν ὄντων ὧν τὰς ἐπιστήμας κατ' ἐνέργειαν ἔχομεν. Cf. 514–515. There is here a distinct advance in discrimination not only on Plato but on Plotinus: see above, p. 51.

[2] 496, 8–10: καὶ ὅλως ἀρέσκει τοῦτο σχεδὸν ἅπασι τοῖς ἀρχαίοις καὶ ἡ συνήθεια συνομολογεῖ τῇ δόξῃ τῶν παλαιῶν. Another opposition to a Stoic paradox may be noted: against the ascription of all passion to wrong opinion, the influence of feeling and will on opinion is recognised (550–551).

[3] 500.   [4] 575–578.

beautiful, the just. Beauty mediates between the wider notion of goodness and the more limited notion of justice. The underlying reality of the triad is one, but the terms in their explicit meaning differ[1]. Ultimately the political art, as it ought to be, is one with justice[2].

Citing from the Dialogue[3] the proof from wars that men in general cannot know accurately what is just and what is unjust, since it is precisely through differences of conviction on this point that they go to war, Proclus rejects the inference that they know nothing at all on the subject. These extremest differences, provoking the extremest evils, indicate the priority of the notion in our minds. Because we have this so firmly fixed, and think ourselves right about the application, we fall into contentions such as do not arise in the case of health and disease, where we know that we do not know, and trust the experts[4]. In truth, men have the right notion innate in them: where error comes is in the application to particular circumstances. Moreover, justice and injustice are an affair of the whole of life: compared with them, questions of health and disease are only about the parts. These last we might even cast aside as questions that do not concern that in us which is of most value; but by nature we hold to the distinction between the just and the unjust as having here our very being. Deprived of justice, our life becomes to us a life in death and no longer a living reality[5].

---

[1] 577, 21–22: τὸ μὲν ὑποκείμενον ἕν, οἱ δὲ λόγοι διάφοροι.

[2] 501.   [3] Alcib. I. 112.

[4] 537, 21–28: περὶ μὲν γὰρ τῶν ὑγιεινῶν ἁπλῆν ἔχομεν ἄγνοιαν καὶ ἴσμεν ὅτι οὐκ ἴσμεν, κἂν πρὸς ὀλίγον διενεχθῶμεν, τοῖς τεχνίταις τῶν τοιούτων ἐπιτρέπομεν· περὶ δὲ τῶν δικαίων οἰόμεθα ἐπιστήμονες εἶναι διὰ τὸ λόγους ἔχειν αὐτῶν τὴν ψυχήν, καὶ τοῦτο οἰόμενοι κατὰ φύσιν οὐ βουλόμεθα προέσθαι τὸ δίκαιον.

[5] 538, 3–9: καὶ νοσῶδες καὶ ὑγιεινὸν κἂν πρόοιτό τις, ὡς οὐ περὶ τὸ τιμιώτατον γινομένης τῆς βλάβης· δικαίου δὲ καὶ ἀδίκου κατὰ φύσιν ἀντεχόμεθα πάντες, ὡς τὴν οὐσίαν ἡμῶν ἐν τούτῳ σύμπασαν ἔχοντες· μόνον οὖν οὐκ ἀνούσιοι καὶ νεκροὶ καὶ τὸ μὴ ὂν ὑπάρχοντες νομίζομεν γίνεσθαι, στερόμενοι τῶν δικαίων.

ON THE *PARMENIDES*[1]

Fʀᴏᴍ the more elementary theory of knowledge with ethical
applications, the transition comes appropriately to the more
abstruse doctrine developed out of the *Parmenides*. The Commentary begins with a prayer to the gods for enlightenment.
This prose hymn, detached from the context, has gained some
celebrity as a composition. A translation is given in Maurice's
Moral and Metaphysical Philosophy. There is here, as in many
other places, a grateful recognition by Proclus of what he owes
to his master Syrianus, who stands for him, among all his
predecessors, next in authority to Plato[2].

The views of different commentators are first set forth.
Some said the Dialogue was written merely for logical exercise,
and as an illustration of method. Others insisted that the
method was developed only for the sake of the theory of
reality. Again, some took this reality to be the Being of
Parmenides himself considered as One (ἐν ὄν). Others found
that Plato, in his series of distinctions, began with the One
before Being; not all the assertions and denials being true of
the One in the same sense. Syrianus, whom Proclus follows,
decisively adopted the position of those who regarded the
Dialogue as concerned with the theory of reality. This was
in his view not only an ontology but a theology. The One is
identical with God[3].

Proclus has some judicious remarks on the composition.
The dry style (χαρακτὴρ ἰσχνός), contrasting with that of the
mythological poets, is, he points out, admirably adapted to
the dialectical purpose[4]. In the poem itself of Parmenides he
finds something of the same character[5].

He ingeniously reconciles the prohibition of dialectic to
youth in the *Republic* with the commendation of it in the
Parmenides to the youthful Socrates. The prohibition is a

---

[1] 126 ᴀ–141 ᴇ.

[2] In this Commentary (1061, 24), the Homeric λοῖσθος ἀνὴρ ὥριστος (*Il.*
xxiii. 536) is applied to him.

[3] 641, 10: θεὸς καὶ ἐν ταὐτόν. Cf. 643, 1: ὁ γὰρ κατὰ τὸ ἐν θεὸς οὐ τίς θεὸς ἀλλ'
ἁπλῶς θεός.

[4] 645–647.   [5] 665.

legislative decision for average natures; the commendation is advice given in a small circle to an exceptional nature[1]. The kinds of dialectic he classifies into (1) mental gymnastic; (2) discovery of truth; (3) refutation of error.

A dialogue of Plato is an organism. To treat the prologue as alien to the contents is incompatible with all critical judgment. The setting of the *Parmenides* must therefore first be considered in detail.

The arrival of Cephalus at Athens from Clazomenae to hear from Antiphon the discourse of Parmenides symbolises the relations between the Ionic, the Italic and the Athenian philosophy. The Ionic philosophy dealt with nature as in flux, the Italic with stable ideal existences. The theories of these, which are both realities though of different orders, were brought together and completed by the mediation of Socrates and Plato. Accordingly, the Ionian comes to Athens to be initiated by an Athenian in what had been taught by the Eleatic Parmenides about the higher, or mental, order of reality[2].

In the chance meeting of Cephalus with Adeimantus and Glaucon, the brothers of Antiphon, the need is symbolised for the gifts of good fortune not only in external things but also in the soul's pursuit of the things that belong to itself[3]. Proclus is conscious that some of his interpretations may appear too subtle; but, he says, even if they were not part of Plato's own meaning, they are profitable to us as mental exercise, and are an aid to the apt soul in passing from images to the realities that are their pattern[4].

[1] 651–653. Cf. 992.

[2] 660, 26–30: ἡ μὲν οὖν Ἰωνία τῆς φύσεως ἔστω σύμβολον· ἡ δὲ Ἰταλία, τῆς νοερᾶς οὐσίας· αἱ δὲ Ἀθῆναι, τῆς μέσης, δι' ἧς ἄνοδός ἐστι ταῖς ἀπὸ τῆς φύσεως εἰς νοῦν ἐγειρομέναις ψυχαῖς.

[3] 664, 11–14: ὡς οὐκ ἐν τοῖς ἐκτὸς μόνον δεόμεθα τῶν ἀπὸ τῆς ἀγαθῆς τύχης δώρων, ἀλλὰ καὶ ἐν ταῖς αὐτῆς τῆς ψυχῆς ἀναγωγοῖς ἐνεργείαις. Cf. *in Tim.* i. 197–198. Commenting on the words ἀγαθῇ τύχῃ χρὴ λέγειν (*Tim.* 26 E), Proclus observes that Plato refuses to say, as the Stoics did, that the good man has no need of fortune.

[4] 675–676: ὥστε εἰ μὴ καὶ ταῦθ' οὕτως σύγκειται πρὸς αὐτοῦ τοῦ Πλάτωνος, ἀλλ' ἡμῖν γε τὸ πρᾶγμα λυσιτελές· γύμνασμα γάρ ἐστι τῆς εὐφυοῦς ψυχῆς καὶ ἀπὸ των εἰκόνων ἐπὶ τὰ παραδείγματα μεταβαίνειν δυναμένης καὶ τὰς ἀναλογίας τὰς πανταχοῦ διατεινούσας κατανοεῖν φιλούσης.

The presence of Aristoteles, afterwards one of the Thirty, in the company, starts a disquisition on a possible alternation of the same soul between the lives of the philosopher and the tyrant[1]. Proclus again develops the thought, which from very slight hints in Plato he has made effectively his own, that souls more loftily-minded, and therefore figured as having lived with the gods in heaven and seen the movements of the whole under supreme unity, are apt to aspire to power and despotic authority. He does not fail, however, to add that the tyrannic life, as it actually comes to be, is a sinking to the life of the earth-born giants, symbolising the dominance of passionate violence in the soul[2].

A characteristic position of Proclus himself, that the highest reality manifests itself furthest down in the scale, the next highest a stage short of this, and so forth[3], is here applied to the personages. Aristoteles, the youngest and least in the philosophic life, can receive instruction only from Parmenides, the eldest and greatest. For minds of the first order make an appeal reaching to all ranks of intelligence, while minds of the second order can influence only intelligences less removed from themselves[4].

Parmenides, Zeno and Socrates in this dialogue correspond to the μονή, the πρόοδος and the ἐπιστροφή[5]. The dialectic of Zeno, by which the thought of Parmenides is made more explicit, is of the second order, proceeding by synthesis through division and antithesis. That of Parmenides goes directly to the unity which is its object[6]. This is prior to multiplicity and fundamental; yet a real multiplicity, as distinguished from spatial separation which is only phenomenal, is not to be denied. In some sense plurality as well as unity

---

[1] 690–691.

[2] 692, 24–28: ἐπεὶ καὶ αὐτὸ τὸ τοὺς τριάκοντα τυράννους κρατῆσαι τῶν Ἀθηνῶν ἔμφασιν ἔχει τῆς Γιγαντείου καὶ γηγενοῦς ζωῆς κρατούσης τῶν Ἀθηναϊκῶν καὶ Ὀλυμπίων ἀγαθῶν· ὁ γὰρ ὄντως Γιγαντικὸς πόλεμος ἐν ταῖς ψυχαῖς ἐστι.

[3] See above, pp. 168–9.

[4] 691–692.   [5] 712–713. Cf. pp. 166–7, above.

[6] 701–702. Cf. in Alcib. I. 519, 2–6: μετὰ δὲ τὴν ἐπιστήμην καὶ τὴν ἐν αὐτῇ γυμνασίαν τὰς μὲν συνθέσεις καὶ τὰς διαιρέσεις καὶ τὰς πολυειδεῖς μεταβάσεις ἀποθετέον, ἐπὶ δὲ τὴν νοερὰν ζωὴν καὶ τὰς ἁπλᾶς ἐπιβολὰς μεταστατέον τὴν ψυχήν.

exists causally; that is, in the primal metaphysical reality[1]. What Parmenides affirmed was that Being in itself is One; what Zeno denied was that a plurality absolutely dispersed and without any unity that it participates in can be real at all. This granted, he did not deny the Many. And indeed, Proclus adds, there is multitude not only with the unity that is Being, but with the unity beyond[2].

One name applied by the Neo-Platonists to unity in a generalised sense needs elucidation in view of the historical change in its significance. It would be misleading, in the absence of explanation, to translate the term μονάς by "monad." A monad in its modern sense, as fixed by Leibniz, signifies a minimum of real or mental being containing implicitly or potentially the order of the universe. In Neo-Platonism this idea is not absent, but it is expressed by the term "microcosm." The monad or unit is not the atomic individual, but the unity of a group. The units become more inclusive till at length the "Monas monadum[3]," the Demiurgus or mind of the universe, is reached. It is possible, however, that in this commentary we come upon the idea that led to the change of sense. In one place Proclus speaks of "the monads in individuals" (τὰς ἐν τοῖς ἀτόμοις μονάδας)[4]. This means that the specific or generic unity of the individuals is not only over them but exists in each[5]. The transition, we see, was obvious; but the difference remains that by Proclus the individual as such, or the minimum, is never called a monad[6].

---

[1] 712, 2–3: ἡ δὲ αἰτία τοῦ πλήθους ἐστί πως καὶ αὐτὴ κατ' αἰτίαν τὸ πλῆθος. Cf. 620, 5–8: δεῖ μὲν γὰρ καὶ ἓν εἶναι τὸ ὂν καὶ πολλά· καὶ γὰρ πᾶσα μονὰς ἔχει τι σύστοιχον ἑαυτῇ πλῆθος, καὶ πᾶν πλῆθος ὑπὸ μονάδος τινὸς περιέχεται τῆς αὐτῷ προσηκούσης.

[2] Cf. 764, 28–30: πλῆθος καὶ ἓν οὐ μόνον οὐσιῶδές ἐστιν, ἀλλὰ καὶ ὑπὲρ οὐσίαν.

[3] 733, 35–36: μονὰς γοῦν ἐστιν ὁ δημιουργὸς μονάδων πολλῶν περιληπτικὴ θείων. This phrase was taken up by Bruno, in whom perhaps the transition first appears to the later sense of "monad."

[4] 735, 10–11.

[5] Cf. in Tim. ii. 222, 5–13. The monad in relation to which the other parts of the soul are ordered is not to be considered as the minimum of quantity and the basis of numeration, but as the first principle of the soul's essence and the root of its powers.

[6] Cf. in Tim. iii. 221, 25–26: ἡ τῆς ἑτερότητος δύναμις κατακερματίζει τὸ ὅλον εἰς τὰ μέρη καὶ τὰς μονάδας εἰς τοὺς ἀριθμούς.

For the rest, differences of terminology allowed for, it must be clear from the general exposition that Neo-Platonism contains an analogue of Leibnizian monadism. The essential contrast is that the Neo-Platonic real individual is primarily an idea, not, as with Leibniz, a force; and that it is not purely self-evolving, but interacts with other metaphysical beings. For Proclus, as for Plotinus, there are "Ideas of individuals"; and, if he does not carry real individuality below the rational soul, this does not mean that the permanent soul consists only of the reason; within its unity are included certain "roots," as we may call them, of the irrational life that is part of the life in time[1]. But prior to individuals and their energies are certain intellectually defined modes of existence, such as "likeness" and "unlikeness," to which all active manifestation is secondary. In the unity of Mind that contains the Ideas, all opposites pre-exist with creative power. There they are at peace, like the antenatal Caesar and Pompey in Virgil. Violence and mutual destruction arise only when they become embodied in matter[2].

> Illae autem paribus quas fulgere cernis in armis,
> Concordes animae nunc et dum nocte premuntur,
> Heu quantum inter se bellum si lumina vitae
> Attigerint, quantas acies stragemque ciebunt![3]

Each soul is one by participating in the unity of the whole (ultimately in virtue of the transcendent unity beyond the whole); but it is one as being itself, not as identical absolutely with that unity and therefore in essence one with every other soul. Alcibiades and Socrates and other apparent persons are not really the same soul disguised by differences of perceptible appearance. These differences have indeed an inferior degree of reality in contrast with the unity of the person; but the differing individuality is not a mere illusion arising from them. This is stated definitely against a doctrine of the "identity of opposites" already formulated. Must we, asks Proclus, say that likeness is unlikeness and unlikeness likeness, and sameness otherness and otherness sameness, and

---

[1] More is said on this theory later. See pp. 289–90.
[2] 739–742.   [3] *Aen.* vi. 826–829.

multitude one and the One itself multitude; from which it
would follow that each is all the rest, and that there is nothing
that is not all, and that thus the part is no less than the
whole[1]? This, he shows, would lead to a quest for smaller and
smaller parts, each identical with the whole, and so to an
infinite dispersion incompatible with the limitation that is
essential to knowledge. Again, if there is in reality nothing
but the Self-same, and all else is unreal distinction resting on
names, the identity, being itself a term of the distinction,
exists only as bare notion; and so, the cause of the appearances being gone as reality, nothing remains[2]. Yet, he allows,
the identification of opposites is a way of indicating the unity
in which all distinctions are implicit[3]. In the unity of Mind,
each exists as itself, but not as "itself alone[4]."

Perhaps we find in the course of this disquisition a nearer
anticipation than is to be met with elsewhere of the Hegelian
dialectic, though the terms are differently ordered. The progress of a good mind, says Proclus, has three stages, illustrated
in the Socrates of the Dialogue. First there is the starting
away from and denial of something strange; then the suspicion that it may be true; lastly the recognition that it is
true in one sense while the denial is true in another[5]. Hegel's
ordering of the stages—that the first is to assert an accepted
position, the second to find contradictions in it, and the third
to reaffirm it with modifications—seems to indicate a more
conservative temperament than that of his Greek precursor.

Before discussing in detail the criticism of the Ideas that is
ascribed to Parmenides, Proclus sets himself to prove by an
argument of his own that they must exist. The argument is
essentially that a metaphysical reality is necessary to explain
the physical universe, which is not explicable from itself.
This reality cannot proceed by deliberation and choice; for
these are secondary causes within the whole: but, on the
other hand, it must not be a mere good to which things aspire
(as with Aristotle), but which produces nothing[6]. Thought

---

[1] 751, 15–25.   [2] 751–753.   [3] 760.   [4] 755.   [5] 757–758.
[6] 788, 27–28: οὐ μόνον ἔσται τελικὸν ἐκεῖνο τοῦ παντὸς αἴτιον, ἀλλὰ καὶ
ποιητικόν.

indeed is prior, and does not exist for the sake of production; yet production follows as its effect[1]. The order of the universe is to be conceived as determined necessarily by more generalised intellectual existences acting downwards through mediate stages to bring into being the more special. That this is the necessity of the case is argued from the power of the human mind to geometrise, for example, with more accuracy than is to be met with in external nature even in astronomical phenomena, to reason with probative consequence from generals to particulars, and so forth. As this in us is inexplicable from the particulars of experience, but makes them intelligible, so also, in the whole, a higher intellectual order of causes is needed to explain that which is manifested physically. And so we arrive at the fundamental thought of the Platonic doctrine of Ideas; that generals have more being and more causal efficacy than particulars[2].

Side by side with this, however, we must not fail to notice the constant repetition by Proclus of the position that in experience the imperfect always genetically precedes the perfect. This is no casual thought, but deliberate antithesis. It would be correct to say that for him the process of nature is upward, not downward. If he treats the causal order—the order of realities—as the reverse, that is because he is looking for an adequate explanation of the final perfection of each thing: the cause of this, he holds, must be in its real existence superior, not inferior, to that which it produces. The succession of stages in time, therefore, is antithetic to the order of implication in the whole.

At first sight contradictory to what has been said about the doctrine of individuality held by Proclus, is a passage expressly opposing the theory of Plotinus that there are Ideas of particular individuals (τῶν καθ' ἕκαστα)[3]. What Proclus opposes, however, is an accident and not the essence of the theory[4]. The position of Plotinus that he rejects is one that

---

[1] 791, 21: τῷ νοεῖν ἑαυτὸν ποιητὴς ἔσται πάντων.

[2] 796–797: τὰ καθόλου...καὶ οὐσιώτερα καὶ αἰτιώτερα τῶν καθ' ἕκαστα.

[3] 824. Cf. Enn. v. 7.

[4] I find that in my own exposition (pp. 61–2 above) I had stated only the portion of the theory that is common to both philosophers. Later study of

seems to make the merely empirical individual, even of all
animal races, in some sense eternal[1]. Against thus carrying
down the idea of the individual, he raises the objection that
on this supposition the empirical individuality of Socrates
would be immortal. But this is a product, to speak generally,
of the cosmic order, and, when we descend to detail, of
seasonal and climatic influences and all sorts of special
causes[2]. He is quite clear that the composite individual,
Socrates or Plato, thus brought to be, has only one mortal
life, and at the end of it disappears. This, however, is to be
distinguished from the soul of which it is a temporary embodiment. In his view as in that of Plotinus, each individual
human soul is permanent and goes on from life to life as the
manifestation of a permanent "mind," which is an eternally
distinct thing within universal Intellect[3]. According to
Proclus, indeed, each mind is not realised in one soul only,
but in several. These have intermittent lives in time, while
the "mind," or intellectual type, under which they are
grouped, is eternally active[4]. For animal souls, below some
never exactly defined stage, the permanence (as has been said
before) appears to be conceived as belonging to the species
rather than to the individual[5].

In these complexities, it may be well to mention, Proclus
confesses that he is not very sure of his ground. To carry our
thinking down to the ultimate individual, he says, is beyond

the objection taken by Proclus was necessary to bring out more exactly the
implications in the argument of Plotinus.

[1] In like manner Spinoza appears to say that there is in infinite intellect a
necessary and eternal concept of every human body that was and is and is to
be (*Eth.* v. Prop. 22). The phrases of Plotinus that suggest a similar infinity
of concepts are these: τὴν δὲ ἐν τῷ νοητῷ ἀπειρίαν οὐ δεῖ δεδιέναι· πᾶσα γὰρ ἐν
ἀμερεῖ (Enn. v. 7, 1); ἆρ' οὖν καὶ ἐπὶ τῶν ἄλλων ζῴων, ἐφ' ὧν πλῆθος ἐκ μιᾶς γενέσεως, τοσούτους τοὺς λόγους; ἢ οὐ φοβητέον τὸ ἐν τοῖς σπέρμασι καὶ τοῖς λόγοις
ἄπειρον, ψυχῆς τὰ πάντα ἐχούσης (v. 7, 3).

[2] 825.

[3] Cf. *in Tim.* iii. 72, 20: ἄλλος μὲν ὁ φαινόμενος Σωκράτης, ἄλλος δὲ ὁ ἀληθινός.

[4] Cf. *in Tim.* ii. 143–145.

[5] Cf. *in Tim.* i. 53, 20–23: αἱ γὰρ κατελθοῦσαι ψυχαὶ πάλιν ἀνίασιν, οὐχ ὅσαι
τὴν ὑπόστασιν ἐξ ἀρχῆς εἶχον ἐν τῇ γενέσει καὶ περὶ τὴν ὕλην, οἶαι δή εἰσιν αἱ πολλαὶ
τῶν ἀλόγων. This particular passage denies true individuality of most, but
not of all, irrational animals.

the powers of the human mind, which is more adapted to theorise on the universal or general[1]. About the particular, he is sure only that, in its smallest details, it is not uncaused[2].

This is quite consistent with its not having its causation wholly in the Ideas. For causality, in his view, begins above intellect, from the One and Good, and does not end till unformed Matter is reached. The Ideas thus constitute only a portion of the causal series. Evils, for example, arise through complexes of causation among the interacting parts of the whole; but there are no "Ideas of evils[3]." There is, nevertheless, an eternal idea, a παράδειγμα, of the knowledge of evil in relation to good; for this knowledge is a good and ignorance an evil[4].

As is well known, the most destructive criticism to which the doctrine of Ideas was ever subjected is put by Plato himself in the mouth of Parmenides discoursing with the youthful Socrates. Coming to this part of the Dialogue, Proclus, first quite generally and then in detail, tries to determine precisely what is the effect of the criticism. Of course he does not fail to observe that in the discussion Parmenides recognises the necessity of some theory concerning the realities corresponding to general names if there is to be knowledge[5]. His own view is that all the criticism is directed towards showing the inadequacy of comparisons with things in space to describe relations between incorporeals. The relation of particulars to the reality signified by a general name is not physical, but of another kind. Image in a mirror, impression of a seal on wax, imitation of an object by plastic or pictorial art, may put a beginner in the way of thinking on the subject; but participation in the Ideas is not of corporeal things in their like; for it is neither participation in the whole nor in a part as the terms are understood of bodies[6]. The puzzle arises from

---

[1] 813, 17–21: ἐπὶ γὰρ τὰς ἀτόμους καὶ τὰς ἰδίας πάντων διαφορὰς χωρεῖν κρεῖττόν ἐστιν ἢ κατὰ ἀνθρώπειον νοῦν, τὸ δὲ πάντη ἢ ἐπὶ πλεῖστον διατεινόντων μᾶλλον ἡμῖν θεωρῆσαι δυνατόν.

[2] 835, 11: παντὶ γὰρ ἀδύνατον χωρὶς αἰτίου γένεσιν ἔχειν.   [3] 829–831.

[4] 833, 8–12: καὶ γὰρ ἡ ἄγνοια κακόν,...ὥστε πάλιν τὸ παράδειγμα οὐ κακοῦ, ἀλλ᾽ ἀγαθοῦ, τῆς τοῦ κακοῦ γνώσεως.

[5] 838, 9–11.   [6] 858.

bringing in an antithesis that has no proper application. The youthful Socrates was imperfectly prepared. He had indeed already the notion of a general idea as a unity, but, through want of sufficient introspective analysis of the notion, he imagined the unity as somehow distributed among things set apart[1]. The criticism ascribed to Parmenides is thus, according to Proclus, intended by Plato to make clear to his own disciples that, in his theory of Ideas, he meant them to apply their minds to a kind of reality which is not that of the things that furnish him with metaphors. In virtue of his clear insight beyond these, he could himself use them with the utmost freedom and variety. His mode of turning on them reveals his full possession of that insight.

That the Ideas are realised as notions in the soul[2] Proclus recognises in accordance with the traditional Platonic doctrine[3]; but Parmenides, he points out, corrects the suggestion of Socrates that they may be *only* in the soul. They imply intelligible objects of thought; and the object is more distinctively the Idea than is our thought of it. The notions by which the Ideas are realised in the soul do not come as generalisations from perception, which are "notions" in another sense, but make generalisation possible[4]. They are products of Intellect contemplating its own being, and are more properly said to be "in the mind" than "in the soul"[5]; but it is enough for us if our souls participate in their universality[6].

Proclus thus saw quite clearly that Plato's theory of ideas, while it had psychological references, could not be understood as merely psychological. His own development has strikingly

---

[1] 864, 23–36. Cf. 865, 1–2: ἅτε τὴν νόησιν τὴν ἔνδον μήπω διαρθρῶσαι δυνάμενος.

[2] 892, 8: ἐν νοήμασί τισιν οὐσιῶσθαι τὰς ἰδέας.

[3] 892, 24–25: τὴν ψυχὴν πάντα εἶναι τὰ εἴδη φαμέν, καὶ τόπον τῶν εἰδῶν τὴν ψυχήν.

[4] 893, 17–19: οὔτε γὰρ [τὸ γιγνῶσκον] παρ᾽ αὐτῶν τῶν αἰσθητῶν λαμβάνει τὸ κοινόν. Cf. 894, 24: πᾶσα ἀπόδειξις ἐκ τῶν προτέρων. Again, 896, 31–33: ἔνδοθεν ἄρα καὶ ἀπὸ τῆς οὐσίας ἡμῶν αἱ προβολαὶ γίγνονται τῶν εἰδῶν, καὶ οὐκ ἀπὸ τῶν αἰσθητῶν. Cf. in Alcib. I. 545, 7: ὅτι προβάλλουσιν ἀφ᾽ ἑαυτῶν αἱ ψυχαὶ τοὺς λόγους.

[5] 930, 24–25.

[6] 931, 17–18: ἡμεῖς δὲ ἀγαπῶμεν ἂν τῶν νοερῶν ψυχικῶς μετέχοντες εἰδῶν.

Kantian turns; and it may be said in his favour that, by his distinction between "soul" and "mind" (the associate of a particular body and the intellect in which it shares), he makes clearer than Kant did that it is not the merely individual intelligence that is conceived as "projecting" the forms of knowledge. Another glimpse confirms the general impression made. The term *ego* did not become a technical term with the Neo-Platonists; but Proclus uses it in one place in a sense very like Kant's "transcendental unity of apperception." In serving to indicate every mental act, perceptive, volitional, intellectual, it points, he says, to "some one life" that moves the soul to assert each psychical state in turn, to some one indivisible thing in us that knows all our energies, ἐφ' ἑκάστῳ λέγον τὸ ἐγὼ καὶ τὸ ἐνεργῶ[1]. This he applies as an analogy to show how there can be an indivisible divine knowledge, knowing things not as they appear but in their causes or essences, and at the same time creative by its activity which is one with its thought.

Theory of knowledge thus passes into ontology. In his theory of reality, Proclus carefully distinguishes that which he regards as the all-inclusive doctrine of Plato[2] from Aristotelianism on the one side and Stoicism on the other. Each of these has an element of truth. The things in the universe co-operate in its processes by their aspiration to Mind; but the Mind that is the end does not stand apart in complete isolation from the things that aspire[3]. Its thinking is also creative[4]. This the Stoics recognised when they conceived a providential order as running through matter; but they did not recognise that transcendence of the divine intellect which, by the too exclusive emphasis on it, makes the pure monotheism of Aristotle "dark with excessive bright[5]." The refutation of this exclusiveness is put in the form of the questions: How can the physical universe strive after the divine if it has not its origin thence[6]? How can we know the object of

---

[1] 957–958.   [2] 921, 10–13.

[3] 842, 26–28: τοῖς μὲν οὖν τὸν νοῦν τελικὸν αἴτιον ποιοῦσιν, ἀλλ' οὐχὶ καὶ δημιουργικόν, ἐξ ἡμισείας ὑπάρχει τὸ ἀληθές.

[4] 844, 1–2: ὡς νοεῖ, ποιεῖ, καὶ ὡς ποιεῖ, νοεῖ, καὶ ἀεὶ ἑκάτερον.   [5] See *e.g.*, 955.

[6] 922, 3–4: πῶς γὰρ ὁ οὐρανὸς ὀρέγεται τοῦ θείου, μὴ γενόμενος ἐκεῖθεν;

aspiration if we neither have our existence from it nor participate in the laws that express its true reality[1]? The Ideas, for Proclus, thus represent the intellectual diversity by which the unity of the universe is mediated to its parts; for it is the Ideas that are meant by these "intelligential laws[2]."

The philosophic impulse, says Proclus, is called by Parmenides "divine" as looking beyond visible things to incorporeal being, and "beautiful" as leading to the truly beautiful, which is not in things practical, as the Stoics later deemed, but in the intellectual energies. This impulse to beauty the philosophic life has in common with the life of the true lover[3]. To urge Socrates to pay special attention to the apparently useless dialectic called by the vulgar "idle talk" ($\dot{a}\delta o\lambda\epsilon\sigma\chi\acute{\iota}a$), is a way of indicating that this is the true salvation of souls, and is one with the power of theorising on being and judging of truth[4]. This is how it is put "enthusiastically[5]"; but Proclus can also soberly point out the danger of approaching ontological questions without a sufficient training in theory of knowledge[6]. The aim is to discover one method for solving many problems, not to be able plausibly to attack or defend every rival solution[7]. This showy sort of accomplishment in the forms of logic the multitude admires[8]. The preliminary gymnastic advised by Parmenides is troublesome, and force must be used to drag oneself away from a direct attack on those problems of being that excite impassioned interest. The season for it is youth, when there is vigour for toil, and plenty of time, and when discipline can be applied so that the procedure shall be by orderly stages.

Proclus himself gives one or two illustrations of the kind of search commended. Starting from the *Sophist*, he sets forth a theory of relative not-being. Of this there are various kinds. Matter, as we know, is a kind of not-being because it

---

[1] 923, 2–4: πῶς δὲ καὶ ἡμεῖς ἐκεῖνο γιγνώσκομεν, μήτε ὑποστάντες ἐκεῖθεν, μήτε λόγων μετέχοντες τῶν ὄντως ὄντων;

[2] Cf. 888, 2: νοερούς λόγους εἶναι τὰς ἰδέας.   [3] 988.

[4] 990, 7–11: παρὰ μὲν τοῖς πολλοῖς ἀδολεσχίαν προσαγορευομένην, κυριώτατα δὲ οὖσαν ἀληθινὴν σωτηρίαν τῶν ψυχῶν, ἐξ ὧν φανερὸν ὅτι ταὐτόν ἐστι τῇ θεωρητικῇ τῶν ὄντων καὶ κριτικῇ τῆς ἀληθείας δυνάμει. Cf. 1024, 33–38.

[5] Cf. 987, 18–21.   [6] 989–991.   [7] 984–985.   [8] 990, 13–14.

is in itself unformed. Material things phenomenally are, but in the proper sense of being are not[1]. On the other hand, the cause of all is a kind of not-being because it is set over against the forms of being[2]. There is no absolute not-being[3]. This was the truth affirmed by Parmenides in the poem.

Next Proclus tries to apply the method of the Dialogue to the soul. What will be the result to itself and to other things if we say, in one sense or another, that it is or that it is not? Here the most interesting remark occurs at the close: that it would be easier to begin from bodies than from the soul, since we are better acquainted with bodies and the consequences of their animation or non-animation than with what happens to the soul itself[4].

While commending slow, methodical approaches to philosophical questions, Proclus finds it to be a merit in the *Parmenides* that the relation of dialectic to the things themselves about which truth is desired is never left out of view in a round of mere unapplied logical generalities[5]. So difficult was the combination found to be that none of Plato's successors composed any treatise in this form[6]. Again, while approving of toil over dry distinctions as good for philosophic youth, he singles out expressly for notice the proposal of Parmenides that the youngest in the company shall answer his questions, because he will be the most docile and will give the least trouble; grounding on this the observation that "to energise with ease is divine[7]." This is a Hellenic point of view. The power, bearing with it the appearance of struggle and volition, which the ancients sometimes called "daemonic" and which we call "Titanic[8]," seemed to the Greek spirit, now retired

---

[1] 999, 26–27: τὸ ἔνυλον πᾶν, ἅτε φαινομένως μὲν ὄν, κυρίως δὲ οὐκ ὄν.

[2] 999, 36–39.   [3] 999–1000: τὸ μὲν μηδαμῇ μηδαμῶς ὂν οὐδέποτε ὑποθετέον.

[4] 1006, 29–35: καὶ ὁρᾷς ὡς ἐν ταύταις ταῖς ὑποθέσεσι γένοιτ' ἂν ῥᾷον ὁ λόγος οὐκ ἀπ' αὐτῆς ἡμῶν ἀρξαμένων τῆς ψυχῆς, ἀλλ' ἀπὸ τῶν σωμάτων· ταῦτα γὰρ γνωριμώτερα τῆς ψυχῆς, καὶ τῶν ἐπομένων ἐκείνῃ καὶ οὐχ ἐπομένων τὰ τούτοις ἐπόμενα καὶ οὐχ ἑπόμενα, τῷ μετέχειν ἢ μὴ μετέχειν ψυχῆς.

[5] 1018, 25–27: τὸ διὰ τῶν πραγμάτων αὐτῶν ὁδεύειν αὐτὴν καὶ μὴ ἐν ψιλοῖς ὑφεστάναι τοῖς λογικοῖς κανόσι.

[6] 1020, 31–35.

[7] 1037, 37–38: θεῖόν ἐστι τοῦτο τὸ μετὰ ῥᾳστώνης ἐνεργεῖν.

[8] Through the Orphic myth of the tearing in pieces of Dionysus by the

into its watch-tower, to be of the second order. The highest life attainable by man is the life of intellectual contemplation beyond effort[1].

It is only after this wide expatiation on the preliminary matter that we arrive at direct discussion of the hypotheses concerning the One. Of these nine were enumerated. All the rest of the Commentary that survives is devoted to the first. This was indeed the most important for Neo-Platonism; comprising as it did the proof that no predicates are applicable to the One. All the hypotheses, with their various affirmations and negations, Proclus says, are true of it though in different senses, just as all the paradoxes on the Ideas are in some sense true[2]. For him, however, as for his school, the highest truth is in what has since been called the "negative theology." Not only is the One unknowable to us, but we do not even know that it is knowable to itself[3]. Thus it is properly nameless. Yet it undoubtedly is[4]. The meaning of the negations is that, since it is the cause of all, it is not distinctively any of the things that it produces. On the other hand, all the affirmations of real existences that are not the One have for their causes the negations applied to it[5]; for it is above all determinate being, as matter, or bare possibility, is below all determinate being. Its positive reality is apprehended by the unity

Titans, the "Titanic" had come to be interpreted as symbolising the principle of diremption in the world-process. See *in Cratyl.* 64, 17–20; cf. 77–78.

[1] 1025, 32–34: μόνη δὲ ἡ κατὰ νοῦν ζωὴ τὸ ἀπλανὲς ἔχει, καὶ οὗτος ὁ μυστικὸς ὅρμος τῆς ψυχῆς.

[2] 972, 9–11.

[3] 1108, 25–29: καὶ οὐχ ἡμῖν μὲν ἄγνωστον, ἑαυτῷ δὲ γνωστόν ἐστιν· εἰ γάρ ἐστιν ὅλως ἡμῖν ἄγνωστον, οὐδὲ αὐτὸ τοῦτο γιγνώσκομεν ὅτι ἑαυτῷ γνωστόν ἐστιν, ἀλλὰ καὶ τοῦτο ἀγνοοῦμεν.

[4] 1065, 31–33: ἀνάγκη δήπου πάντως εἶναι τοῦτο τὸ ἕν, οὗ πάντα ἀποφάσκεται.

[5] 1075, 16–19: ἀλλ' εἴ με χρὴ συντόμως εἰπεῖν τὸ δοκοῦν, ὥσπερ τὸ ἓν αἴτιόν ἐστι τῶν ὅλων, οὕτω καὶ ἀποφάσεις αἰτίαι τῶν καταφάσεών εἰσιν. We are reminded of Spinoza's saying that determination is negation: see Ep. 50 (ed. Bruder), where also he says that to speak of God even as one is to apply a term that is not properly applicable. The sentence in which this is put would have been accepted by a Neo-Platonist as correct if we are to speak with the utmost rigour. "Quoniam vero Dei existentia ipsius sit essentia, deque eius essentia universalem non possimus formare ideam, certum est, eum, qui Deum unum vel unicum nuncupat, nullam de Deo veram habere ideam, vel improprie de eo loqui."

262 THE COMMENTARIES OF PROCLUS

of existence at the summit of our intellect, a kind of bloom of the mind, ἄνθος τοῦ νοῦ[1]. It is itself completely transcendent, "imparticipable" (ἀμέθεκτον, χωριστόν, ἀπὸ πάντων ἐξῃρημένον). It is God simply and absolutely. The conception of gods as makers or fathers is the partial conception of a kind of divinity, not of divinity simply[2]. Divinity is properly unity[3]. Are we to call it Limit or Unlimited? Unlimited, Proclus finally answers; for it is not subject to the limits which we say in relation to other things that it fixes for them[4].

This, Proclus recognises, goes beyond anything in the poem of Parmenides[5], which demonstrates only the unity of that which is (τὸ ἓν ὄν), not the unity beyond being. At the same time, he holds that there was a theology behind the doctrine of Parmenides himself, though he did not give it the explicit form that it has in Plato. Some commentators, it appears, doubted whether the developments in the *Parmenides* were really Platonic; but Proclus establishes their Platonic character from the *Sophist*, with its connected line of argument[6].

---

[1] Cf. *in Cratyl.* 66, 11–12.

[2] 1097, 1–3: εἶδός τι θεότητος μερικόν, ὃ δὴ ποιόν ἐστι θεῖον, ἀλλ' οὐχὶ ἁπλῶς. Cf. 1096, 30: ὁ γὰρ δημιουργὸς καὶ ὁ πατήρ τις θεός.

[3] 1069, 8–9.

[4] See the interesting dissertation on the kinds of infinity and the kinds of limit, pp. 1117–1124. There is infinity in matter as itself formless; in body without quality, as divisible without limit; in the qualities of bodies, admitting of continuous differences in intensity (τὸ μᾶλλόν τε καὶ ἧττον, *Phileb.* 24 B); in the perpetual renewal of birth; in the rotatory movement of the heaven; in the soul with its continuous transitions from thought to thought; in time, limitless as to the numbers with which it measures the motions of the soul; in intellect, ever present in the intelligential life with no limit to its duration; and in eternity (ὁ πολυύμνητος αἰών), which is prior to intellect and is the potency of all infinities. In the reverse direction, the notion of limit can be applied at all stages short of formless matter; for all in one aspect involve measure and number. Eternity is the measure of mind, time of the soul; the movement of the heaven takes place by the repetition of a measurable period; the Ideas manifested in the succession of births are finite in number; body is finite in extension.

[5] The Parmenides of the poem is always distinguished from the Parmenides of Plato. The phrase is: ὁ ἐν τοῖς ποιήμασι Παρμενίδης (1177, 3), ὁ ἐν τοῖς ἔπεσι Παρμενίδης (1177, 12). Cf. 1240, 32–37.

[6] 1103, 6–8: ὥστε ἢ ἐκείνοις ἀπιστείτω τις ὡς οὐ Πλάτωνος θεάμασιν, ἢ καὶ τούτοις συγχωρείτω.

Proclus no doubt read into his predecessors, including Plato, some distinctions not developed till later; but he was quite aware that he might be "reading between the lines"; and, as the philologists who have recently discussed or edited the texts fully recognise, "historical sense" cannot be denied to him or to the Neo-Platonic school. If he is unwilling to admit as some did, that Plato corrected Parmenides, he does not hesitate to allow that he added a new point of view[1]. The demonstration of Parmenides, he observes, is not directly of the One, but of Being, and he proceeds by affirmation of that which is. Plato, in the first hypothesis, proceeds by denying all attributes to the One itself; only afterwards, in the second hypothesis, where he combines Being with the One, does he assert the unity of Being. The higher point of view is attained by denying, through a methodical process, everything that can possibly be asserted of the One. It is beyond expression even by the "rest" or "quiet" or "silence" of the mystics[2]. Yet, though it is in a sense "not-being," it may be better spoken of as a kind of being to avoid confusing it with the not-being that is below all positive existence[3]. Different modes of speech are allowable from different points of view. Thus Proclus allows himself to use the language of personal theism characteristic of the *Laws*, while treating it definitely as exoteric. Assertions such as that God is beginning, middle and end are, he says, only relative to other things, and are not properly applicable to the incomprehensible existence of the One itself[4].

What then, it may be asked, is there of positive insight in the final result? There is, it seems to me, the clear notion that we apprehend ultimate reality by the "synthetic unity"

---

[1] 1135, 2–5: οὐκ ἔλεγχός ἐστι ταῦτα τῆς Παρμενίδου φιλοσοφίας, ἀλλ' ἐκείνης μενούσης πρόσθεσις τῆς ὑπέρτερας.

[2] 1171, 4–8: εἴτε οὖν γαλήνη τίς ἐστιν ὑμνημένη νοερὰ παρὰ τοῖς σοφοῖς, εἴτε ὅρμος μυστικός, εἴτε σιγὴ πατρική, δῆλον ὡς ἁπάντων τῶν τοιούτων ἐξήρηται τὸ ἕν, ἐπέκεινα ὂν καὶ ἐνεργείας καὶ σιγῆς καὶ ἡσυχίας.

[3] 1079–1082.

[4] 1113–1116. The One is not even "in itself," for all place must be denied of it: μόνον δὲ τὸ ἓν ἁπλῶς οὐδαμοῦ ἐστιν (1135, 40). This means that it alone has no cause in which it can be said to be.

in our own minds. This, of course, could not be said by Parmenides; and Plato himself could not yet say it in the subjective terms that would have appropriately conveyed his
thought. Even Plotinus has to help out theoretical insight
by mystical experience. The last degree of self-conscious
clearness was reached only by Proclus at the end of the long
development. If the One is now more firmly than ever declared to be objectively unknown and unknowable, it is at
the same time definitely made the correlate of what is subjectively the principle of cognition[1]. The distinction between
the One and the Mind of the Whole, as Berkeley with his
kindred subtlety perceived, had become the metaphysical
analogue of the psychological distinction between self and
intellect[2]; the ultimate self in each and in the whole being a
kind of unknowable point of origin of all determinate forms
of thought or reality. It is the nature of human language,
applied primarily to things outside, that compels philosophers
to speak of that which is most real as a negation of all that is
customarily described as "being."

ON THE *TIMAEUS*[3]

To justify the order in which I am taking the Commentaries,
the words of Proclus himself can now be cited. The *Timaeus*
being a physical treatise, he observes, it proceeds downwards
from intelligible reality, and in the logical order follows the
Parmenides[4]. He quotes Iamblichus with approval to the
effect that these two dialogues contain the whole theoretical
philosophy of Plato[5]. Through the absence or loss of the
portion of the preceding commentary treating of the other
meanings assigned to the One, there must of course be a gap
in the exposition. For it was not immediately from the One
without predicates, the unknowable source, that Proclus
made the transition to the theory of nature, but from the
unity of Being and Mind.

[1] 1044, 26–28: λείπεται δὴ τὸ ἕν, τοῦ νοῦ τούτου καὶ τὴν ὕπαρξιν καὶ τὸ οἷον
ἄνθος, τοῦτο εἶναι τὴν πρώτην ἀρχήν. Cf. 1047, 1: τὴν μίαν ἀρχὴν τῆς γνώσεως.
[2] *Siris*, § 352.   [3] 17 A–44 D.   [4] i. 12–14.
[5] i. 13, 14–17: ὀρθῶς ἄρα φησὶν ὁ θεῖος Ἰάμβλιχος τὴν ὅλην τοῦ Πλάτωνος θεωρίαν ἐν τοῖς δύο τούτοις περιέχεσθαι διαλόγοις, Τιμαίῳ καὶ Παρμενίδῃ.

In spite of the gap, the positions taken up at the opening can be directly connected with what has just been said about the subjective basis of the Neo-Platonic ontology. Since man is a microcosm[1], knowledge of man and of the world are necessarily correlated. As God or the One can only be apprehended as the cause by the principle itself of the mind, so the Being of which the universe is a manifestation can only be understood by mind in its explicit activity. To place the theory of thinking beside the theory of the object of thought is declared to be a Pythagorean point of view[2]. This meant what we now call an idealistic position. The remark has special relevance because the historical Timaeus was said to have been a Pythagorean[3].

In accordance with that which had become the general presupposition of the commentators, the minutest details in the setting of the Dialogue are interpreted as symbolism[4].

The City, as well as Man, is a microcosm[5]. Hence analogies can be found between the distributions of functions to the classes in the State (recapitulated in the opening summary of the Republic) and the orders of beings in the universe. A point of interest in detail is that Proclus, with Theodore of Asine, firmly upholds the position that men and women have the same virtue and perfection, being not two different races, but portions of the same race, which as such is human, not male or female[6]. The secret arrangement of marriages by the guardians under the appearance of leaving them to be determined by casting lots he interprets as indicating the reality of metaphysical causation in the universe behind apparent chance-collocations[7].

When Socrates tells the company that he cannot represent

---

[1] i. 5, 11–13: μικρὸς κόσμος ὁ ἄνθρωπος καὶ ἔστι καὶ ἐν τούτῳ πάντα μερικῶς, ὅσα ἐν τῷ κόσμῳ θείως τε καὶ ὁλικῶς. Cf. i. 202, 26–27.

[2] i. 5, 22–23.

[3] Proclus supposed the work ascribed to Timaeus Locrus, Περὶ ψυχᾶς κόσμω καὶ φύσιος, to be by Timaeus himself.

[4] i. 26, 8–10: ταῦτα μὲν οὖν γυμνασία προτεινέσθω τῆς τῶν πραγμάτων θεωρίας ἐν τοῖς προοιμίοις αὐτῆς εἰκονικῶς ἐμφαινόμενα.

[5] i. 33, 24–25: οὐ γάρ που μικρὸς μὲν κόσμος ὁ ἄνθρωπος, οὐχὶ δὲ μικρὸς ἡ πόλις κόσμος.

[6] i. 46.   [7] i. 51, 6–8.

his City bodied forth, but must limit himself to abstractions, Proclus finds this to be a mark of superabundant power, not of weakness[1]. The philosophic mind is analogous to the higher cause, remaining at the summit of the productive series, and not itself descending to particulars[2]. Like many interesting and subtle ideas in Proclus, this has its "occasional cause" in the effort to justify every detail in Plato. It resembles what is said by Comte in the *Philosophie Positive* when he treats science and philosophy as more originative than art, and therefore prior in the directive order. It might be defended by incidental expressions in the poets themselves. Milton, for example, places the "thoughts more elevate[3]" of moral philosophy above song. In the celebrated passage in praise of beauty, Marlowe, where he speaks of the poets' work, might be taken as conceding the superiority of abstract ideas even to

> all the heavenly quintessence they still
> From their immortal flowers of poesy,
> Wherein, *as in a mirror*, we perceive
> The highest reaches of a human wit[4].

The italicised words are in fact curiously coincident with the Neo-Platonic doctrine for which imagination is analogous to a mirror placed as a mean between thought and sense. Proclus, however, made this high claim only for thought which, in its moments of enthusiasm, becomes, like Plato's, itself a kind of poetry. Inspired poetry ($\check{\epsilon}\nu\theta\epsilon\sigma\varsigma$ $\pi\sigma\acute{\iota}\eta\sigma\iota\varsigma$) is for him at the summit. We find it, he holds, in Plato as in Homer.

An error in the Commentary is that the Critias of the Dialogue is taken to be the member of the Thirty. Modern commentators also have generally assumed this. As Prof. Burnet has recently shown[5], he is not the oligarch, but his grandfather and the great-grandfather of Plato. Alexander of Aphrodisias still had the relationships right. Once recognised,

---

[1] i. 62, 31: καὶ ἔστιν ἡ τοιαύτη ἀδυναμία δυναμίας περιουσία.

[2] This must not be confounded with the Aristotelian view that providence does not descend to particulars, but only to generals. The Neo-Platonists held that it descends, but through grades, more and more lowered as they are more removed from contemplation and more immersed in practice.

[3] *Paradise Lost*, ii. 558.   [4] *Tamburlaine the Great*, Part I. Act v. Sc. 2.

[5] *Greek Philosophy*, Part I. (1914), § 256, p. 338.

they make the account of the tradition from Solon chronologically possible. Proclus was evidently a little puzzled about
this; but he was more interested in the symbolism than in the
exact chronology[1]. Critias, for him, like Alcibiades and Aristoteles, is the naturally gifted mind aspiring to tyranny. The
coming from heaven of such a mind signifies, as we have
already seen, the fascination exercised on it by the power
manifested in the hierarchical direction of the whole. Again,
as before, Proclus observes that the ambition for power belongs after all to a mind of the second order; for principality
and sway and dominion are not the highest, but are only in
the middle place[2]. With this it is in harmony that Timaeus,
having a position in the dialogue corresponding to that of
the Demiurge in the universe, symbolises the personally-
governing Zeus subordinated to Adrasteia[3].

To any who think that the Neo-Platonists represent a
swamping of Greek thought in Orientalism, I commend the
passage in this Commentary on the interview between Solon
and the Egyptian priest. Proclus has a very clear idea of
progress as the principle for which Athens stands against a
fixed order like that of Egypt. Pride in mere length of memory
of the past, he finds, savours of conceit. "The learning of
many things does not bring forth mind (πολυμαθείη νόον οὐ
φύει), says the noble Heraclitus[4]." Turning his philosophic
rationalism against the prestige of an old historic order, he
dwells on the thought that memories and sense-perceptions
do not suffice to produce knowledge[5]. We ourselves project

---

[1] i. 82, 19–21.

[2] i. 71, 10–11: τὸ γὰρ ἡγεμονικὸν καὶ τὸ ἐπὶ πολλὰ διατεῖνον καὶ ὅλως ἡ δύναμις
τῶν μέσων ἐστί.

[3] i. 69, 24–26.   [4] i. 102, 24–25.

[5] i. 102, 29–31: τὰς μνήμας καὶ τὰς αἰσθήσεις ποιητικὰς εἶναι τῆς ἐπιστήμης, ὥς
φησιν ὁ Ἀριστοτέλης, ἀδύνατον. From a scholium on this passage we learn
incidentally what various possibilities could still be realised by the Greek
intellect. The writer distinctly suggests the "radical empiricism" of a "psychology without the soul." If there are no souls, he says, it is not only not
impossible, it is necessary, that memories and sense-perceptions should be
productive of knowledge: εἴ τις λόγος δείξει, φίλε Πρόκλε, μὴ ὑπάρχειν τὰς
ψυχάς, οὐ μόνον οὐκ ἀδύνατον, ἀλλὰ καὶ ἀναγκαῖον τὰς μνήμας καὶ αἰσθήσεις
ποιητικὰς εἶναι τῶν ἐπιστημῶν (i. 463).

on the particulars the unity of the universal[1]. The priest, it is true, in his insistence on the claims of age, has hold of the principle that the elder, that is, the ontologically prior cause, is that which preserves the stability of the whole. Yet, great as is this conservative order in the cosmos, the principle of renewal figured by the creative action of Athena[2] goes back to a higher point of the all-inclusive causal series, in which fixity and alternating cycles alike have their source[3]. And he could put stress on this against what seemed too arrogant in the claims of the East while fully recognising the spirit of unification in the old order, admired by Plato as afterwards by Comte in its opposition to the dispersiveness of the new[4].

Nor is his Greek rationalism unaccompanied by a feeling for the importance of historic memory. To acquire knowledge of the past from the stable orders, where these have kept records, he remarks, contributes in the highest degree towards perfecting human wisdom[5]. In a later passage[6], he dwells on the value for scientific theory of the empirical results attained by the long-continued observations of Egyptian and Chaldaean astronomers; setting these against the mere agreement with hypothesis of what can at present be observed. A true conclusion, he points out, can be reached from false assumptions; and the consonance of phenomena with hypotheses is an insufficient test of the truth of these.

When the priest reconstitutes from recorded history that memory of past cycles which had been lost by the younger world, Proclus finds this procedure to be imitated by the Pythagoreans, who set themselves to show how individuals may restore the memory of their former lives. For the different periods of a race may be compared to the different lives

---

[1] i. 103, 1: τὸ ἕν...εἶδος προβάλλομεν.

[2] i. 103, 8–9: τὴν νέαν δημιουργίαν τὴν ὑπὸ τῆς Ἀθηνᾶς συνεχομένην.

[3] i. 103, 30: τὸ νεώτερον ἐξ ὑπερτέρας ἥκει τάξεως.

[4] i. 104, 14–17: σύμβολον γὰρ τὸ μὲν πολιὸν νοήσεως καὶ ἀχράντου ζωῆς καὶ πόρρω γενέσεως οὔσης, τὸ δὲ νέον τῆς μερικωτέρας γνώσεως καὶ τῆς ἐφαπτομένης ἤδη τῶν γιγνομένων. Cf. 127, 23–27.

[5] i. 124, 11–13: αἱ τῶν πρόσθεν περιόδων ἱστορίαι μεγίστην εἰς φρόνησιν παρέχονται συντέλειαν.

[6] iii. 125–126.

of one man, or rather, of one soul[1]. Whatever may be the case
with the soul's history, it seems to me that this image is truer
to the facts of progress as hitherto known than that which
was taken over by Comte from Pascal, *viz.*, that the history of
Humanity may be compared to the life of one man continually
living and learning. The choice has been, so far as experience
yet shows, between Egyptian or Byzantine fixity on the one
side and movement through upheavals and submergences on
the other. Proclus gives a rationale of the theory, stated in
the Dialogue, of catastrophic destructions. Composite unities
such as races and cities, he says, occupying an intermediate
position between the imperishable whole and individual organic things, which are easily dissoluble, are destroyed only
at long intervals; for it is only at rare conjunctures that the
causes destructive of their parts all co-operate; usually, what
is destructive of one part is preservative of another[2]. Briefly
glancing at his own time, he suggests that the cause of the
depopulation now said to exist in Attica, being neither fire nor
flood, as in former depopulations, is "a certain dire impiety
utterly blotting out the works of men[3]." This is said merely
in passing. Like Plato, he assumes in his general theory that
remnants are always left.

The wonder that Solon said he felt at the history (*Tim.*
23 D) is made the occasion of observing that in us wonder is
the beginning of knowledge of the whole[4].

Proclus finds that the political order of Egypt described by
the priest is a stage below that which has been set forth by
Socrates[5]. For the ruling priestly class is inferior to the ruling
class of guardians in the *Republic*, who as philosophers go
back by insight to primal reality. Moreover, Plato in the
Politicus subordinated the priests to the statesman, and gave

---

[1] i. 124, 7–9: ὡς γὰρ ἐφ' ἑνὸς ἀνδρός, μᾶλλον δὲ ψυχῆς μιᾶς, διαφόρους βίους,
οὕτως ἐφ' ἑνὸς ἔθνους τὰς διαφόρους περιόδους προσήκει λαμβάνειν.

[2] i. 116.

[3] i. 122, 11–12: δεινῆς τινος ἀσεβείας ἄρδην τὰ τῶν ἀνθρώπων ἀφανιζούσης.
On this a Byzantine annotator has commented: ὑμεῖς ἀσεβέστατοι, ἡμεῖς δὲ τὸ
τῶν Χριστιανῶν γένος ἔνθεον καὶ εὐσεβέστατον (Scholia, i. 463).

[4] i. 133, 7–8.

[5] i. 152, 1–3: δῆλον...ὅτι τῆς Σωκρατικῆς πολιτείας ὑφεῖται τὰ νῦν παραδιδόμενα
καὶ δευτέραν ἂν ἔχοι μετ' ἐκείνην τάξιν.

them no share in political power. And the Egyptian military caste, being wholly specialised for war, is inferior to Plato's class of auxiliaries, who share with the guardians in the higher education[1]. It is evident that Proclus would have been able to criticise shrewdly the analogy often drawn between the republic of Plato and the hierarchical order of mediaeval Europe.

A prayer to Athena, conceived in a generalised and symbolical way[2], may have suggested Renan's famous prayer on the Acropolis[3].

The resistance of prehistoric Athens to the extension of a Titanic or Gigantic world-power, Proclus accepts as fact restored from actual records; but he assigns to it also a cosmic meaning. Athens represents the higher cause, like the Olympian gods in the myth of the giant-war. The dominion of the kings of Atlantis, before it is broken, succeeds in prevailing over a portion of the higher order. This is in accordance with the frequent enslavement found to take place of the last in the superior order to the first in the inferior[4]. Of the kings of Atlantis the power is celebrated, of the Athenians the virtue[5]. Their virtue, which prevails over power, is a whole including philosophic wisdom as the higher associate of warlike strength.

Discussion of the meaning of prayer is suggested by the invocation of the gods[6]. Proclus finds its end to be ultimately mystical[7]. At every point in the series of existences, it is possible to turn back to the Highest from which all proceed; for production is not merely continuous through the intermediate stages, but direct even to the lowest, and so the return also at every step can be direct[8]. The virtues by which the mystical unification is to be attained are especially the

---

[1] i. 151, 19–28. Cf. i. 154, 18–20, where the theoretic class (τὸ τῆς φρονήσεως ἐπιμελούμενον καὶ θεωρητικόν) is found to be marked off from all the specialised classes, including the priests.

[2] i. 168–169.   [3] In *Souvenirs d'Enfance et de Jeunesse*.   [4] i. 182–183.

[5] i. 185, 7–10: τοῖς μὲν Ἀτλαντίνοις μόνον ἀπονέμει τὴν δύναμιν...τοὺς δὲ Ἀθηναίους κρατεῖν φησι τῆς δυνάμεως διὰ τῆς ὅλης ἀρετῆς.

[6] *Timaeus*, 27 β.   [7] i. 211, 24: τελευταία δὲ ἡ ἕνωσις.

[8] i. 209, 19–20: οὐδενὸς γὰρ ἀφέστηκε τὸ θεῖον, ἀλλὰ πᾶσιν ἐξ ἴσου πάρεστι.

triad, faith, truth, love; with hope, receptivity of the divine light, and a standing apart (ἔκστασις) from all else.

After a dissertation on the nature of "becoming" in the world, Proclus finds again that Plato sets out from theory of knowledge; which begins not by examining things, but by asking what the mind can know[1]. To learn the meaning of "being" and "becoming," we must discover in what way each is known. To try to find out directly what they are in their own nature would lead only to confusion[2]. In defining "being" as the object of thought and reason, "becoming" as the object of opinion, Proclus of course simply repeats Plato; but he soon goes on to a notable development. To explain how he came to put the question in the way he did, we have to remember the age-long controversies of Epicureans, Stoics and Sceptics on the universal criterion[3]. Returning from these to Plato, but bearing them in mind, he insists on Plato's breadth as compared with other thinkers in assigning a place to all the criteria. The soul is not only unitary, but also manifold; and so there is a place for intuitive thought (νοῦς, νόησις), for reason or understanding (λόγος, διάνοια), for opinion (δόξα), and for sense-perception (αἴσθησις). But to judge belongs to the soul as a unity. What then is its common power of judgment? Discursive reason (λόγος), answers Proclus. Whatever the human mind at one extreme may grasp by intellectual intuition, or at the other extreme may apprehend from experiences of sense, it must, for proof, be able to assign the grounds of its belief through an articulate process expressing itself in general terms[4].

The mystical state beyond mind by which the One is directly apprehended, Proclus assigns from this point of view to a kind of "spurious intellect" (νόθος νοῦς) comparable to

[1] i. 242, 15: ὁ ἀπὸ τῶν γνώσεων ἀφορισμός.

[2] i. 242, 19-21: ἀλλ' εἰ μὲν αὐτὴν ἐφ' ἑαυτῆς τὴν τῶν πραγμάτων φύσιν ἡμῖν παρεκελεύσατο θηρᾶν, ἔλαθεν ἂν ἀσαφείας ἐμπλήσας τὴν σύμπασαν διδασκαλίαν.

[3] I note in passing that the phrase of Xenophanes, δόκος δ' ἐπὶ πᾶσι τέτυκται, is interpreted as meaning: "The universal criterion is opinion" (i. 254).

[4] i. 254-255. Proclus mentions that he has developed his view at greater length in a commentary on the *Theaetetus*. This we do not possess; but there is some restatement later in the present commentary.

the "bastard reasoning" by which, according to Plato, that
which afterwards came to be called Matter is seized without
sensation[1]. This of course does not mean that the apprehension of either of these extremes is illusory; the apprehension
of that which is beyond intellect by a power that is also beyond it is indeed superior[2]; but the distinctly formulated
doctrine is that the common test is ultimately coherence in
a total system of knowledge[3]. Neo-Platonism in its finished
form thus presents itself, if we are to give it a definition, as
in principle a decidedly circumspect rationalism[4].

On the theory of beauty in art, the discriminating attitude
of Plotinus was maintained by Proclus. Works of plastic art,
he says, are beautiful not by mere imitation of generated
things, but by going back directly to the source itself of their
beauty in its Idea. To what was said by Plotinus[5], he adds
that if Phidias could have raised his mind beyond the Homeric
Zeus to the metaphysical conception of Deity, he would have
made his work still more beautiful[6]. This, however, does not
imply aversion from the beauty of the world. Even those who
talk abusively about the Demiurge, he remarks, alluding to
the Gnostics, have not dared to say that the world is not most
beautiful; on the contrary, they say that its beauty is a lure
to souls[7].

The immediate cause of the cosmic order Proclus finds to

---

[1] *Timaeus*, 52 B: αὐτὸ δὲ μετ' ἀναισθησίας ἁπτὸν λογισμῷ τινι νόθῳ. On the
theories concerning the "Platonic Matter," see above, pp. 70–1.

[2] i. 257–258. The scholiast has an admiring note: τίς οὐκ ἄν σε θαυμάσειε
καὶ χάριτας μεγάλας ἐς ἀεὶ μεμνήσεται, φίλε Πρόκλε. νοῦν νόθον λέγει τὸ ἕν καὶ
οἷον ἄνθος τῆς ψυχῆς (i. 472).

[3] Cf. i. 283, 5–11. The grasp of the whole by "enthusiasm" is characteristic
of philosophy at its highest; but it does not dispense the philosopher from
subsequent proof of his propositions. This is illustrated by the procedure of
Timaeus.

[4] Cf. i. 351, where the caution of Plato is contrasted with the extreme confidence of some other philosophers, such as Heraclitus, Empedocles and the
Stoics.

[5] Enn. v. 8, 1. See above, p. 90.

[6] i. 265, 18–22: ἐπεὶ καὶ ὁ Φειδίας ὁ τὸν Δία ποιήσας οὐ πρὸς γεγονὸς ἀπέβλεψεν,
ἀλλ' εἰς ἔννοιαν ἀφίκετο τοῦ παρ' Ὁμήρῳ Διός· εἰ δὲ πρὸς αὐτὸν ἠδύνατο τὸν νοερὸν
ἀνατείνεσθαι θεόν, δηλονότι κάλλιον ἂν ἀπετέλεσε τὸ οἰκεῖον ἔργον.

[7] i. 333, 6–9.

have been described correctly, by a distinction of Plotinus, as intellect immanent in the world[1]. This mediates between the world and the supra-mundane intellect which contains the Ideas. While the higher reality—"the divine intellect that is the cause of the whole creation[2]"—is not subject to the flux that it sets in order, this flux of things itself is not merely something external set in order, but pre-exists in a manner in its ever-productive source[3]. What he desires to make clear by these distinctions is the continuous intellectual necessity that runs through the whole and the parts. He cannot, with Aristotle, admit any element of the casual: that there is no such thing follows from Aristotle's own recognition that the universe is one system[4].

The things of nature, but not those of the instrumental arts, are formed on the model of the Ideas[5]. If Plato in the *Republic* speaks of the "bed in itself" and the "table in itself," this is easy illustration for learners, not formal doctrine. The ideas that find expression in the mechanical arts are therefore, according to Proclus, at a greater remove from reality than "natural kinds." They are only "here," not in the intelligible world, and they are "made." The ideas embodied in nature are not made[6].

That the Good—not properly an Idea, though so called[7]— is beyond Intellect, means for Proclus ultimately that

---

[1] i. 305, 16–20: Πλωτῖνος ὁ φιλόσοφος διττὸν μὲν ὑποτίθεται τὸν δημιουργόν, τὸν μὲν ἐν τῷ νοητῷ, τὸν δὲ τὸ ἡγεμονοῦν τοῦ παντός, λέγει δὲ ὀρθῶς· ἔστι γάρ πως καὶ ὁ νοῦς ὁ ἐγκόσμιος δημιουργὸς τοῦ παντός.

[2] i. 317, 17: νοῦς θεῖος τῆς ὅλης ποιήσεως αἴτιος.

[3] As it is put in one passage, γένεσις must be included among the causes that precede the generated world (i. 325–328).

[4] i. 262. In the *Philebus*, he adds, causation is further generalised by its application to things mixed. This means, in modern language, that the causes are to be sought not only of events, but of collocations.

[5] i. 344, 21–24: ἀπείκασται δὲ πρὸς τὸ νοητὸν τὰ ἔργα τῆς φύσεως, οὐχὶ καὶ τὰ κατὰ τέχνην, ὡς οὐδὲ τὰ καθ' ἕκαστα διωρισμένως, ἀλλ' αἱ ἐπ' αὐτοῖς κοινότητες.

[6] i. 344, 13–14: τῶν δὲ ἰδεῶν (as distinguished from τῶν ἐνταῦθα ἰδεῶν) οὐκ ἔστι δημιουργός.

[7] See, for example, i. 424–425: τἀγαθόν is not τι τῶν εἰδῶν, nor yet ὅλον τὸ νοητόν, but πρὸ πάντων τῶν νοητῶν. Cf. *in Remp.* i. 286–287. The ground for identifying the Idea of the Good in the *Republic* with the One is of course that it also is said to be beyond Being: cf. *in Parm.* 1097, 11–20. Necessarily therefore it is not properly an Idea; for the Ideas are at once being and thought.

world is a teleological order[1]. The highest cause being the
Good, it follows that goodness is highest in each. Merely to
assert, however, as many do every day, that "God is good,"
implies no insight. Without virtue, as Plotinus said, "God is
a name[2]."

Causation, we have already seen, while embracing the Ideas
and their manifestation, includes more. The causal series begins with the One and Good, and descends to Matter unformed
by the Ideas. Since the One before Being, with a certain coexistent infinity that precedes the One as Being, is its cause,
Matter is in a sense both good and infinite[3]. Only by abstraction is the world of material things described as a godless
realm of disorder, such as Plutarch and Atticus[4] and those
who took the imagination of the creative Demiurge literally,
supposed it to have been in the beginning. In the description
of it as such, Plato imitates the theological poets, with their
wars of the Titans against the Olympians[5], but his own meaning is philosophical. For the circumstantial refutation of
Atticus, Proclus takes over the argument of Porphyry[6], who
seems to have put it very clearly that in the cosmogony of the
Timaeus Plato intended to indicate the factors into which the
composition of the ordered world can be analysed; body, considered in abstraction from formative intellect, having no
order of its own[7]. The saying of Timaeus that it was not
lawful[8] for the best to produce anything but the most beautiful, is taken as meaning that Right which is identical with
Necessity (Θέμις with Ἀνάγκη)[9] presides over the universal
order.

When the Demiurgus is spoken of as reasoning (λογισά-

---

[1] i. 369, 4: διὰ ταῦτα μὲν οὖν τὴν τελικὴν αἰτίαν τὴν κυριωτάτην ἀρχὴν προση-
γόρευσε. This refers to *Tim.* 29 E.

[2] See above, p. 86.

[3] i. 385, 12–14: ἡ ὕλη πρόεισιν ἔκ τε τοῦ ἑνὸς καὶ ἐκ τῆς ἀπειρίας τῆς πρὸ τοῦ
ἑνὸς ὄντος, εἰ δὲ βούλει, καὶ ἀπὸ τοῦ ἑνὸς ὄντος καθόσον ἐστὶ δυνάμει ὄν. διὸ καὶ
ἀγαθὸν πῇ ἐστι καὶ ἄπειρον.

[4] Atticus lived in the reign of Marcus Aurelius. On his doctrines, see
Zeller, iii. 1, pp. 808–810.

[5] i. 390–391.   [6] i. 391–396.   [7] i. 394, 25–31.

[8] *Tim.* 30 A: θέμις δὲ οὔτ᾽ ἦν οὔτ᾽ ἔστι.

[9] i. 396–397. Cf. *in Remp.* ii. 207, 19–22.

μενος), this does not imply the uncertainty of deliberation, but means that there is a regular causal succession from the general order of the world to the special orders of its parts[1]. The mindless itself, Proclus subtly argues, is prefigured in mind, but always under the form of intellect, not as a "mindless idea," which is impossible[2]. Thus, while there are particular bodies without a soul of their own, and particular souls that are irrational, there is no part of the world which, as a part of the whole, is not animated, and no soul that does not, as part of the whole of soul, participate in intellect[3]. By participating in mind through the mediating stage of soul, the world is the most beautiful, by participating in the super-intellectual good through mind, it is the most divine of works[4].

The question whether there may not be more worlds than one is discussed at some length. All views were held: that there is one world, that there are many, and that there are infinite worlds[5]. Proclus decides with Plato that there is one world, on the ground that the unity of divinity has its necessary manifestation in unity of system. Some, it appears, argued that there may be many worlds formed according to the one pattern of a world, as there are many men formed according to the Idea of Man, ὁ αὐτοάνθρωπος[6]. The reply of Proclus amounts to this: that man is at a greater remove from the archetype than the system to which he belongs, and so is more pluralised. In the ascent from the pluralised forms, if there is to be continuity, we must at last reach an all-inclusive whole, most resembling the pattern as absolutely one. We thus necessarily arrive at the unity of the universe (τὸ πᾶν).

---

[1] i. 399, 18–20: ἔστι γὰρ ὁ λογισμὸς τῶν μερῶν διῃρημένη διέξοδος καὶ ἡ διακεκριμένη τῶν πραγμάτων αἰτία.

[2] i. 399–401. [3] i. 407.

[4] i. 409. The question, how the world as a whole is not made inferior to the superior parts of itself by the addition of worse parts, is answered by an anticipation of Mr G. E. Moore's principle of "organic value": εἰ γὰρ τὸ μέν ἐστιν ἐν τῷ ὅλῳ κρεῖττον, τὸ δὲ χεῖρον, πῶς τὸ ὅλον οὐ καταδεέστερον τοῦ ἐν αὐτῷ κρείσσονος προσθήκῃ τοῦ χείρονος γέγονε; λύεται δὲ τὸ ἄπορον, διότι τοῦ χείρονος ἡ πρὸς τὸ κρεῖττον σύνταξις ἐν ποιεῖ τὸ ὅλον καὶ τέλειον, ὅταν δὲ ἀσύγκλωστα ἀλλήλοις ᾖ, τηνικαῦτα ἡ μῖξις τοῦ χείρονος ἀφανίζει τὴν τοῦ κρείττονος δύναμιν (i. 423–424).

[5] i. 436, 10–12. [6] i. 439, 22–25.

This admitted, he is not inclined to dogmatise with complete theoretical confidence about the number of systems there may be within it[1]; but actually he holds to the cosmology common to Plato, Aristotle, and the orthodox science of later antiquity, for which the universe was one finite world, with the spherical earth at the centre, surrounded by revolving spheres bearing the heavenly bodies. The positions taken by these go through certain revolutions which bring back at intervals precisely the same relative order; and so the movement of the whole is cyclical. This is the outline; but within it he shows himself to the end eager to find and discuss as many open questions as possible.

The first question raised in detail is about the elements of the world. These Proclus tries to determine by relation to the senses of which they are the objects. Fire and earth he distinguishes, after Plato (*Tim.* 31 B), as the elements that respectively give visibility and tangibility to the phenomenal world of becoming. The senses of sight and touch, by which they are perceived, are extremes; the object of touch being perceived immediately, that of sight not immediately[2]. Theophrastus asks, in criticism of Plato, why are not the other senses also taken into account? The reply is, that the external world is known to us by actual touch directly, by sight indirectly; actual taste, hearing or smell is no necessary part of our perception of the object. Not weight, Proclus remarks, but tangibility, is the characteristic property of earth[3]. The physical and the mathematical solid are distinguished, the first as tangible, the second as intangible[4]. Of these the former is primary, as the first resistant[5].

To bring together in one world the two most opposed elements, there is need of a mean or means. These of course

---

[1] i. 452, 12–15: εἰ δὲ λέγοις, ὅτι δεῖ καὶ ἄλλας αἰτίας εἶναι δευτέρας, πρὸς μερικώτερα παραδείγματα ποιούσας, εὖ μὲν λέγεις, ἐν δὲ ὅμως φυλάττεις τὸ πᾶν.

[2] ii. 6, 10: τὸ μὲν ἀμέσως αἰσθητόν, τὸ δὲ οὐκ ἀμέσως.

[3] ii. 11, 20: οὐ γὰρ τὸ βάρος ἴδιον γῆς, ἀλλὰ τὸ ἁπτόν.

[4] ii. 13, 3–4: φυσικὸν γὰρ ἄλλο στερεὸν καὶ μαθηματικὸν ἄλλο, τὸ μὲν ἀναφές, τὸ δὲ ἁπτόν.

[5] ii. 13, 10–12: πρῶτον οὖν ἁπτὸν ἡ γῆ καὶ πρῶτον ἀντίτυπον καὶ διὰ τοῦτο πρῶτον στερεόν.

are found to be the other two elements of air and water. Here it is interesting to notice how Bruno long afterwards partly took over and partly modified the physical theorising of Neo-Platonism; bringing in the "bond[1]" between fire and earth in much the same way. As with Bruno, so already with Proclus, metaphysically and physically everything is in everything; fire has something of the nature of earth, and earth of the nature of fire, and both participate in moisture[2]. In some bodies in the universe fire predominates, in others earth. This again was taken over by Bruno, who follows the Neo-Platonists in omitting the "fifth element" imagined by Aristotle as the substance of the heavenly bodies. Where he differs is in rejecting also the notion, retained by Plotinus and Proclus, that the fire in the heavenly region is a finer or purer fire[3]. For him, not only the same elements, but the same kinds of the same elements, are universal[4].

In exactitude of thought, Proclus, for all his antiquated cosmology, is still in advance of the revived Platonism of the early modern period, and, by his remarks on the order of the sciences, suggests comparison rather with later thinking. When he says, for example, that things physical are images of things mathematical[5], he means definitely that science has to proceed from mathematics to physics. At the same time, this insistence on the intellectual order is guarded by the recognition that physics is not simply applied mathematics. The sciences form indeed a continuous series; but the physical point of view introduces complications that do not permit of mathematical accuracy[6]. In each body are these three, number and mass and force[7]. There is on these subjects a pre-

---

[1] ii. 18.

[2] ii. 26, 24–31: μιμεῖται γὰρ καὶ ταύτῃ τὸν νοητὸν κόσμον ὁ αἰσθητός, καὶ ὥσπερ ἐν ἐκείνῳ πάντα ἐν πᾶσίν ἐστιν, ἀλλ' οἰκείως ἐν ἑκάστῳ,...τὸν αὐτὸν τρόπον καὶ ὁ αἰσθητὸς κόσμος πάντα ἔχει κατὰ πάσας ἑαυτοῦ τὰς μοίρας· καὶ γὰρ τὸ πῦρ καθόσον ἁπτόν ἐστι, γῆς μετέχει, καὶ ἡ γῆ καθόσον ὁρατόν, πυρός, καὶ ὑγρότητος ἑκάτερον.

[3] ii. 44, 1: τὸ οὖν εἰλικρινὲς πῦρ ἐν οὐρανῷ. Cf. ii. 49, 15: ἐν ᾧ πάντων αἱ ἀκρότητές εἰσι.

[4] With the qualification about differences of kind, stated above, the same elements are universal for Proclus. See iii. 128, 18–19: πᾶς μὲν ὁ οὐρανὸς ἐκ πάντων ἐστὶ τῶν στοιχείων. [5] ii. 39, 18. [6] ii. 23, 25–30.

[7] ii. 25, 23–24: τοῦ τριττοῦ τούτου, λέγω δὲ ἀριθμοῦ καὶ ὄγκου καὶ δυνάμεως.

cision of thinking which, amid much obsolete science, reminds us of Leibniz and Kant and Positivism rather than of the Renaissance.

Of the highly speculative developments that follow, it may be said that they are represented most in the most recent thought. Pampsychism is very distinctly stated in outline as one result of the metaphysical doctrine. The world as a whole, though it has no organs of special sense, has a kind of general sensibility (οἷον συναίσθησις)[1]. This Proclus compares to the "common sensibility" of Aristotle. From the total common sensibility our own is derived[2]. The consciousness of the world has a perfection which ours has not[3]; but of course it is itself, in the view of Proclus, not ultimate, but dependent on a supramundane cause, with which it is united by love[4]. This, he recognises, is Aristotelian; but in his own doctrine the love is not merely on the part of the things that return; there is also a love at the intelligible source, which the creative cause directs in its outward process, ποιμαίνων πραπίδεσσιν ἀνόμματον ὠκὺν Ἔρωτα[5].

Thus the heaven or world is a derivative, though not mortal, god. On its immortality Proclus insists against the apparent concession of Plato that it is by nature dissoluble[6]. The only God in the full sense is, however, as he uniformly declares, the One. From this proceeds the derived divinity of everything else that is called divine[7].

When the soul of the world is said to be "elder" as compared with the body, this does not refer to an order in time, but in being[8]. Soul has metaphysically a higher degree of

---

[1] ii. 83, 23.

[2] ii. 85, 19–21: πόθεν γὰρ καὶ ἐν ἡμῖν ἡ μία αἴσθησις πρὸ τῶν πολλῶν ἐστιν ἢ ἐκ τοῦ παντός;

[3] ii. 84, 28–30: ὁ μὲν οὖν κόσμος ἔχει τὴν πρώτην αἴσθησιν, ἀμετάβατον, ἡνωμένην τῷ γνωστῷ, παντελῆ, κατ' ἐνέργειαν ἐστῶσαν.

[4] ii. 85, 29–31: οὕτω δὴ οὖν καὶ τὸ πᾶν συνῆπται δι' ἔρωτος τοῖς πρὸ αὐτοῦ, τὸ ἐν ἐκείνοις κάλλος διὰ τοῦ ἐν ἑαυτῷ βλέπον, τοῦτο δὲ οὐ μερισταῖς αἰσθήσεσιν ὁρῶν.

[5] ii. 85 (Orph. Fr. 68). This is quoted again, iii. 101, 23.   [6] ii. 55–56.

[7] ii. 113, 5–10: ἕκαστον γὰρ ἐκθεοῦται διὰ τὸ πρὸ αὐτοῦ προσεχῶς, ὁ μὲν σωματικὸς κόσμος διὰ ψυχήν, ἡ δὲ ψυχὴ διὰ νοῦν,...νοῦς δὲ διὰ τὸ ἕν '...οὐκέτι δὲ τὸ ἓν δι' ἄλλο θεός, ἀλλὰ πρώτως θεός. Cf. i. 363, 20–23.

[8] ii. 115, 3: τῇ τάξει τῆς οὐσίας.

reality: in time, as regards the whole, soul and body are perpetually coexistent. Yet in a sense the soul is older as regards time; for its time and motion are prior (again metaphysically) to the time and motion of body[1].

To the objection of Theophrastus that, since the soul is a primal thing, its generation (the ψυχογονία of the *Timaeus*) is not a rational problem[2], Proclus answers that what is set forth as an account of its generation is to be understood scientifically as an analysis. Since the soul is not only a unity, but also in another aspect a plurality, it can in a manner be anatomised like the physical organism[3]. The parts into which it can be resolved by analysis are its constituent powers and energies. These are numerable, not innumerable like the parts of body, with its infinite divisibility[4]. For the unitary nature in soul is not divisible into like parts[5]. Of course the parts of soul never exist by themselves; but in a manner they can be distinguished in time because the soul cannot energise with all its powers at once, but only successively. Every soul contains both Limit and Unlimited (πέρας and ἄπειρον), being at once unitary as dependent on Intellect, and in infinite process as associated with the dispersion of body. The limit of the soul of the world is more unitary and its infinity more comprehensive than those of all other souls; for not every limit is equal to every limit and not every infinity to every infinity[6].

Proclus has a careful and skilful argument to show that the soul cannot be literally a mixture of an indivisible and a divisible nature[7]. What Plato intends in so describing it is to

---

[1] This belongs to the subtle theory of time and its kinds, expounded later.
[2] ii. 120.　　　　　　　[3] ii. 123–124.
[4] ii. 138. Cf. ii. 152, 11–14: αὐτὸ τὸ σῶμα οὐκ ἔστι μεριστὸν εἰς πολλά, ἀλλ' εἰς ἄπειρα, ἡ δὲ ψυχὴ διῃρημένη εἰς πολλὰς οὐσίας ἔχει καὶ τὸ ἡνῶσθαι, χωριστὴν λαχοῦσα σωμάτων ὑπόστασιν.
[5] ii. 164, 26–28: ἀδιαίρετος εἰς ὅμοια καὶ ταύτῃ τοῦ ἐν σώμασιν ἑνὸς διαφέρουσα, ὃ διαιρεῖται εἰς ὅμοια ἐπ' ἄπειρον. Cf. ii. 192, 29: δύο γὰρ μέρη τὰ αὐτὰ ψυχῆς οὐκ ἔστι. The unity of bodies is only a phantom of unity: τὸ δὲ τῶν σωμάτων οὐδὲ ἁπλῶς ἕν, ἀλλὰ φάντασμα ἑνὸς καὶ εἴδωλον (ii. 204, 17–19).
[6] ii. 141, 25–27: οὔτε γὰρ πᾶν πέρας ἴσον παντὶ πέρατι,...οὐδὲ πᾶσα ἀπειρία πάσῃ ἀπειρίᾳ ἴση.
[7] ii. 147–154.

convey by analogy the notion of the soul as a distinctive existence, combining a unity like that of pure intellect with a plurality, not indefinite like that of body, but composed of a finite number of powers. To place it in its intermediate position by distinguishing these aspects is the proper aim of the ψυχογονία, not to show how it was formed out of elements that existed before it. It does not even derive the kind of divisibility that it has from its relation to body. This belongs to the soul in its own nature[1]. As Proclus explains elsewhere, the particular soul comes into relation with body because its own nature causes it to lapse periodically from the timeless unity of intellect; not because it is drawn down by body into a dispersion that is not its own.

The principles enumerated as constitutive of soul are, in a very generalised statement, (1) totality, (2) unity and duality[2], (3) division and harmony, (4) connecting bond, (5) multiplicity with simplicity. Here it becomes especially difficult to do justice to the subtlety of the thinking. The insight of Proclus into the subject-matter was beyond the tradition behind him; for a part of this was the search for mathematical and musical analogies to the mental life. He knows, and occasionally says, that the formulae of which he gives an elaborate statement do not touch the nature of the soul[3]. Plato's use of mathematical terms he compares to the use of mythology by the speculative theologians and of symbols by the Pythagoreans[4]. It is not a mode of discovering the truth about mind and soul, but only of setting it forth—or wrapping it up—in external figurations[5].

---

[1] ii. 150, 22–24: αὐτὴ καὶ οὐσία πῃ οὖσα ἀμέριστος καὶ γιγνομένη μεριστή, ἀλλ' οὐ περὶ σώμασιν, ἀλλὰ καθ' αὑτὴν μεριστὴ γιγνομένη καὶ μηδὲν δεομένη σωμάτων εἰς τὸ εἶναι ὅ ἐστι.

[2] The soul is δυοειδής in so far as it has two kinds of life, one turning back to the unity of intellect which is before it, one exercising care over the things of nature which come after it (ii. 242, 17–19).

[3] ii. 174. Cf. ii. 212, 5–6: οὐ γὰρ ἐκ μαθηματικῶν ἀριθμῶν ἐστι καὶ λόγων ἡ οὐσία τῆς ψυχῆς.

[4] ii. 246, 4–7: ὁ δέ γε Πλάτων δι' ἐπίκρυψιν τοῖς μαθηματικοῖς τῶν ὀνομάτων οἷον παραπετάσμασιν ἐχρήσατο τῆς τῶν πραγμάτων ἀληθείας, ὥσπερ οἱ μὲν θεολόγοι τοῖς μύθοις, οἱ δὲ Πυθαγόρειοι τοῖς συμβόλοις.

[5] ii. 247–248.

Here he is concerned, as he tells us, no longer with theory of knowledge, but with ontology[1]. He proposes to set forth certain abstract metaphysical principles that are of the soul's essence; and, following Plato's imagery applied to the world-soul, he does his best to show how these are imaged in mathematical relations[2]. Primarily, he always refers to the world-soul; particular souls have the character of soul imperfectly[3], and are to be understood from the theory of soul in its perfection as rationally defined. In this perfection of reality, it is never a mere identity. The principle of unity and identity is indeed, according to the true interpretation of Plato, always the highest; but an identity with distinction latent in it is better than the undistinguished uniformity of the mean[4].

Starting from Plato's alternate description of the soul as placed within the body of the world and as extending beyond it[5], Proclus shows in more directly subjective language how this is true of the relations between body and soul in general. Soul in one aspect appears to animate the body from some position within. In another aspect, when it turns back upon itself, it finds itself not to be included in the mass, but to know it as a part of its own existence. The first point of view he describes, in his distinctive terminology, as that of the πρόοδος, the second as that of the ἐπιστροφή[6]. By its outgoing powers soul animates the whole mass; in its introspectively known reality it remains always beyond the limits of body[7]. When soul, in contrast with body, is said to revolve in itself and not in place, this means that it thinks itself and finds itself to be all things[8].

---

[1] ii. 192, 32–33: οὐ γὰρ τὴν γνῶσιν νῦν τῆς ψυχῆς, ἀλλὰ τὴν οὐσίαν ἐπισκοπούμεθα.

[2] Cf. ii. 195, 11–15: ὁ δὲ τρόπος τῆς περὶ αὐτὴν ἐξηγήσεως ἔστω τῇ οὐσίᾳ συμφυής...ἀπὸ τῶν εἰκόνων ἐπὶ τὰ παραδείγματα ἀναπεμπόμενος.

[3] ii. 311, 16–20.

[4] ii. 263, 7–9: τὸ μὲν γὰρ οὕτω ταὐτόν, ὡς ἐν τῇ ταυτότητι τὴν ἑτερότητα κρυφίως περιέχειν, κρεῖττόν ἐστιν ἢ κατὰ τὴν μεσότητα τὴν ψυχικήν.

[5] Timaeus, 30 B, 34 B, 36 DE.   [6] ii. 102–103. Cf. i. 406–407.

[7] ii. 282, 25–27: καὶ πᾶν τὸ σωματικὸν ὁμοίως πανταχόθεν ἐψύχωται, καὶ πᾶσα ἡ ψυχὴ πανταχόθεν ἐξῄρηται τοῦ σώματος.

[8] ii. 286, 15–17: τοῦτο [τὸ σῶμα] μὲν γὰρ στρέφεται τοπικῶς, ἡ δὲ ψυχὴ ζωτικῶς καὶ νοερῶς, νοοῦσα ἑαυτὴν καὶ ἑαυτὴν εὑρίσκουσα τὰ πάντα οὖσαν. Cf. ii. 296, 14–18.

Proclus now goes on to discuss, as a question about the soul's distinctive being, that "reason" which was found to be the criterion of human knowledge. If, he says again, there is to be a common knowledge of things knowable, the reason (λόγος) by which they are known must be a common power of dealing with them all, not merely one for one thing, another for another; though the aspect of plurality also is not to be neglected[1]. This common reason is the realisation of the soul's essential part[2]. Through this we describe the whole soul simply as rational[3]. It is the one common knowledge of the soul[4]. With it Proclus etymologically connects speech (τὸ λέγειν)[5]. The soul's distinctive nature is to be reasoning intellect (νοῦς λογικός)[6]; the common form to which all its activities are reducible being the discursive form[7].

This does not exclude a kind of acquired intuition (νοῦς καθ' ἕξιν), which, in distinction from knowledge proper (ἐπιστήμη), takes in the whole at a glance, while knowledge proceeds from cause to effect, by synthesis and division of concepts[8]. Formed individual intuition, however, like the sense-perception from which the knowledge of each person sets out, does not speak the last word. The decisive word can only be spoken by that which is common; and this for the soul, which as such is not eternally unmoved intellect, is movement from point to point within a demonstrative system connecting principles with applications and applications again with principles.

---

[1] ii. 301, 6–17.

[2] ii. 299, 18–19: ἐνέργεια, ὡς ἂν ἐγὼ φαίην, τοῦ οὐσιώδους τῆς ψυχῆς.

[3] ii. 299, 21: λογικὴν λέγομεν ἁπλῶς τὴν ὅλην ψυχήν.

[4] ii. 299, 22–32: ὁ δ' οὖν λόγος οὖτος ἡ μία ἐστὶν γνῶσις τῆς ψυχῆς....καὶ οὗτός ἐστιν ὁ εἷς λόγος οὐσιώδης,...καὶ διὰ τοῦτο οὐ μόνον ἐστὶν δυοειδὴς ἡ ψυχή, ἀλλὰ καὶ μονοειδής.

[5] ii. 300, 21–22: λόγος γάρ ἐστιν ἡ ψυχή, λόγου δὲ ἐνέργημα τὸ λέγειν, ὡς νοῦ τὸ νοεῖν, ὡς φύσεως τὸ φύειν.

[6] ii. 301, 7.

[7] ii. 315, 7–8: πᾶσαι γὰρ αἱ γνώσεις αὗται καὶ λογικαί εἰσι καὶ μεταβατικαί.

[8] See ii. 313–314, and compare i. 438–439, where Proclus accepts the position of Aristotle, that the principles of demonstration are from intuitive intellect: πᾶς γὰρ ὁ ἀποδεικνὺς ἀπὸ νοῦ λαμβάνει τὰς ἀρχάς, νοῦς δὲ ᾧ τοὺς ὅρους γινώσκομεν, φησὶν Ἀριστοτέλης, ἁπλαῖς ἐπιβολαῖς τὰ ὄντα γινώσκοντες.

On time, stárting from Plato's description of it as the "moving image of eternity," Proclus reaches a subtlety of thought and expression never surpassed, but not easy to make perspicuous outside the context of the system. Time, for him, has an existence not barely notional[1], and almost unreal because incorporeal, as the Stoics said: on the contrary, its existence is more real than that of the things that come under it, whether souls or bodies. Soul is in time, as mind or pure intellect is in eternity. As eternity ($al\acute\omega\nu$) is more than mind, which it contains, so time, in this real significance, is more than soul[2]. It measures the duration of all, not merely of the mental or the animated: lifeless things, even as such, participate in time[3]. Being in all things, it exists everywhere indivisibly[4]. Its essence is to be productive, not destructive, since things that are in process need it for their perfection[5]. Because of its productive energy, the theological poets have called it a god[6]. Considered as subsisting in its unapparent causes, it has rightly been deified[7]. The world moves in an orderly way ($\tau\epsilon\tau\alpha\gamma\mu\acute\epsilon\nu\omega s$)[8] because it participates in mind, of which time is a mode. Properly, time itself does not move, but it is said to be in motion because movements participate in it[9].

The "parts of time," nights and days and months and years, pre-exist in the reality of Time before their manifestation[10]; but this does not mean that there was time before the world.

---

[1] iii. 95, 10: κατ' ἐπίνοιαν ψιλήν.   [2] iii. 27, 18–20.

[3] iii. 23, 4: οὐ γάρ ἐστιν ὅπου μὴ πάρεστιν ὁ χρόνος.

[4] iii. 23, 17: πανταχοῦ ἐστιν ἀμερίστως.

[5] iii. 47, 2–6: ἡ μὲν οὖν γένεσις καὶ παρακμάζει καὶ δι' αὐτὸ τοῦτο προσδεῖται τοῦ ἀνανεώσαντος αὐτὴν χρόνου καὶ ἀτελής ἐστι τὴν ἀρχὴν καὶ χρῄζει τοῦ τελειοτέραν αὐτὴν ποιήσοντος καὶ πρεσβυτέραν χρόνου. (Contrast Aristotle, *Phys.* iv. 12, 221 b 1; cf. 13, 222 b 19.)

[6] iii. 27–28. Cf. iii. 39–40.

[7] iii. 89–90. Night, Proclus ingeniously observes, is mentioned by Plato (*Tim.* 39 bc) before day because in the intellectual order the unapparent is prior to the apparent.

[8] iii. 28, 21.   [9] iii. 32, 2–4.

[10] iii. 36, 6–9: αἱ γὰρ ἀφανεῖς τούτων αἰτίαι μονοειδεῖς εἰσι πρὸ τῶν πεπληθυσμένων καὶ ἐπ' ἄπειρον ἀνακυκλουμένων, καὶ ἀκίνητοι προϋπάρχουσι τῶν κινουμένων καὶ νοεραὶ πρὸ τῶν αἰσθητῶν. Cf. iii. 55, 5–7: πᾶν γοῦν τὸ γενόμενόν ἐστι πρὸ τῆς γενέσεως ἀφανῶς ἱδρυμένον ἐν τῇ ἑαυτοῦ αἰτίᾳ.

The "before and after" and the world and time everlastingly coexist[1]. Their coexistence expresses itself in a total movement that may be figured as a circle or a spiral[2] because it ever repeats itself. Motion is not time, but temporal intervals are measures of motions[3].

Like a modern psychologist, Proclus notes the element of negativity in "was" and "will be." Yet, though characterised by "no longer" and "not yet," they also participate in being, as is indicated by their grammatical derivation from the verb to be[4]. The things that have their becoming in time are inferior to time as regards being. The world of genesis becomes perpetually, but there is no birth or dissolution of time, unless one should apply these names to its necessary relations of periodic process and return[5]. In this sense, the heaven or universe also might be said to be dissolved or born; but this can be rightly said only in a sense compatible with the assertion that for all time it is and was and will be[6].

Proclus expressly dissents from the apparent meaning of Plato's teleology (*Tim.* 39 B), by denying that the light of the sun came to be in order that we might have a measure of time[7] The whole does not exist for the sake of the parts; and the time that is as it were perceptible may be considered rather as a last result of higher (that is, dominant and imperishable) causes, than as that for the sake of which they exist. Time itself is a real measure prior to the notional measure[8] in our minds. It is not, as many of the Peripatetics have called it, "an accident of motion," for it is everywhere, not only in moving things[9]. Proclus equally rejects, as we have seen, the view of those who would limit it to the "inner sense." External things also have part in it. It measures all things, moving or at rest, by a certain permanent unit (μονάς);

---

[1] iii. 38, 8–9: οὐκ ἄρα καὶ τὸ 'ἦν' καὶ τὸ 'ἔσται' πρὸ τῆς τοῦ κόσμου γενέσεως ἦν, ἀλλ' ἅμα τῷ κόσμῳ καὶ ταῦτα καὶ ὁ χρόνος.

[2] iii. 21, 2; 40, 29.   [3] iii. 90, 16–17.

[4] iii. 45–46: καίτοι καὶ τὸ 'ἦν' καὶ τὸ 'ἔσται,' καὶ εἰ τῷ μὴ ὄντι μᾶλλον χαρακτηρίζεται τὸ μὲν τῷ μηκέτι, τὸ δὲ τῷ μηδέπω, ἀλλ' οὖν μετέχει γε πάντως ἀμηγέπη τοῦ ὄντος, ἦ οὐδ' ἂν κατὰ παρέγκλισιν ἀπ' αὐτοῦ κατωνομάζετο.

[5] iii. 50, 10–14.   [6] iii. 51, 7–12.   [7] iii. 81, 23–25.

[8] iii. 83, 19: τὸ ἐπινοηματικὸν μέτρον.   [9] iii. 95, 15–16.

and this it does "according to number[1]." The time of subordinate periods is "the number of the apparent life of each[2]." The whole of cosmic time measures the one life of the whole[3]. Descending from mind, its determinations run through the system of the animated universe down to all its parts in their degrees. Like the nature of Soul, the nature of Time also, as between the ungenerated and the generated, can only be described by combining opposites[4].

To the oppositions in the description of time itself, we must add the opposition between the grades of its reality and our mode of acquiring knowledge of it. Logically, time as a whole is prior to its parts. Genetically, our knowledge proceeds from the partial, but orderly, measures of time to the whole of time[5].

In further discussing the "organs of time," the heavenly bodies, which for us mark out different parts of it phenomenally[6], Proclus repeats some of the physical doctrines already set forth. Developing these, he takes occasion to state his sceptical position about the machinery of epicycles and eccentrics invented by the later astronomers. That it has not the authority of Plato counts with him for something as an argument[7]; but his criticisms are quite direct and rational, turning essentially on the artificiality and want of simplicity of the devices[8]. He allows their value for convenience of

[1] iii. 19, 2–9: μένει τοίνυν καὶ ἡ τοῦ χρόνου μονάς,...μένων οὖν ὁ χρόνος τῇ ἀμερεῖ ἑαυτοῦ καὶ ἔνδον ἐνεργείᾳ τῇ ἔξω καὶ ὑπὸ τῶν μετρουμένων κατεχομένη πρόεισι κατ᾽ ἀριθμόν.

[2] iii. 90, 18: ἀριθμὸς τῆς ἑκάστου ζωῆς τῆς ἐμφανοῦς.

[3] iii. 92, 24–25. Cf. iii. 95, 5–6: ὅλος δέ ἐστι χρόνος ὁ τέλειος ἀριθμὸς τῆς τοῦ παντὸς ἀποκαταστάσεως.

[4] iii. 25, 19–24: τί δ᾽ ἂν εἴη νοητὸν ἅμα καὶ γενητόν; τί δ᾽ ἂν εἴη μεριστὸν ἅμα καὶ ἀμέριστον; ἀλλ᾽ ὅμως ἐπὶ τῆς ψυχικῆς οὐσίας πάντα ταῦτα προσηκάμεθα, καὶ οὐδ᾽ ἄλλως δυνάμεθα τῆς μεσότητος ταύτης κατακρατῆσαι τελέως εἰ μὴ τρόπον τινὰ τοῖς ἀντικειμένοις ἐπ᾽ αὐτῆς χρησαίμεθα.

[5] iii. 55, 9–12: αὐτὸς μὲν ἀπὸ τῶν ὁλικωτέρων εἰς τὰ μερικώτερα πρόεισιν ἄχρι καὶ τῶν ἐσχάτων οἷον ζῴων καὶ φυτῶν, ἡμῖν δὲ ἀπὸ τῶν μερικῶν μέν, τεταγμένων δὲ μέτρων ὅλως γίγνεται γνώριμος.

[6] iii. 39.   [7] Cf. ii. 264, 19–21.

[8] iii. 56, 28–31: οὐδὲ γὰρ αὗται τὸ εἰκὸς ἔχουσιν αἱ ὑποθέσεις, ἀλλ᾽ αἱ μὲν τῆς ἁπλότητος ἀφίστανται τῶν θείων, αἱ δὲ ὥσπερ ὑπὸ μηχανῆς ὑποτίθενται τὴν κίνησιν τῶν οὐρανίων, ἐσκευωρημέναι παρὰ τῶν νεωτέρων.

calculation; but, he says, they remain only an affair of
specialist calculators, who miss the nature of the whole,
which Plato alone laid hold on[1]. Returning to the subject,
he admits their usefulness as means of analysing complex
motions into simple ones[2]. In this they are not vain, although
no such mechanisms exist in nature[3]. What he desires is to
arouse attention and to stir up more exact inquiry[4]. His own
suggestion is that, without any such hypotheses, we may
suppose the planets, in accordance with their intermediate
position in the universe, to revolve according to types of
motion intermediate between the circular and the rectilinear.
For cause, he can only assign regularly changing impulses
from the planetary souls[5]. The philosophic insight, as in the
case of Bruno and Kepler, whose astronomical conceptions
were of course larger but whose causal explanations are not
in advance of this, was in discarding the external contrivances.
A genuinely scientific explanation was not reached before
Newton; and this, when it came, had what Proclus calls the
simplicity of divine things.

With Proclus, the divinity of the earth is as much an article
of faith as the divinity of the stars. The Earth, he argues[6],
cannot be a mere inanimate mass. If it were such, of course
it would not be divine; for, as Theophrastus says: οὐδὲν τίμιον
ἄνευ ψυχῆς[7]. From the mind of the Earth, "our nurse," as
Plato calls it, our own mind receives impulses[8]. Taking up
the phrase of Plato, that it is "the first and eldest of the gods
within the heaven," Proclus shows how the element of earth,
though darker and more material, as some insist, exceeds the
other elements in the comprehensiveness with which all are

---

[1] iii. 96, 31–32: καλὴ μὲν ἡ ἐπίνοια καὶ ψυχαῖς ἐμπρέπουσα λογικαῖς, τῆς δὲ
τῶν ὅλων ἄστοχοι φύσεως, ἧς μόνος ἀντελάβετο Πλάτων.

[2] iii. 148–149.   [3] iii. 146.

[4] iii. 149, 5–8: ἀλλὰ ταῦτα μὲν ἐπιστάσεως ἄξια, καὶ διὰ τοῦτο καὶ πλεονάκις
αὐτὰ τοῖς φιλοθεάμοσιν εἰς ἐπίσκεψιν προτείνω καὶ ἀνεγείρω ἐν αὐτοῖς καὶ τὰς περὶ
τούτων ἀκριβεστέρας κατανοήσεις.

[5] iii. 147.   [6] iii. 135–136.

[7] iii. 136, 1. Cf. ii. 122, 16, where the same quotation from Theophrastus
occurs.

[8] iii. 136, 26–28: εἰ γὰρ δὴ ἡμετέρα τροφός ἐστιν, οἱ δὲ ὄντως ἡμεῖς ψυχαὶ καὶ
νόες, κατ᾽ ἐκεῖνα ἂν μάλιστα τελεσιουργὸς ἡμῶν εἴη, τὸν ἡμέτερον κινοῦσα νοῦν.

represented in it[1]; whence its generative potency; for, as it is at the end of the outward progression, it is also at the beginning of the return. Evidently we are here much nearer to Bruno's exultation that the earth also is one of the stars than to the mediaeval view which made it the dregs sunk to the lowest depth.

The view of some ancient commentators, adopted by Grote[2], that according to Plato (*Tim.* 40 BC) the earth revolves on its axis, is discussed but rejected. As in the cosmology of Proclus himself, so in his interpretation of Plato, it is stationary at the centre of the universe[3]. This does not imply that in magnitude it is first. He knows that it is smaller than the sun, and, as Aristotle had said, insignificant in bulk compared with the whole.

On another much-debated passage of the *Timaeus* (40 DE), which some, both in ancient and in modern times, have held to be ironical[4], while some have regarded it as seriously deferential, or even as commending literal faith in the popular stories about the gods, Proclus has a brief but interesting disquisition, in which he makes no reference to either view. We cannot, Timaeus is made to say, disbelieve those among us who, according to their own assertion, were descendants of the gods, when they tell us, even without probable or demonstrative evidence, things concerning their ancestors. Now Proclus undoubtedly held that the world is full of divine powers, of the nature of minds and souls[5]. Such powers he treats nominally as the gods or angels or daemons or heroes (in this order of dignity) of the popular stories; but for the whole Neo-Platonic school, as has been said, these stories themselves are simply not true. In accordance with this general position, his method of interpreting the passage of Plato is to rationalise it without irony. What is meant by

---

[1] In his physical as in his metaphysical theory, we know, all things are in all.

[2] See *Plato*, 3rd ed., vol. iii. p. 257.   [3] iii. 136–138.

[4] See above, p. 143, n. 3.

[5] iii. 155, 9–12: εἰ γὰρ ὅλος ὁ κόσμος θεὸς εὐδαίμων ἐστίν, οὐδέν ἐστι τῶν συμπληρούντων αὐτὸν μορίων ἄθεον καὶ ἀπρονόητον. εἰ δὲ καὶ θεοῦ πάντα μετέχει καὶ προνοίας, θείαν ἔλαχε φύσιν.

the knowledge that some have of their divine ancestors is this: while all souls are children of gods—that is, are linked by causation to higher intellectual powers—not all know their own god; but some who have chosen the mode of life assigned to a certain divinity—for example, Apollo—do know it, and are therefore called children of gods in a special sense[1]. From these, whose knowledge is a kind of enthusiastic insight, others, if they will apply their minds even without this enthusiasm[2], may learn of what nature the divine powers are.

On the whole, it may be said that while Plato had less respect for mythological modes of expression than his successors, his thought, on its positive side, remained more dependent on them. In denying that the cosmogony of the *Timaeus* really meant creation by an act or acts of volition, they were doubtless right; but the meaning they found in it is certainly not on the surface. On the other hand, their own use of mythology is transparent. In all his fanciful genealogies of gods, taken over from the elaboration of myths by the theological poets, the underlying thought of Proclus is quite clearly the continuity of metaphysical being. The great problem of knowledge, he puts it, is to find mean terms[3]. And historically, it seems very probable, the Leibnizian doctrine of continuity, and so in the end the continuity that has insensibly become one of the presuppositions of modern science, descends from the Neo-Platonic metaphysics.

In the metaphysical doctrine the element of pluralism, as already noted, becomes more evident on closer examination. The many minds, says Proclus, exist as something intrinsic in the divine mind, and are ungenerated[4] and uncreated[5]. When, in the *Timaeus*, the mundane gods, *i.e.*, the heavenly bodies,

---

[1] iii. 159, 29–31: πᾶσαι μὲν οὖν ψυχαὶ θεῶν παῖδες, ἀλλ᾽ οὐ πᾶσαι τὸν ἑαυτῶν ἐπέγνωσαν θεόν· αἱ δὲ ἐπιγνοῦσαι καὶ τὴν ὁμοίαν ἑλόμεναι ζωὴν καλοῦνται παῖδες θεῶν.

[2] iii. 160, 23–24.

[3] iii. 153, 13–15: καὶ ὅλως τοῦτο καὶ μέγιστόν ἐστι τῆς ἐπιστήμης ἔργον, τὸ τὰς μεσότητας καὶ τὰς προόδους τῶν ὄντων λεπτουργεῖν.

[4] iii. 205, 26–27: ἀνεκφοίτητοι γάρ εἰσιν οἱ νόες τοῦ θείου νοῦ καὶ ἀγένητοι παντελῶς.

[5] iii. 209, 18–21: οἱ δὲ νόες οἱ ταῖς ψυχαῖς ἄνωθεν ἐπιβεβηκότες οὐκ ἂν λέγοιντο ἔργα τοῦ πατρός· οὐδὲ γὰρ γένεσιν ἔσχον, ἀλλ᾽ ἀγενήτως ἐξεφάνησαν.

are said to be indissoluble except by the will of the Father,
who wills to preserve and not to destroy them, the real meaning is that they are indissoluble (ἄλυτοι) by their own nature
in so far as that nature is divine. They are said to be at the
same time resoluble (λυτοί) not in the sense that they are
destructible, but because, not being perfectly simple, their
components, as contained in universal Mind (signified by the
Father and Maker), can be discriminated in thought; in other
words, they are mentally analysable[1]. In the end, their inde-
structibility, not dependent on any will, is stated with emphasis[2]. Plato's expressions are finally interpreted as meaning
that they are indissoluble and immortal in a secondary sense;
not as simple and eternal beings, but as synthesised in their
pre-existent causes (figured by the common bond, σύνδεσμος),
and as having a perpetuity of becoming in time[3].

Of human souls, alternately descending to birth and re-
ascending, there is a particular life that is altogether mortal.
This the historians, in their summarising manner, declare to
be the irrational life. Proclus, they say, only preserves the
rational part of the soul[4]. The actual doctrine of Proclus is
more subtle and complex. In his view, it is only at the end
of a cosmic cycle that all the individuality disappears except
that of the rational soul. The soul then starts from a new
beginning; but even then it still retains the necessity of re-
descent; and this is conceived as a kind of ultimate irrational
element inherent in its innermost nature. To all the successive
lives within a cycle, there is attached the soul's permanent
vehicle, consisting of finer matter[5], together with certain
"apices" of sense and motion (ἀκρότητες τῆς ἀλόγου ζωῆς)[6].
From these, as from the growing points of a plant, the irrational life is extended into the system of perceptions and
habits that subserves each embodiment[7]. This system dis-

---

[1] iii. 212, 2–5. Cf. iii. 213, 12–18.

[2] iii. 214, 33–35: οὐκ ἄρα δεῖ λέγειν, ὅτι φθαρτὰ μέν ἐστι καθ᾽ αὐτά, διὰ δὲ τὴν
βούλησιν τοῦ πατρὸς ἄφθαρτα μένει, ἀλλὰ κατὰ τὴν αὐτῶν φύσιν ἄφθαρτά ἐστι.

[3] iii. 216–217. [4] See above, p. 156, n. 4. [5] See above, p. 179. [6] iii. 236, 32.

[7] iii. 237, 18–24: αἱ δὲ ἡμέτεραι ψυχαί...ἔχουσι τὴν ἐν τῷ ὀχήματι ζωὴν ἄλογον
οὖσαν ὡς πρὸς αὐτάς, πλεονάζουσι δὲ τῷ καὶ ἄλλην ἄλογον προσλαμβάνειν, ἔκτασιν
οὖσαν τῆς ἐν τῷ πνεύματι ζωῆς,...ἡ δὲ προσθήκη τῆς δευτέρας ἐστὶ θνητοειδής.

appears; but the modifications acquired go on in a latent
form, and, by carrying the whole soul forward to its appropriate reincarnation, furnish the basis for the reality that
corresponds to the myths of the choice of the soul, the punishments in Hades, and so forth. Thus, though the concrete
individuality in its fullness is dissolved, much more is left
than in Aristotle's doctrine of the immortality of the intellect,
even on the interpretation that this refers to the individual
mind, and not simply to the Deity, as was held by Alexander
of Aphrodisias, or to the general mind of man, as the Averroists
later maintained[1].

The doctrine held by Theodore of Asine and some of the
later Neo-Platonists, that the human soul is equipollent with
divinity[2], Proclus will not allow to be compatible with the
teaching of Plato, who indicates the gradation of souls by the
successive "mixtures" (*Tim.* 41 D)[3]. In accordance with the
inferior rank of souls that descend to birth instead of remaining always among the gods, is the changing of life from thought
to action, the coming under external necessity, the association
with perishable things[4]. For the differences among particular
souls belong to them not from relations to particular bodies,
as some say, but from their own essence[5].

The Demiurgus is described as revealing to the souls the

---

[1] A theory that our mortal part is resolved at death into elements separately imperishable is alluded to as held by some, but is rejected. The unity
being lost, we could not say that the identity of the reality is preserved; for
the irrational part is not a mere conflux of lives, but a life one and multiple:
ἀλλὰ τοῦτο καὶ καθ᾽ ἑαυτὸ μὲν ἄτοπον· τῆς γὰρ ἑνώσεως ἀπολομένης πῶς ἔτι τὸ
αὐτὸ διαμένειν φήσομεν; οὐ γάρ ἐστι ζώων συμφόρησις ἡ ἄλογος, ἀλλὰ μία ζωὴ
πολυειδής (iii. 236, 20–23).

[2] iii. 245, 19–21: οὐκ ἄρα ἀποδεξόμεθα τῶν νεωτέρων ὅσοι τὴν ἡμετέραν ψυχὴν
ἰσάξιον ἀποφαίνουσι τῆς θείας ἢ ὁμοούσιον ἢ οὐκ οἶδ᾽ ὅπως βούλονται λέγειν.

[3] iii. 246, 27–28: ἡ γὰρ τοιαύτη μεγαλορρημοσύνη πόρρω τῆς Πλάτωνός ἐστι
θεωρίας. It would have been interesting to know more exactly what Theodore
meant. We are told (iii. 265) that he put forward the remarkable thesis
that the vehicle of each particular soul is the universe (τὴν τοῦ παντὸς
φύσιν).

[4] iii. 258, 28–30: τὸ μεταβάλλειν τὴν ζωὴν ἀπὸ νοήσεως εἰς πρᾶξιν, τὸ ὑπὸ τὴν
εἱμαρμένην τελεῖν ποτε, τὸ συμμίγνυσθαι τοῖς ἐπικήροις πράγμασιν.

[5] iii. 264, 14–16: οὐκ ἀπὸ τῶν σωμάτων οὐδὲ ἀπὸ τῶν τοιῶνδε σχέσεων αἱ
διαφοραὶ τῶν ψυχῶν εἰσι, καθάπερ φασί τινες, ἀλλ᾽ ἀπὸ τῆς ἰδίας αὐτῶν οὐσίας.

nature of the whole and as telling them the fated laws[1]. Discussing this, Proclus treats as characteristic of Fate the manifold connexion of causes[2], not exclusively natural in the sense of mechanical[3], but, to the souls that come under it, appearing to be externally imposed[4]. The natural causation in which it consists is really divine as part of the complete order, and is only separable from the unitary direction of Providence by an abstraction, as in the myth of the *Politicus*, where the world is figured as in a certain period going on by itself. It is also not to be conceived as really external to the souls that undergo it, but as written in them in the form of laws which are realised according to the choices they make.

Every particular human soul must by inherent destiny descend to birth at least once in each cosmic cycle[5]. The rest depends on its choice: through this comes subjection to Fate[6]. When Plato speaks of the first birth ($\pi\rho\omega\tau\eta$ $\gamma\epsilon\nu\epsilon\sigma\iota\varsigma$), he means descent from the intelligible world to manifestation in time; and so, when he goes on to describe further stages of descent, this is to be understood as a classification of souls, not as an actual genetic order. He cannot mean literally that the first birth in time is as a man; that the second, in case the soul deteriorates, is as a woman; and that, if the deterioration continues, the same soul will become reincarnate as an irrational animal. Similarly in the *Republic*, the account of the degeneration of political constitutions is really a classification. The stages of descent from aristocracy, through timocracy, oligarchy and democracy, to tyranny have no historical necessity: there is no reason why there should not be transition directly from timocracy to tyranny or from aris-

---

[1] *Timaeus*, 41 E: τὴν τοῦ παντὸς φύσιν ἔδειξε, νόμους τε τοὺς εἱμαρμένους εἶπεν αὐταῖς.

[2] iii. 272, 24–25: τοῦτο δὲ εἱμαρμένης ἴδιον, ὁ τῶν πολλῶν αἰτίων εἱρμός, ἡ τάξις, ἡ περιοδικὴ ποίησις.

[3] iii. 272, 16–20.

[4] iii. 275, 15–17: ὅτε τοίνυν ἐγκόσμιοι γεγόνασιν αἱ ψυχαί, τότε καὶ τὸ κράτος θεῶνται τῆς εἱμαρμένης ἄνωθεν ἀπὸ τῆς προνοίας ἐξηρτημένον καὶ τοὺς νόμους ὑποδέχονται τοὺς εἱμαρμένους.

[5] iii. 277, 3–7. Cf. iii. 278, 25–27.

[6] iii. 277, 18–20: κρατηθεῖσαι δὲ ὑπὸ τοῦ θνητοῦ εἴδους τῆς ζωῆς δοῦλαι γίγνονται τῆς εἱμαρμένης· χρῆται γὰρ αὐταῖς ὡς ἀλόγοις τὸ πᾶν.

tocracy to democracy[1]. In the *Timaeus*, the production of
all animal souls is figured under that of the human soul, taken
as a convenient starting-point to set forth, as imaginary
descent to lower stages, a classification according to rank in
the scale[2]. What is meant by placing the male of the human
species first is that the masculine mind is better adapted to
attach itself to intellect and to principles. Yet, when Socrates
has to learn from Diotima how to find the way to the Idea of
the Beautiful, it would be absurd to say that no soul can
become incarnate at the highest stage as a woman[3]. Is there,
Proclus goes on to ask[4], a difference of sex in souls prior to
birth? He answers that there is, but that the male soul has
a female element and the female soul a male element: this is
indicated by the myth ascribed to Aristophanes in the *Sym-
posium*[5]. Hence a soul predominantly male may descend to
birth as a woman, and a soul predominantly female as a man[6];
just as a soul in a particular life may become attached to the
wrong presiding deity,—may, as we say, miss its vocation[7].
For the difference of sex is not a difference of kind, but is
analogous rather to the differences between modes of life; and
the virtues of men and of women are the same.

Proclus denies that a human soul can ever become the soul
of a lower animal; though he seems to admit that it might
attach itself to and direct a brute soul[8]. The language of Plato
about transmigration into animals he takes to be mythical[9].
Its meaning is that every kind of vice ends by embodiment in
some brutish mode of life; the brutality that there is in injustice, for example, being described as the life of a wolf.

---

[1] iii. 282.   [2] iii. 240.   [3] iii. 281.   [4] iii. 283.   [5] iii. 293.   [6] iii. 284.

[7] This is not identical with moral failure in life. A soul may guide its course
wrongly within, or rightly outside, its proper vocation. Proclus minutely dis-
criminates the cases (iii. 279–280). Vocation itself is not simple: within the
domain of the presiding deity, the right or the wrong power may be chosen;
and so there are many possible combinations. The happy life is the life
completely in accordance with vocation: ὁ δὲ εὐδαίμων βίος ἐστὶν ὁ κατὰ τὴν
ἰδιότητα τῶν ἡγεμόνων ἀφοριζόμενος (iii. 290, 30–31).

[8] iii. 294, 29–295, 3. Milton's description of the entrance of Satan into the
serpent is too similar not to recall: compare *Paradise Lost*, ix. 187–190.

[9] Cf. iii. 293, 30–31: ἄλλως τε καὶ τοῦ Πλάτωνος πολλὰ καὶ διὰ τῶν συμβόλων
κρύπτειν σπουδάζοντος.

Quite consistent with this view that there is no passage of a soul from one species to another is the traditional conception, worked into his system by Proclus, of the eternal Man as mediating between the individual man and the life of the whole[1]. His doctrine of continuity, with its search for means between extreme terms, of course serves as the recipient for this as a special example[2]. Each human soul is Man and the first Man[3]. At the same time, as we have seen, each is not only a particular rational soul, distinguished in essence from all others, but also contains the roots of differentiating irrational elements, which pre-exist and survive the body of the individual[4].

For the body, says Proclus, the way to that which is contrary to nature, and the deprivation of life, produces pain; the way to that which is according to nature, and the attunement with life, pleasure[5]. These affections of pleasure and pain he finds to be the sources of the other affections[6]. We cannot help being reminded of Spinoza's definitions in the third Part of the *Ethics*[7]. Unlike Spinoza, however, Proclus regards the living body as characterised not primarily by its *conatus*, but by perception, to which appetition is secondary[8].

The intellectualism (in modern phrase) of Proclus appears when he says that the decrees of the Demiurge (*Tim.* 42 D)

---

[1] Compare Comte's mnemonic verse: "Entre l'homme et le monde il faut l'Humanité."

[2] iii. 298, 5–11: καὶ πῶς γὰρ ἀπὸ τῆς τὸν κόσμον ὅλον διοικούσης ζωῆς εἰς τὸ μερικώτατόν ἐστιν ἡ κάθοδος;...ἀλλὰ πάντως εἰς τὸ μέσον πρότερον ἡ κάθοδος, ὃ μή ἐστι τι ζῷον ἀλλὰ πολλῶν βίων περιεκτικόν· οὐδὲ γὰρ εὐθὺς τὸν τοῦ τινὸς ἀνθρώπου προβάλλει βίον, ἀλλὰ τὸν ἀνθρώπου πρὸ τούτου.

[3] iii. 307, 15–17. Cf. iii. 166, 28: ἄνθρωπον γὰρ καὶ τὸν νοητὸν καὶ τὸν αἰσθητὸν λέγομεν.

[4] Cf. iii. 299–300: τῆς ἄρα ἀλόγου ζωῆς οὐκ ἔστι καθ' ἕκαστον τὸν βίον ἐξαλλαγὴ καθάπερ τῶν σωμάτων.

[5] iii. 287, 17–20: τοῦ γὰρ σώματος ἡ μὲν ἐπὶ τὸ παρὰ φύσιν ὁδὸς καὶ ἡ στέρησις τῆς ζωῆς τὴν λύπην ἀπεργάζεται, ἡ δὲ ἐπὶ τὸ κατὰ φύσιν ἐπάνοδος καὶ ἡ πρὸς τὴν ζωὴν ἐνάρμοσις ἡδονήν.

[6] iii. 287, 22–23: πρωτουργὰ μέν ἐστι τὰ δύο ταῦτα πάθη καὶ πηγαὶ τῶν ἄλλων παθῶν.

[7] "*Laetitia* est hominis transitio a minore ad maiorem perfectionem. *Tristitia* est hominis transitio a maiore ad minorem perfectionem."

[8] iii. 288, 9–13. Cf. *Eth.* iii. Prop. 7, with Prop. 9, Schol.

are not commands like those of a city or a legislator, but are implanted in the being of souls so that these may govern themselves. Only thus can the fault be their own if they do not[1]. The distribution of souls is not by chance, nor yet by a bare will that determines their places beforehand, nor is each simply identical with the whole; but there is a total order accordant with intellect, in which each takes its part by the cooperation of its own will, which is from within[2].

The mortal body assumes form before the soul is present; and the presence of the merely animating principle is before that of the immortal principle[3]. The first is produced along with the body[4]. This is always the order of genesis, from the imperfect to the perfect by a regular process[5]. In the timeless order of being, mind and soul precede body; but this is not the order of birth, but, as has often been said, of causal derivation. The immortal soul is not bound in relation to the body till the body has become compacted into one whole[6].

Describing, after Plato (*Tim.* 43 BC), the troubles brought by the nutritive life and the life of the senses, Proclus denies that these are troubles of the soul. It is as if one standing on the bank were to see his image distorted in all sorts of ways by the currents in a river, and were to imagine that this affected him in his reality. So it is only the soul's image that is tossed about in the stream of birth[7]. This seems almost coincident with expressions of Plotinus; but Proclus goes on

---

[1] iii. 302, 29–31: ἵν' οὖν ἀναίτιος ᾖ τῶν ἁμαρτημάτων ὁ θεός, ἐν ταῖς οὐσίαις αὐτῶν ἀπέθετο τοὺς εἱμαρμένους νόμους.

[2] iii. 304.

[3] iii. 321, 25–29: μετὰ δ' οὖν τὴν ἕνωσιν τῶν πολλῶν καὶ ἀνομοίων ἡ ψυχὴ παραγίγνεται, πρώτη μὲν ἡ θνητὴ πάντως...δευτέρα δὲ ἡ ἀθάνατος.

[4] iii. 321, 31: ἀπογεννᾶται μετὰ τοῦ σώματος.

[5] iii. 322, 1–2: πᾶσα γὰρ ἡ γένεσις ἀπὸ ἀτελοῦς ἄρχεται καὶ ὁδῷ πρόεισιν ἐπὶ τὸ τέλειον.

[6] iii. 322, 21–23: ὅταν οὖν ἓν γένηται καὶ ὅλον τὸ σῶμα, τότε ἡ ἀθάνατος ψυχὴ περὶ αὐτὸ καταδεῖται. In the terms applied to the corresponding patristic and scholastic theories, the Stoics were "traducianists," the Neo-Platonists "creationists"; at least so far as they held that the rational soul is not immanent in the seminal matter, but is superinduced. According to Proclus, the attachment is at the moment of birth, when the new body acquires a separate existence.

[7] iii. 330.

to oppose the view of Plotinus and Theodore of Asine that something in us remains passionless and always thinks[1]. The soul descends as a whole, and errs in its choice both as regards action and judgment. The reconciliation of this with what goes before is to be found in the distinction between the soul's essence and its powers and energies. Its essence indeed remains identical[2]; but its powers and energies are perturbable throughout; so that it cannot be said that anything of them dwells always in serenity amid the flux. In short, Proclus agrees with Plotinus that the trouble is illusory; but he asserts against him that the illusion may affect the whole soul while it is here, and make it inwardly, not as in a mere dramatic representation, unhappy[3]. The return to the rational order of the soul is to be accomplished by unbinding the Prometheus in ourselves[4].

ON THE *REPUBLIC*

As compared with the commentaries hitherto dealt with, the Commentary on the *Republic* has the advantage of being at once approximately complete and more manageable in size. It does not, like the others, set out to go over the whole of the Dialogue in detail, but consists of dissertations on selected topics. The first part is the most generally interesting and the most literary of the writings of Proclus; and the second contains some of his profoundest thoughts. The drawback is the imperfect text of this second part, due to the unfortunate condition of the manuscript. Not until 1901 did a complete edition appear; and the editor has had to make much use of conjecture. In spite of this drawback, students of Greek philosophy may now read the whole with profit; and some, if I may judge from my own experience, will find pleasure in the reading even apart from any purpose.

---

[1] iii. 333, 29–30: παρρησιασόμεθα πρὸς Πλωτῖνον καὶ τὸν μέγαν Θεόδωρον ἀπαθές τι φυλάττοντας ἐν ἡμῖν καὶ ἀεὶ νοοῦν. Cf. iii. 323. For the position of Plotinus, see above, p. 64, n. 5.

[2] iii. 335, 24: ἡ μὲν οὐσία παντελῶς ἡ αὐτὴ διαμένει. Cf. iii. 340, 15; 343, 4.

[3] iii. 334. .   [4] iii. 346. Cf. *in Remp*. ii. 53.

In the exposition, some points brought out before will have to be repeated; but, as elsewhere, I shall try to make repetition as infrequent as possible.

Early in the Commentary, we find ourselves again on the ground rapidly gone over in the sketch given of the short treatises on Theodicy. Matter is not the cause of evils. There was no one cause. They arise episodically in a world of strife among differentiated existences; and such a world was necessary to fill up all the grades of possible being. Of this order of the world as conceived in the Neo-Platonic system, mythology is found to be symbolical. Apollo is the universal poet, giving harmony to the cosmos. Ares is a kind of general of the forces of evil; but, since he is conceived as divine, he must be regarded as setting wars in motion with insight in relation to some universal end[1]. The agents of evil in the lower parts of the causal chain have not the idea of marshalling it for good, having no insight into the whole, and so they become liable to punishment for their ill-will; but the punishment also is beneficent. The final victory is always to the good; but the power of the worse may not be destroyed, since the whole must consist of opposites. Above strife is the life of intellect. Philosophy is the highest kind of $\mu o \nu \sigma \iota \kappa \dot{\eta}$ and $\dot{\epsilon} \rho \omega \tau \iota \kappa \dot{\eta}$. The soul possessed of it imitates Apollo Musegetes; for the philosopher, though this is not obvious to the multitude, is a kind of enthusiast[2].

This leads up to the predominant purpose of the first part of the Commentary; which is in effect to defend poetry and mythology against the master. Among Plato's successors, Aristotle had vindicated the drama against his indiscriminate attack on the imitative arts; Plotinus had shown that sculpture and painting are not at a greater remove from the Idea than the natural things that exemplify it, but, on Platonic principles, must go back to something more real because more general; Proclus now sets himself to rehabilitate the Homeric epic and its mythical stories.

He cannot indeed formally admit that Plato did not in his

---

[1] i. 68–69. Cf. ii. 295–296.

[2] i. 57. Here of course Proclus starts from Plato in the *Phaedrus*.

own mind see and allow for everything; but his criticisms are
none the less keen for that. It is of course true that with
Plato's irony on the poets as teachers there is mixed real
admiration; and on this Proclus, with something of the
orator's art, insists, without fully recognising the irony. He
has, however, no scruple in saying that Plato would have been
turned out of his own republic both as a poet and as a jester;
that his underworld is not less terrifying than Homer's,
against which he protests[1]; that he borrows some of his own
myths from Homer as well as from the Orphics[2]; that if we
take everything literally he is full of contradictions; that
these can only be excused by allowing for the dramatist in
Plato himself and the consequent dramatic element in the
Dialogues[3]. Finally, he remarks that doubtless the reason for
Plato's attack on Homer was that he saw his contemporaries
despising philosophy as useless, and, in their excessive admiration of poetry, treating it as sufficient for the whole of
education. We must not, however, blame the divine poet
for that, any more than we ought to blame the philosopher
because some, in their admiration of his dialogues as literature, have made his style the sole object of their imitation;
or, Proclus adds, than we ought to blame the Maker of the
world because particular souls are content to revolve in the
world of birth without rising higher. But some of these
things, which it is lawful for him to say to his pupils, they are
not to repeat to outsiders[4].

At the attempt to show that the Homeric myths contain
the principles of Platonic theology the modern world, having,
so far as its best minds are concerned, outgrown the mode of
thought since the seventeenth century, now only smiles; but
interesting ideas are brought out by the way. The deceptions
wrought by the gods, as for instance Agamemnon's dream in
the second Book of the *Iliad*, are ultimately for the good of
the deceived; just as the Platonic Socrates enjoins on the

---

[1] i. 118–119.
[2] i. 168–169. Cf. ii. 110–111 : τοῦ Πλάτωνος τὰ τοιαῦτα πλάττοντος μὲν οὐδαμῶς,
κατὰ δὲ τὴν χρείαν τῶν προκειμένων ἀεὶ παραλαμβάνοντος καὶ χρωμένου πᾶσι μετὰ
τῆς πρεπούσης περιβολῆς καὶ οἰκονομίας.
[3] See above, p. 160.   [4] i. 202–205.

guardians of his State the use of falsehood for the benefit of
those who have not sufficient insight into their own good[1].
Goodness is above truth; and the two, united in the whole,
often become separated and incompatible in the parts. Why
are the gods represented as causing one of the Trojan heroes
to break the truce? They do this not by a mere arbitrary
external use of him as an instrument, but by bringing into
action his own predisposition. Thus, though no doubt his
will is made to contribute towards a cosmic end, he is not
purely and simply sacrificed to it; the temptation is also for
the sake of his own soul, as physicians sometimes have to
bring a physical malady to a head before it can be cured[2].

On poetry itself, Proclus has many good observations. He
anticipates Shelley's thought[3] that in a tyrannically-ruled
State even those less elevated kinds of poetry which in their
lowered type bear the marks of that order tend to make those
who live under a tyranny better and not worse[4]. In placing
highest the poetry with an element of "divine madness" in
it[5], he follows Plato; adding that Plato, as is fitting, puts this
above every other human art[6]. From an incidental phrase of
Plato (ἀπαλὴν καὶ ἄβατον ψυχήν)[7], he educes a description of
the poetic mind as receptive of inspiration because not fixed
in some stable habit of its own, but at the same time resistant
to miscellaneous opinions and impressions from outside[8]. The
second order of poetry he finds to be the poetry of wisdom and
understanding. Of this Theognis is the best example[9]. The
third kind is the poetry that imitates things as they are or as

---

[1] i. 116.

[2] i. 105, 26–30: ἔδει γὰρ τοὺς τῶν μεγίστων ἀδικημάτων ἄρξαντας ἀνακληθῆναί
ποτε πρὸς τὴν δίκην· τοῦτο δὲ οὐκ ἄν ποτε συνέβη, μὴ τῆς μοχθηρίας αὐτῶν ἀνα-
πλωθείσης· πολλαὶ γοῦν τῶν ἕξεων ἀνενέργητοι μένουσαι τῆς προσηκούσης θεραπείας
τυχεῖν ἀδυνάτους ποιοῦσιν τοὺς ἔχοντας. This idea of the Greek theodicy,
starting from the doctrine of Plato that punishment is for the good of the
offender, was applied by Origen to the "hardening of Pharaoh's heart"; as
Proclus applies it here to the "breaking of the oaths."

[3] In the *Defence of Poetry*. [4] i. 48.

[5] i. 178, 24: μανία σωφροσύνης κρείττων.

[6] i. 182, 14–16: ταύτην δὴ τὴν ἐκ τῶν Μουσῶν ὑφισταμένην ἐν ταῖς ἀπαλαῖς καὶ
ἀβάτοις ψυχαῖς ποιητικὴν ἀπάσης ἄλλης τέχνης ἀνθρωπίνης εἰκότως προτίθησιν.

[7] *Phaedrus*, 245 A. [8] i. 181. [9] i. 186–188.

they appear. In the first case it is the poetry of representation; in the second, of fancy[1]. All the kinds are illustrated in Homer.

Several remarks on the relation between ethics and politics show the persistence of thought on the subject even when all influence of political philosophy on practice had for the time ceased. Comparing the virtues of the city and of the individual, Proclus allows that, as the city is greater in magnitude, its virtues are more conspicuous: on the other hand, they are only images of the virtues in the particular soul, in accordance with the rule that greater perfection is found in the smaller quantity or number[2]. Plato's ruling class, he goes on to show, is selected, though Plato did not expressly say so but only implied it, for proficiency in the "musical," —that is, literary and ethico-religious—branch of training, and not specially for proficiency in the gymnastic or physical branch. After their selection, at once for natural capacity and progress made, they are to be trained in science and philosophy (mathematics and dialectic)[3]. In another passage, he touches upon the question whether women should take part in the government. The reason, he says, why women, although their virtues, according to Plato, are the same as men's, share in the highest offices in the first State (that of the *Republic*) but not in the second (that of the *Laws*), is that in the second private property and separate families are permitted. For the sympathies of women are by nature with private rather than with public interests and with the part rather than the whole[4]. This is no doubt the most plausible argument ever

---

[1] i. 188–192.

[2] i. 217, 10–16: τῷ γὰρ ὄγκῳ μιᾶς ψυχῆς μείζων ἡ πόλις, <εἰ> καὶ εἰκόνες εἰσὶν αἱ τῆς ὅλης πόλεως ἀρεταὶ τῶν τῆς μιᾶς ψυχῆς, κἀνταῦθα δήπου τοῦ λόγου κρατοῦντος, ὅς φησιν τὰ ἀμερέστερα τῇ δυνάμει κρατεῖν τῶν εἰς πλείονα μερισμὸν ὑποφερομένων, καὶ τὰ ἐλάττω κατ' ἀριθμὸν ὑπερφέρειν τῇ δυνάμει τῶν πλειόνων κατὰ τὸ ποσόν. There is a strikingly similar thought in Victor Hugo's *William Shakespeare*. "A beauté égale, le Râmayana nous touche moins que Shakespeare. Le moi d'un homme est plus vaste et plus profond encore que le moi d'un peuple."

[3] i. 218–219. The point about order in time is not put quite so distinctly by Proclus, but seems to be implied.

[4] i. 257, 1–6: καὶ γὰρ συμπαθέστερον φύσει τὸ θῆλυ περὶ τὸ ἴδιον τοῦ ἄρρενος·

used against political equality between the sexes: Herbert
Spencer's argument is practically identical. The answer, on
the ground taken by Proclus, might be that, since the virtues
of men and of women are the same, both ought to take part
in public affairs so that the latent capacity for political virtue
may be educed in all; for of course Proclus recognised the
spiritually educative function of the State. It was worth
while to make this remark because it is essentially his own
reply to one of Aristotle's arguments against the Platonic
communism as an ideal. Men, says Aristotle, neglect what
concerns only the public, and take more interest in what is
their own. True, answers Proclus, but Aristotle himself has
pointed out, in reply to those who would have the human
mind restrict itself to human affairs, that there is also a divine
part in us with an aptitude for speculative contemplation, and
with this also we ought to energise as far as the conditions of
human life permit. So, in politics, we must be taught by
institutions to turn from our merely private interests to those
that concern the whole State[1].

Before we go on to the abstruser discussions of the second
part, one position may be selected from various observations
on psychology and metaphysics, because it is not repeated
elsewhere, and because it illustrates the advance made by the
Neo-Platonic school on Plato himself. Proclus notes[2] that
the perceptive part of the soul (τὸ αἰσθητικόν) is distinct from
the three classified by Plato (reason, spirit, desire) and is the
foundation of all. This is, scientifically considered, an improvement on Plato's psychology, which, as Proclus himself
observes, has primarily a political and educational aim.

The principal topics of the second part are the celebrated
puzzle or mystification known as the "nuptial number" (Rep.
viii. 545–546), and the myth of Er (Rep. x. 614–621). This
last is dealt with in the circumstantial manner characteristic
of the commentaries of Proclus generally.

 οὐκ ἦν οὖν ἀσφαλὲς μερισμὸν εἰσαγαγόντα καὶ χρημάτων καὶ παίδων καὶ εἰς γυναῖκας
ἄγειν τὴν τῶν ὅλων ἀρχήν, ὑπ᾽ αὐτῆς τῆς φύσεως ἠναγκασμένας τοῖς ἰδίοις συμ-
πάσχειν ἀντὶ τῶν κοινῶν καὶ τοῖς μέρεσιν ἀντὶ τῶν ὅλων.

[1] ii. 367–368. This argument occurs in a fragment imperfectly deciphered,
but the meaning is quite clear.   [2] i. 232–233.

In the exposition by Socrates of the degenerations from the
best State, there is a certain "geometrical number" on which
the goodness or badness of births is said to depend. Of this
number the guardians will at some time fail to take account;
marriages will be wrongly arranged; and, through the deterioration of offspring, the decline of the polity will set in. Here
Proclus, as often, refuses to take Plato literally. He repeats
a position we have already met with: the degenerations from
the best State are not necessary phases in a historical process,
but represent gradations in the actual continuous order of all
things. The meaning of the formula is cosmical, not properly
political. The best State, once established, could perish only
by violence; for its citizens would choose to be completely
destroyed rather than descend to a base mode of life[1].

This made clear, Proclus allows himself some applications
to the State considered as part of the whole. What the
mysterious number indicates is that human life can never be
entirely self-dependent. It is dependent finally on the astronomical order; and the total revolution of this would have its
scientific expression, if that were discoverable, in a mathematical formula. As suffering from disease, in the case of
those who have knowledge, comes almost exclusively from
the cosmic system, not by their own fault, so dissolution comes
to the best State. Its immediate cause he finds to be, as suggested by Amelius[2], that the guardian sages, most apt and
educated as they are for theory, that is, for the science of
principles, miss the right appreciation of perception. For it
is through perception that we have to learn the contexture of
causes in the parts of the world; reasoning here is fallible.
This is εἱμαρμένη, external fate: the control of practice fails
through the complexity of the order in its detail.

The guardians, Proclus observes, did not receive all knowledge as a gift, but were left, as wise men, to seek the appropriate kinds themselves; as every order of being receives
something from the order above and adds something of its
own[3]. The legislator gave them the hint that, among other
things, knowledge of the cosmic periods was needed. It was

[1] ii. 2, 16–20.   [2] ii. 29–30.   [3] ii. 74.

for them to discover and apply that knowledge. Fallibility
in the application of knowledge is latent in the system of
causes. Everything in the world of becoming is unfolded in
time; but not everything is unfolded at the right time for
attaining the good that would arrive if its coming to be were
concurrent with developments in the rest of the world making
for its perfection[1]. Thus the impossibility of complete deduction from the superior order of causes is recognised. Since
Proclus cannot admit the emergence anywhere of something
from nothing, this means, as has been noted before, that
there is an element of explicit pluralism in his doctrine. In
the present section of the Commentary, indeed, he once more
repeats that if a root of discord had not been latent in the
soul's being, discord could not have appeared in its lives[2].

In one passage of this section not otherwise remarkable, we
come upon what I venture to say is a most indisputable
example of progress in philosophy,—a thing of which the
existence is often denied. However highly we may think of
Proclus, we cannot put him, any more than he would have
put himself, on a level with Plato in genius; and still less can
his age be compared with Plato's age as a social medium for
dialectical discussion. Yet, out of a passing generality of
Plato, after the continuous thinking of eight centuries, he is
able to educe a statement of philosophical rationalism equal
in precision to any that is to be found in Kant after the much
longer but profoundly discontinuous period since. Knowledge of truth, says Plato, is acquired by experience, judgment and reason[3]. Taking these three terms consecutively,
Proclus defines experience as a kind of precursory knowledge,
supplying matter to the judgment[4]. In judging, we ourselves

---

[1] ii. 79.

[2] ii. 49, 12–15: εἰ δὲ μὴ προϋπῆρχεν ἐν τῇ οὐσίᾳ τῆς ψυχῆς καὶ τῆς ἀσυμφωνίας
ῥίζα, τῆς συμφωνίας ἀκράτου καὶ μόνης οὔσης, οὐδ᾽ ἂν ἐν ταῖς ζωαῖς αὐτῆς ὤφθη καὶ
ταῖς δυνάμεσιν διάστασις καὶ ἀναρμοστία. But down even to the lowest stage,
symbolised by the iron race of Hesiod, there is imitation of reason: ὥσπερ
καὶ σίδηρος ἀμυδρὰν ἔχει πρὸς τὸν ἄργυρον τῆς χρόας ἀπεικασίαν μέλας ὢν κατὰ
τὸ πλεῖστον· καὶ γὰρ τὸ παθητικὸν ἔχει φαντασίαν μιμεῖσθαι νοῦν ἐθέλουσαν καὶ
λόγον, ἀσθενοῦσαν δὲ διὰ τὴν μετὰ τῆς ὕλης ἐνέργειαν (ii. 77, 14–18).

[3] Rep. ix. 582 A: ἐμπειρίᾳ τε καὶ φρονήσει καὶ λόγῳ.

[4] The specialisation of φρόνησις in this exact sense is due to Proclus, who

project the bond of causation; experience declaring only the
"that." Reason turns into an object of knowledge, and veri-
fies, by using method, that which the judgment has discerned,
thus making manifest the inward energy of the judgment
itself[2].

We now proceed to the myth concerning the soul's destiny.
For the detailed study of this, two speculative doctrines are
postulated, *viz.*, that there are separable souls and that there
is a providential order[2]. Of these the first is regarded as
demonstrable for the rational part of the soul, the second as
capable of establishment by probable arguments. The principle of the opposite view is taken to be that the superior,
i.e., reason and mind, is a product of the inferior, *i.e.*, spontaneous and irrational movement[3]. As a general argument
against it, we are reminded of astronomical science, a symbolical account of which Socrates works into his narrative.
The myth has for its aim to reinforce the idea that providence
extends not only to the whole but to individuals[4].

Against those who would extrude myths altogether, Proclus
argues that they are fitting for the instruction of souls like
ours that are imaginative as well as intellectual. So much is it
the nature of our souls to be imaginative that some of the
ancient thinkers treated phantasy and intellect as the same,
and some even who distinguished them denied the existence
of any thought without imagery[5]. The mind that is insepar-

---

declares it to be the critical power: δῆλον δήπουθεν, ὡς ἄρα ἡ μὲν ὡς ἀληθῶς
κριτικὴ τῶν ὄντων τῆς ἀξίας ἐστὶν ἡ φρόνησις (ii. 82, 4–5).

[1] ii. 82, 6–14: προηγεῖται δὲ ταύτης [τῆς φρονήσεως] ἡ ἐμπειρία, πρόδρομος οὖσά
τις γνῶσις καὶ τὴν ὕλην παρέχουσα τῇ φρονήσει (δέονται γὰρ οἱ ἔμφρονες ἐσόμενοι
τῆς ἐμπειρίας, ἀλλ' ὡς ὕλης προϋποκειμένης, αὐτοὶ τὸν τῆς αἰτίας προβεβλημένοι
δεσμόν, τῆς ἐμπειρίας μόνον τὸ ΄ὅτι΄ λεγούσης)· ὁ δὲ δὴ λόγος ἐκ τρίτων, ὅσα
διέγνωκεν ἡ φρόνησις, γνώριμα ποιεῖ καὶ πιστοῦται μεθόδοις χρώμενος, δι' ὧν
ἐμφανίζει τὴν ἔνδον ἐνέργειαν τῆς φρονήσεως.   [2] ii. 101.

[3] ii. 102, 10–14: οἱ μὲν οὖν τῷ αὐτομάτῳ καὶ τῇ τύχῃ τὸ πᾶν ἐπιτρέψαντες οὐδὲν
γίνεσθαί φασιν κατὰ πρόνοιαν καὶ δίκην, νοῦν δὲ καὶ λόγον ὕστερα ποιοῦσιν τοῦ
αὐτομάτου καὶ γεννῶσιν ἀπὸ τῶν χειρόνων τὰ ἀμείνονα καὶ ἐκ τῶν ἀλόγως κινουμένων τὰ κατὰ λόγον ζῶντα.

[4] ii. 103, 4–5: ὅτι μέχρι τῶν ἀτομωτάτων οἱ μισθοὶ τῆς τε δικαιοσύνης εἰσὶ καὶ
τῆς ἀδικίας, καὶ οὐ τὰ ὅλα προνοεῖται μόνον, ἀλλὰ καὶ τὰ καθ' ἕκαστα.

[5] ii. 107, 18–20: ὥστε καὶ τῶν παλαιῶν τινας τοὺς μὲν φαντασίαν ταὐτὸν εἰπεῖν
εἶναι καὶ νοῦν, τοὺς δὲ καὶ διακρίναντας ἀφάνταστον νόησιν μηδεμίαν ἀπολείπειν.

able from phantasy is not indeed the mind that we are, but
it is the mind that we put on, and through this we take
pleasure in myths as akin to it[1]. Myths are not themselves
speculative truth, but they keep the soul in contact with
truth. And they have an effect on the many. Else how is it
that with the ancient myths and mysteries all places on earth
were full of all kinds of good, whereas now without them all
is devoid of the breath of life and of divine illumination[2]?

If the philosopher had been asked how he reconciled this
with his optimism, he would doubtless have pointed to various
implications brought out by him in the doctrine of cosmic
cycles. Living in a period, soon to cease, of precarious philosophical liberty, he could still hint at what he meant, but no
more. Even Sallust, the friend of Julian, in setting forth about
a century earlier a creed for the reformed paganism, had put
only in cryptic language his explanation of the change that
had come over the world. The guilt, he says, that is now
punished in some by total ignorance of the true divine order
may be that of having deified their kings in a former life[3].
Thus it appears that in Julian's circle Christianity was regarded as nemesis for the deification of the Emperors. We
know that he himself had satirised the apotheosis in his
Caesares. For Proclus, of course, this was all in the past; and
he lived in a still older past. The Athenian democracy was to
him a more living reality than the imperial monarchy; which,
for anything he tells us, might not exist.

In the part of the Commentary now reached, we are met

---

[1] ii. 107–108.

[2] ii. 108, 27–30: ἢ πῶς μετ' ἐκείνων μὲν πᾶς ὁ περὶ γῆν τόπος μεστὸς ἦν παν-
τοίων ἀγαθῶν, ὧν θεοὶ προξενοῦσιν ἀνθρώποις, ἄνευ δὲ ἐκείνων ἄπνοα πάντα καὶ
ἄμοιρα τῆς τῶν θεῶν ἐστιν ἐπιλάμψεως;
Damascius, when the Byzantine age had closed in, has put on record
philosophic opinion at the time in the form of a sketch of the three kinds of
polity founded respectively on λόγος, θυμός and ἐπιθυμία (*Vita Isidori*, 238).
The first was realised in the Saturnian or Golden Age; the second in the
military States famous in history; the third in the life to which the world has
now run down, φιλοχρήμονα, μικροπρεπῆ, δουλεύειν ἀσφαλῶς ἐθέλουσαν, οἷα τῶν
ἐν τῇ νῦν γενέσει πολιτευομένων ἡ ζωή.

[3] See Περὶ θεῶν καὶ κόσμου, c. 18. The commentators note that ἀθεΐα was
the cryptic expression for Christianity.

by the question how far credulity about the marvellous, in
Neo-Platonists like Julian and Proclus, who show some sympathy with it, actually extended. The reply, I think, must be
that all the really confident belief they had was founded on
what they took to be metaphysical demonstration; but that
they were willing to indulge in fancies that there might be
elements of truth in the many strange things commonly believed. Thus Proclus brings in an account from Clearchus, a
disciple of Aristotle, relating how a wonder-worker convinced
the philosopher that the soul is separable by drawing that of
a young man out of its body, and then bringing it back, like
the doctor in Gautier's *Avatar*[1]. Generally, however, he is
little given to anecdote; and, when we come to his scientific
doctrine, we find the only shade of difference from that of
Porphyry, for example, to be that he is even more strenuous in
keeping it clear of dualistic animism.

The departure of the soul from the body, like its entrance
into it, is not to be regarded as a local motion; for the soul is
not in place, and not in the body as in a subject (ὑποκειμένῳ).
Its "entrance" is the name given to a mode of relation
(σχέσις); its departure, to dissolution of the relation[2]. This
is conceived as in its inner reality a mode of psychical relation,
not as an association of two coordinated realities called soul
and body. Soul contains in itself, as the prior reality, pre-existent forms of all corporeal motions[3]. In modern language
(occasionally used by Proclus) these last are purely phenomenal. What draws it to the kind of life it attains is a certain
emotion of sympathy and desire[4]. It finds its proper life and
destiny, whether in this phenomenal world or in another, by
a sort of spontaneous impulse without conscious choice[5]. Remaining always the same in essence, it changes its lives[6].

---

[1] ii. 122–123.

[2] ii. 125, 6–8: ἀλλὰ εἴσοδος μὲν αὐτῆς ἡ πρὸς αὐτὸ καλεῖται σχέσις, ἔξοδος δὲ ἡ
τῆς σχέσεως ἀπόλυσις.

[3] ii. 125, 23–25: πασῶν γὰρ τῶν σωματοειδῶν κινήσεων ἐν τῇ ψυχῇ τὰ παραδείγματα προϋφέστηκεν.

[4] ii. 127, 2–4: δεῖ γὰρ τὸ ὅμοιον πᾶν φέρεσθαι πρὸς τὸ ὅμοιον, νικᾶν δὲ ἐν ταῖς
κινήσεσι τὸ πλεονεκτοῦν.

[5] ii. 128, 1: οἷον αὐτομάτως καὶ ἀπροαιρέτως.

[6] ii. 137, 13–14: μένουσα γὰρ ἀεὶ ἡ αὐτὴ κατὰ τὴν οὐσίαν ἐξαλλάττει τὰς ζωάς.

Beneath Plato's mythological language, Proclus finds a meaning that places the supreme control above all personal agency. The judgment of souls does not really come to pass by a discourse of judges, but by a process running through the life itself of those that are judged and of the agents of destiny[1]. Justice itself is one[2], but it takes multiplex form according to the variety of lives. The process by which it is realised, depending on the inward disposition to receive a certain impulse, the myth calls a command[3]. "God," "mind," "reason," "order," along with the perversion of reason and the disposition to excess of passion or appetite and to disorder, are all latent in the soul. "Above" and "below," applied to the direction in which it goes, are merely analogical terms. The better souls know themselves and the providential destiny that leads them, the worse not[4].

The souls both from above and from below are represented as coming with joy to the world of birth; those from the underworld naturally, as having undergone penalties; but those from heaven also, because they have grown weary of the life there[5]. For even the souls in heaven desired the heavenly life only with one part of themselves. The other part, remaining unrealised (ἀνενέργητον), and desiring to realise itself, conveyed its weariness to the whole, and made it glad to see that which put birth before its eyes. This craving belongs not merely to that which as body is perishable, but to the imperishable also. For the soul is a whole, with unexercised energies always latent; and the realisation of all of them at some time cannot fail[6].

To the heaven or intelligible world, the notion of an incorporeal vision, as set forth by Plotinus, is applied with little modification. Recognition in that world is by renewal of

---

[1] ii. 145.   [2] ii. 145, 18: μίαν...μονάδα θείαν, τὴν δίκην.

[3] ii. 146, 16: κέλευσιν προσεῖπεν ὁ μῦθος.

[4] ii. 152. This is also the view of Plotinus; for similar positions compare pp. 66–7, above.

[5] ii. 159–160: ταῖς οὐρανίαις οὖν καὶ ταῖς χθονίαις ἡ μεταβολὴ τῆς ζωῆς ἀσμένη ἐστί, καμούσαις ἐν ταῖς προτέραις ἐνεργείαις, ταῖς μέν γε εἰκότως, ἐν τληπαθείαις οὔσαις, ταῖς δέ, εἰ καὶ ἐν εὐπαθείαις, ἀλλ' ἀποκαμούσαις καὶ πρὸς ἐκείνην τὴν ζωήν.

[6] ii. 162, 14–17.

memory; the images of the past life having been deposited in the phantasy. This, however, is put quite generally: the remarkable theory of the separability of memory from the brain, which Plotinus had thought out in a very independent way in relation to the physiology of his time[1], Proclus nowhere discusses. The completely purified soul, he adds with Plotinus, at last puts aside all the impressions received from perception, and passes on to the state of intellectual intuition[2]. But this purification itself is only for a world-period, not for endless time.

So, at the other extreme, the greatest of criminals, the tyrant, is punished for a whole cosmic period. The period of a thousand years of punishment or reward assigned to most souls between one birth and another is not to be understood as an actual period of which the portions can be counted, but as indicating a certain type of periodicity belonging to genesis[3]. The soul of the despot differs from the other souls that are punished in being incurable for a whole great cycle of the world of birth. He cannot repent of his crimes, but can only try to escape[4]; his escape being, in the myth, prevented by the closing of the egress and by certain demons. Repentance means self-accusation and the inward return to a right mind before there is external justice: when it does not arise from within, it has to be brought about by the agency of the whole world-order. This is figured by the tortures to which Ardiaeus is subjected. Ardiaeus will never come to the upper earth again; but, as he began to be bad in time, he can cease to be bad in time; being immortal, he cannot be destroyed; and at last salvation will be brought to him by the Whole[5].

Passing to the astronomical symbolism, which comes next, Proclus interprets the "pillar of light" as signifying the cor-

---

[1] See above, pp. 47–8. [2] ii. 177, 26–29.

[3] ii. 169, 5–8: λεγέσθω καὶ παρ' ἡμῶν ἡ χιλιὰς οἰκεῖός τις ἀριθμὸς εἶναι ταῖς ἀπὸ γενέσεως στελλομέναις εἰς γένεσιν ψυχαῖς, πρὸ τῆς τελείας, ὡς εἴπομεν πρότερον, ἀποκαταστάσεως.

[4] ii. 180, 6–8.

[5] ii. 178. Cf. ii. 184, 26–28: καὶ εἰ μὴ θέμις τελέως ἀπολέσθαι τὸ ἀθάνατον, ἑαυτῷ μὲν ἀπόλλυται, τοῖς δὲ ἀπὸ τῶν ὅλων εἰς αὐτὸ καθήκουσιν σῴζεται.

poreal, unmoved, indivisible, all-inclusive place of the universe,—a view suggested by Porphyry[1]. This plenum of space is not to be conceived as incorporeal, since it has parts that can be marked off from one another (though not actually separated) and so is not all in each part, like true incorporeals[2].

The Necessity that involves all things in its order and gives them their revolution is not that of Matter, which is at the remotest extreme from active causation, but is the divine necessity of Mind. This, the Mother of the Fates and disposer of all, the theologians call Themis, which it is unlawful to attempt to transgress, and which cannot be transgressed[3]. The adamant in the composition of the distaff that spins round upon the knees of the goddess signifies the indissoluble character of intellectual necessity[4].

As if to correct the impression that this is conceived as a mere "abstract unity," Proclus notes with emphasis that the impulse to knowledge contains in itself the effort to distinguish and pluralise as well as to unify[5].

Discussing again the question about the epicycles and generally the complicated mechanical hypotheses of the later astronomers such as Ptolemy, he expresses admiration of Plato for not introducing them; but excuses the astronomers on the ground that, although the mechanisms do not actually exist, such hypotheses are necessary aids to calculation[6]. As against the view that they are real, his criticism is here more stringent than elsewhere. The hypotheses are not only in

---

[1] ii. 196.

[2] ii. 198, 7–10: ἢ ἀσώματός ἐστιν [ὁ τόπος] ἢ σωματικός. ἀλλ' ἀσώματος μὲν οὐδαμῶς εἶναι δύναται· τό τε γὰρ χωριστὸν σώματος ὅλον πανταχοῦ ἐστιν, ὁ δὲ τόπος οὐχ ὅλος πανταχοῦ.

[3] ii. 207, 21–22: ἦν τὸ ὑπερβαίνειν ἐγχειροῦν ἀθέμιτον μὲν εἶναι λέγομεν, ὑπερβαίνειν δὲ ὅμως μὴ δύνασθαι.

[4] ii. 211–212: καὶ γὰρ τὸ ἄλυτον κυριώτατα τῆς νοερᾶς ἦν ἴδιον οὐσίας.....εἰ οὖν τὸν ἀδάμαντα σύνθημα τῆς ἀλύτου οἰητέον οὐσίας...ταὐτὸν ἂν εἴη νοῦν τε θεολογοῦντας λέγειν καὶ ἀδάμαντα μυθολογοῦντας.

[5] ii. 225, 11–14: καὶ γὰρ ἡ γνῶσις καὶ τοῦ ὄντος ἐπορέγεται καὶ τῆς ζωῆς, διότι κίνησίς τίς ἐστιν, καὶ τῆς ἑτερότητος, διακρίνειν ἐθέλουσα τὰ ὄντα καὶ οὐ μόνον ἐκ πολλῶν ἕν, ἀλλὰ καὶ πολλὰ ποιεῖν ἐξ ἑνός.

[6] ii. 233–235.

themselves irrational; they do not even save the appearances[1]. The true rule of method is the Pythagorean precept,
to bring the apparent anomalies in the celestial motions to
uniformity by the fewest and simplest hypotheses[2]. Why not,
he asks, anticipating Bruno, let the stars move of themselves
unimpeded by their medium and without the aid of external
devices? The actual motions that calculators have to treat
as compositions of simple motions are not thus composed, but
belong to kinds of their own[3].

On the "choice of lives" in the myth, Proclus develops in
more detail the solution of the traditional problem concerning
fate and free-will already stated by Plotinus. This contains
in a subtler form the doctrine of the "intelligible character"
taken over from Kant by Schopenhauer, who himself discovered and pointed out the anticipation of it in Proclus.
The general statement of the modern theory is that in the
timeless order, before the phenomenal life of the person, a
character is fixed by an act of will that might have been other
than it was. When the character becomes manifest in the
phenomenal world, all events in its life proceed as determined
according to laws of natural causation; yet in reality it is free,
because it once for all determined (or, more exactly, always
determines) itself. The theory of Proclus is subtler in two
ways: first, the notion of "choice" is not left as if it meant
here or anywhere pure undetermined volition by which any
mind or will might have become anything that it simply chose
to be; and, secondly, the identity of the person to whom a
particular life comes to be assigned does not exclude the power,
within certain limits, to modify the character. This will become clearer in a fuller statement.

The postulates of Proclus are the same as those of Kant and

---

[1] ii. 229–230.

[2] ii. 230, 3–5: δι' ἐλαχίστων καὶ ἁπλουστάτων ὑποθέσεων χρῆναι τὴν φαινομένην ἀνωμαλίαν τῶν οὐρανίων ἀπευθύνειν εἰς ὁμαλότητα καὶ τάξιν. Cf. in Alcib.
I. 425, 6–10: τὰς ὑποθέσεις πανταχοῦ τῶν λόγων ἐλαχίστας εἶναι δεῖ καὶ ἁπλουστά-
τας· ὅσῳ γὰρ ἂν μᾶλλον ὦσι τοιαίδε, τοσούτῳ τῆς ἀνυποθέτου λεγομένης ἐπιστήμης
ἐγγυτάτω τυγχάνουσιν οὖσαι.

[3] ii. 234, 13–14: ἐκείνων τοιούτων οὐσῶν καθ' αὐτὰς ἀσυνθέτων, οἵας οὗτοι
ποιοῦσι διὰ συνθέσεως.

Schopenhauer. Individual choice must exist if we are to be anything; but it must be consistent with universal causation. If all the links of causation in the series of events in a life could be traced, it is true that all would end in necessity[1]. The causation, however, would be incomplete if the soul's original nature were not taken into account[2]. The reality behind the myth of the soul's antenatal choice is that each soul has a distinctive nature of its own, from which choices proceed that would go otherwise if the soul were different. This essence of the individual is itself timeless, but it manifests itself by choices in time. In the myth there is not one life given without choice to each, nor are all lives offered to each indiscriminately[3]. This excludes at once fatalism and chance. The souls that in the myth are said to take the first places by lot, and therefore to have most choices of lives, are not to be conceived as taking their places in reality by chance-distribution. The real order is that of discriminating justice according to rank in the universe[4]. Those that come first are the better-endowed souls. When it is said that the rank of the soul is not inherent in it (ψυχῆς δὲ τάξιν οὐκ ἐνεῖναι)[5] this does not mean that the soul has no intrinsic nature, but that its acquired character is not fixed by its nature, but is consequent on the mode of life chosen[6]. The best-endowed souls do not necessarily use the best judgment: in the myth, the first in order chooses ill, the last well. And even when the choice has been made, and the type of life fixed with its events[7], it is not determined as good or bad; the soul can live well or ill within it[8]. In short, Proclus had the idea of those modern deter-

---

[1] ii. 275, 17–19: καὶ οὕτως ἔοικεν καὶ πᾶν τὸ ἐνδεχόμενον εἰς ἀναγκαίαν μεταπίπτειν δύναμιν διὰ τῆς ἀκολουθίας, καὶ τῶν ἐνδεχομένων ἀναγκαίως ἐνδεχομένοις ἄλλοις ἐπομένων.

[2] ii. 276.

[3] ii. 263, 5–8: λείπεται τοίνυν μήτε ἑνὸς προτεινομένου πάσαις μήτε πάντων πάσαις τοὺς προτεινομένους βίους τινὰς εἶναι ταῖς ψυχαῖς καὶ ἄλλους ἄλλαις. Cf. ii. 264, 18–19: οὔτε εἷς τις μιᾷ βίος ἀπονέμεται τῶν ψυχῶν οὔτε πάντες ὁμοίως πάσαις, ἀλλὰ τινὲς τισίν.

[4] ii. 273–274.   [5] Rep. x. 618 b.   [6] ii. 284.

[7] ii. 275, 15–16: ἐνεδέχετο γὰρ καὶ ἄλλον βίον ζῆν, ἀλλὰ πρὸ τῆς αἱρέσεως, μετὰ δὲ τὴν αἵρεσιν ἀδύνατον.

[8] ii. 266, 23–26.

minists who make personality something deeper than character. Character he holds to be still plastic to inward impulses;
so that, while the soul had never open to it all choices without
limit, it never loses the power of choice consistent with its
limitations.

The "daemon" assigned to each presides over a kind of
life[1], and is not to be imagined as the guardian spirit of one
soul alone. What appears as chance coming from outside is
part of the whole destiny of the soul, and is pre-determined
like the rest[2]. Mind and reason are from God ($\theta\epsilon\acuteo\theta\epsilon\nu$), or are
the divinity in us[3]. If we do not choose in accordance with
them, the fault is not in God, but in our individual determina-
tion; and this is the meaning when it is said, $a\i\tau\acute{\iota}a$ $\epsilon\lambda o\mu\acute{\epsilon}\nu o\nu$,
$\theta\epsilon\grave{o}s$ $\grave{a}\nu a\acute{\iota}\tau\iota os$[4].

Plato represents the first to choose as seizing upon the most
absolute despotism. This illustrates the rule that the greatest
evils are done by the best-endowed souls through grasping
indiscriminately at the whole[5]. By a partial anticipation of
Descartes, the cause is said to be, along with the blinding of
the understanding, the infinity of the will[6]. And here Proclus
starts a speculation of which he accentuates the audacity by
drawing attention to it[7]. The fall of spirits in its typical form,
he argues, is symbolised by the first god imagined as a king
ruling by despotic compulsion[8]. In accordance with this

---

[1] ii. 272, 20: πολλῶν εἶς ἄρχει τῶν ὁμοειδῶς ζώντων.

[2] ii. 282, 12–15: ὅτι δὲ ὁ βίος οὐ μόνον τὸ εἶδος ἔχει τῆς ζωῆς, ἀλλὰ καὶ τὰ
ἀκόλουθα ἑκάστῳ παρὰ τοῦ παντὸς ἀπονεμόμενα, πολλάκις ἤδη προείπομεν.

[3] ii. 280, 6–7: οὐδὲ γὰρ ἄλλως ἐνεργοῦσιν εἰς ἡμᾶς οἱ κρείττους ἡμῶν ἢ ἔνδοθεν.

[4] Rep. x. 617 E.

[5] ii. 297, 1–5: καὶ ὅλως πάντων τῶν μεγάλων κακῶν αἱ πράξεις ψυχῶν εἰσιν
μεγάλῃ μὲν φύσει χρωμένων καὶ εὐφυῶν, δι' ἐννοίας δὲ ἀδιαρθρώτους ἐξεργαζομένων
τὰ μέγιστα τῶν κακῶν (καὶ εἴρηται ἡμῖν ὁ λόγος καὶ ἐν ἄλλοις πολλάκις).

[6] ii. 291, 11–14: τὰ μὲν οὖν αἴτια τῆς τοιαύτης τραγῳδίας εἶναί φησιν ἀφροσύνην
καὶ λαιμαργίαν, ὧν ἡ μέν ἐστι τῆς γνωστικῆς δυνάμεως τύφλωσις, ἡ δὲ τῆς ὀρέξεως
ἀπέραντος ἔκτασις.

[7] ii. 297, 6: εἰ χρὴ τολμήσαντα εἰπεῖν. Cf. ii. 298, 9: ἀλλὰ ταῦτα μὲν εὔστομα
κείσθω.

[8] This occurs in an imperfectly deciphered passage (ii. 297–298), but there
is no doubt about the interpretation. The god in whose history the symbolism
is found is Cronos, who seized the kingdom from his father and afterwards
devoured his own children,—a misfortune assigned by Plato to the soul that

exemplar, the souls that come from heaven have acquired
their tyrannic phantasy from beholding the powers one above
another that govern the world of birth; forgetting that, for
power to be rightly used, it must, as in heaven, be conjoined
with goodness and intellect[1]. The particular soul whose
destiny was so unfortunate, Proclus recalls from Plato, had
in its previous life lived virtuously in an ordered State, but
by habit, without having studied philosophy. And so, he
generalises, having taken the upward path without the exercise of their own intellect, such souls are unable to recognise
in heaven the intellect in accordance with which power determines the order of the whole; for like is known by like[2].

Plato's observation that most choices are determined by
the custom established in the previous life[3], leads to a disquisition on the modes in which certain customs or laws rule
the periods of human history. In this passage[4] there is at
least an adumbration of the view that tradition changing from
age to age is characteristic of human society, in distinction
from the stability of the cosmos on one side and of animal
habit on the other.

When the metempsychoses[5] of heroic souls like those of
Orpheus, Ajax and Agamemnon into animals are described,
Proclus declares this, taken literally, altogether absurd; especially as coming from Plato, who in the same work cries out
against the poets for letting the heroes, while they are in the
body, feel as men[6]. In the myth, adoption of the life of a

---

grasps at the tyranny. On the "fall" in general, compare ii. 296–297: ἐπεὶ
καὶ τὸ τῇ μεγίστῃ τῶν τυραννίδων ἐπιτρέχειν ἀπόπτωσίς ἐστιν τοιαύτης τινὸς ζωῆς
τῆς πάντα τὸν κόσμον διοικούσης, ἧς ἔχουσα φαντασίαν ὑποφέρεται πρὸς τὴν τοιάνδε
πολλῶν ἄρχουσαν μετὰ ἀνάγκης δύναμιν.

[1] ii. 301, 18–23: ἐοίκασι δὲ καὶ τὴν φαντασίαν ταύτην ἔχειν τὴν τυραννικὴν αἱ
ἐξ οὐρανοῦ, θεασάμεναι τὰς τῶν οὐρανίων ἀρχὰς καὶ δυνάμεις κυβερνώσας πᾶσαν τὴν
γένεσιν καὶ ἄλλας ἄλλων μείζους καὶ δυνατωτέρας, ὅθεν καὶ αὐταὶ δυνάμεως ἐφίενται·
δέοντος γιγνώσκειν, ὅτι παρ' ἐκείνοις μὲν τὰ τρία σύνεστιν, ἀγαθότης δύναμις νοῦς.
Cf. ii. 326, 15–16: ἐπεὶ καὶ τὸ τυραννίσιν ἐπιτρέχειν διὰ τὰ κράτη τῶν οὐρανίων
ἐγγέγονεν ταῖς ἐξ οὐρανοῦ κατιούσαις.

[2] ii. 326, 19–25.   [3] Rep. x. 620 A.   [4] ii. 305–308.

[5] It is of interest for the philologist that the actual word, μετεμψύχωσις,
which has been treated as doubtful Greek, occurs in this commentary of
Proclus (ii. 340, 23).

[6] ii. 312–313.

swan, a lion or an eagle signifies the predominant use of some
power that we have in common with other animals, instead of
the power of reason by which man is distinguished. The
animals into which the heroes transmigrate symbolise their
respective modes of life,—the musical (Orpheus), the brave
with wrathful feeling (Ajax), the kingly (Agamemnon), and
so forth[1]. The most distinctive portion of the interpretation
refers to Orpheus. A soul resembling in type the divine or
heroic soul of the singer and lover can descend to a life symbolised by the form of a swan because music has in it an appeal
to irrational passion. Irrational animals also can be charmed
by it, whereas none can philosophise. From the lapse into the
irrational, the soul can be preserved only by philosophy, with
its proof that neither hearing nor seeing gives accurate knowledge, but that for this we must take reason and mind as our
guides. Music and love take the senses, though at their
highest. Only when accompanied by philosophy can they
lead the soul upward.

On the nature of irrational souls themselves, I find the
teaching of Proclus to the end uncertain. An Orphic fragment
quoted by him[2] gives a clearer statement than he himself ever
makes. Simply as dogma, it perfectly agrees with the distinction reasoned out by Leibniz between the mere "metempsychosis" of animal souls conceived as perceptive monads,
and the immortality—that is, continuity of memory and consciousness—to be attributed to monads at the stage of "apperception." The souls of animals too are conceived as permanent
individuals going on to shape for themselves new bodies.
This was no doubt the view of Plotinus; but it is not definitely that of Proclus. For him, only rational souls are
certainly both individual and immortal; though these, as we

---

[1] ii. 315–317. Cf. ii. 310, 9, where Proclus finds a point of contact for this
view in Plotinus: cf. Enn. III. 4, 2: ὅσοι δὲ αἰσθήσει μόνον ἔζησαν, ζῷα. ἀλλ'
εἰ μὲν αἰσθήσει μετὰ θυμοῦ, τὰ ἄγρια....τοὺς δὲ φιλομούσους μέν, καθαρίους δὲ τὰ
ἄλλα, εἰς τὰ ᾠδικά· τοὺς δὲ ἀλόγως βασιλέας [εἰς] ἀετούς, εἰ μὴ ἄλλη κακία παρείη.

As we have seen in the Commentary on the Timaeus, he does not deny the
possibility of attachment (imagined as penal) to an animal life; but he
absolutely denies that a human soul can become the soul of a brute.

[2] ii. 339 (Fr. 224).

have seen, are not, even in their immortal part, purely rational[1].

In going on, after these speculative discussions, to end the Commentary, he lays stress on the warning against drinking too deep of the Lethe that symbolises descent to the world of birth. Our task must be, by purification from the passions incident to this, to restore our memory of the truth of being. This was appropriate in pages dealing with the close of the *Republic*. Yet the more distinctive thought of Proclus, running through this and other commentaries, seems to be that for the perfection of the universe and of each soul all possibilities must be realised, and that the possibilities of a soul can be completely realised in no one life, even when it chooses and finds the best.

---

[1] Incidentally, he interprets Aristotle as teaching, with Plato, that there is a limited number of souls individually immortal; but the immortal part for Aristotle, he points out, is only the potential intellect. See ii. 338, 25–27: τὸ δὲ ὁμολογεῖ σαφῶς, ὅταν λέγῃ περὶ τοῦ δυνάμει νοῦ· καὶ ' τοῦτο μόνον ' τῶν ἐν ἡμῖν ἀθάνατον.

INDEX OF NAMES

Aedesius, 121, 131, 132, 133

Aenesidemus, 32

Aeschylus, 2

Agathias, 182

Alcibiades (in Dialogue), 242 ff.

Alexander of Aphrodisias, 157 n., 266, 290

Alfred the Great, 186

Alypius, 121, 122

Amelius, 28, 33, 35, 99, 109, 301

Ammonius Saccas, 26, 28, 31, 32

Ammonius (pupil of Proclus), 184

Anaxagoras, 10, 23

Antiochus Epiphanes, 108

Antoninus, M. Aurelius. *See* Aurelius

Antoninus (Neo-Platonic philosopher), 132

Apollonius of Tyana, 22, 113, 115 n., 137

Aquinas, St Thomas, 191, 193

Archer-Hind, R. D., 71 n., 183 n.

Archimedes, 226

Aristophanes, 23, 216, 292

Aristotle, 3 n., 7 n., 8, 10, 11, 12, 13 n., 15, 18, 19, 20 n., 22, 23, 33, 41 n., 43, 46, 51, 52, 54, 56, 70, 72, 73, 91, 92, 96, 101, 105, 110, 118, 124, 132 n., 156 n., 157, 158, 161 n., 179 n., 183, 186, 188, 189, 195, 205, 212, 217, 222, 225, 232, 246, 253, 258, 267 n., 273, 276, 277, 278, 282 n., 283 n., 287, 290, 296, 300, 305, 314 n.

Asclepiodotus, 184

Atticus (Platonist), 274

Augustine, St, 185, 192, 196 n.

Aurelius, M., 3, 4, 32, 274

Avicebron (Ibn Gebirol), 194

Bacon, Francis, 200, 232

Bacon, Roger, 194

Baeumker, Cl., 71 n.

Bardesanes, 120

Benn, A. W., 11 n., 14, 71 n., 205

Berkeley, 29, 40, 49, 50, 201, 202, 264

Bigg, C., 36

Boccaccio, 194

Boethius, 110, 186, 238

Bosanquet, B., 90 n.

Bouillet, M. N., 192 n.

Bruno, Giordano, 21, 196, 197, 198, 214, 251 n., 277, 286, 287, 309

Brutus, 3

Burnet, J., 7 n., 9 n., 266

Caesar, 3, 252

Caligula, 4 n.

Cambyses, 1 n.

Campanella, 198

Carneades, 118

Cato the Censor, 120

Cato of Utica, 3, 12 n.

Celsus, 136, 139, 144

Chaignet, A. E., 181 n.

Chosroes, 182, 183

Chrysanthius, 121, 132, 133, 134

Chrysippus, 118

Cicero, 1 n., 12, 27 n., 32, 186

Claudius, 3 n.

Clement of Alexandria, 26

Commodus, 4

Comte, 5 n., 159, 207, 208, 217, 218, 222, 227 n., 232, 233, 266, 268, 269, 293 n.

Constantine, 3, 121, 122 n., 131, 141 n.

Constantius, 131, 150 n.

Critias, 266, 267

Cudworth, 19, 199

Cyril, St (Bishop of Alexandria), 144, 145, 155

Damascius, 180, 181, 182, 304 n.

Dante, 6, 191–194

Democritus, 9, 10, 198, 199

Descartes, 8, 33, 43, 71 n., 198, 199, 200, 201, 232, 311

Dexippus, 134
Diocletian, 3, 137
Diogenes (the Cynic), 138
Diogenes (Neo-Platonist), 182
Dionysius the Areopagite, 187, 188, 191
Diotima, 292
Dodwell, H. (the elder), 122 n.
Drummond, J., 35 n.
Duns Scotus, 193, 194

Empedocles, 10, 120, 210, 211, 272 n.
Epictetus, 138, 183
Epicurus, 11, 27 n., 199
Erigena, John Scotus, 187, 188, 194, 203, 222
Euclid, 225
Eulalius, 182
Eunapius, 27, 107, 108, 113 n., 121, 122, 131, 132, 133, 134, 139
Euripides, 21
Eusebius (Bishop of Caesarea), 31, 137
Eusebius (Neo-Platonic philosopher), 133
Eustathius, 131

Ficino, Marsilio, 195, 196
Firmus, Castricius, 113

Gallienus, 28, 29
Gautier, Th., 305
Gibbon, E., 132 n., 181
Goethe, 198
Gordian, 28
Grote, G., 132 n., 242, 287

Hadrian, 117
Hatch, E., 18 n.
Hegel, 203, 204, 233, 253
Heraclitus, 9, 35, 36 n., 72, 267, 272 n.
Herennius, 31
Hermes Trismegistus, 220, 221
Hermias (of Alexandria), 184
Hermias (of Athens), 182
Herodotus, 1 n., 2 n., 7 n.
Hesiod, 17 n., 99, 302 n.

Hierocles (of Alexandria), 31, 155, 156
Hierocles (Pro-consul of Bithynia), 137, 144
Hippocrates, 93
Hobbes, 8, 198, 199, 206, 217
Homer, 17, 95, 109, 148, 160, 231, 237 n., 266, 297, 299
Honorius III, 188
Hugo, V., 299 n.
Hume, 203
Hypatia, 27, 155, 187

Iamblichus, 15 n., 22, 26, 92, 109, 121–131, 134, 155, 156, 163, 225–228, 264
Innocent III, 224
Isidore, 181 (not identical with the "Isidorus" mentioned at p. 182)

Jerome, St, 108, 132 n.
Jowett, B., 222 n., 242
Julian, 3 n., 16, 108, 121 n., 122, 131, 132, 133, 134, 135; ch. VIII; 304, 305
Justinian, 144, 155, 157, 181, 182, 183
Juvenal, 21

Kant, 203, 222, 225, 258, 278, 302, 309
Keim, Th., 19 n., 137 n.
Kepler, 286
Ker, W. P., 238 n.

Leibniz, 200, 203, 251, 252, 278, 313
Lipsius, R. A., 219
Locke, 200, 201
Longinus, 31, 33, 35, 72, 107
Lucian, 21
Lucretius, 11 n., 27 n., 199
Lyall, A. C., 237 n.

Macarius Magnes, 145
Machiavelli, 6
Macrobius, 186
Maine, H. S., 4 n.
Maistre, J. de, 15 n.
Marcella, 108

Marinus, 143, 157–160, 180, 187, 234 n.
Marlowe, 266
Matteo, J., 26, 219, 220 n., 224
Maurice, F. D., 135 n., 248
Maximus, 133
Melite, 132
Milton, 266, 292 n.
Mirandola, Pico della, 163 n.
Moore, G. E., 275 n.
Morbeka, William of, 161, 234
More, H., 199
Moses, 38, 139, 140, 145 ff.

Nemesius, 185
Nero, 4 n., 16 n.
Neumann, C. J., 137 n., 144 ff.
Newton, 199, 286
Numa, 150
Numenius, 33–38, 137, 156 n.

Ockham, William of, 194
Olympiodorus (teacher of Proclus), 156 n., 157
Olympiodorus (commentator on Plato and Aristotle), 156, 184
Origen (the ecclesiastical writer), 26, 31, 137 n., 196, 237 n., 298 n.
Origen (Platonic philosopher), 31

Parmenides, 9, 56, 215, 243; (in Plato), 248 ff.
Pascal, 269
Paul, St, 147, 150, 151, 152, 187, 191, 222
Pericles, 245
Petrarch, 6, 194
Phidias, 90, 272
Philo Judaeus, 26, 33–37, 87 n., 105, 137, 221
Philoponus, 157 n., 182 n., 184 n.
Plato, 3 n., 8, 9, 10, 11, 12, 13, 14, 15, 17, 18, 19, 22, 23, 24, 27, 34 n., 35, 36, 37, 38, 40, 41, 43, 46, 52, 54, 55, 70, 71, 72, 83, 85 n., 87, 90 n., 92, 93, 95, 98, 99, 101, 105, 106, 107, 116, 117, 121, 122, 124, 132 n., 134, 137, 143, 147, 155, 156 n., 157, 160, 161, 162, 180,

183, 195, 202, 205, 208, 213, 216–218, 224, 225, 228; Supplement, *passim*
Plotinus, 13, 24; chs. IV, V, VI; 107, 108, 109, 110, 111, 112, 113, 121 n., 123, 124, 134, 155, 156 n., 157, 158, 162, 163, 170, 173, 181, 185, 192, 193, 194, 195, 196, 197, 198, 201, 202, 208–215, 220, 231, 232, 234, 235, 236, 237, 240, 244, 246 n., 252, 254, 255, 264, 272, 273, 274, 277, 294, 295, 296, 306, 307, 309, 313
Plutarch (of Athens), 155–158
Plutarch (of Chaeronea), 32, 71, 119, 120, 274
Pompey, 252
Porphyry, 22; ch. IV *passim*; 45 n., 56, 82, 92, 99, 100, 101, 103, 105 n., 107–120, 121, 123, 129, 134, 135 n., 137, 140, 144, 145, 146, 155, 156, 161 n., 163, 186, 192, 195, 196, 228 n., 274, 305, 308
Portus, Aemilius, 161 n.
Posidonius, 220
Preller, L. *See* Ritter
Priscianus, 182
Priscus, 133, 134
Proclus, 19, 27, 34, 37 n., 110, 123, 124, 134, 143, 144 n., 156, 157–180, 181, 182, 184, 187, 192, 205, 208–215, 222, 225–228, 231–314
Prohaeresius, 122
Ptolemy (the astronomer), 231, 308
Pythagoras, 7, 22, 110, 113, 120, 122 n., 123, 129, 146, 226, 227

Read, C., 208 n.
Reinach, Th., 38 n.
Reitzenstein, R., 219 ff.
Renan, E., 4 n., 139 n., 183 n., 189 n., 270
Ritter, H. and Preller, L. (cited as R. P. The references are to *Historia Philosophiae Graecae*, 7th ed.), 15 n., 20 n., 29 n., 34 n., 38 n., 41 n., 111 n., 124 n., 162 n., 181 n., 182 n., 210 n.

Roberts, W. Rhys, 31 n.
Rogatianus, 28
Rohde, E., 17 n.

Sallust (Pretorian Prefect under Julian), 135, 304
Salonina, 29
Schopenhauer, 309, 310
Scotus, John. *See* Erigena
Scotus, John Duns. *See* Duns
Sextus Empiricus, 32
Shakespeare, 299 n.
Shelley, P. B., 202, 298
Sidney, P., 196
Siebeck, H., 43, 52, 71 n., 205, 222
Simon, J., 26, 37 n., 76 n., 83 n., 108, 113 n.
Simplicius, 182, 183, 210, 233
Socrates (the philosopher), 10, 12, 18, 27, 41, 143 n., 162, 205, 222 n., 232; in Supplement as interlocutor in Dialogues
Socrates (ecclesiastical historian), 155
Solomon, 151
Solon, 267, 269
Sopater, 122 n., 131
Sorel, G., 18 n.
Sosipatra, 132
Spencer, H., 213, 216, 217, 300
Spenser, E., 202
Speusippus, 156 n.
Spinoza, 100, 161, 173, 200, 203, 244 n., 255 n., 261 n., 293
Stobaeus, 110, 156 n.
Suetonius, 3, 4 n., 16 n.
Swinburne, A. C., 241
Synesius, 155, 187
Syrianus, 156–158, 184, 248

Tacitus, 3, 4 n., 139
Tannery, P., 9 n.
Taylor, T., 161 n., 192 n.
Tertullian, 20, 185
Thales, 205
Themistius, 131, 157 n.
Theodore of Asine, 134, 163, 265, 290, 295
Theodoret, 137
Theodoric, 186
Theodosius II. 144
Theognis, 298
Theophrastus, 115, 119, 276, 279, 286
Tiberius, 4 n.
Timaeus Locrus, 265 n.

Vacherot, E., 26, 34 n., 83 n., 92, 157 n., 197 n., 221 n.
Valens, 133
Virgil, 252

Xenocrates, 121, 156 n.
Xenophanes, 9, 20, 271 n.
Xenophon, 12
Xerxes, 1 n.

Zeller, E. (The references are to *Die Philosophie der Griechen*, II. 1, 4th ed.: II. 2, III. 1, III. 2, 3rd ed.), 12 n., 22, 32, 34, 35 n., 71 n., 76 n., 83 n., 93, 101, 104, 105, 110 n., 122 n., 131 n., 134 n., 135, 156 n., 157 n., 158 n., 159 n., 160 n., 162, 163 n., 181, 182 n., 183, 184 n., 231, 235 n., 274 n.
Zeno (the Eleatic), 250, 251
Zeno (the Stoic), 12
Zoroaster, 109